THE CAMPBELL REVOLUTION?

The Campbell Revolution?

Power, Politics, and Policy
in British Columbia

Edited by

J.R. LACHARITE and TRACY SUMMERVILLE

McGill-Queen's University Press
Montreal & Kingston · London · Chicago

© McGill-Queen's University Press 2017

ISBN 978-0-7735-5102-2 (cloth)
ISBN 978-0-7735-5103-9 (paper)
ISBN 978-0-7735-5233-3 (ePDF)
ISBN 978-0-7735-5234-0 (ePUB)

Legal deposit fourth quarter 2017
Bibliothèque nationale du Québec

Printed in Canada on acid-free paper that is 100% ancient forest free (100% post-consumer recycled), processed chlorine free

This book has been published with the help of a grant from the University of Northern British Columbia.

McGill-Queen's University Press acknowledges the support of the Canada Council for the Arts for our publishing program. We also acknowledge the financial support of the Government of Canada through the Canada Book Fund for our publishing activities.

Library and Archives Canada Cataloguing in Publication

The Campbell revolution? : power, politics, and policy
in British Columbia / J.R. Lacharite and Tracy Summerville, eds.

Includes bibliographical references and index.
Issued in print and electronic formats.
ISBN 978-0-7735-5102-2 (hardcover). – ISBN 978-0-7735-5103-9 (softcover). –
ISBN 978-0-7735-5233-3 (ePDF). – ISBN 978-0-7735-5234-0 (ePUB)

1. British Columbia – Politics and government – 2001–.
2. Campbell, Gordon, 1948–. 3. British Columbia – History – 21st
century. I. Summerville, Tracy, 1963–, editor II. Lacharite, J. R., editor

FC3830.2.C36 2017   971.1'05   C2017-904264-5
                                              C2017-904265-3

This book was set by True to Type in 10.5/13 Sabon

This book is dedicated to Dennis Woodward (1952–2011)
– scholar, mentor, and friend.

Contents

Tables and Figures

Acknowledgments

There are many people to whom we are grateful for bringing this volume together. First, we would like to thank our authors for sticking with us as we moved through to publication. Your patience and support have been deeply appreciated. Thank you for the fine scholarship that makes this volume eminently readable and informative to a wide audience.

We would also like to thank all of the reviewers for their suggestions and comments. The agreements and the disagreements with the reviewers' comments are a critical part of the work. Indeed, our readers helped us to question and rethink our ideas and arguments at a number of critical junctures. Ultimately, the interaction between reviewers and authors makes the scholarship better. We are, of course, in your debt for this.

We owe a debt of gratitude to the Department of Political Science at the University of Northern British Columbia as well – especially Gary Wilson, Michael Murphy, and Boris DeWiel. We are proud to be among such a great group of colleagues and scholars.

Unsurprisingly, no volume comes together without a team of amazing editors. From the beginning, McGill-Queen's University Press was supportive of the project and we are particularly indebted to Ryan Van Huijstee and Jacqueline Mason for all of their encouragement and guidance, and to Joanne Richardson and Kathleen Fraser for all of their work on the text.

We would like to give a special thanks to Kathy Plett, who indexed this volume. We are so very, very appreciative of the care she gave to this task.

Finally, we would like to thank our families for their support. Tracy would like to thank Keith and Neyve for their understanding and patience, while Jason would like to extend a long overdue thank you to Lara, Isabelle, and Daniel. You motivate us to work hard, have fun, and pursue all life's challenges with determination.

THE CAMPBELL REVOLUTION?

Introduction

The Campbell Revolution?

J.R. LACHARITE AND TRACY SUMMERVILLE

During his ten years in power, former BC premier Gordon Campbell was a deeply polarizing figure. As with any elected official in a position of authority, he experienced both the highs and lows of leadership. His public approval ratings soared after his election victory in 2001 (a very John F. Kennedyesque 70 per cent according to one Ipsos-Reid poll [2007]) but eventually hit rock bottom by 2010 (a miserable 9 per cent after the harmonized sales tax [HST] was announced) (Burgess 2010). What was especially interesting about Premier Campbell, however, was that at times he appeared to be pursuing mutually incompatible and contradictory policy programs. On the one hand, he was described as an uncompromising proponent of privatization, deregulation, and individual responsibility – that is, as an adamant supporter of neoliberalism. On the other hand, he seemed to conform to a variant of reform liberalism marked by determined efforts to preserve large tracts of ecologically sensitive old-growth rainforest, arrest the root causes of anthropogenic warming through a much maligned carbon tax, and settle long-standing land rights disputes with First Nations groups. These labels, of course, are convenient and give observers of BC politics an easy way to discuss his so-called ideological orientation. They are, to put it differently, a useful way to make sense of his policy choices and actions. Yet viewing former premier Campbell's accomplishments and failures through a narrow conceptual and/or ideological lens tends to obscure a more nuanced, instructive, and enticing narrative.

At its heart, this book is a policy evaluation piece that examines the contexts under which Gordon Campbell was adaptive, pragmatic, and/or ideological. The central question that we have taken on is: In what fundamental way(s) did the policy landscape change while Campbell was in power? To be more explicit, we asked our contributing authors to complete a chapter in an area of public policy in which they hold considerable expertise. We did not suggest a predetermined hypothesis about a specific ideological tendency but, instead, wanted them to critically appraise the former premier's policy initiatives and reforms outside of the framework of personality.

Even so, there was an unmistakable neoliberal twist to how Campbell managed BC politics and policy from 2001 to 2011 (Harvey 2005). But, on occasion, it seemed to exist within a more pragmatic and self-conscious leadership style that recognized the complexity of the province's politico-economic system. Therefore, while issues of privatization, de-regulation, and public-sector reform always seemed to be on the BC Liberals' agenda, there were clearly times when Campbell asserted his own odd combination of populism and rational choice. Importantly, it is this dimension of his leadership style that explains why the analysis in the following chapters addresses both neoliberal and, at times, other policy options.

Public preferences appeared to be evolving in the 1990s – especially in the aftermath of a series of dysfunctional New Democratic Party (NDP) governments – and what we attempt to demonstrate is that, while Campbell helped to propel the province's politics in a certain direction, he was far from an uncomplicated figure. Indeed, many common perceptions of the former premier continue to linger (probably because he deployed a range of policy options during his decade in power), but they are not always borne out by the evidence. Unsurprisingly, he wasn't just "a monochromatic ideologue bent on commercializing BC politics and government," nor was he simply "a hackneyed politician attempting to curry favour with environmental activists and/or Indigenous communities." These are the sorts of reflexive responses we encountered when we tried to explain to our friends, family members, and colleagues the purpose of our book. Occasionally, some even drew on his pre-election spending activities (i.e., expansionary infrastructural projects) to disparage his "free market" credentials.

From the outset, we generally felt uncomfortable with these types of straightforward and informal depictions of Campbell's time in public office. Was it fair to reduce the former premier to a set of competing caricatures? Did he not inherit a legacy of sorts? To what extent did he simply adopt a form of neoliberalism that had already proven itself to be both potent and effective in Alberta and Ontario? We also thought that it would be instructive to consider the contextual and proximate factors that contributed to his style of governance and policy agenda from 2001 to 2011. What we have discovered is that Campbell's policy record appears to reflect a considerable measure of both pragmatism and ideological zeal.

On the social welfare front, for example, some of our contributing authors convincingly argue that he was typically unsympathetic to the experiences and impoverished circumstances of marginalized groups such as single mothers, low-income families, and minimum wage earners in service-sector jobs. In these instances, ideology appeared to motivate decisions to restrict various forms of social assistance and subsidization. When it came to other state programs and services, however, he seemed more inclined to apply a measure of pragmatism that could be judged to be largely inconsistent with what are otherwise considered strict (neoliberal) ideological tenets of one variety or another. Hence, we thought it would be productive to pursue a line of inquiry that would uncover the degree to which he was a policy pioneer and the concrete impact his policy decisions had on the province's political milieu. What we have found is that the "Campbell effect" has not been as obvious as you (the reader) might think.

Campbell did not initiate BC's turn to "laissez-faire government." Nor did he gift the province with an uncompromising glorification of individualism. Some depoliticization and commercialization of public life had already taken root several years before Campbell had even embarked on his political career. As a province, BC was relatively late to the so-called "neoliberal party." Former Alberta and Ontario premiers Ralph Klein (1992–2006) and Mike Harris (1995–2002) had installed a successful brand of populism well in advance of Campbell's ascent to power. In hindsight, Harris's "Common Sense Revolution" may have even served as a template for Campbell. More to the point, however, Klein and Harris were merely promoting and executing a neoliberal reform package established by the likes of Margaret Thatcher, Ronald Reagan, and, to a lesser extent, Brian Mulroney in the 1980s (Gutstein 2014). To use a surfing analogy, Canada's more anti-Keynesian and fiscally conservative-leaning premiers seemed to be riding the groundswell of support that had already been accepted in a central government context. Recognizing its appeal, provincial leaders such as Harris and Klein applied it to their own regional and/or sub-state situations. It took BC a bit more time to transition away from a well-entrenched NDP-inspired social democratic framework, but it, too, would eventually succumb to the public's demands for more "responsible government" and more personal freedom.

Attacks against the welfare state, government over-regulation, and deficit spending became the norm by the time Campbell was officially proclaimed premier in 2001. It was, for all intents and purposes, a highly successful and sophisticated electoral strategy – and political reality – that generated results. But again, we feel compelled to reiterate that there was more to Campbell's legacy than a desire to transform BC into a simple replica of the Klein and Harris regimes of the 1990s and early to mid-2000s.

Hence, there are very good reasons for producing a book like *The Campbell Revolution?* Principal among them is that too little has been written on the public policy record of influential sub-state actors in federal regimes like Canada. Certainly, there are important works that chronicle the "life and times" of high-profile premiers such as Ralph Klein (Dabbs 1995; D. Martin 2002) and Mike Harris (Ibbitson 1997), but they tend to either be adulatory in orientation and tone or lack the breadth and depth of a scholarly piece dedicated to policy review and evaluation.[1] Not to be outdone, several authors have produced impressive biographies detailing the life history and policy accomplishments of former BC premiers Mike Harcourt (Gawthrop 1996), Bill Bennett (Plecas 2006), and W.A.C. Bennett (Mitchell 1983). These contributions, it must be said, have been extremely valuable in that they have given readers some insight into what may have motivated these party leaders to pursue one course of action over another. Still, they are limited to the extent that exhaustive policy analysis is not the main focus or even a major priority of the overall presentation. This is why we wanted to do something different. We felt that it would be valuable to construct a more highly specialized account of Campbell's key "policy moments" – supplemented, of course, by a requisite amount of context. Ultimately, we instructed our authors to focus on the former premier's policy and outcomes, and not on his "cult of personality."

We also felt compelled to complete this book because we thought it was important to more carefully examine the idea of policy making as a highly circuitous enterprise – one characterized by meaningful twists and turns. One of the more critical ideas advanced in *The Campbell Revolution?*, as has already been indicated, is that many of Campbell's policy decisions as well as his style of leadership were merely adaptive and not very revolutionary at all: it is for precisely this reason that we include a question mark in our title. The idea that Campbell's leadership was revolutionary is a common misperception that, in some ways, we hope to dispel.

The conventional wisdom before Campbell's Liberal Party supplanted the province's crisis-prone "leftist" alternative was that BC, in the 1990s at least, had universally embraced a social democratic program and that it could be fairly understood by the sum total of logging protests in Clayoquot Sound, the siege at Gustafsen Lake, or the general hostility that characterized public-sector contract negotiations. There remains this misguided belief that BC, in some crucial ways, is the antithesis to neoconservative and/or neoliberal values because it possesses a moderately irreverent political culture and identity. When confronted by two environmentalists at a resource and energy development conference in Vancouver in January 2014, former prime minister Stephen Harper reinforced this view of the province when he quipped "it wouldn't be BC without some sort of protest" – forgetting of course that expressions of dissent are also common in Quebec and Ontario and that contesting and/or questioning power and policy is simply part of Canada's broader liberal democratic reality. The bottom line is that BC has not been immune to the practical appeal of neoliberalism. In other words, it has not been able to insulate itself from the putative "successes" attributed to commercializing politics, governance, and administration.

Some of Campbell's political strategizing, policy initiatives, and policy reforms, then, can be seen as adaptive in the sense that, in the 1990s, anti-government and anti-tax rhetoric, and an emphasis on classical liberalism (a major component of which is the strength and sanctity of individualism), had already been expressed and adopted by other governments across Canada and, to a limited degree, in BC. To be sure, the BC NDP encouraged public-private partnerships (P3s) in relation to the revised 1998 Municipal Act – a policy initiative established under Premier (Glen) Clark and intended to help "governments expand opportunities for P3s for the delivery of public facilities and services," tested the waters of austerity budgeting, and firmly entrenched an ascetic social assistance program with the implementation of the BC Benefits plan in 1993. Incidentally, none of this should come as a great shock since, as Peck and Tickell (2002) have suggested, the process of neoliberalization is itself a highly adaptive phenomenon. Granted, it took on divergent forms and occasionally confronted the overarching and persistent challenge of public regulation, but neoliberalism ruled in the 1990s and early to mid-2000s, and, with the exception of Ottawa's generous stimulus program in response to the 2008 global financial crisis, it continues to rule. Fundamentally, then, this continued trend indicates that even left-of-centre parties have been at a loss to assail its apparent and growing suitability and acceptability: Britain's national Labour Party is a stunning illustration of this seemingly inevitable conversion of the left (Lund 2008).

Be that as it may, there was still a revolution of sorts in the making. More specifically, as was alluded to above, smaller government, lower taxes, and balanced budgets began to resonate with an increasingly larger segment of the province's active ballot casters – and well in advance of the BC Liberals' 2001 election victory. Naturally, Campbell was a populist committed foremost to winning elections. But again, the ideas of leaning up public services (trimming the so-called fat from government institutions and agencies), privatizing public assets, and modifying tax systems to better benefit citizen-consumers had already been embraced by a significant portion of Canada's voting population by the 1990s. In particular, putting government bureaucracy to the sword seemed to genuinely restore many western Canadians' interest in federal and provincial politics (if only temporarily), as can be evidenced by the popularity of the federal Reform Party and Canadian Alliance Party platforms throughout the decades preceding Campbell's rise to prominence (as both mayor of Vancouver and leader of the province's official opposition). Hence, the "real" revolution that was taking root was a small, but not insignificant, shift in popular attitudes and opinions. BC was no longer a hard left-to-centre political regime committed solely to the principles of Keynesian redistribution and public enrichment; rather, attitudes reflected a more ideologically complex socio-political system that embraced shades of neoliberalism and accepted a form of "rational action" also found in Ontario and the country's midwestern provinces. A quick glance at BC's most recent election results bears this observation out. It could be argued that, while strong pseudo-social democratic tendencies seem to prevail on Vancouver Island and in coastal electoral districts, there remains consistently solid support for neoliberal values in the Lower Mainland and large parts of northern BC. In essence, BC, like many of its provincial counterparts, embodies a polarization of values and beliefs that is ultimately expressed through the ballot box but that has found some comfort in broadly accepted pro-business (i.e., anti-government) and hyper-individualistic preferences.

It could be reasonably asserted, then, that former premier Campbell wasn't really doing anything especially perverse, unexpected, original, or even unanticipated. Curiously, though, Campbell did pursue some strikingly anti-neoliberal policy initiatives. He was a champion of safe injection sites for substance abusers in Vancouver's Downtown Eastside. As premier, he cast himself as a defender of the province's environmental riches by implementing a carbon tax and by establishing legislation designed to expand upon the conservation and protection of several of BC's fragile ecosystems along the province's central and north coasts. Campbell also followed through on referenda relating to treaty negotiations with First Nations groups, provincial electoral reform, and repealing the dreaded HST. Finally, as mayor of Vancouver he was responsible for significant infrastructural projects such as the redevelopment of Yaletown and the construction of a new Vancouver Public Library – the second-largest public library system in Canada – from 1993 to 1995. Yet we feel that all of these accomplishments – significant though they may be – simply personify his versatility as a political operator. So, while the province seemed to be experiencing an evolution of sorts in terms of its predominant value structure, Campbell's policy legacy, on balance, reflected a carefully planned political strategy that took its cue from, and advantage of, well-established pro-market maxims and policy reforms advanced by progenitors like Margaret Thatcher (UK) and Ronald Reagan (US).

In all, Gordon Campbell was a very complex politician. He was competent, had a vision for the province, and possessed exceptional management skills. At the same time, he could be obstinate, impulsive, and even detached from the myriad views and values that inform and energize provincial politics. The temptation, of course, is to focus on the negative because it creates controversy and conforms to certain peoples' preconceived opinions of Campbell. But as authors and editors we felt compelled to offer a more even-handed appraisal of his time in public office. Ultimately, our hope is to shed more light on his approach to policy making and to expose the various triggers – both internal and external – that contributed to his policy regime. As a result, an intriguing collection of viewpoints is presented throughout this volume.

Instead of offering a traditional introduction to each chapter, we want to demonstrate thematically how the book in general speaks to the Campbell legacy. Broadly speaking, *The Campbell Revolution?* makes the case that Campbell was driven by a set of ideas that had started to inform many Anglo-liberal regimes from the early 1980s onward (Gray 2009). We think that there are four central themes that are critical to understanding an assessment of Campbell's time in Victoria. First, the

1990s appeared to be marked, in part, by a pent up-anger with the Mike Harcourt–, Glen Clark–, and Ujjhal Dosanjh–run NDP governments. Public discontent, though isolated to certain quarters, seemed to simmer after the introduction of the BC Benefits Plan (1993–95) and eventually manifested itself in the form of an entirely unconvincing election win in 1996, in which Campbell's Liberal Party actually won a higher percentage of the popular vote than did the NDP. This was followed by an even more spectacular outcome in 2001, when the NDP was reduced to a mere two seats out of a total of seventy-nine. Of course, the party was also plagued by a series of scandals, such as "Bingogate," the fast-ferry initiative, and "Casinogate" (see CBC 1999; Mickleburgh 2000a, 2003); only moderate economic growth; and defections from core supporter groups that felt betrayed. However, the party also failed to adapt to the populism that had reinvigorated disgruntled voters – of both the core and marginal variety – in Ontario and Alberta. Rhetorical salvos that consisted largely of promises to invest more generously in social, health, and educational services fell upon deaf ears. By the late 1990s, BC voters had become justifiably suspicious of NDP intentions and wanted change. Moreover, they seemed to fully accept the notion that only a Liberal government could address the root causes of BC's social, political, and economic problems.

Second, an undermining of the collective sense of identity that had previously underpinned most social policy initiatives began to intensify under Campbell's watch. That is to say, a more entrepreneurial environment in which the role of the state became less concerned with collective outcomes started to gain significantly more traction.

Third, Campbell championed a brand of fiscal austerity that looked very similar to the economically conservative financial proposals advanced by the Reform Party under Preston Manning in the 1980s. Yet, he also seems to have drawn considerable influence from the "Common Sense" redevelopment platform pursued by Ontario premier Mike Harris from 1995 to 1999. What is particularly striking is how Campbell essentially emulated Harris's income tax cut program, health care surtax initiative, deficit reduction mantra, aggressive confrontations with public-sector unions, and sale of government assets.

Finally, a noticeable level of politicization pertaining to the institutional structures of government and communications methods also became more apparent at this time, ensuring the prevalence of relative control over, and uniformity of, policy options. Looking back, it is clear that Campbell – and his army of public relations personnel – tried to carefully manage the way initiatives, reforms, scandals, and so on were delivered or publicly resolved. This is not to suggest that he was always successful but, rather, to point out that, as premier, he developed a communications strategy that spoke to a populist agenda (see Pilon, chapter 2, this volume; Smith, chapter 11, this volume; and Belanger, chapter 3, this volume).

Throughout this book, it is argued that, from his early career in politics, Campbell subscribed to what could be called conservative economics and the politics of ideas. He supported developers and private enterprise as a way to move the economy towards the entrepreneurial class. In chapter 1, Kevin Ginnell takes us through the early years of Campbell's career and notes that his time as Vancouver mayor was marked by his pragmatism, even though his economic policies tended to favour capital. Furthermore, the rhetoric related to "big government" had thoroughly taken shape during this period and Campbell used it to make the case for belt tightening in the municipal budget. In chapter 4, Tracy Summerville makes the case that, during his time as premier, his policy options were drawn from a limited toolkit of policy alternatives that were already in play in other jurisdictions. In chapter 10, Marjorie Griffin Cohen writes about Campbell's privatization of BC Hydro. She argues that the public was generally happy with this provincially owned corporation, but Campbell managed to "circumvent the popularity of the Crown corporation to promote the development of privately supplied electricity" (206). She asserts that the consequences of these changes to BC Hydro may not be known for some time. In chapter 5, Lacharite credits the populist language of "low taxes" and "big government" as the impetus to reform BC tax policy. While Campbell did bring in the carbon tax, Lacharite suggests that, overall, his "'taxing' legacy was neither too progressive nor too regressive" (109). In chapter 9, George Hoberg notes the complex legacy of Campbell as "champion" of the environment. While he delivered a climate change policy unique to Canada (at the time, at least), he did significantly reduce the government's "capacity for sustainable resource management" (193). Summerville and Hoberg make slightly different arguments about Campbell's reasons for engaging First Nations participation in resource management, but, without doubt, Campbell did extend a significant olive branch in terms of Aboriginal/state reconciliation. In chapter 3, Yale Belanger suggests that Campbell's concessions were extended after he became aware of, or rather educated about, Aboriginal law and Canadian Aboriginal policy. Despite Campbell's change of heart, the context of BC provincial-Aboriginal politics was, and continues to be, extraordinarily complicated.

With regard to "big ideas," Campbell found policy initiatives driven by the notions of a "creative class" and "urban entrepreneurs." As Duncan Low demonstrates in chapter 12, Campbell captured some of the elements of the creative economy by focusing funding on large-scale projects that would enhance the profile of the province. The arts community generally lost out as part of the administration's assertion of fiscal discipline, but, as Emmanuel Brunet-Jailly argues in chapter 13, Campbell took advantage of the 2010 Olympic bid to make Vancouver a world-class city. By and large, Campbell's approach to the economy was based on his self-professed belief in "classical liberalism," which, in many ways, had been rebranded as "neoliberalism" by the time Campbell came to office.

Campbell managed to frame his premiership as broadly democratic and inclusive, but his brand of democracy was really Western populism. He linked his political strategy to the power of individualism and, as Dennis Pilon shows in chapter 2, Campbell essentially redefined the public by suggesting that group interests were special interests. This type of rhetoric undermined the province's collective consciousness in terms of social policy. In chapter 8, Gillian Creese and Veronica Strong-Boag claim that the neoliberal agenda set up the context within which advances towards equity were dismantled. They show how the "austerity state" tends to disproportionately affect women and the poor. Moreover, they show how undermining the collective was reinforced by neoliberal policies dating back to before Campbell became premier. This argument is also examined in chapter 6 by Gary Teeple, who shows how labour relations were reconstituted in the era of neoliberal reform. Teeple points to changes to the labour code that weakened the collective spirit of bargaining, which was once at the centre of labour union strength. He notes the specific case in which adding "the individual employee into the code along with unions and employers ... undermines the collective force of the union by providing a formal regulatory path for individual dissent and by implying that workers on their own can negotiate as good a contract as can a union" (129). The implications of the shift from the collective identity to the individual identity are profound and marked a dramatic change in political attitudes that is evident not only in the decline of union membership, but also in the acceptance of the idea that we must undermine the social contract in order to achieve sound fiscal management. One area in which Campbell remained a pragmatist was in the realm of health care reform. In chapter 7, Neil Hanlon asserts that Campbell did not seek to make dramatic policy changes along neoliberal lines but that he did take aim at health care unions.

While Campbell's approach was populist, he was also oddly authoritarian, which likely reflected his desire to stay the course in what he might have perceived to be critical areas of policy reform. Kevin Ginnell and Dennis Pilon illustrate this point well by highlighting (1) his leadership style during his first two terms as mayor of Vancouver and (2) the way that he instructed senior bureaucrats and his own caucus to ensure there was a strict adherence to party directives or, more accurately, "Campbell directives." Chapter 11, in which Patrick Smith looks at local government, also demonstrates the tension between populism and control. Certainly, Campbell argued for strong decentralized municipal governments when he was mayor of Vancouver, but when push came to shove as premier, he could not release power to local governments for fear that principles of new public management would be undermined.

In closing, the four central themes of this book recur over and over. The first theme concerns capitalizing on a form of populism that had generated success at the federal and provincial levels of government. Campbell was able to cast a long dark shadow over the Harcourt, Clark, and Dosanjh eras by convincing voters that government was too big, that taxes were too high, and that the way to move forward was to accept that the market would fix issues of unemployment and inequality. The second theme concerns a decline in the social contract that diluted the collective sense of identity, the third a consistent conservative economic policy that favoured the market and undermined labour, and the fourth a reasonably effective command-and-control strategy that ensured that policy options were limited to those that fit within the dominant discourse of a "BC-is-open-for-business" refrain. These neoliberally oriented ideas had been brewing for a long time in other places, and Campbell was able to benefit from public distrust of government institutions to promote a perceived radical transformation in BC politics and policy. We believe that you will see this narrative emerge throughout the book and that you will conclude, along with us, that Campbell was a formidable figure who rode the wave of a legacy that had already hit the shore.

ACKNOWLEDGMENTS

Several years before Gordon Campbell became premier of British Columbia, Brian Costar and Nicolas Economou published an edited volume entitled *The Kennett Revolution: Victorian Politics in the 1990s*, which surveyed the life, leadership, and policy of one of Australia's more notorious state premiers, Jeff Kennett. We would like to acknowledge and thank them for their efforts and inspiration.

NOTE

1 The exception here is Kevin Taft's *Shredding the Public Interest* (1997), a short and wonderfully crafted book that chronicles Klein's approach to fiscal policy and public services support.

1

Charting Gordon Campbell's Rise to the Top

The Pragmatic Mayor and the Politics of "Efficiency"?

KEVIN GINNELL

His defiant attempts to avoid the old labels of right and left have produced deep suspicion on both sides in BC's polarized political landscape. The left thinks he's lint in the pockets of the business community, while the business community suspects he might be too much of a wussy consensus-builder to do the tough stuff. One side suspects he's a right-winger in yuppie disguise; the other thinks he's secretly just a book-reading liberal. The less attentive – that would be most of us – can't figure out what he stands for. (Bula 2001a)

Frances Bula, writing about Gordon Campbell's political career in the *Vancouver Sun*, captured the essence of his approach to politics throughout his career both at the local and provincial levels of government in Vancouver and British Columbia. Regardless of one's ideological viewpoint, there can be no denying that Gordon Campbell was one of the most important political figures in British Columbia from the late 1980s until his resignation as the premier on 14 March 2011.

This chapter focuses on Campbell's career as an alderman and as mayor of Vancouver from 1986 to 1993. It was in his capacity as mayor that he developed into a well-rounded, pragmatic, and adaptive local politician. Indeed, he tended to utilize "new public management" strategies to attempt to improve the efficiency of service provision at the local level while supporting several "progressive" policy initiatives.

This chapter is divided into several parts. Part 1 considers Gordon Campbell's early life and part 2 discusses his time as a young alderman on City Council. This is followed by a section that examines his three terms as mayor of Vancouver, chair of Metro Vancouver's (formerly the Greater Vancouver Regional District [GVRD]) Planning Committee, and chair of Metro. My central contention is that Gordon Campbell's early local political experience offers insight into his nearly three terms as premier of British Columbia.

I argue that, given Campbell's early political activities, it is possible to identify clues to understanding his later proclivities as BC's premier from looking at his much earlier, more formative proclivities. Specifically, these include: (1) a penchant for hard work and even over-achievement; (2) an ideological tendency (leaning to the right) tempered by a more pragmatic, and at times, progressive streak; and (3) a quixotic inclination to intensify focus on an issue, or set of related issues, and then eventually drift off to other policy areas.

EARLY LIFE

Gordon Campbell spent his early life living on the University of British Columbia (UBC) campus with his father Dr Charles "Chargo" Gordon Campbell, the assistant dean of UBC's Faculty of Medicine, his mother Peg, and his three siblings. Dr Campbell died when Gordon (his oldest child) was only twelve years old. From that point on, Gordon was raised by his mother. Following the death of his father, Campbell began to focus heavily on athletics and academics. He excelled at athletics and became a student leader at University Hill Secondary School (student council president), which eventually earned him a full scholarship to Dartmouth College, New Hampshire, in 1970, where he would earn a bachelor of arts (English) with an additional focus on urban studies (Bula 2001a).

Campbell developed a taste for local government and politics at the age of twenty in the summer of 1969 while serving as an intern at Vancouver City Hall. He "was in the bowels of Vancouver's Art Deco city hall, colouring maps and making friends with one of the TEAM councillors, Art Phillips, who was older but shared the same wacky sense of humour" (Bula 2001a, D2). This initial connection with Phillips led to Campbell's later entrance into civic politics in Vancouver.

Prior to his more political involvements, and following his stint at Dartmouth, Campbell married Nancy Chipperfield on 4 July 1970, and the couple travelled to Yola, Nigeria, to work for the Canadian University Service Overseas (CUSO). During this period Campbell and his wife read extensively, coached sports teams, and helped build a local library (Bula 2001a). Bula (2001a) suggests that Campbell's interest in reading manifests itself further later in his career:

> He buys books by the cartload, grabbing at every idea in the world – knowledge through pounds of print accumulated – sucking in a chapter here and a chapter there from the landfills of print piled around the various beds he owns; goes on reading binges in particular mineral lodes (used to be leadership, recently it's high tech and Thunderbolt Thinking!, one of those messianic positive-thinking theories that "teaches the participants how to manage his or her own thinking and do away with the belief system" in order to ignite the spirit and compete in the global economy).

In 1972, after his CUSO placement, the Campbells returned to Vancouver. Nancy received her teaching certificate, and Gordon entered law school at the University of British Columbia (Bula 2001a). Campbell's career in local government started as a summer job working in the city of Vancouver's planning, social planning, and engineering departments before he became an executive assistant to his former friend/mentor Mayor Art Phillips (1972 to 1976).

Campbell left his administrative job and entered the business world in 1976, joining Marathon Realty (the real estate arm of the Canadian Pacific Railway) for five years as a project manager. In 1969, Marathon Realty had submitted a plan to the city of Vancouver for the development of a large North False Creek site called La Ville Radieuse (Punter 2003, 187). Campbell's primary responsibility with Marathon was management of this False Creek project (Gutstein 1986, 69). The plan involved "nineteen towers, each 150 to 200 metres tall, set along the shoreline away from a major highway (Pacific Boulevard). The city had its own priorities in mind so Marathon withdrew the initial plan and introduced a different plan in 1974 that involved the creation of four distinct neighbourhoods and requested a rezoning for them" (Punter 2003, 187). Marathon was finally given city approval for its redevelopment when a thirty-eight-hectare (ninety-five-acre) parcel of land between the Cambie Street Bridge and the Granville Street Bridge was rezoned from industrial use to comprehensive development. In 1981, Campbell struck out on his own and started the Citycore Development Corporation, working on such projects as the Georgian Court Hotel (Moya 1984).[1]

In support of Expo '86, on 6 November 1980, BC premier Bill Bennett finalized a $60 million deal ($30 million in cash, $30 million in a land swap) with Campbell and Marathon for seventy-one hectares (175 acres) of the company's False Creek land (Punter 2003, 187). The land that was given by the province to Marathon in the land swap included "valuable downtown properties and other undisclosed benefits including, at least, some valuable forest lands" (Gutstein 1986, 72). Yet Gutstein suggests that the real cost of the deal may never be known:

> That the CPR did receive other benefits became clear in January 1981 when MLA Don Lockstead (NDP-Mackenzie) charged that a swap of timbered for recreational land by the government and the CPR-owned Pacific Logging Co. was a multi-million dollar giveaway of public assets. The BC government gave Pacific Logging about 5000 acres of prime timberland on the Sunshine Coast in return for 9800 acres of logged off recreational property on central and northern Vancouver Island. Basing his estimates on statements by forestry officials, Lockstead charged [that] the timber values alone were more than $60 million and the property value could exceed $100 million for the land being traded to Pacific Logging. (97)

During the late 1970s and early 1980s, Vancouver city politics mirrored the partisan nature of BC provincial politics, which had been evident since the election of 1941 (Phillips 2010).[2] Provincial party politics was epitomized by a simple dynamic: on the one side, free enterprise parties seeking to exploit the rich resources of the province to achieve economic prosperity, and, on the other, the "socialist rabble." Coalitions, particularly on the right, would form to either gain or maintain power. Two municipal parties in Vancouver regularly competed for control of City Council, the School Board, and the Parks Board, mostly along ideological lines. These were (1) the Non-Partisan Association (NPA), a right-leaning civic party based in the west side of the city, and (2) the Committee of Progressive Electors (COPE), a left-leaning civic party based in the east side of the city. Historically, the NPA was seen as the party that favoured a conservative program supportive of business and development, while COPE was seen as having links to organized labour and a "left-progressive" platform. From 1941 onward, the NPA was the dominant civic party electorally representing free enterprisers – although there were occasional interludes of independent mayors and a very brief COPE period from 2002 to 2005.

VANCOUVER ALDERMAN 1984

Campbell became president of the Non-Partisan Association in 1983. His career as an elected politician at the local government level began in 1984 at the age of thirty-six, when he finished eighth in his first attempt at running for office and was elected as alderman as part of an NPA slate (Moya 1984). Two years later, after one term as alderman, Campbell would be elected the youngest mayor in the city's history, replacing Michael Harcourt who had moved on to provincial politics, first as leader of the New Democratic Party and then as premier. The 1986 Vancouver mayoral election was fought between Campbell and sixty-six-year-old COPE alderman Harry Rankin. Rankin, a criminal lawyer who had served as treasurer to the BC Law Society and Queen's counsel, was famous for his extreme left-wing views and his unabashed socialism. It was a fiercely contested election. The main point of contention was the future development of the Expo '86 site on the north side of False Creek, and there were concerns about each candidate's suitability to deal with the provincial Social Credit government (Cruickshank 1986). Campbell campaigned on a platform of "rationaliz[ing] the planning and permit process to make it more efficient," working to "get a ward system in place for 1986," and showing "council how a north gate for Expo [could] be built" (Moya 1984). Campbell's term as alderman was uneventful, and he was a relatively unknown entity heading into the mayoral election. However, the electorate's values appeared to be shifting to the right, and Campbell won with 55.7 per cent of the votes cast (*Toronto Star* 1987). Campbell attributed his electoral success to "hard campaigning, Phillips's endorsement, and many hard-working supporters" (Moya 1984).

FIRST TERM AS MAYOR OF VANCOUVER (1986–89)

Writing in the *Vancouver Sun*, Peter McMartin (1987c) described Campbell's first six months as mayor as follows:

> He has exhibited more inclination toward real decision-making than Mike Harcourt did in four years. Maybe he took to heart the size of the mandate he was handed and interpreted that as a message to act decisively. With the overwhelming majority he has on the council, he does not have to make any pretense about refereeing. He makes sure he has his way. He has also won the respect of

his department heads, crucial to the mayor. One said he is a "real toughie and smarter than most."

Yet, despite these positive words, McMartin also described Campbell as "secretive" and "arrogant" and as having the ability to "brown-nose if it suit[ed] his purpose" (McMartin 1987c).

During Campbell's first term as mayor of Vancouver he was "variously accused by friends and foes as being 'a wimp, a moral eunuch, an opportunist, a one-man show and the developers' mayor.'" He was also accused of "being short-tempered and impatient with city hall staff" and "mak[ing] others feel incompetent." One thing that every commentator agreed on was that Campbell's work ethic was astonishing. Alderman (later Mayor) Philip Owen remarked that "Campbell's production level was unbelievable" (Fayerman 1988).

At the new council's first meeting on 9 December 1986, the NPA dominated assembly-made headlines and raised howls of fury when it[3]

> repealed the shops closing bylaw; raised aldermanic salaries by
> 27.3% and the mayor's by 12 percent; reversed the practice of re-
> quiring an outside contractor to pay its workers "fair wages" and
> benefits on a par with those of civic staff; turned down a peace
> group's request for a grant; agreed to remove two traffic diverters
> in east Vancouver, and approved, in principle, a championship car
> race without consulting neighbourhood residents. (Volkart and
> Cox 1987)

Council also passed bylaws cracking down on, or eliminating, illegal suites and mega-houses, irresponsible dog owners, support for a rental aid society, and bed and breakfasts in Vancouver (Volkart and Cox 1987). Early in his first term, Campbell showed no hesitation in tackling contentious local issues, which is similar to how he would later implement massive policy change during his first term as premier. Less controversial actions included fighting for the preservation of the Vancouver-Kingsway federal riding, providing increased funding to AIDS Vancouver,[4] and seeking closer relationships with other levels of government. Campbell sought inter-governmental cooperation on a variety of local issues, just as he did as premier (when, for example, he connected with California governor Schwarzenegger on environmental issues). Council also opened Granville Street to limited car traffic and passed a plan to transform the Granville strip into "a lively arts-

and-entertainment district with new housing and parks nearby" (Volkart and Cox 1987). Campbell's moving liquor licences to the strip, along with limiting traffic and encouraging returning the street to a neon-lined entertainment district, plus encouraging residential developments in Yaletown, could be seen as an early attempt to ensure that his legacy as mayor remained intact.

Campbell's ideological focus was apparent quite early in his first term as mayor. Indeed, he sought a decrease in local government spending by cutting services by $5 million (Cox 1987). He was motivated to deepen the cuts because he believed that it was necessary for increased costs in local government to match the rate of inflation. He considered budgetary restraint to be a "cautious" management of city spending that was centred on "changing city services," not on "cutting" them (Cox and Palmer 1987). Some of the more controversial cuts included the "elimination of the city fireboat, reduced pumper truck crews, a reduction in city social workers and nursing positions, and reduced garbage pickup and park maintenance" (ibid.). Campbell justified his administration's austerity by claiming:

> Without these cuts, the costs of civic government in this city would go up 8 ½ per cent by next year, two times the rate of inflation. In the economic climate we have in Vancouver, we can't afford that. The cost of the Iona sewage outfall is part of that $60 million, plus the cost of the Cambie Street bridge, and the four-year capital plan we passed last year. We also have salary negotiations coming up this year. (McMartin 1987a)

The $1.9 million in cuts to the fire department budget included decommissioning the city's only fireboat, reducing the number of firefighters on the city's pumper trucks from five to four, and eliminating thirty-nine administrative general staff positions (Cox 1987). Campbell not only moved quickly to institute budgetary cuts at city hall, he also aggressively consolidated his power base within council, ignoring the two COPE aldermen in his appointments to the Greater Vancouver Regional District – now referred to as Metro Vancouver – and the board of the Pacific National Exhibition. Campbell stated that "it was his prerogative to assign aldermen to whatever committees he want[ed]" (Lee 1988d). Campbell did not hesitate to use his political power when necessary or expedient – a trait that he would regularly display later on as he embarked on his provincial career.

Suspicions over Campbell's connections to the development community persisted during his first term as mayor. During the 1986 mayoral campaign Campbell had included development of city land along Marine Drive in his party's election platform. He was subsequently lobbied by George Weston Ltd of Toronto, Westfair Foods, and Real Canadian Superstore to allow for large-scale "box stores" for the first time in the city. He used his NPA majority on council to create a task force to consider the possibility of large-scale development in this area and appointed himself chairman of the committee (McMartin 1987b). Campbell's interest in development issues was evident during this first term – later he would show this interest in a regional sense as he became the chair of the GVRD's planning committee.

The Vancouver Land Corporation Properties Ltd (VLC) deal arranged by Campbell and developer Jack Poole had severely damaged the cohesiveness of the NPA caucus during the first term, with several aldermen, particularly Baker, opposing the arrangement that would see the city of Vancouver paying $2 million for 10 per cent (400,000 special shares) and giving the company access to a minimum of $48 million worth of city land (fifteen city-owned lots in ten locations) (Bramham and Buttle 1989). Poole had raised about $18 million from union pension funds and investors to set up VLC. Campbell had directly negotiated with Poole and union pension fund administrators to give the company access in "exchange for moderately priced rental units." According to Baker, "the city should have tendered the property and sold it to the highest bidder and, failing that, it should have had an independent analysis of the deal by outside, experienced consultants." He continued: "The integrity of municipal government and the way it deals with land has been severely compromised ... [W]hat's good for Jack Poole and the investors is not necessarily good for the city" (Bramham 1989a).

Campbell's scheme did have support in the community from surprising sources, despite the opposition within his own caucus. For example, one person who advocated for the arrangement was the president of the BC Federation of Labour, Ken Georgetti, who agreed to sit on the company's board of directors. His comment: "This should help take the pressure off the low end of the market and the units that are now occupied by people with better means ... and it will put union members to work" (Bramham and Buttle 1989).

Campbell's response to internal challenges was to blame previous councils for having inadequate housing plans and to blame "senior" governments for providing the city with insufficient funding. He suggested that his council was attempting to meet the issues with a "comprehensive plan" that featured such steps as: the direct involvement in Vancouver Lands Company Properties Ltd to build rental properties in the downtown core; a proposal to set up a series of "neighbourhood housing centres" that would act as pilot projects for high-density demonstration projects; supporting the redevelopment of Expo by Concord Pacific and the redevelopment of Coal Harbour by Marathon Realty Ltd; facilitating a large Bosa Bros. development alongside Science World; stopping the construction of mega-houses in single-family areas; and meeting the challenges of increased immigration.

Campbell was an unabashed promoter of one strategy to deal with the development issues in Vancouver: "[We] have to be willing to double, triple or quadruple our densities" (Bramham 1989b). He supported the notion of creating a new attitude towards development in Vancouver concerning the plan for the former Expo '86 lands when he became mayor in 1986. The city "undertook a new approach to major land holdings in three areas – False Creek, the Burrard Inlet Waterfront, and the Fraser Lands" – featuring a "public process to establish what the city wanted on the lands" (Gordon Campbell, personal communication, 26 June 2013). The city came up with sixteen guidelines to clearly indicate that "these [were] the public objectives on these lands" (ibid.).[5] The guidelines put the onus on the development community to conform to the desires and needs of the city rather than the other way round.

> If a developer wanted to engage in the redevelopment then that was the framework into which any proposal should fit – my theory was that it was not an effective use of time, energy, or resources if the city just kept saying what it DID NOT want, it was our job to say what we DID want in the public interest. (Gordon Campbell, personal communication, 2013)

This was consistent with the "friendly" relationship between the city administration and developers during Campbell's first term, and it intensified during his second term.

By the middle of his first term in 1987, Campbell began to be criticized for running what his opponents were calling "a one-man show" (Cox 1987). This criticism was not limited to the COPE opposition; it also came from his colleagues within the NPA. NPA alderman Jonathan Baker suggested that Campbell "would take issues he did not consider big and 'just try to ram [them] through without consultation' and that

[he] tended to 'go off on his own, believing he's doing the right thing and expecting we'll all agree with him'" (ibid.). Baker's dissatisfaction with Campbell deepened as the mayor pushed for an early vote on the prospects of a ward system and appeared to crest when he began advocating for a lease arrangement with VLC Properties Ltd involving eighty-year leases and $48 million worth of city-owned land (Bramham 1989b). This type of intense effort on major policy initiatives, and the lack of hesitancy to move forward on his own as mayor, are consistent with his later activities as premier. However, Campbell's attention would eventually shift to other policy challenges.

The controversy over the institution of the ward system brought internal turmoil within the NPA caucus into the open in July 1987. Campbell had lobbied the provincial government hard to obtain support for allowing a plebiscite to be held on whether the city should adopt a ward system for municipal elections. Traditionally, the NPA did not favour the ward system for Vancouver, with "at least four NPA aldermen [having] spoken against it" (McMartin 1987d). Alderman Baker led the internal opposition, suggesting that the ward plebiscite be held in conjunction with the municipal election in 1988 (so that the system could be used in 1990), while Campbell argued for an early "stand-alone" vote late in 1987 or early in 1988 (so that the system would be in place for the 1988 election). Council voted six to five against the mayor's motion for an early plebiscite date, handing Campbell his first political defeat (ibid.).[6]

Despite flashes of an ideologically driven right-wing modus operandi (cost-cutting, support for private enterprise, anti-union firefighter cuts, and so on), one must counter-balance this with the recognition that Campbell also led a council that took on several very progressive programs during his first term. For example, Campbell said that the city of Vancouver would not oppose the building of a stand-alone medical clinic when Bill Vander Zalm's government was debating whether or not to fund abortions in the province (Bolan and Mason 1988). Furthermore, Campbell supported the development of a civic AIDS policy and chaired a task force on council to examine the city's role in combating the epidemic. He also supported the city's hosting of the Gay Games, called Celebration '90, which would bring five thousand athletes from seventeen countries and about ten thousand visitors to the city. Campbell commented: "One of the reasons I feel it's a privilege for Vancouver to host these Gay Games is they're one of the few events possible where anyone who wants to experience the thrill of international competition can" (*Vancouver Sun* 1987a). Campbell also supported the

Vander Zalm government's "province-wide sex education program for public schools," stating: "it is important that our educational program include information about all aspects of life including sex" (Bolan and Baldrey 1987).

Donald Gutstein asserted that, during Campbell's first term as mayor, he found a way to lead a moderate local government: "He's found the secret to governing a social democratic city by voting on the left for inexpensive social issues and on the middle to right political spectrum for all else" (Fayerman 1988).

Mayor Campbell's first term in office was clearly more right of centre than left of centre, especially in terms of how he approached the fiscal operations of the city's administration. The cuts to city services, which included fire services, nurses, and social workers, point to a desire for smaller government and a focus on balancing budgets ahead of the needs of often unionized public services. The efforts to consolidate power, his aggressive behaviour towards his opponents both inside and outside of the NPA, and the criticisms of his go-it-alone style did indicate a strong desire to lead – but frequently in a narrowly focused direction. This pragmatic approach meant that Campbell did not necessarily follow strict neoliberal tenets at all times. Still, his support of "more" progressive social issues, such as the construction of abortion clinics in Vancouver, the hosting of the Gay Games, and the development of AIDS protocols, suggests a pragmatic and adaptable leader rather than an ideologue driven by a set of unrelenting neoliberal values.

Campbell's early activities as mayor mirror the approach he would later follow in his first term as premier: that is, an intense focus on policy change favouring free enterprise, deficit reduction, program rationalization, and pushing the political culture of the city and (later) the province towards the right. What has been largely ignored by his opponents is Campbell's concern for several progressive policy initiatives during his first term. Unquestionably, his focus was clearly on the internal operations of Vancouver and on seeking fundamental changes in the way the city conducted its business. This focus began to change when Campbell won his second term as mayor in 1988.

SECOND TERM AS MAYOR OF VANCOUVER, 1990–93

Campbell's second term as mayor of Vancouver began with his election on 19 November 1988. He defeated the unity candidate, Jean Swanson, supported by COPE, the civic New Democrats, and the Vancouver and District Labour Council. The election featured a voter turnout of 43.3 per cent, down from 49 per cent in 1986, with Campbell obtaining 75,545 votes (59.5 per cent) versus Swanson's 45,178 (35.6 per cent) (Lee 1988f, A1).

The ward plebiscite held in conjunction with the civic election failed as it did not achieve the necessary 60 per cent threshold set out by the province: in the end, it received 56 per cent support. Campbell, responding to the defeat, pointed to his government's first term as the reason for the lack of support for the plebiscite: "I think the fact that we provided such good government hurt the ward system's chances. I've always been in favor of it, but I think the most important thing for governments is to respond to what people want and the people in this city obviously want to keep the system as it is" (Lee 1988b).

Development issues were clearly at the forefront of the election campaign and would dominate most of Campbell's time and attention during his second term as mayor. In the run-up to the 1988 election, he began advocating a development plan for lands along False Creek that had contained the former Expo '86 site and the Coal Harbour waterfront. For example, he wanted the city to purchase $20 million worth of land for two thousand housing units from the developers of both areas to "ensure an adequate mix of seniors, family and subsidized rental housing" (Fayerman 1988).

Under this Strategic Housing Opportunities Program, Campbell suggested the use of the city's property endowment fund over ten years to "acquire land for 1,500 units (out of a total of 8,000) at the Expo site being developed by Hong Kong owner Li Ka-shing, and 500 (out of a total of 2,500) at the Coal Harbour site owned by Marathon Realty" (Fayerman 1988).[7] Not surprisingly, the development community supported the idea. "We think this is very appropriate and we have always maintained that the only way we can allocate is if the city and others are involved," said Jack Birkett, land manager for Marathon Realty (ibid.).

One of the first things that occurred shortly after the new council was elected – and, as it turned out, a harbinger of things to come – was the resignation of long-time city planning director Ray Spaxman. The NPA's opponents, most notably Michael Harcourt, suggested that Spaxman was forced from his job over philosophical differences concerning the future of development in the city. According to Harcourt: "Ray was fired. They got him. This NPA developers' council got Ray Spaxman because he stood in the way of everything they want" (Lee 1988c).

During Campbell's second term, he began to feel increasing pressure from several disparate sources:

> Midway through his second term Campbell gets daily complaints about how housing prices have skyrocketed, mega-houses are still replacing bungalows, elderly tenants are being evicted to make way for luxury condominiums, single-family neighbourhoods are being rezoned to legalize secondary suites, immigration has increased and the vacancy rate is virtually zero. (Bramham 1989b)

Further evidence of the ongoing and intensifying relationship between the city administration and the development community can be found in the development of a "joint planning process" for megaprojects that "allow[ed] the city to extract from developers much of the cost of staff time it takes to process (development) applications" and, according to its supporters, theoretically "allow[ed] city planners and developers to work together to develop projects that benefit everyone" (Buttle 1990). Mayor Campbell asserted that the development process that had been used previously was "confrontational" and "often meant [that] developers presented the city with a proposal that the city would then either accept or reject"; he much preferred the consensual approach, which had resulted in about $100 million worth of amenities from developers for the city (ibid.).

Campbell did show signs of placing political expediency ahead of maintaining electoral support during his second term as mayor, and this included implementing policies that would not be supported by his traditional base of support – most particularly, the business community. A dramatic increase in commercial property taxes caused by provincial reassessments heightened small business distrust of the NPA regime during Campbell's second term. Indeed, four hundred west-side merchants and landlords booed Campbell at a meeting held in June 1989 as he suggested that there was nothing city council could do and that businesses would "have to work towards unspecified long-term changes in the municipal financing structure" and "adjust to the situation of rising land values" (Buttle 1989).

Campbell also worked directly against the interests of local developers in response to public pressure against the demolition of low-cost housing when he supported the imposition of a new thousand-dollar fee "to be paid to the city by developers for each rental unit they demolish and the establishment of a service to help relocate displaced tenants" (Balcom 1989). In essence, he made a political decision to ignore the concerns of developers as a large-scale residents' group from his power base in the west side of the city forced a delay in the demolitions. The Concerned Citizens for Affordable Housing collected petitions, mostly from seniors in Kerrisdale, and lobbied the Campbell administration for assistance for "long-time renters that were increasingly being forced from their homes as land values [rose] and apartment owners [sold] out to developers" (ibid.).

Consistent with his adoption of more progressive public policy, Campbell also participated in the GVRD's choosing the Our Future program, which sought citizen input for enhancing the region's livability. Moreover, he formed the Fraser Cities Coalition with mayors from municipalities along the Fraser River and set up, with council, the Environmental Action Secretariat.[8] He was instrumental in the development of the "False Creek Loop,"[9] and he was purportedly responsible for substituting foam coffee cups with china mugs at city hall. Campbell also took a leadership role in January 1990 by organizing a meeting of ten environmental groups "to learn what they believe[d] [were] the city's most pressing environmental concerns" (Kavanagh 1990). Several priorities were identified throughout this process, including "Vancouver's curbside recycling program, ecological issues in Stanley Park such as the controversial reforestation program and zoo expansion, logging in local watersheds, and toxic wastes in Vancouver real estate" (ibid.).

Gordon Campbell's second term as mayor of Vancouver was marked by a continuation of many of the themes that were initiated over his first three years in public office. However, he did intensify his consolidation of political power both in his internal relations within the NPA and in confidently facing external opposition both from elected and non-elected directions. There was significant evidence of continuous power consolidation and retribution with Campbell's and the NPA's manipulation of the nomination process leading to the 1990 civic election in which Alderman Jonathan Baker was dumped from the NPA slate. This brought to light the fact that support for the mayor within his own party was not unanimous.

Campbell had no problem taking on members of his own party and traditional business supporters (including developers) who were against increased development fees. He did continue his close relationship with business and, more important, the development community during his second term, thus facilitating major projects that would forever change the complexion of the downtown core and the city in general. Throughout this term he continued to make politically expedient decisions to support or oppose issues that were important to maintaining his electoral base.

However, a few key differences are worth pointing out since they put him at odds with a number of important stakeholders. Most notably, opposition started to form against the mayor's increasingly overt support for development and the planning processes being undertaken by the city's administration. In addition, he faced considerable pressure from the local business community, which perceived his response to the provincial government's increase in commercial property tax rates to be disingenuous.

Consistent with his efforts in the first term, Campbell also continued to pursue progressive social issues, most notably those connected to the environment, alongside issues that would appear to be more ideologically consistent with his later political program. As with his efforts in the first term, concern for the environment and other progressive policy initiatives were similar to his later efforts as premier, when he began to further a more environmentally friendly program, including instituting the provincial carbon tax. The concern for environmental policy mirrored Campbell's actions during his second term as premier, when he began actively pushing for a "greener" agenda.

Campbell's focus, entering his third term of office, shifted to a more outward-looking perspective. Indeed, he began to concentrate more heavily on issues not necessarily internal to the city's operations, taking a major role at the regional level through his leadership of the GVRD and the Union of British Columbia Municipalities. He continued exercising considerable political strength at the local government level in Vancouver and maintained a fairly consistent policy focus, which he had displayed in the first two terms. However, his attention appeared to be shifting towards building a legacy and setting the foundation for a role on a larger political stage as first leader of the BC Liberal Party and later as premier of British Columbia.

THIRD TERM AS MAYOR OF VANCOUVER, 1993–96

The election campaign leading to Campbell's third term as mayor of Vancouver in November 1990 was the most tense, and competitive, of his three mayoral campaigns.[10] The Downtown Eastside Residents' Association's high-profile organizer, Jim Green, emerged as a challenger to Campbell following COPE incumbent alderman Libby Davies's decision not to challenge the mayor for the position. COPE had also entered into an agreement to "split the field of candidates for all council, park board and school board positions, and run a unity mayoral candidate" (Lee 1990a).

Libby Davies referred to Green as having "great knowledge, and [being] right off the street in the public's eye," having "wisdom and commitment and [the] backing needed to do the job" – "a breath of fresh air" (Lee 1990a). Green saw himself as the "everyman" (and woman) and was known for speaking out against the gentrification and eviction issues related to Expo '86, and for his advocacy of social housing in the city's Downtown Eastside. In stark contrast to Campbell's perceived privileged early life on the city's west side, Green's early working years saw him take up positions as a taxi driver and longshoreman upon arriving in Canada as one of a wave of American Vietnam War resisters (Spencer 2012).

Green saw the central issues of the 1990 campaign as "the destruction of neighbourhoods, developers running the city and an increasing crime rate," with his main campaign focus being that he was "be running for the people of the city of Vancouver against the megadevelopers" (Bramham 1990).

The election was about several issues that emerged from various sources rather than on any type of east-west bias. These sources included angry Kerrisdale residents who were opposed to the demolition of rental stock and its replacement with condominium developments; the city's new ban on illegal suites; South Shaughnessy residents who bemoaned the lack of zoning and design controls over "monster houses"; businesspeople and west-side home owners who were still upset over property assessments that had been increased in 1988 (and that forced council to cap taxes and institute a rebate program); opposition to Concord Pacific's False Creek and Marathon's Coal Harbour developments and the failure to provide sufficient social housing amenities; and criticism of the land lease deal with VLC Ltd, which had built fewer units than promised and at a higher rental rate than originally proposed.[11] Concern over the dislocation of residents because of a lack of affordable housing was an issue that "city hall confronted[,] with [the] spectacle of young squatters moving into abandoned apartment buildings slated for demolition" and "a noticeable increase in the number of homeless people on the streets" (Lee 1990b). Formal plebiscite questions being considered alongside the 1990 civic election included: an approval of an $80 million capital plan (including $29.5 million for a new library); $500,000 for a controversial new otter display at the Stanley Park Zoo;[12] and funding for a new fireboat program (ibid.).[13]

During his mayoral campaign, Campbell highlighted his successes over the previous two terms, including the provision of rental housing units, "$300 million in city services paid by developers," "better eviction notice provisions," the Cassiar Connector, and the Vancouver Charter provisions intended to help renters in the city (Lee 1990d). The mayor, in defence of his first four years, suggested that "action, not ideology" drove his agenda. He went on to say: "I've never claimed we have all the answers. There are a whole series of questions, and if we keep our destination in view, then we can get there, slowly but surely" (Lee 1990c). Campbell pointed to the focus of his potential third term suggesting that "the NPA [would be] the only alternative for voters who don't like confrontational politics that threaten to bankrupt them." Furthermore, he reiterated that "the new reality in Vancouver is the need for affordable government that works ... There is a limit to what the taxpayer can pay" (Lee 1990b).

More specifically, the Campbell/NPA election platform during the campaign included the following proposals to:

a) Establish an "affordable home-ownership task force" to find ways for young people and first-time buyers to buy in Vancouver;
b) Press the province for annual property assessments, removal of school tax levies from city tax bills, three-year averaging of taxes and a flat-tax option for commercial properties;
c) Establish "rental-use" zones where designated rental properties will be encouraged;
d) Create "neighbourhood profiles and housing action plans for West Point Grey, Kerrisdale, Grandview-Woodlands, Riley Park and Mount Pleasant;
e) Push for more provincial and federal involvement in housing programs, and for Vancouver to be given the right to roll back excessive rent increases; and
f) Create a "regulatory review commission" to help streamline civic regulations and make them more cost-effective. (Lee 1990d)

The results of the 1990 Vancouver civic election saw Mayor Campbell receive 67,950 votes to Jim Green's 56,814. Campbell actually lost votes compared to his 1988 totals, with his margin of victory over his COPE/NDP opponent dropping from 30,300 in 1988 to 11,100. Campbell's share of the popular vote dropped from 60 per cent to 53.7 per cent as well, and council was split down the middle, with five COPE aldermen and five NPA aldermen. In addition, the otter habitat referendum failed, but the new main library funding and parks/recreation funding passed (Fayerman 1990).

In his inaugural address for his third term Campbell recognized the mood of the citizenry, suggesting that "[the] electorate is tired of the old answers to the old problems. The electorate sent council a strong message for change and they know that we can handle the problems. We accept the responsibility for Vancouver's future" (Lamb 1990). Consistent with a change in focus towards more outward-looking issues, observers at the inauguration noted that part of Campbell's speech focused on "larger challenges" that involved "regional and provincial matters" and the need for greater "cooperation between local, regional, and federal governments" and that this could possibly indicate the mayor's desire to "move on to the chairmanship of the Greater Vancouver regional district, [and] then [to] move on to the chairmanship of the Union of British Columbia Municipalities as a springboard to provincial politics" (ibid.).[14]

Following his election victory Campbell's own personal focus appeared to shift away from the day-to-day inward-looking micromanagement of the city's affairs to a more outward-looking vision that involved greater connections and influence with the surrounding regions, the provincial government in Victoria, and the federal government in Ottawa. A good first indicator of Campbell's increasingly outward vision and rising regional profile was his election as chair of the GVRD shortly after the civic election in early December 1990 (Gram 1990). Traditionally, the mayor of Vancouver was not selected as chair as others feared the city would wield too much power in the regional district.[15] Campbell had previously chaired the region's development services committee and had overseen the Creating the Future regional plan.

His commitment to regional transit centred on seeking systemic change to the funding of the region's transportation system. He pointed to the "poor financial planning" at the regional level to ensure the long-term fiscal health of the system and called for several reforms regarding how the regional transportation system could be funded.

In his annual *State of the City* report in 1992, Campbell specifically began criticizing both levels of government for shifting costs unfairly to local taxpayers by transferring responsibilities to municipalities without funding mechanisms to meet the new-found commitments. He called for a municipal government "bill of rights" and argued for a "municipal-provincial constitutional conference" that would "maintain the momentum for reform" (Lee 1992a).

In 1993, following his election as chair of the UBCM, Campbell would further increase his provincial profile. At this point he began pressuring the NDP government in response to Harcourt's program of belt-tightening, which included a reduction in municipal grants, an elimination of the supplementary homeowner's grant, and the shifting of other services that had a direct effect on the main source of municipal revenues – property taxes. Campbell commented on the province's plan to gain access to some forms of municipal revenue to meet provincial budgetary goals: "The property tax is not a bottomless pit. The property taxpayer was thoroughly fleeced in 1992, and we don't want that to happen in 1993" (Lee 1993a).

In his third term, Campbell was faced with a council that was evenly divided between COPE and NPA councillors, which meant that the internal politics of the city became particularly acrimonious. In several ways, Campbell's approach to governance began to represent more of a prime ministerial and/or cabinet-centred model (especially in a minority government) of local government as opposed to the presidential or dictatorial model that was evident from time to time in his first two terms.

This rebalancing of power may have encouraged Campbell to turn his attention to what he believed to be more pertinent issues. For one, he began to openly challenge the provincial government on municipal taxation and transit issues in order to further the concerns of the city and surrounding region, and, as a by-product, his regional and provincial political profile began to increase. Finally, as was the case throughout his first two terms, Campbell continued prioritizing efforts in the city in socially progressive areas such as housing, child care, AIDS assistance, and development. All of these areas indicate, to some extent, that he was more of a value-pluralist and populist – cherry-picking policies and causes that would yield instant public support – than a monochromatic defender of free-market philosophy.

Campbell's desire for legacy building and moving towards more macro issues during his third term as mayor of Vancouver is consistent with the foreshadowing that was evident after his first two terms. In the waning days of Campbell's tenure as premier of British Columbia it was evident that he had begun looking outward and towards legacy building, which can be seen in relation to his efforts to organize the Federation of the Provinces, the Olympics, and the construction of several large-scale infrastructure projects.

CONCLUSION

In this regard, the record shows that Canadian mayors, regardless of opposition from city councillors, can often accomplish a great deal if they are competent, shrewd and, most important, popular with the electorate. Not surprisingly, then, the office of mayor in Canada has often attracted persons with large egos and dictatorial passions – headline seekers with visions of grandeur who think they know what is best for their cities. Often they have been right. (Sayre and Kaufman 1960)

Gordon Campbell's three consecutive terms as mayor of Vancouver were characterized by considerable systemic change in the way the city was managed, and it could be considered a period of accomplishment. Campbell was clearly competent and shrewd, and he enjoyed significant popularity among the city's residents. Analyzing Gordon Campbell's three terms as mayor of Vancouver is more complex than one would expect – particularly in terms of how he was perceived as premier from 2001 to 2011. On the one hand, especially at the beginning of his first term as mayor, Campbell would embark on a fairly conservative program (some would argue neoliberal) that featured budgetary cost-cutting, challenges to unions, attention to rationalizing systems and improving accountability mechanisms, and implementing policies favourable to capital. Many of these efforts were facilitated through the NPA's control of council and Campbell's efforts to consolidate power in the mayor's office. Campbell's program, however, did not just focus on right-wing policies as he spent a considerable amount of time, energy, and political capital on progressive issues such as combatting AIDS, supporting school lunch programs, embarking on environmental issues within the city and region, and so on.

This approach to public policy at the local government level in Vancouver continued throughout his second and third terms. He managed to maintain his base of free enterprise support while addressing significant social issues within the city. The nature of his policy focus, however, changed from a relentless drive to rationalize the city's budget and operations in his early days as mayor to a concern for legacy and more macro-related issues involving the regional, provincial, and federal governments.

Campbell certainly enjoyed substantial electoral, policy, and political success during his years in Vancouver: he rarely lost a political battle. It must have been an especially intense jolt to his psyche when his initial foray into provincial politics resulted in defeat as leader of the Official Opposition Liberal Party rather than being elected immediately as premier of British Columbia: his loss to Glen Clark in 1996 would likely have been even more disappointing given that he won the popular vote.

I contend that, given Gordon Campbell's early political activities, it is possible to identify clues to understanding his proclivities as BC's premier. Specifically, these included an excellent work ethic combined with a pragmatic, and at times progressive, focus, with an inclination to place intense attention on an issue before eventually moving on when he lost interest or some other challenge presented itself.

As one examines Gordon Campbell's early political career as mayor of Vancouver, it becomes apparent that he was far from the one-dimensional ideologue portrayed by his detractors. The evidence suggests that he adopted a much more pragmatic approach to policy – at this early point in his career – than he was/has been given credit for. Furthermore, it should become apparent as one makes one's way through this volume that the threads of his earlier political behaviour permeate his later provincial career and are consistent with this multi-dimensional profile.

NOTES

1 During his time at Marathon Realty, Campbell was heavily involved in the development of the North False Creek Lands. Campbell, along with Martin Zlotnick and Frank Rigney (who would later develop the Georgian Court Hotel next to the stadium site), former mayor Art Phillips, and architect Randle Ireland, organized the "Stadium for Downtown Vancouver Association" to lobby for the False Creek location for Expo '86 (Government of Canada 1986, 11).

2 In the 1936 election, members of the CCF won three seats on city council, motivating local business owners to form the NPA in 1937.

3 COPE had been reduced to two seats on council, one held by Bruce Ericksen and the other held by former NDP MP Libby Davies.

4 Council actually passed a motion prohibiting discrimination against city employees found to be carrying the AIDS virus and formed a mayor's study group on AIDS.

5 As part of my doctoral dissertation, in 2013 I conducted an "interview" with Gordon Campbell that consisted of a series of e-mail conversations.

6 The 1988 plebiscite failed, with only 56 per cent voting in favour of the motion, thus falling well short of the 60 per cent threshold needed to pass.

7 Campbell's connection to Marathon as a former employee was fodder for his opponents and the media.

8 Set up to direct civic efforts and to coordinate environmental policy among city departments.

9 The loop was a circuit of bicycle paths around False Creek.

10 This was Campbell's first "three-year-term" election contest.

11 The mayor had originally promised these suites would average $615, which was not the case by the time the 1990 election came around.

12 Critics of the otter display suggested that its approval would be the first step in a $40 million six-phase expansion of the zoo.

13 Campbell had included getting rid of the fireboat program and reducing staffing on fire trucks as part of the $5 million in cuts during his first term. In preparation for the 1990 election, he suggested the city would fund four new fireboats and a barge.

14 Campbell would become chair of the GVRD in December 1990 and, later in 1992, the president of the UBCM.

15 Campbell was only the second chair from Vancouver in almost forty-five years. The first was Alderman Earl Adams, who was elected in 1967.

2

Assessing Gordon Campbell's Uneven Democratic Legacy in British Columbia

DENNIS PILON

At the commemorative event marking the end of the innovative and widely lauded British Columbia Citizens' Assembly (BCCA) process, BC Liberal premier Gordon Campbell was credited by participants and the media with being a democratic visionary for his government's role in creating and supporting its work. "No government, in any democracy, has ever given such a charge to non-elected citizens," claimed assembly chair Jack Blaney. "You set new rules – the new gold standard – for the true engagement of citizens in democratic governance" (Blaney, as cited in Hall 2004). At a glance, Gordon Campbell's Liberal government does appear to have been very active on democratic reform in its first term, introducing fixed election dates, holding open cabinet meetings, and not only sponsoring the BCCA but also preparing to hold a public referendum on its proposed alternative voting system. Yet a closer inspection reveals a more uneven performance. Not all of the reforms promised while in opposition were introduced when Campbell became premier, while others were limited by a fine print that often weakened the impact of the changes.

How should we approach unpacking Gordon Campbell's uneven democracy legacy? Why did his government move quickly on some issues, slowly on others, and not at all in a number of cases? Clear answers have not been forthcoming from the politicians, who have tended to offer self-serving rationales for their actions (or inaction, as the case may be). Attempts to understand decisions by recourse to an examination of the actors themselves have generally not proven much more illuminating. For instance, countless scribes have declared Gordon

Campbell an enigma or cipher, with no clear political philosophy other than gaining and holding power (Rossiter, as cited in McMartin 1995; Fotheringham 1994; Palmer 1993b).

Awkward and uncomfortable as a public persona, Campbell is seldom cast with the more charismatic populist reformers that emerged in the 1990s. If anything, he is typically described as a neoliberal, especially in light of the deep cuts to taxes and services that his government made in its first term in office (Teghtsoonian 2010). Even so, in terms of discourse and the character of their reform proposals, there is a striking overlap between the populism of Preston Manning's Reform Party and the Campbell reboot of the BC Liberal Party post-1993 (as Lacharite echoes in chapter 5, this volume, where he looks at tax policy in BC under Campbell). As many scholars have noted (Laycock 1994; Patten 1996; Barney and Laycock 1999), the democratic imaginary of this reformist right-wing politics is actually about narrowing the space of democratic participation through a redefinition of the public (not "special interests") and legitimate public space (i.e., less government, more market). In reviewing the election platforms and public statements of the BC Liberals, and Gordon Campbell in particular, we see that the similarities with the Reform Party are strong. But it would be wrong to suggest that Campbell's BC Liberals were merely mimicking Reform. In power, Campbell quickly dispatched elements of his reform package that proved inconvenient. Indeed, after 2005, his government largely abandoned a programmatic democratic reform agenda altogether.

In this chapter, I demonstrate how Gordon Campbell's uneven democracy legacy is a product of an opportunistic marriage between plebiscitarian populism and an older tradition of municipal nonpartisanism. I do this by examining the development and execution of the democratic promises he made while leading the provincial opposition and government, and noting their antecedent links with his past political experience at the civic level. My method is simple: I compare what he claimed he would do with what he actually did. I deal with these reforms under four broad themes: openness, consultation, accountability, and reforming politics.

POLITICAL IDEAS/POLITICAL PRACTICE

Before Gordon Campbell became leader of the BC Liberal Party, it had been described as clearly centrist, both in terms of its traditional party members and its leadership (Blake and Carty 1995–96, 65). The right-

wing economic and populist policies associated with the post-1993 it-
eration of the party coincide with the arrival of Gordon Campbell as
leader and the influx of new members that supported him (68). As
such, it makes sense to attend to his influence on the programmatic
changes that followed in the wake of his leadership victory. But here
many commentators struggle to define Campbell's worldview. It has
been said that he does not really fit the mould of conventional party
politics. It is often claimed that he either is post-politics or simply does
not believe in anything – other than Gordon Campbell (Cernetig 2009;
Palmer 1993b). However, his views are recognizably on the right –
economically, often the far right – of the political spectrum. And, in
countless interviews since his arrival at Vancouver City Hall in 1984,
Campbell expressed an understanding of politics that echoes the clas-
sic themes of municipal non-partisanism, with, after 1993, an added element of plebiscitary populism.

When Gordon Campbell first entered electoral politics he did not
immediately make an impression. In his first run for mayor of Vancouver in 1986, commentators described his two-year stint as an alderman as "competent but unremarkable" (Farquharson 1986a) and
his mayoralty campaign as a "fresh but positive approach to leadership
based more on style than policy pronouncements" (Farquharson
1986b). But an early indication of Campbell's political views could be
found in his book review of Donald Gutstein's *Vancouver Ltd.*, published in the academic journal BC *Studies* in 1976. Gutstein's book was
highly critical of the property development industry and what he saw
as its cozy and self-serving links with city politicians. Campbell's review was mostly an intemperate ad hominem attack on Gutstein's
character and abilities as a journalist. But when he did finally dig into
the details of a False Creek development deal that Gutstein criticized,
it was clear that Campbell was fairly sympathetic to the developers
and the politicians working with them (Campbell 1976, 88–9). This
was not surprising as Campbell was just finishing his term as assistant
to Vancouver mayor Art Phillips and embarking on a career in the
property development field himself. In other words, he was essentially defending himself.

Campbell's impatience with Gutstein and other critics of development
bore the markings of an older non-partisan tradition at the civic level,
one that typically denied that there were any real divisions in local politics. In his first campaign for mayor, he dismissed political disagreements
at city council as the product of "ideology and politicking" (Harper 1986).

Later he would applaud longer terms for council so councillors could spend "more time on government and less on politics" (*Vancouver Sun* 1987b). In his first bid for re-election as mayor he complained that he was "tired of governments that [were] trying to set up oppositions" (Lee 1988a). And, when the civic wing of the New Democratic Party failed to make a breakthrough in the 1988 council election, he suggested the results proved that voters preferred his "non-partisan" approach (Lee 1988e). In making such claims, Campbell was drawing on a long tradition in Vancouver that eschewed party-like politics at city hall (Tennant 1980). His own electoral vehicle, the Non-Partisan Association, had been formed in the 1930s expressly to push a left-wing party out of civic politics (among other priorities), something it had succeeded in doing for the better part of four decades (Vogel 2003).

But municipal non-partisanism, far from being truly apolitical, proved, throughout the twentieth century, to be a very effective *political* strategy employed by pro-business forces to counter organized challenges to their influence at the local level. Its roots were in the American municipal reform movement of the 1920s, which claimed as its purpose the end of "log-rolling" and corruption in city decision making (Anderson 1972, 11–18). The idea that city decisions should be outside politics appealed to reformers from left to right, tapping into strong anti-party and anti-immigrant sentiment. But the end of obvious politicking at the local level often meant that business groups were the only coherently organized players left standing. In Canada, non-partisanism emerged in reaction to labour and left-wing breakthroughs at the civic level in the 1920s and 1930s (18–19).

Campbell's non-partisanism was also in evidence in his coyness to identify with political parties at other levels of government. In a 1984 interview he claimed, "I've been called a socialist by Grace McCarthy, a Liberal by the Tories and a Tory by the Liberals, and I'm sure there are some New Democrats who think I'm a Socred" (as cited in *Vancouver Sun* 1993). Later, when pressed about running for a provincial or federal party seat, Campbell dismissed the importance of party labels altogether: "What's a Liberal? What's a Conservative? What's a New Democrat?" he responded. "These are just names that don't mean anything anymore. What matters is discipline, not dogma" (Lamb 1989). Even when he became leader of the BC Liberals, Campbell still leaned on anti-party rhetoric. When questioned about whether his party and Social Credit should merge, he claimed: "I don't think it is a question of parties. Frankly, I think that is obsolete thinking. It is not [about] bringing parties together, it is [about] bringing people together that will make a difference" (Lee 1993d).

Despite his efforts to be seen as beyond party labels, Campbell was consistently associated with the federal Liberal Party both before and during his municipal political career, having worked for former mayor Art Philips (who would go on to become a federal Liberal candidate) and having attended various political fundraisers with Liberal activists and MPs (Ward 1990). As mayor, Campbell appeared consistently "liberal" on social issues and even a few regulatory ones, supporting the extension of spousal benefits to gay employees and the return of a provincial rentalsman office to address the city's housing crisis in the 1990s (Austin 1990). Donald Gutstein claimed that Campbell "found the secret to governing a social democratic city by voting on the left for inexpensive social issues and on the middle to right [of the] political spectrum for all else" (Gutstein, as cited in Fayerman 1988). Later, journalist Barbara Yaffe would describe Campbell as a "Blue Liberal" for his mix of social liberalism and fiscal conservatism. "I believe in the classical definition of a Liberal," he told Yaffe in 1994, "not in the publicly eroded definition of a Liberal. And that is, I believe, in individuals, individuality, [and] in individual choice" (Yaffe 1994). Campbell's electoral success and flexible ideological profile made him an attractive candidate for other political contests. In 1990, both the Liberal and Progressive Conservative parties approached him to run federally (Canadian Press 1990).

Campbell's political balancing act was possible not simply because of his efforts but also because of a marked shift in the character of Canadian liberalism that occurred from the 1970s on. As Summerville argues (chapter 4, this volume), the economic crisis of the 1970s raised the profile of neoliberal critiques of the postwar Keynesian approach to managing the economy, gaining adherents for their countermeasures – shrinking the welfare state, cutting taxes, and deregulating the economy. But supporters found access to what they thought should be their traditional home on the right blocked by conservative parties that remained committed to province-building (e.g., the Ontario Conservatives and the BC Social Credit Party) or maintaining support in Quebec (e.g., the federal Progressive Conservatives and Quebec Liberals). This created an opening for new parties (e.g., the western-based Reform Party and the Action Democratique Party of Quebec) or a redefinition of various Liberal parties to champion aspects of the neoliberal program (the post-1993 BC Liberals and federal Liberals being two good examples).

Gordon Campbell's embrace of strong neoliberal economic policies after 1993 was, then, neither that original nor that surprising, given developments elsewhere in the country. By contrast, his adoption of a clearly populist, right-wing discourse to frame his campaign for leadership of the provincial Liberal Party was seen as a departure, at least for him. While always pro-business, the Gordon Campbell who arrived on the provincial scene was now an avowed tax fighter, committed to rolling back government and unleashing the power of individual initiative. As he told the assembled crowd when he won the Liberal leadership: "The choice that British Columbians face is clear. They can continue to support a party that believes in big government solving all of our problems, or they can support the Liberal Party of British Columbia, which believes in individual rights, individual responsibilities, [and] economic opportunities matched with social obligations" (White 1993). Less than a year later, Campbell had crafted a reworked platform for the BC Liberals that echoed both the federal Reform Party's substance and, importantly, style. As Yaffe (1994) described it after emerging from her interview with Campbell: "The platform is straightforward. Get government out of people's faces and pockets, giving individuals more choice with what they do with their own cash. That means reducing government, eliminating duplication, paring back regulations, downsizing the public service and forcing government to live within its means."

The anti-tax, "power-to-the-taxpayer" populism of the post-1993 Gordon Campbell bears a striking resemblance to what Barney and Laycock (1999) dub "plebiscitary populism." Over the past century, various populisms have claimed to be just giving voice to "the people" against "powerful interests." But Steve Patten (1996, 103) argues that Canada's latest right-wing variant was not merely a reflection of public wants but, rather, an "ideological instrument for the construction of ... political identities," one that sought to redefine both "the people" and "powerful interests" of traditional populist discourse. In this new version, "the people" are "individualized and detached from broader social relations," while "powerful interests" are no longer the banks or the moneyed classes but, instead, anything than can be deemed "special interests" – basically any organized group that makes claims on the state (Patten 1996, 109; Laycock 1994, 217). Thus, the Reform Party project was about legitimating certain actors and activities as appropriate. As David Laycock notes, for the Reform Party "citizen participation is encouraged if it mobilizes opposition to bureaucrats and misguided egalitarians, or if it eschews intermediate organizations of representation." But it is not encouraged if people rally support for government spending or programs. In this populist redefinition of "the people" such actors must be, by definition, "special interests" and thus illegitimate (Laycock 1994, 230–45). Rather than allow politics to be contaminated by these special interests, plebiscitary techniques – such as recall, referenda, and initiatives – are preferred to establish a "direct" connection between the people and their preferred policies (Barney and Laycock 1999, 318).

As with municipal non-partisanism, the democratic credentials of plebiscitary populism are illusory – that is, a cover for obscuring the real politics that is going on. Indeed, Barney and Laycock (1999, 320) suggest that the real world of plebiscitarian politics is paradoxical: "private, direct (i.e., unmediated by institutionalized organizations) links between citizens and their policy preferences" are combined with "heavy leadership structuring of citizen attitudes towards these policies." The public think they are gaining control, but what they get access to has been heavily circumscribed and vetted. Again, Barney and Laycock remind us that the "combination works best if the 'grassroots' believe that they actually drive the agenda of a party or party government, and that the little delegation of power to which they have formally acceded is checked by a tight relationship of accountability" (320).

Gordon Campbell's democratic imaginary post-1993 mirrors many aspects of the plebiscitary populism sketched out above. As he told *Globe and Mail* columnist Craig McInnes in 1995, his main issues were "cutting the size of government and giving people back more control over their own lives." His vision of "the people" was one of individual taxpayers seeking freedom from government programs and financial commitments. His concrete democratic reforms involved making it easier to recall politicians, launch citizen-initiated referenda, and hold provincewide votes on key issues, like Aboriginal land claims. His political discourse invoked Reform's idea of there being legitimate versus illegitimate actors and activities. For instance, in a 2002 television address defending his steep budget cuts, Campbell declared: "We are doing everything we can to put your interests ahead of special interests" (*Vancouver Sun* 2002). And, as we shall see, Campbell sponsored a host of public consultation efforts that invited public leadership but that bore the heavy stamp of elite design and control. Attending to the influence of municipal non-partisanism and plebiscitary populism on Gordon Campbell will help us make sense of his uneven performance as a democratic reformer.

DEMOCRATIC REFORM:
PROMISES AND PERFORMANCE

In their 1996 election platform, *The Courage to Change*, under the heading "Making Government More Accountable," the BC Liberals promised to introduce "effective and workable" recall and initiative legislation, fixed election dates, a fixed legislative calendar and budget day, free votes on all issues (except the budget and Throne Speech), a ban on government advertising before elections, an end to the NDP "gag" law restricting third-party political advertising during elections, and a requirement for full disclosure of election donations, including support from labour organizations (British Columbia Liberal Party 1996, 13). In their 2001 election platform, *A New Era for British Columbia*, they added many more items to their democratic reform list (see table 2.1), among them: open cabinet meetings, a referendum on the principles to guide treaty making with Aboriginal peoples, and a promise to create an innovative citizens' assembly to examine electoral reform (British Columbia Liberal Party 2001, 27–30).

When the BC Liberals won the 16 May 2001 election, they quickly set out to introduce many (but not all) of these proposals. Some reforms, like fixed election dates, were introduced immediately; others, like the citizens' assembly, only got off the ground more than halfway through the government's term. And some promised reforms, like an overhaul of the recall and initiative referendum legislation, never materialized at all. This section examines Campbell's reforms under four broad themes – openness, consultation, accountability, and reforming politics – to assess the extent to which his accomplishments lived up to the promises he made as opposition leader and during the 2001 provincial election contest (before he came to power), and why he acted on them (or not) when he became premier.

Openness

Campbell's Liberals promised a new era of openness in government to counter the "trend toward centralization of power, closed-door decision making, and legislation by cabinet order without proper debate," a trend they claimed had led to "scandal, mismanagement and misplaced priorities" (from a Liberal policy document, as cited in V. Palmer 2000c). To counter this, the Liberals promised a number of reforms: open cabinet meetings, improved freedom of information rules, stable

Table 2.1
Campbell/BC Liberals democratic reforms, 1993–2006

Openness	Consultation	Accountability	Reforming politics
open cabinet meetings	task forces	90 days to introduce election promises	fixed election dates
improved freedom of information rules	citizens' assembly	fixing direct democracy	free votes
independent officer funding	native treaties referendum	fixed legislative calendar	improved committees/ MLA influence on cabinet
election donations disclosure (labour)	Conversation on Health	ban on government ads during elections	community charter
longer Question Period		removal of third-party spending limits	joint MLA/MP meetings

funding for the independent officers of the legislature, better disclosure of who was donating to political parties (specifically unions donating labour to NDP campaigns), and an increase in Question Period from fifteen to thirty minutes.

Of all these proposals, the open cabinet meetings gained the most attention. To open up the traditionally secretive cabinet decision-making process to public scrutiny seemed like a stunt to many observers, but Campbell defended the initiative as merely taking up the municipal practice of holding open council meetings (Farquharson 2001). As a Liberal policy document of the period claimed, "We want to lift the veil off cabinet secrecy forever by holding full cabinet meetings at least once a month in public" (as cited in V. Palmer 2000c). Some political opponents quickly dismissed the idea as a gimmick, while others warned of the practical difficulties of making cabinet decisions in public (Beatty 1999; Bailey 2001b).

Nevertheless, upon taking office, Campbell did introduce public cabinet meetings, with the first held on 27 June 2001 and the last on 28 January 2005. In their first term, they arguably had forty-seven opportunities for a monthly cabinet meeting but held only thirty-two, with the frequency declining as the term wore on. The media judged the open cabinet meetings as PowerPoint-heavy show-and-tell sessions for the government, with the real cabinet meetings occurring somewhere beyond the cameras (Yaffe 2001a; Danard 2001). As a *Province* newspaper editorial complained: "Let's be real: decisions aren't reached [at the open cabinet meetings] and some – perhaps all – of the information is staged. While we support the concept of open government decision-making, those who have sat in on the televised meetings say they smack of a taxpayer-paid publicity stunt" (*Province* 2001). They did not improve over time. Two years later, columnist Vaughn Palmer (2003b) complained the meetings were expensive infomercials: "The government figures it costs about $25,000 to televise each open cabinet meeting on the cable channel. Which would be worth it at twice the price, in my opinion, if the public could actually witness cabinet ministers engaged in genuine discussion and decision-making." But that didn't happen. Instead, the government terminated the experiment after the last session held in 2005. As Norman Ruff (2010b, 2004) notes, the open cabinet meeting eventually "outlived ... its limelight utility for government messaging."

Other promises for greater openness in government were not acted on in such a direct way. In opposition, the Campbell Liberals were heavy users of the province's freedom of information (FOI) provisions, and they complained bitterly when they felt the NDP government was limiting access or levying unreasonable fees. As Campbell told the legislature in 1998, "Make information available when people request it, as opposed to trying to stop them and sending them large bills to get the simplest information" (Francis 2005, 88). But in power the Liberals introduced new fees for FOI requests and created a database to track just who was requesting what, and how often, in an attempt to control the disclosure of information that might be damaging to the government (Francis 2005, 89; Rees 2005, 76–9). They also restricted the range of records to which FOI applied, excluding various legislative committees, BC Ferries, and government advertising, and they increased the maximum waiting times to receive the records (Smyth 2003c). Campbell's deputy minister Ken Dobell hinted in 2003 that his bureaucrats routinely avoided writing things down to get around FOI requests and that he regularly deleted his e-mail despite government policy to the contrary (Smyth 2003d). On a related issue, the Campbell Liberals had promised to stabilize funding for the independent officers of the legislature but pursued an opposite course while in power, raising them slightly upon taking office only to cut them after the midway point of their first term (Smyth 2003a; *Vancouver Sun* 2004).

Another issue that the Liberals promised to address concerned increasing the transparency of who funds political campaigns. Here they were concerned that organized labour was aiding their foes, the NDP, by providing the party with salaried labour bureaucrats who could then run campaigns for them at no cost. Not surprisingly, the Liberals acted quickly to require that such donations of time be declared as campaign contributions. There was some irony in the Liberals leading this charge as Campbell had repeatedly avoided disclosing the funders of his mayoralty campaigns in 1988 and 1990 (Cox 1988; Lee 1988d; Sarti 1990) and his 1993 Liberal leadership bid (Hauka 1993; V. Palmer 1993a). He also resisted revealing the donors to his provincial by-election in 1994, only producing the list after much media pressure when the campaign was over (Ward 1994; *Vancouver Sun* 1994a; *Province* 1994; *Vancouver Sun* 1994b). Two years later, columnist Vaughn Palmer complained that the Liberals were still unwilling to disclose who contributed to the party's pre-election fundraisers (V. Palmer 1996).

The Liberals did increase the length of Question Period from fifteen to thirty minutes, but they only introduced this reform at the beginning of their second term. Near the end of their first term their only reform to Question Period was to introduce time limits on questions from opposition members, with some limits as brief as twenty seconds (Smyth 2005b).

Consultation

Gordon Campbell's Liberals promised to consult the public directly through a number of mechanisms: provincewide referenda, topic-specific task forces, roving panels that would gather public input on key issues like health, and an innovative citizens' assembly process. While each strategy had merit, the manner in which they were carried out raised questions about what the government really intended to accomplish with them and, more specifically, what politics might have been animating their design and/or conclusions.

Possibly the most political of Gordon Campbell's consultation proposals involved his insistence that the public help craft the principles that should guide the treaty negotiations with the province's Aboriginal peoples. Critics complained that the promise was either populist opportunism, stoking public fears about the impact of possible land claims, or simply a useless exercise, given recent court decisions and the necessarily strong federal role in the negotiations process (V. Palmer 2001b; Hume 2002a). Both before and after the election, countless public bodies and media outlets counselled Campbell to abandon his pledge to hold a referendum (V. Palmer 2000b; Fong 2001). But Campbell persevered, with a 2002 mail-in ballot referendum registering more than 80 per cent approval for each of his eight proposed principles for negotiating treaties. Despite a low return rate on the mail-in ballot (36 per cent of registered voters), Campbell nonetheless declared the results a sound reading of the public's views (Ruff 2010a, 201; V. Palmer 2002c; *Edmonton Journal* 2002).

Setting aside the ethical concerns surrounding the use of a referendum in this case, there were a number of inconsistencies with how Campbell's government utilized this kind of public consultation (e.g., Hon 2005). First, it appeared that Campbell was keen on referenda for certain issues that his more rural supporters opposed, like Aboriginal treaties, but not for others with which they might have a problem, like Vancouver's Olympic bid. He had strongly defended consulting the public on Aboriginal treaties, arguing: "we have got to stop being afraid to include the public in the development of public policy" (Lavoie and Sekeres 2002). But when it came to consulting the public on the Olympics bid he argued against it, suggesting that it might make the city look bad internationally (Beatty 2002b).

Second, Campbell appeared inconsistent in his application of decision rules for different votes, setting the bar at 50 per cent plus one for the Aboriginal treaties referenda but requiring more than 60 per cent for any voting system referenda that his BCCA might decide to hold. Campbell also seemed strangely indifferent to questions of voter turnout, setting no minimum participation levels for the various votes. This seemed particularly problematic in cases in which he demanded a super-majority for victory given that his whole argument had been that such decisions required strong public support (McLintock 2003). But this was not a new scenario for Gordon Campbell. As mayor of Vancouver he had also insisted on a 60 per cent super-majority rule to replace the city's at-large voting with a ward system, and he had been prepared to hold a vote in a non-election year, despite being counselled that voter turnout would be low (Volkart 1987a; Volkart 1987b).

Another method of getting public input involved the creation of a number of issue-specific task forces. Over Campbell's three terms he established task forces on such varied themes as leaky condos, offshore oil and gas projects, and local government elections, among others (Ruff 2010b, 207). While these committees offered an important role for back-bench MLAs (particularly in Campbell's first term, when his caucus comprised nearly the whole legislature) and arguably produced some important reports, concerns emerged that membership on certain key task forces (e.g., energy) was stacked in favour of those supporting pre-determined government objectives. In 2009, the Friends of Bute Inlet urged their supporters to complain about the appointment of pro-industry representatives on the Green Energy Advisory Task Force, while the David Suzuki Foundation wrote the premier complaining that the body was going to take submissions in secret and produce no publicly available report. Again, Gordon Campbell had a lot of experience with using committees for political purposes while at Vancouver City Hall, where his critics argued he used them to bring handpicked outsiders into the policy process and to marginalize his political opponents (Cox 1987; Lee 1988e).

A fairly blatant exercise of "politics by task force" was the Liberals' Conversation on Health in 2006. Though allegedly formed to take the pulse of the province on the current performance of, and challenges facing, health care, Campbell's own view that fundamental change would be required – change in a direction that would involve more private care – was well known. When the report of the cross-province meetings was compiled, however, it became clear that the public thought the status quo should be bolstered rather than privatized. Ignoring the results, Campbell's government introduced changes to the province's Medical Care Protection Act to dilute the public's universal access to care to "reasonable access" and to add financial "sustainability" as a new principle guiding government implementation of the act (Davidson 2010, 303–4). Nor were ostensibly "independent" commissions free from political tampering. In 2008, Campbell interfered with the BC Electoral Boundaries Commission, publicly threatening to overrule its preliminary recommendation to reduce the number of rural ridings to equalize representation in the province if it remained in its final report (MacLeod 2008). The commission dropped the proposed reduction.

One area of public consultation sponsored by the Campbell Liberals that has been almost universally lauded is the British Columbia Citizens' Assembly. The particulars of the assembly's design, process, deliberations, and results are detailed extensively and effectively elsewhere (Warren and Pearse 2008). The politics behind the BCCA is less well explored. This is partly because Campbell is often praised simply for following through on his promise to examine the provincial voting system via a citizens' assembly, a model he had initially proposed to address questions of Canadian unity (Yaffe 1996; Proctor 1997). But embedded within his BCCA design was a number of decidedly political decisions. For instance, banning from membership in the BCCA anyone with elected experience deprived it of some valuable, practical insights (Redekop 2005), though it did fit with Campbell's populist anti-politics. Yet this was nothing compared to two other crucial decisions that arguably rigged the process to fail: (1) the requirement of a super-majority for any change to pass and (2) the failure to seriously inform the public of the BCCA proposal once a decision was made. As columnist Michael Smyth (2003b) argues regarding the threshold: "There's no compelling legal reason to set the bar so high. If Campbell is sincere about letting the people decide, why not let this be settled by a simple majority. A simple majority was all that was required in the 1991 referendum that brought us the recall law, as well as the Liberals' recent referendum on native treaties." Indeed, there was no precedent in Canadian history for requiring a super-majority for a voting system change at the provincial or federal level (Pilon 2007).[1] On funding for communication, the logic of spending $5 million on a process, only to fail to let the public know about it at the crucial moment, seemed like political interference by indifference (Pilon 2010).

Accountability

After campaigning against the NDP for essentially four years on accountability questions, the Liberals were keen to be seen as keeping promises. In opposition, Gordon Campbell had argued that, to rebuild public trust, his government would fix the province's direct democracy legislation, set a regular legislative calendar, ban government ads during elections, and repeal the NDP's "gag" law restricting third-party spending during election campaigns. And, to demonstrate his commitment to delivering on promises, Campbell set out twenty-one legislative goals that would be implemented within ninety days of taking office. Additionally, Campbell suggested that his cabinet ministers would have an incentive to meet budget-cutting targets or risk losing some of their pay.

Ninety days after taking office, Gordon Campbell declared that the Liberals had done as promised, introducing all twenty-one items. "It's been incredibly hard work," Campbell enthused to reporters. "We're changing the culture of government. We're changing it to a service-oriented culture. We're changing it to a culture of openness and accountability. We don't claim for a minute that we've done everything that needs to be done but I think we've made a good start" (Beatty 2001). Some critics argued that Campbell had met the deadline by fudging on the details of more than a few promises. For instance, his promise to quickly introduce a new community charter for local government was downgraded to a promise to study the issue further. Or, instead of appointing an independent officer of the legislature to assure that government hiring was based on merit and not party connections, he simply assigned a bureaucrat to do the job. But no one could deny that the government had been busy. Even so, its handling of the "big ticket" accountability issues was not the best example of accountability in action.

As he campaigned for the leadership of the Liberal Party in 1993, one of Gordon Campbell's first promises involved direct democracy: "The first item on the order paper should be legislation for recall. That establishes accountability" (Lee 1993e). When the NDP introduced its version of a recall and initiative referendum law in 1994 Campbell was vitriolic: "The NDP's recall and referendum legislation is a slap in the face to every British Columbian voter because it is unworkable and too expensive" (Hunter 1994). In 1995, Campbell introduced his own private member's bill to make the recall legislation easier to use (*Vancouver Sun* 1995). Later, the BC Liberals would dedicate pledge 9 (of nine pledges) of the BC Liberal Taxpayers' Pledge (a document signed by every candidate for the party) to fixing it: "I will vote for workable recall legislation so that you can kick me out if I don't do what I say" (British Columbia Liberal Party 1996, 5). When Liberal efforts to recall NDP MLAs came under criticism in the late 1990s, Campbell defended its use by saying: "there are very few jobs where you do not have the right to fire someone who is not doing their job" (as cited in Willcocks 2003). Finally, the 2001 Liberal election platform, *A New Era for British Columbia*, promised to "establish workable recall legislation, to make it easier for citizens to hold MLAs accountable" (British Columbia Liberal Party 2001, 30). Seldom has a policy direction been so clearly and adamantly spelled out and so doggedly pursued – at least while in opposition.

Yet, by 2002, as public opposition to the steep Liberal cuts in services started to make an impact on local communities, and various recall campaigns against Liberal MLAs started to gear up, government enthusiasm for easy recall rules began to wane (*Province* 2002; V. Palmer 2002a). In 2003, Campbell claimed that the reform was still on his agenda (Bailey 2003b), though media support was noticeably slipping ("Recall Bids Are a Tough Challenge: Legislation Is Designed to Be Used in Extreme Cases, Not Simply to Change Election Results," *Times-Colonist*, 19 November 2002; "Recall Legislation Must Be Repealed: It's Being Used Too Often for the Wrong Reasons," *Vancouver Sun*, 3 February 2003). After a number of Liberal cabinet ministers, including the premier, were subjected to recall campaigns, Campbell and others began to complain that people were misusing the recall legislation to simply "refight the last election" and that they were primarily NDP activists and their union friends (Jang 2003a; Jang 2003b; V. Palmer 2003c). In the same year, Liberal attorney general Geoff Plant, the man responsible for the recall file, blamed too many priorities for the delay, complaining: "I have found that it's not possible to move everywhere at high speed all at the same time" (McInnes 2003). But, by 2005, Plant finally admitted that reform of the recall legislation was not going to happen because, as journalist Craig McInnes (2005) put it, "there is now little enthusiasm in the Liberal caucus at the prospect of having to campaign for their seats between elections."

The Liberals did move quickly to introduce a fixed legislative and budget calendar shortly after taking power, but, as Norman Ruff points out, by 2004 the government started altering the sitting days to suit its purposes, a trend that only increased over time. Ruff (2010a, 194) argues that "[b]y 2008[,] it was clear that the exigencies of the government had undermined the 'fixed' notion of the calendar." On another promise, the Liberals did not have to repeal the NDP's "gag law," as they called it, because the BC Supreme Court struck down the restrictions on third-party spending in February 2000. But after a number of unions mounted creative third-party ad campaigns targeting the Liberals in 2005, Campbell's government surprised many by passing its own restrictions on third-party advertising in 2008. The Liberal rules were much more stringent than were the NDP's, applying not just to election campaigning but also to the period sixty days prior to the start of an election. These rules were struck down by the courts just before the start of the 2009 provincial election (Phillips 2010, 123–4).

The Liberals had promised to ban government advertising in the run-up to an election, having felt that, all through 2000 and into 2001, the NDP had saturated the media with "good news" government ads that were thinly veiled propaganda. But that didn't stop the Liberal government from using ads to trumpet its own accomplishments between elections. Journalist Michael Smyth complained that Campbell had seethed when the NDP spent $500,000 to tout its "facts" on Medicare. At the time, Campbell had vowed: "I'm not going to run ads saying what a great job we are doing in health care. When I look at how much money government spends on advertising, I think people are appalled by that" (Smyth 2003e). But, in 2003, the Liberals sent out an eight-page brochure on health care highlighting what Smyth thought were "highly selective" facts. Nor would the Liberals divulge how much the mail-out cost. Meanwhile, as the election approached in 2005, no law restricting government ads before or during elections had materialized, though Campbell assured the media that he had intended to pass such legislation. Instead, he sent a policy directive from the Premier's Office saying that all government bodies should shut down non-essential government advertising four months before the start of an election (V. Palmer 2005a).

Campbell had long taken the moral high road on questions of accountability, promising a new kind of politics and politician. In one of his first speeches as Liberal leader, in hammering home his promise to balance budgets, Campbell made it personal. "If there are budget overruns in my term of office [as premier] I will personally face the same penalties which thousands of other British Columbians face when they overspend," he claimed. "I will take a percentage cut in my salary equivalent to any percentage overruns in the budget. I will also require the same discipline from senior management within the provincial public service" (Needham 1993). When he came to power in 2001, Campbell made much of his promise to hold back a portion of every cabinet minister's pay unless they made their budget targets (McInnes 2001). Yet, as Norman Ruff observes, by 2010 no actual salary reductions had ever occurred, in part because the act allowed for an expedient revision of defined operating expenses for all sorts of reasons. As the opposition complained, ministers could essentially offer a "dog-ate-my-homework" excuse and face no real consequences (Ruff 2010a, 196).

Reforming Politics

In his long spell as opposition leader, Gordon Campbell spent a lot of time talking about plans to reform *how* politics would be done, both inside and outside the legislature. He claimed that he wanted to weaken the power of leaders and elites and strengthen the role of MLAs to speak up on behalf of their constituents. Fixed election dates would remove the arbitrary power of a premier to call a snap election; more free votes in the legislature and a properly functioning committee system would empower individual MLAs; and a new community charter would grant municipalities more power to make key decisions. Altogether, the thrust of the Liberal reform package was to counter the trend towards executive dominance in BC politics by weakening the power of the premier vis-à-vis government caucus, the legislature, and other levels of government.

The Liberals moved quickly to introduce fixed election dates, utilizing them for the 2005 and 2009 provincial elections. The party wavered slightly when Christy Clark won the Liberal leadership in 2011, but talk of an early election evaporated amid poor polling results. The fixed election date proved a popular reform with governing elites and was soon copied in eight other provincial locales and at the federal level in 2006. Of course, part of its popularity was that it didn't really affect very much politically. Whatever benefit might accrue to a premier in control of setting an election date was offset by the benefits that fixed election dates offered party managers in the new "information control" mode of campaigning. Having a fixed date helped with information gathering, targeted messaging, media buys, and fixed campaign costs like space rental and printing costs (Marland et al. 2012).

Hopes were higher for the Liberals' Community Charter, an addition to the Local Government Act designed to strengthen municipal power. Dubbed "Gord's Baby" by the press, a version of the proposed changes had already been introduced as a private member's bill by Campbell when he was in opposition. Thus some in the media were surprised when it was shuffled off to a committee in the first ninety days of the Liberal government (V. Palmer 2002b). When legislation finally emerged in 2003, the media read the new act as simply granting local government the power to assess new taxes (V. Palmer 2003a). In fact, experts complained: "the Community Charter has been as much a case of false hope as it has been a harbinger of true jurisdictional, financial, and policy independence" (Smith, Ginnell, and Black 2010, 254). The charter claimed to recognize local government as an independent order of government, while granting it powers to offer new services, establish public/private partnerships, and insist on consultation with other levels of government. It did not, however, create any new revenue streams for municipalities. As such, as Smith and Stewart complained, it did little to alter their "creature-of-the-province" status or their suboptimal policy capacity (as cited in Smith, Ginnell, and Black 2010, 255).

In opposition, Campbell had promised to improve the functioning of the legislature with more free votes and more powerful legislative committees (*Times-Colonist* 1994; V. Palmer 2001a). In 1999, Vaughn Palmer reported on Campbell's claims from the Liberal Party convention: "Mr. Campbell says the effect of his proposals would be to weaken the power of the premier to do as he pleases behind the closed doors of the cabinet room, backed up every step of the way by a docile legislative majority" (Palmer 1999). In an overview of the Campbell committee reforms, Norman Ruff (2010a, 197–8) suggests that the Liberal era legislative committees were markedly re-energized, particularly in the government's first term, but with few exceptions operated in a fairly conventionally partisan manner. Campbell's novel hybrid cabinet/caucus committees were a departure for BC; however, as they fell under cabinet confidentiality rules, it is hard to assess how well the experiment worked out (Ruff 2010b, 207).

On the question of free votes, it is hard to tell just how "free" government MLAS were under Campbell. While there were a few high-profile departures from party discipline, legislative voting was strongly partisan in the Campbell decade. As Ruff points out, this could be because MLAS agreed with the government's legislative program or because the process of running for office internalizes strong party discipline in individual MLAS. But more likely, he argues, political ambition won out. Voting against one's party is unlikely to be popular with cabinet colleagues or a "fast-track route out of a lowly backbench status" (Ruff 2010a, 198). As for improving the legislative atmosphere, Campbell set the tone early in his first term when he refused, against all credible evidence and advice, to recognize the NDP's two-person caucus as the Official Opposition. While he tried to hide behind a technical defence of his decision, his actions appeared to most as "narrow, quibbling, [and] anti-democratic" (V. Palmer 2005b). Even his usual supporters on the political right and the media condemned his intransigence (Spector 2001; *Vancouver Sun* 2001; *Times-Colonist* 2001). Another promise that came to naught was the proposal for joint BC MLA/MP meetings. Again, Campbell had tried this at the civic level, holding meetings of Vancouver city councillors, MLAS, and MPS, but critics argued that they were just for show (Volkart 1988). Campbell did manage to schedule in a number of joint cabinet meetings with Alberta in 2003, 2005, and 2008, eventually including Saskatchewan as well in 2009 and 2010 when it, too, had elected a populist right-wing government.

In opposition, Campbell claimed his democratic reforms would reverse the trend towards executive dominance in BC. But the reforms proved unequal to the task. Furthermore, there is a great deal of evidence that Campbell's leadership style worked against them. Commentators have described his approach to governing as "presidential" and, less flatteringly, "authoritarian" (McInnes 1995; McMartin 1995). As one reporter described him, "he has methodically taken on the task of leading the province like a Chief Executive Officer" (Lunman 2001b), a leadership style not often characterized as "democratic." Campbell's CEO-style leadership can be seen in a host of examples, ranging from some of the very first directives to emerge from his Premier's Office, to his takeover and leadership of the provincial Liberal Party, to his unparalleled control over Vancouver City Hall and his municipal political machine.

In government, Campbell set his CEO tone early with individualized ten- to twelve-page letters delivered to every cabinet minister detailing exactly what he expected them to do. Though on the campaign trail he had made much of letting MLAs freely express themselves, the letters told a different story (Farquharson 2001). He also reminded his ministers that all deputy ministers, assistant deputies, ministerial aides, and support staff were appointed by either the premier or the premier's chief of staff, which was a way of saying that they ultimately worked for him and not the minister (V. Palmer 2001c).

Campbell's plan to find places to cut government spending also appeared very corporate. Instead of relying on ministers to prepare reports, he brought in the deputy minister for corporate planning and restructuring to conduct a core program review that would look at every government program to see what could be cut or provided by someone else (Willcocks 2001). Next, Campbell centralized all government communication through the Premier's Office, effectively politicizing what had been a non-partisan part of the civil service (Beatty 2002a). As he took control of more and more, the Premier's Office ballooned in size in 2002, expanding from forty full-time staff and an annual budget of $3 million to 470 staff and an annual budget of $56 million (though this was later reduced in 2009 to 110 staff and an annual budget of $14.1 million) (Ruff 2010b). Campbell also had conflicts with some of his MLAs, who complained about his domineering approach, ill temper, and bad language. One departing MLA described the Liberal caucus as a "cult" (Kines and Rudd 2004). Over time, the media noted derisively that Campbell was less and less available.

Province reporter Michael Smyth complained in 2003: "Campbell won't even do media scrums in the hallways of the legislature after question period anymore! Now he's whisked back to his west-wing office to huddle with his spin-doctors. Then the media are invited down to ask him questions. Sometimes. Not even Glen Clark or Bill Vander Zalm went running for cover when times got bad" (Smyth 2003c).

Campbell's approach to governing and the complaints that accompanied it were not new. As mayor of Vancouver, Campbell managed to dramatically increase the power of his office, transforming what had often been a ceremonial position into an executive one (Lee 1993b). His secret was in gaining control over the political machine that dominated city hall. As Vaughn Palmer (1993b) notes, "Campbell quickly took charge of the NPA (Non-Partisan Association), infiltrating the membership with his own people and transforming the party apparatus into a relatively sophisticated machine." After one term as mayor, Campbell had wrested control of the NPA nominating process from its membership and placed it within an executive he dominated (McCune 1990). Councillors who did not see eye to eye with the mayor often found themselves on the losing side of an NPA nomination race (Lee 1993a). Campbell also had a reputation as a one-man show, dropping policies and projects on council with little or no input from other politicians. As Vaughn Palmer (1994a) puts it, "he is not the kind of leader who goes out of his way to court strong individuals, people he might regard as equals, or potential rivals."

Campbell appeared to take the same operating approach to his campaign for the BC Liberal Party leadership. Again, he used his considerable financial backing to gain control of the party executive, helped craft rules that would aid his campaign, and then spent enormous sums of money signing up new members and professionally organizing to pull his voters (V. Palmer 1993a; V. Palmer 1993c). Reporters at the leadership convention underlined the organizational acumen and confidence of Campbell's team, noting: "one Campbell aide boasted that his team had more workers to help confused Liberal voters yesterday than did the party itself" (McLintock and Hawthorn 1993).

Once ensconced in the leadership, Campbell moved to solidify his control over the party, gaining a veto over local Liberal nominations and carte blanche to recruit MLAs from other parties (Kieran 1994; V. Palmer 1994b). In a 1994 by-election, early in Campbell's leadership, local Liberal members complained of being shut out of the decision-making process by "the crowd from the city" (V. Palmer 1995). Com-

plaints of central party dominance would surface again and again over
the next two years, leading to the resignation of a number of constituency presidents and one Liberal MLA quitting the party just before
the 1996 election (Yeager 1995; Barrett 1996; Hunter 1996). Yet, by 2001,
the Liberals would appear to be a well-oiled machine, operating under
a tight media script, one that critics argued meant that Liberal candidates avoided engaging in public debate (Mulgrew 2001) or responding
to public enquiries (the latter being vetted by central Liberal campaign
headquarters) (Smyth 2001).

Democratic reform lingered on into Campbell's second term, but without any enthusiasm. The results of the voting system referendum – 57
per cent for the BCCA's single transferable vote option – embarrassed
the government into holding another vote on the issue in 2009 (when
it was finally – clearly – defeated). The Liberals' 2005 election platform,
*Real Leadership, Real Progress for British Columbia: A Proven Plan for a
Golden Decade*, devoted a whole page to democratic reform, but it focused solely on their past. In the end, the abandonment of democratic
reform appeared to cost them little. After all, the stunning 2001 Liberal victory had little to do with such promises (Palmer 2001a). As a senior Liberal backer complained to Vaughn Palmer in 2000, "I've told him
there are no votes in those proposals, but he believes [that there are],
and he won't give up" (V. Palmer 2000b).

    Why had Campbell pursued democratic reform in the first place?
Part of the commitment was clearly based on political opportunism,
an attempt to channel the federal Reform Party's rising popularity into
solidifying a new vehicle for BC's centre-right electorate. But a considerable part was driven by Gordon Campbell's own gut instincts about
who "the people" are and just what they wanted from politics. As ex-
emplified in his critique of Donald Gutstein's *Vancouver Ltd.*, Campbell felt the need to defend another view of "the people" – that is, the
ones who wanted development, or approved of housing towers and
shopping malls, or did not attend public meetings or demonstrations
(Campbell 1976). As he remarked in a 1992 interview: "Ninety percent
of people don't belong to organizations. We hear from people who
want more inclusion. We also hear from people who want government
to stay out of their lives" (Horn 1992).

Campbell's zeal for reform was thus partly rooted in his (over)confidence about who and what would be heard. When the results did not match his preconceptions or became inconvenient for accomplishing other, usually neoliberal, goals, he did not hesitate to jettison the commitments. The gap between his promises and their delivery in terms of openness, consultation, accountability, and reforming politics was usually papered over or simply ignored. Ironically, after setting himself up as a reformer, as being above politics and parties, his policy reversals, omissions, and scandals ended up reinforcing the very cynicism and public hostility to politics he claimed his reforms would reverse. As political columnist Craig McInnes (2004) put it:

> Despite what some might call a blinkered determination to carry out his platform, however, Campbell has failed to deliver on his underlying promise of restoring trust. He has failed because on too many occasions he has insulted the intelligence of British Columbians by insisting on a lawyer's version of truth, the version that relies on the small print on the back of the contract that no one ever reads until it's too late.

Some of those prepared to applaud Campbell as a democratic reformer in media and academe also seem a bit like lawyers in making their case, crediting him with simply putting ambitious proposals before the public and enshrining a good many in legislation. But judging a legacy requires assessing the substance of what was accomplished. Here Campbell must be judged to have come up short. In four areas of democratic reform – openness, consultation, accountability, and reforming politics – he consistently moved quickly only on reforms that either were dressed-up public relations exercises (e.g., open cabinet meetings) or had little real impact on political power (e.g., fixed election dates). In most areas, he introduced reforms only to undermine them by backsliding on them later (e.g., promises to fund independent officers of the legislature, improve the FOI process) or have their effect countered by other actions of the government (e.g., limiting legislative oversight by centralizing power in the Premier's Office). But, in the most crucial areas (i.e., the reforms that had the greatest potential to alter the democratic balance of power in the province), Campbell reneged on his promises (e.g., to make it easier to initiate legislative referenda or recall politicians), rigged them to fail (e.g., the voting system referendum), or gutted their legislative substance (e.g., the community charter). This being the case, his legacy in democratic reform for BC would appear to be how to wield it as rhetoric while frustrating it as practice.

NOTE

1 Campbell's insistence on a super-majority threshold for voting system change in BC has been defended by some as reasonable, given the potential impact of the reform. For support, Campbell argued that such a threshold was common at the municipal level in BC. But neither Campbell's logic nor his evidence is very compelling when analyzed more closely. First, BC's voting system is just a piece of legislation like any other. It was passed initially by a simple majority vote. Thus, it is illogical to subject it to a quasi-constitutional super-majority process to reform it. Second, BC's voting system was twice changed historically (1951, 1953), both times by a simple majority vote of the legislature. Further, Ontario, Manitoba, and Alberta all experimented with alternative voting systems historically, adopting and re-pealing them by simple majority votes. Comparatively, the three national referenda on voting system reform in Western countries (Switzerland, France, and New Zealand) were all decided by 50 per cent plus one thresholds. Even Campbell's municipal evidence is wrong – Vancouver's at-large voting system was introduced in 1935 under referendum rules calling only for a simple majority verdict. Since then, the city's critics of at-large voting have consistently rejected attempts to impose a super-majority rule on any referendum to change the system. For more background on this question see Pilon 2006, 2009, and 2013.

3

The Road to "Reconciliation"?
Premier Gordon Campbell and BC Aboriginal Policy

YALE D. BELANGER

Gordon Campbell's legacy as Aboriginal advocate was assured following his resignation as BC premier in November 2011. Dating to his efforts to promote the $5.1 billion Kelowna Accord tabled in 2005 by Prime Minister Paul Martin in an attempt to improve Aboriginal education, housing, economic development, health, and water services (and which in part helped to convince his fellow premiers of the need to improve Aboriginal well-being), Campbell had by 2011 become a nationally recognized Aboriginal supporter. This was a significant achievement considering that, in October 2000, long-time political adversary and Union of British Columbia Indian Chiefs (UBCIC) grand chief Stewart Phillip declared: "I don't believe that Gordon Campbell and the Liberals really have the depth of experience with respect to aboriginal people and aboriginal issues. We could be in for some very difficult times if Mr. Campbell sweeps into power ... I'm deeply concerned" (V. Palmer 2000b). Triggering Phillip's concern was Campbell's campaign promise to pursue a provincial referendum to ascertain "public opinion on the 'principles' best able to resolve the interminable issue of aboriginal treaties" (Macqueen 2002). Thus, in what amounted to a little more than one decade, Gordon Campbell had transformed his public persona from intolerable opponent to celebrated Aboriginal advocate. An impressive about-face, to be sure, and one that demands we chronicle Campbell's efforts and experiences in this area of public policy.

Like the majority of provincial premiers, Gordon Campbell entered politics with a narrow understanding of Aboriginal issues. However, contrary to most of his peers (publicly at least), Campbell became immediately known as a staunch opponent of Aboriginal self-government. So what was it that led to his makeover from Aboriginal opponent to believer? This chapter traces Gordon Campbell's political evolution by exploring BC Aboriginal politics during three key periods. The first period (1992 to 2000) precedes his time as BC's premier, when, as Vancouver's mayor and then as leader of the official opposition, he publicly contested the pith and substance of Aboriginal self-government – specifically, its negative impacts on municipal agency. He also challenged the self-government provisions of the Nisga'a Treaty (ratified in 2000), which is discussed below. The second period (2000 to 2003) overlaps with his first term as premier, when he introduced and presided over a socially and politically contentious referendum that Aboriginal leaders insisted was purposely intended to undermine the provincial treaty process established in 1992. The third period begins in 2003 with Campbell's second term as premier and ends with his resignation in 2011, and it is symbolized by his public efforts to improve the BC-Aboriginal relationship. Central to this discussion is the failed, albeit prominent, effort to implement the Indigenous Recognition and Reconciliation Act in 2009. By the time of his 2011 resignation, Campbell's self-described "third solitude" – that is, the idea that Aboriginal people form an as yet unrecognized nation within a united Canada, or as John Ralston Saul (2008; 1997) would have it, operate as a concealed third tier of Confederation alongside the French and the English – remained firmly nested in BC's political and social peripheries.

Several important themes anchor the following discussion. Campbell's successes and failures as they relate to Aboriginal politics were arguably grounded by his lack of knowledge of federal Canadian Indian policy. As I discuss, this led him to initiate two legal challenges that most legal experts maintained would fail. This, however, is not the entire story. From the earliest days of his premiership Campbell expended minimal effort to advance his personal awareness of Aboriginal issues, despite steering a staples-dependent province increasingly subject to Aboriginal claims. Although he would ultimately concede BC's objectionable history, characterized by the government physically dispossessing First Nations through a series of illegal provincial land acquisitions, he never linked that history to the contemporary barriers to improved Aboriginal well-being. And, as discussed below, ensuring political progress in the world of provincial-Aboriginal politics was, and remains, a difficult venture. It is with these ideas in mind that I explore

BC's quest for a "new relationship" with the province's Aboriginal community under Campbell's premiership.

OPPOSING THE NISGA'A TREATY'S
SELF-GOVERNMENT PROVISIONS

Gordon Campbell became a provincial celebrity among BC's Aboriginal leaders in 2000 with his opposition to the Nisga'a Treaty. As the Liberal leader of the provincial opposition, he argued that the Nisga'a Treaty illegally created a third order of government, which violated the Canadian Constitution. To this point, Campbell's rise from executive assistant to Vancouver mayor Art Phillips in the early 1970s to a Vancouver city councillor from 1984 to 1986 had culminated in a three-term run as the mayor of Vancouver (1986–1993) (see Ginnell, chapter 1, this volume). During the early 1990s, he served as the vice-president of the Union of British Columbia Municipalities while chairing the Greater Vancouver Regional District, and he first spoke publicly about Aboriginal issues in 1992. His target was the provincial treaty process, which had been established earlier that year to ensure that long-standing land claims and their associated governance issues were dealt with in a non-coercive environment. Encouraging open communications between First Nations and provincial leaders, the BC Treaty Commission was immediately beset with problems. In particular, the set of nineteen principles developed to help guide negotiations was vague, and it is apparent that little thought was given to expanding the Treaty Commission's mandate beyond simply promoting treaty negotiations (Woolford 2005; McKee 2009). By the late 1990s, Campbell had taken firm aim at the treaty process (in particular, its glacial pace of negotiations) while publicly questioning whether a treaty agreement could legally confer self-governance upon a First Nation.

As the UCBM's vice-president, Campbell publicly objected to municipal government exclusion from the treaty process. In September 1992, he informed the media that "the UCBM's position has been very clear ... we should be present at the negotiating table when they are discussing the creation of self-governments throughout the province for first nations." He added: "too often, the federal and provincial representatives don't understand the impacts of their decisions on local municipalities" (Lee 1992b). Campbell went so far as to commission a legal opinion from the law firm Bull, Housser, and Tupper, which deduced that, upon being legally recognized as a self-governing body, Aboriginal governmental jurisdiction(s) would extend beyond First Nations territorial limits, thus providing those communities with the authority to govern community members wherever they reside (i.e., Aboriginal self-government could potentially challenge municipal political authority). This decision disputed the growing legal and federal/provincial understanding of Aboriginal self-government, specifically those ideas related to on- and off-reserve jurisdictional issues. Even so, Campbell remained defiant while positing scenarios that did little more than perplex an already bewildered public and that significantly revealed his political inexperience concerning Aboriginal issues. Not only did it appear that Campbell didn't know where First Nations governments potentially fit into the constitutional matrix, or the provincial framework of municipal governments, but he also refused to make the effort to seek out alternative viewpoints to improve his understanding of the issues (Hauka 1992).[1]

The BC Treaty Commission was an early target, and an agency in which Campbell never expressed much confidence. He did concede in 1995 that treaties were an effective means to resolving long-term grievances with provincial Aboriginal peoples, the caveat being that the approved process remained transparent and embraced public involvement. This stance echoed the BC Reform Party's treaty referendum position based on the writings of Mel Smith, who had earlier argued that provincial attempts to accommodate Aboriginal title claims would lead to BC's ruin (M. Smith 1995; McKee 2009). Smith's arguments resonated with both Campbell, who wanted him as an advisor, and the Citizen's Voice on Native Claims Foundation, led by a seven-member board of BC business leaders. Its public voice was Martyn Brown, who would later be appointed Premier Campbell's chief of staff. Brown immediately launched an assault arguing that land claims negotiations would certainly jeopardize BC's title to Crown lands. Referring to the recent *Delgamuukw* decision, which accepted pre-contact forms of government grounded in ongoing and functional legal systems to guide the external affairs and internal relations of Aboriginal peoples, Brown insisted that the court's ruling would have the opposite effect to that intended: "instead of leading to more harmonious relations between aboriginal and non-aboriginal Canadians, it will increase racial tensions, particularly in resource-dependent communities" (de Leeuw 2004, 131). Intensely opposed to the recognition of Aboriginal title, Brown warned that engaging in this type of race-based politics would compromise the "greater equality of all Canadians" by reinforcing Aboriginal peoples' special status. His position was important at the time because it reflected a growing non-Aboriginal constituency's concerns with First Nations title issues.

During this period, Campbell did not try to derail the Treaty Commission; instead, he set his sights on disrupting the Nisga'a Treaty's implementation following its royal assent in 2000. Concluded by the Nisga'a Tribal Council and the federal and provincial governments on 15 July 1998, the Nisga'a Treaty became effective on 11 May 2000. It was BC's first modern treaty, though it was not completed through the BC Treaty Commission (see Molloy 2006; Ponting 2006). Dating back to 1887, the Nisga'a had been persistent in their desire for treaty negotiations and the formal recognition of their Aboriginal title and right to self-government. In the 1890s, Nisga'a hereditary chiefs and matriarchs formed the Nisga'a Land Committee to pursue these ends. After several decades of fits and starts, the Nisga'a Tribal Council, in 1968, petitioned the BC Supreme Court to rule on its claim that the Nisga'a had never surrendered their land base and thus still possessed territorial Aboriginal title. The claim was denied, sparking two separate appeals that culminated in a 1973 Supreme Court of Canada ruling (the *Calder* decision) that formally acknowledged the Aboriginal right to land. Responding to the decision, the federal government initiated treaty negotiations with the Nisga'a Tribal Council in 1976, which BC joined in 1990. The public was kept informed of events, and between 1991 and 1998 federal and provincial negotiators held 250 consultations and public information meetings in northwestern BC. In 2000, the treaty passed into law (see generally Molloy 2006).

During the ratification process, the federal Reform Party of Canada enthusiastically denounced the treaty and publicly declared its intent to delay its ratification (little resulted from this resistance).[2] Campbell cannily supported the Reform Party's position while forcefully channelling Smith's belief that Canada's failure to constitutionally entrench Aboriginal self-government during the failed Charlottetown Accord in 1992 meant that the Nisga'a Treaty could not be ratified absent a provincial referendum on the matter (in addition to the provincial and federal agreement) (see Sullivan 2000). Campbell recruited Liberal attorney general critic Geoff Plant and Aboriginal affairs critic Mike de Jong to contest chapter 11 of the Nisga'a Treaty, which identified Nisga'a law as a prerogative: (1) in cases where local laws about education existed; (2) regarding the use of lands and resources; and (3) in instances in which the preservation of culture conflicted with federal and provincial laws.

Campbell argued that any and all rights to Aboriginal self-government had been extinguished at Confederation in 1867 and that "the exhaustive division of powers granted to Parliament and the [country's] legislative assemblies" signified exclusive law-making authority (quoted in Rasmussen 2008, 48). Aboriginal self-government, according to this logic, could not exist as a third order of government.

Asked to resolve the question, in July 2000 BC Supreme Court justice Paul Williamson began by elaborating Campbell's position:

> The heart of this argument is that any right to such self-government or legislative power was extinguished at the time of Confederation. Thus, the plaintiffs distinguish aboriginal title and other aboriginal rights, such as the right to hunt or to fish, from the right to govern one's own affairs. They say that in 1867, when the then British North America Act (now called the Constitution Act, 1867) was enacted, although other aboriginal rights including aboriginal title survived, any right to self-government did not. All legislative power was divided between Parliament and the legislative assemblies. While they concede that Parliament, or the Legislative Assembly, may delegate authority, they say legislative bodies may not give up or abdicate that authority. To do so, they argue, is unconstitutional. The treaty did enshrine a third order of government.
> (*Campbell v. British Columbia [Attorney General]* 2000)

Justice Williamson ruled that, while the Aboriginal right to self-government may have been diminished, it had not been extinguished: "For the reasons set out above, I have concluded that after the assertion of sovereignty by the British Crown, and continuing to and after the time of Confederation, although the right of aboriginal people to govern themselves was diminished, it was not extinguished." He added: "Any aboriginal right to self-government could be extinguished after Confederation and before 1982 by federal legislation which plainly expressed that intention, or it could be replaced or modified by the negotiation of a treaty. Post-1982, such rights cannot be extinguished, but they may be defined (given content) in a treaty. The Nisga'a Final Agreement does the latter expressly" (*Campbell v. British Columbia [Attorney General]* 2000).

Thomas Berger, representing the Nisga'a, concluded that the inherent right of self-government survived Confederation and that no legislation had been enacted extinguishing that right. It was an existing right recognized and affirmed by section 35(1) of the Constitution Act, 1982. Hence it "was properly the subject of a treaty" (Berger 2002b, 132). Berger later noted that, had Campbell succeeded, his attack would have arguably left the Nisga'a with land they "could not manage or administer, money they could not spend or invest, forests they could not harvest or protect, fish and wildlife they could not distribute or conserve. The treaty would be reduced to an empty shell" (135). Justice Williamson's dismissal of Campbell's petition upheld the Nisga'a Nation's inherent right to a measure of self-government while concluding that "the mere fact of Confederation could not extinguish the right of self-government, because the purpose of that legislation was to provide for the structure of governance as between the federal and provincial governments" (Rasmussen 2008, 50).

Following the decision, First Nations Summit grand chief Edward John expressed his dismay at Campbell's legal adventures: "One would have thought they would be seeking to break from the past and work with us to build a more constructive relationship with First Nations. Let us respect the courts and work together towards realistic and workable solutions" (John 2000). His comment about respecting the court's decision was a direct reply to Campbell's recent assertions that a negative legal outcome would prompt an immediate appeal. John's reference to the historically dysfunctional Aboriginal-provincial relationship is significant for the purposes of this discussion. In particular, John acknowledged that Campbell's reticence to personally engage Aboriginal leaders reflected his predecessors' tendency to ignore Aboriginal concerns. His desire to see Campbell "break from this past" and "build a more constructive relationship" echoes these concerns, as do his comments about respecting the court's decision, which demand attention.

Upon entering Confederation in 1871, BC quickly developed a reputation as a rogue province that frequently chose to politically operate independently of federal proscriptions. Nowhere was this more evident that in its decision to disregard federal demands to negotiate treaties with First Nations. By doing so, provincial officials initiated a process whereby Aboriginal claims tended to be dismissed irrespective of their legal foundation (Harris 2002). Not all provincial officials were duplicitous and seeking to remove "Indians" from valuable lands, even if they generally ignored "Indian" concerns. Campbell – as mayor and then leader of the opposition – fell into the latter category based on two primary observations. The first of these is that Campbell regularly portrayed Aboriginal people as a modern-day "Indian problem." That is, as mayor and UBCM vice-president, he unfailingly railed against federal and provincial inattention concerning the municipal role in creating Aboriginal self-governments. While Aboriginal leaders never bore the brunt of Campbell's criticism directly, they were nevertheless considered a key catalyst of the jurisdictional conflict (Mickleburgh 2000b). First Nations leaders seeking finalized treaties could ultimately affect municipal service provisioning, and this was problematic. Campbell believed he could reduce Aboriginal self-government's impact on municipalities by asking the courts to clarify the operational relationship.

The second observation concerns Campbell's lack of understanding of Aboriginal law and Canadian Indian policy, how this influenced BC's role in the treaty-making processes, and how this translated into Aboriginal self-governing authority. A 1991 study highlights that most Canadians opposed Aboriginal self-government, despite not fully understanding its complexity, and Campbell's early approach reflected the general Canadian attitude of the period (Wells and Berry 1992). By 1998, however, popular opinion had shifted, and the majority of Canadians now considered self-government a priority – even if consensus could not be reached on issues such as how self-government powers were to be formally understood (Martin and Adams 2002). In the interim, the Inherent Rights Policy of 1995 was enacted to help clarify the self-government ideal by adding a greater level of interpretive precision concerning its operational parameters (Belanger and Newhouse 2008). Aboriginal self-government, all the same, remains a poorly understood political phenomenon (see Weaver 1984). Most people tend to conflate Aboriginal self-government with self-determination, when it is more akin to self-administration. Campbell, it seems, likened Aboriginal self-government to First Nations holding the powers of state and consequently not being subject to Canadian federal and provincial laws.

If Campbell did not fully grasp the basics of Canadian Indian policy, comprehend the nuance of Aboriginal law, or grasp the exigencies of BC Aboriginal history, he seemed to care little about how Aboriginal leaders perceived his actions. In particular, to challenge Aboriginal self-government's legal foundations he assembled a "dream team" consisting of Liberal attorney general critic Geoff Plant (later BC attorney general and minister responsible for treaty negotiations from 2001 to 2005) and Aboriginal affairs critic Mike de Jong (later minister of Aboriginal relations and reconciliation from 2006 to 2009) to fight its implementation. Reflecting on these events, one must ask: By using the courts to determine the substance of Aboriginal self-government, was

Campbell truly pursuing legislative clarity? Or was there another agenda at play? Campbell noted from the very beginning that his fight was not with Aboriginal leaders but, rather, with federal and provincial governments seeking to create non-constitutional treaties. These questions are explored below.

MAKING GOOD ON A CAMPAIGN PROMISE: THE 2002 BC TREATY REFERENDUM

Campbell began campaigning for premier in 2000, but it quickly became evident that the previous NDP administration led by Ujjal Dosanjh would not be returning to power. With little effort, then, Campbell had emerged as Dosanjh's de facto successor, and he remained on the offensive and immediately began promoting the need to hold a provincial treaty referendum. When questioned about his motivations, Campbell stated that the referendum would build trust between Aboriginal peoples and the BC government and its residents by ensuring "certainty, equality, and finality" while further enabling politicians to "tap into the goodwill" of British Columbians (Bula 2001b). Campbell refused to meet with Aboriginal leaders, however, which for many signalled the referendum's certainty. Aboriginal leaders responded by threatening international anti-BC marketing campaigns. Proposing direct action was a strategy of last resort, but by March talk of blockades began circulating, replete with references to the 1995 confrontation at Gustafsen Lake (see Lambertus 2004). Campbell remained unfazed and steadfast in his refusal to engage Aboriginal leaders, who, ironically, were being called out for their failure to fruitfully engage provincial officials. Referendum supporter Barbara Yaffe, in particular, concluded that First Nations "do their cause great damage by coming across as petulant bullies who would set up blockades or tarnish BC's reputation abroad if they aren't given their way on treaties." Ignoring previous Aboriginal attempts at dialogue, Yaffe (2001b) asserted: "It's now up to the Indian leaders to make some suggestions to Mr. Campbell. Certainly this would be more helpful than the shameless grandstanding and threats they offered [at the First Nations Summit meeting last week]." Predictably, Aboriginal leaders did not back down and collectively amplified their resistance to what was now being portrayed as a socially polarizing referendum. Arguably, the direct action discourse also awakened political analysts who, to this point, produced lacklustre missives about the treaty process's negative provincial social, political, and economic impacts. For most critics, however, BC's future prosperity was being held captive by a federally imposed process.

With the media now probing the issues, Campbell was seen as promoting an increasingly unpopular referendum. Journalist Ian Mulgrew (2011) would opine, "not since the days of the Social Credit government of Bill Bennett has a group so opposed to resolving land-claims come close to gaining power." Aboriginal leaders had proven effective with their messaging: as a constitutional issue, the treaty process was beyond the scope of provincial modification. But the issue went beyond opposition to land claims. In his enthusiasm to ensure that all British Columbians had a say in the treaty process, Campbell failed to acknowledge that his approach to cultural difference appeared to emulate the same processes that men like Joseph Trutch, BC's first lieutenant-governor, who vigorously dismissed Aboriginal title claims while also ensuring nominal Indian reserve sizes, employed (Belanger, Newhouse, and Shpuniarsky 2008, 203). Similar questionable policies led to the vast and unchecked extraction of resources that were legally (theoretically at least) considered inalienable until Aboriginal title was formally extinguished. One could consequently argue that Campbell's resistance, and that of the people of BC, was historically conditioned. Trutch, for example, denied the existence of "Aboriginal title, actions he considered appropriate, and a way to eliminate the need for treaties or agreements of extinguishment" (Mitchell and Tennant 1996). The provincial legislature then denied Indian people the provincial franchise (Leslie and Maguire 1978). Trutch ignored federal requests to initiate treaty negotiations with First Nations leaders while granting reserve lands he considered sufficient to "fulfil all their reasonable requirements for cultivation and grazing" (Belanger, Newhouse, and Shpuniarsky 2008, 203).[3] First Nations leaders complained about the BC government's failure to politically interact with them and raised concerns about Trutch's ignorance of Aboriginal title right.[4]

Reflecting on BC's failure to enter into post-Confederation treaties and its historic refusal to engage the Indian Land Question (i.e., its failure to extinguish/acknowledge Aboriginal title), the province's origins could be traced along two separate and unambiguous trajectories.

Narrative #1: When whites came to BC the land was relatively empty, the inhabitants' technologically backward. Progressive and cosmopolitan British North Americans developed the undeveloped land. In doing so, they made various attempts to assimilate the native peoples, while setting aside reserves for those who resisted as-similation for one reason or another. The political order they creat-ed, while not perfect, was increasingly democratic, and ready to accept needed people on their own terms. The [Nisga'a] treaty thus represents an unnecessary giveaway of land and tax revenues that belong to all the people of British Columbia and creates a restric-tive and race-based franchise in the native-controlled areas. More-over, it is an attempt to redress possible wrongs that were set in motion more than a century ago and that are best left behind.

Narrative #2: [Before whites arrived in BC there was a] substantial pre-contact population in the region [with] complex social and political structures, particularly along the coast. Strict codes of property ownership, succession, and civil order were handed down through the oral tradition. This version highlights the Royal Proclamation of 1763, which guaranteed the aboriginal right to land and self-government. Any changes were to be effected through negotiations with the Crown. From the time of the gold rush, which brought British Columbia's first major wave of white settlement, a resource hungry white population, supported by provincial governments that were contemptuous of the First Na-tions rights, steadily eroded both the land base and the legal re-dress available to any. In doing so, they not only overrode, ignored, or confused the principles that have shaped the Nisga'a legal codes but also violated the principles laid down by the British crown for governing the white relations in the region. In this version, the treaty represents a long-awaited return to these principles. (Siexas as quoted in Beers 2001a)

A close reading of either narrative suggests that Aboriginal resistance to the referendum should have been anticipated, as should have its ca-pacity to act as "a vehicle for the mobilization of anti-Indian sentiment" (Gibson 2001). In this regard, political scientist Frank Cassidy noted that the blame for the treaty process that Campbell openly criticized had inevitably shifted to Aboriginal people and that the referendum could become an "opportunity for people to vent a lot of their concerns about the economy of British Columbia and I think focus on aborigi-nal people quite unfairly as the cause of a lot of economic woes" (Bar-rett 2001). Exacerbating issues even more was Campbell's token recognition of the First Nations role in BC's development, which, when coupled with his challenge to court-acknowledged Aboriginal claims, intensified provincial economic insecurity (Sayers 2001). In 2009, a PriceWaterhouseCoopers study, as an example, concluded that such uncertainty could cost the BC government $1 billion in lost investment and fifteen hundred jobs per year in the mining and forestry sectors. On the flip side, finalizing treaties with First Nations could lead to more than $10 billion in benefits to the provincial economy during the next fifteen years (PriceWaterhouseCoopers 2009).

The Treaty Referendum Outcome

At a time when a bridge builder was needed, Campbell amplified the growing Aboriginal/non-Aboriginal divide by choosing to forge ahead with a referendum the noted pollster Angus Reid classified as "one of the most amateurish, one-sided attempts to gauge public will that I have seen in my professional career." Reid was especially troubled by the harm that could result from the "false picture it [would] give of the true state of attitudes on this complex question and, even worse, its pretense that this kind of flimsy exercise is a legitimate way to divine the public will" (Reid 2002). Future prime ministerial hopeful Michael Ignatieff weighed in by noting that, if BC's history was an indicator, the public was primed to reject the referendum questions and, perhaps more important, "institutionalize majority tyranny," thus permitting officials to renege on their treaty commitments: "Democracy doesn't simply mean majority rule. It means a balance between majority rule and minority rights and group rights," Ignatieff noted, adding, "What you have a democracy for, is to allow as many different ways of life to flourish as possibly can" (Beers 2001b). First Nations leader Bill Wilson nicely summarized Aboriginal concerns as follows: "Subjecting minority rights, constitutionally protected minority rights, to the will of a majority lies tyranny and oppression and we're worried about that" (Sandler 2001). The federal government would voice its opposition that July as well (Lunman 2001c). In May 2002, former Ontario lieutenant-governor and Canadian Race Relations Foundation chair Lincoln Alexander expressed his concerns regarding what he characterized as the referendum's racist underpinnings and its potential to re-subjugate First Nations to a colonized status (S. Hume 2002b). As referendum resistance was mounting, the Liberal Party swept the NDP from power on 5 June, winning seventy-seven of seventy-nine legislative seats. With little fanfare, one of Campbell's first acts as premier was to eliminate the Aboriginal Affairs Ministry (Lunman 2001c).

It would be more than one year before the proposed referendum was to be held on 3 July 2002, and during that time Aboriginal and extra-provincial resistance to it had grown substantially. Whereas the popular print and electronic media would come to side with First Nations, the majority of the business community professed its support for the referendum. The polls indicated that 60 per cent of British Columbians supported a referendum, even if most agreed that the money should be directed to more important priorities (Matas 2001). Riding this wave of popularity, Campbell pushed forward and First Nations refused to reciprocate. All public engagement was thus confined to the Premier's Office and the (majority) non-Aboriginal public (Bohn 2001). It seemed that non-Aboriginals were again being asked to define the pith and substance of Aboriginal rights. Whatever influence Aboriginal leaders may have exerted disappeared after the 11 September 2001 World Trade Center attacks. Now that terrorism had been thrust into the international spotlight any and all challenges to the state – verbal or otherwise – were being portrayed as potential acts of terrorism. First Nations leaders who had earlier threatened blockades and occupations, such as Lawrence Baird, chief councillor for Vancouver Island's Ucluelet First Nation, now attempted to get ahead of the story: "Maybe now is not the time to be running out with our camouflage clothes on and blockading and whatnot." Concerned that direct action could be mistaken for terrorism, he was worried that his people could potentially "end up on somebody's hit list" (Bailey 2001a). The end result: circumstance had stripped First Nations of a potent resistance mechanism.

The referendum did not produce absolute public support, and critics concerned with its questionable logic and faulty legal scaffold pursued public education in their efforts to unpack its messaging and highlight the potential social costs. Lawyer Thomas Berger (2002a) aptly summarized the process: "Campbell, if he gets the answer he wants, will be bound to refuse to recognize in treaty negotiations the law as laid down by the courts – in fact, as laid down in a lawsuit that he himself brought. And which he obtained the answer he didn't want." He then concluded: "What Campbell is, in effect, saying, is: 'We don't care what the Constitution says about your rights. We don't care that the courts have affirmed your rights. We are going to ask the people of the province to give us a mandate to treat your rights as non-existent. As far as we are concerned, you have no inherent right of self-government."

By the 15 May deadline the $9 million referendum had returned a pal-
try 36 per cent of the ballots sent out (763,480).[5] Over 80 per cent indicated agreement with the eight principles (see Reid 2002).[6] Campbell
identified the response as "a resounding vote of confidence in both the
treaty making process and the principles that my government will take
to the table on the people's behalf" (Campbell 2002). Following the announcement, the provincial Aboriginal services budget was raised from
$1.8 to $3.8 million, and the First Citizens Fund[7] was doubled to $72
million (for 2004–05) (Harnett 2002). Notably, the remainder of 2002
played out contrary to the year's first half: most parties remained silent,
as though the referendum had never occurred.

A NEW RELATIONSHIP:
CAMPBELL AS ABORIGINAL ADVOCATE?

Resistance to Aboriginal concerns so symbolized Campbell's first years
in office that he risked forever alienating BC's Indigenous peoples. Then,
in February 2003, during the Speech from the Throne to open the
fourth session of the 37th BC Parliament, Lieutenant-Governor Iona
Campagnolo surprisingly made the following statement:

> If history has taught us anything, surely it is this: we are always
> stronger as a country and as a province when we work together. We
> are enhanced as a people when we celebrate our diversity and build
> on all we have in common. We are enriched when we listen to one
> another and learn from our mistakes. Nowhere is that truer than
> with governments' relations with First Nations. For too long we
> have been stuck in a rut of our own making, talking past each
> other and heading in opposite directions. There is no mileage in
> the status quo. To make progress, we must all find a new path for-
> ward together. We must move beyond the old approaches and
> flawed policies of the past. It is up to us to accord First Nations the
> respect, support and social and economic opportunities to which
> they are entitled. Errors have been made in the past. Our institu-
> tions have failed Aboriginal people across our province.
>   Your government deeply regrets the mistakes that were made by
> governments of every political stripe over the course of our
> province's history. It regrets the tragic experiences visited upon
> First Nations through years of paternalistic policies that fostered in-
> equity, intolerance, isolation and indifference. Inadequate educa-

tion, health care and housing; rampant unemployment; alcoholism and drug abuse; unconscionably high rates of physical and sexual abuse, incarceration, infant mortality and suicide: these are the hallmarks of despair that have disproportionately afflicted First Nations' families, on and off-reserve. These are the legacies of history that we must act to erase. They are sad reminders that it is always our children who pay the biggest price for society's shortcomings.

No words of regret can ever undo the damage that has been done to First Nations in all the years we have shared this land together. Nor are governments solely responsible for all of the misfortunes endured by First Nations at the cruel hand of history. The point of reflecting on the errors made is not to assign blame or bear guilt for the actions of our forefathers. Rather, it is to assume today's responsibility to heal the wounds that time has wrought. It is to offer our hand in a new partnership of optimism and hope, as one people of many peoples, in pursuit of common goals. (Legislative Assembly of British Columbia 2003)

The following day (12 February), Campbell's Liberal government announced the extension of a three-year $30 million fund to encourage First Nations economic development. This was certainly an exceptional gesture of "good faith." Yet Campbell's actions did not completely eliminate some lingering feelings of distrust. First Nations Summit executive member Ed John, for one, cryptically retorted: "Actions speak louder than words and we will pay attention to how the intentions in the speech are reflected by the action of the government," while conceding, "What is important is that these statements are out there in communities for people to consider and deliberate over" (Bailey 2003a).

Still, for the first time since becoming premier, Campbell appeared willing to work with First Nations and Aboriginal leaders. The unanticipated apology established an interactive framework in that it identified ubiquitous systemic issues grounded in historic injustices that continued to negatively affect First Nations communities while highlighting the need for the Premier's Office to assume responsibility for healing and to forge a new relationship with Aboriginal peoples.[8] A second important development was the proposed improved level of provincial cooperation with federal officials on First Nations issues. While perhaps catching the public off guard, Campbell's about-face was, in fact, a strategic response to a shifting legal understanding of Aboriginal title dating to the 1997 *Delgamuukw* decision (Dacks 2002).

The court in this case ruled that constitutionally protected Aboriginal rights could be infringed upon for the greater good of economic development. However, unregulated access for development was not permitted as the Crown is bound by its fiduciary obligation to Aboriginal peoples (Macklem 2001). Additional cases would expand on the nature of Aboriginal title and the extent of provincial claims to Aboriginal-title lands – the two most important, for our purposes, being the Haida and Taku decisions (see Ross 2005). Dating back to the early 1990s, the Haida Nation challenged several provincial decisions approving the transfer of a tree farm licence from one forestry company to another. The Taku River Tlingit followed in 1994 by challenging a provincial decision to grant a project approval certificate under the BC Environmental Assessment Act to Redfern Resources for an access road to an old mine site.

The BC government challenged First Nations that "took the position that the [court] decisions would affect their aboriginal rights and title, and so the Province had to consult with them about those decisions" (Olynyk 2005, 1–2). It took two years, but the cases found their way to the Supreme Court. All the while, BC business leaders were increasingly pressuring the Premier's Office to resolve Aboriginal grievances to help stabilize increasingly uncertain resource development concerns. Perhaps anticipating the court's decision, Attorney General Geoff Plant, the responsible minister for treaty negotiations, and several prominent provincial business leaders acknowledged the need to develop a new approach to First Nations relations. In the end, the BC Court of Appeal agreed with the First Nations and held that the province should have consulted with them (see *Haida Nation v. British Columbia [Minister of Forests]* 2004; *Taku River Tlingit First Nation v. British Columbia [Project Assessment Director]* 2004).

With the emergence of what was described as "a new constitutional paradigm governing Aboriginal rights" that "recognizes the potential of section 35 as a generative constitutional order – one that mandates the Crown to negotiate with Aboriginal peoples for the recognition of their rights in a contemporary form that balances their needs with the interests of the broader society" (Slattery 2005, 436), Campbell was forced to confront head on the shifting legal winds that, more and more, were at odds with his past approach of denying Aboriginal self-government. This much was evident at a carefully rehearsed "open" cabinet meeting held on 22 November 2002, at which Plant took pains to explain the new context to his colleagues while telegraphing to the public changes to the province's treaty-bargaining approach: "First Nations have told us that they will not accept an extinguishment of rights." He then added: "British Columbia therefore rejects the use of extinguishment or the technique known as cede, release, and surrender" (BC Treaty Commission 2003, 3). Business was identified as a partner in what was being described as a reconciliation process, which, "to be successful, need[ed] clarity about the legal and regulatory regime in which it must operate" (ibid.).

It wouldn't be until March 2005, however, that any substantial progress towards reconciliation would take place. That month Plant announced his leave from politics, and Jessica McDonald, Campbell's new deputy minister for special projects and management of natural resources and environmental issues, was assigned responsibility for developing the "New Relationship" initiative. Later, appointed deputy minister to the premier, McDonald utilized her consulting background and previous efforts with First Nations, companies, and government to negotiate the New Relationship over a six-month period in 2005. Business and First Nations leaders praised her work ethic, and, ultimately, it was her hard work that led to a mutual dialogue that some critics nevertheless perceived as unduly empowering First Nations to render consultation and accommodation as a requirement for consent (see Willcocks 2006). It was apparent that the Campbell government's era of reconciliation was unyielding in its desire to facilitate change. For example, his new cabinet was less overtly hostile to Aboriginal interests due, in part, to McDonald's management approach, which differed dramatically from that of previous Campbell intimates Brown, Plant, and de Jong. He had also by now begun to drift away from Mel Smith's teachings to embrace a more pragmatic approach to promoting improved provincial–First Nations relations that better reflected Supreme Court decisions emphasizing a duty to consult, as well as industry demands for greater political certainty, thus improving developmental capacity.

Many were still surprised at these changes, even following Campbell's public support for Prime Minister Paul Martin's announcement of $700 million in new health programs for Status Indians, Métis, and Inuit in September 2004 (Sallot 2004). The proposal would mature into the $5.1 billion Kelowna Accord, a five-year plan to improve education, housing, economic development, health, and water services (see Patterson 2006).[9] Campbell travelled extensively in the months leading up to the 24 and 25 November First Ministers Conference in Kelowna, BC, to help educate Canadians about the province's New Relationship with

Aboriginal peoples, while contributing his strategy as a potential model
to advance national Aboriginal affairs (El Akkad 2005). His refined message was nevertheless clear: "If you look at the facts, and you stare them
in the face, Canada has been in denial about aboriginal first nations
people for 138 years. We're not going to be in denial anymore" (Cernetig 2005). With Campbell's support, Martin convinced the leaders of
five Aboriginal organizations and the leaders of the remaining twelve
provinces and territories to support the proposal. Martin's minority
government unfortunately collapsed within seventy-two hours of the
agreement, and the newly elected prime minister, Stephen Harper, crip-
pled the Kelowna Accord's potential by allocating substantially less
funding in the May 2006 budget than had originally been outlined.

As the First Ministers' Kelowna meetings garnered the headlines in BC,
the media broke the story of the six-month New Relationship negotiations. Campbell would respond by prophetically declaring before the
BC legislature: "The honour of the Crown is at stake. The trust relationship that was at the core of the Kelowna meeting demands decisive action and unflagging affirmation ... No more excuses" (V. Palmer 2006).
The provincial government was now on notice, and the timing appeared
to be perfect as the previous May the Liberals had retained power in a
provincial election. With a reduced majority of forty-six out of seventy-
nine seats, the Liberals took notice of the fact that, in ten provincial con-
stituencies in which Aboriginal people made up "more than 10 per cent
of the population, the Liberals won four seats and the NDP six. In 2001,
Campbell's party had taken all ten" (Penikett 2006, 257). A stand-alone
ministry dedicated to Aboriginal affairs (previously decommissioned in
2002) was re-established in June as the Ministry of Aboriginal Affairs
and Reconciliation (Smyth 2005a). Adding reconciliation to the name
reflected Campbell's desire to establish a "New Relationship," which
happened also to be the title of a pre-election, five-page agreement that
formally acknowledged the "historic and sacred relationship between
First Nations and their land." Among its highlights was a joint provincial-Aboriginal decision-making framework for land and resources, and
an action plan to achieve "government-to-government agreements for
... land-use, planning, management, tenuring, resource revenue and benefit sharing" (UBCIC 2005). The end goal was to determine how to "bring
about reconciliation through substantive change and develop an effective framework for consultation and accommodation" (UBCIC 2005). Although reconciliation remained ill defined, and minimal terms of
reference and anticipated outcomes were offered, Campbell forged

ahead to advocate on behalf of Aboriginal people, calling upon Prime Minister Harper in November 2006 to declare Aboriginal people a nation within Canada (Cernetig 2006).

The steps towards reconciliation were inspiring, and they forced changes to Aboriginal policy aimed at closing Aboriginal education, health, economic, and opportunity gaps (Palmer 2008a). Campbell's reconciliation model emphasized the treaty process, which made sense given the need to ensure commercial territorial access resulting in orderly provincial economic development. In 2006, however, 60 per cent of the Aboriginal population lived in urban centres with 26 per cent residing on reserves. In the interim, it appeared that satisfying corporate desires trumped formal recognition of the urban Aboriginal population. The multicultural nature of the urban Aboriginal community was likewise ignored in lieu of focusing on First Nations and Aboriginal issues (the interior Métis communities tended to be unnoticed). Prior to first contact, more than fifty-two languages were spoken by multiple First Nations who often claimed overlapping territories. Each of these groups, from its vantage point, is a unique cultural entity that seeks to keep its members united. Napoleon (2004) stresses the heterogeneous nature of BC's Aboriginal communities and, in particular, how historic, economic, social, political, and geographic contexts shape culture and influence how Aboriginal leaders interact with one another and with the federal, provincial, and municipal governments while also exploring the dynamics of internal relationship building and renewal. Carlson (2010) similarly explores how layered identities are forged in response to, and mobilized to confront, the forces of colonialism. The message for Campbell was that no indistinguishable and politically consistent Aboriginal community existed.

Previously, Aboriginal groups had little option but to negotiate with the provincial government in order to achieve their goals (Alcantara 2007), but slowly, beginning in the late 1990s, many pursued agreements with industry, municipalities, and/or the federal government. The reasons for this shift vary, but the sluggish pace of treaty negotiations coupled with the *Delgamuukw* decision's heightening Aboriginal expectations concerning increased values for lands (which provincial officials were unwilling to pay) resulted in a dialogue that was decidedly less focused on Aboriginal rights. And this, in turn, led to the emergence of an innovative claims-based social contract (Dacks 2004). Such institutional developments resulting in an expanded range of options were also appealing. For instance, the Carrier Sekani First

Nations withdrew from treaty negotiations in March 2007 to explore bilateral agreements with private companies to develop their territories' natural resources. The Kamloops Indian Band negotiated four separate agreements with the City of Kamloops to govern issues ranging from infrastructure and service provision to economic development, communication, and land transfer (Nelles and Alcantara 2011). In 2003, the Westbank First Nation and Canada formally signed the Westbank First Nation Self-Government Agreement, which has been used to build capacity and to craft laws reflecting local needs (Alcantara 2007). These examples highlight the political and economic shifts that challenged provincial paramountcy in relation to Aboriginal issues while demonstrating the willingness of First Nations to bypass provincial officials as they pursued improved well-being. In the municipal–First Nations context, in particular, "the patterns of agreement types suggest that both First Nations and municipal governments have progressively recognized the mutual benefits of collaboration and have sought to formalize these new relationships" (Nelles and Alcantara 2011, 325).

Perhaps this is why Campbell failed to concede the BC Treaty Commission's potential, even in the face of First Nations faith in its restorative influence. Yes, Campbell was becoming better informed about Aboriginal affairs under the guidance of Allen Adzerza (Penikett 2006). But, in the spirit of ensuring provincial development, Campbell encouraged all connected parties to pursue treaty-related measures (TRMs). Developed in 2000 by BC and federal officials, TRMs reflected a BC Claims Task Force recommendation to "negotiate interim measures agreements before or during the treaty negotiations when an interest is being affected, which could undermine the process" (First Nations of British Columbia 1991, 23). TRMs have proven successful. For instance, by 2004, four agreements-in-principle were announced, while three hundred side agreements, including eighty TRMs, were noted (Auditor General 2006, 11), followed in the next seven years by an additional three hundred benefit- and revenue-sharing agreements negotiated between First Nations, the provincial government, and private-sector firms (Hoekstra et al. 2014). TRMs are unrelated to actual treaty talks and have led to the subsequent proliferation of local land- and resource development-specific agreements with First Nations. It was with this in mind that the BC Office of the Auditor General explored the province's administrative and management effectiveness in successfully completing treaties with First Nations. It concluded in its final 2006 report entitled *Treaty Negotiations in British Columbia*: "While these options provide temporary reconciliation of issues – similar to 'renting' certainty – ultimately they do not give parties the long-term certainty that treaties offer" (Auditor General 2006, 1). A vital recommendation – greater harmonization of the treaty process with the proposed New Relationship policy – was ignored.

Admittedly, the task of reconciling the conflicting judicial interpretations of what access and consultation necessitated with the New Relationship's goal of working with Aboriginal leaders was massive. And the use of TRMs was considered essential if development was to continue during treaty negotiations, even if this weakened the BC Treaty Commission's authority. Specifically, whereas treaties seek to balance incentives for governments or private firms seeking greater economic or regulatory certainty in negotiating such agreements, TRMs were utilized to facilitate quick agreements and ongoing territorial access. Development may have continued, but First Nations anxiety grew about the potential loss of political, economic, and social control linked with large-scale "transformative" change (Hale and Belanger 2015). It further hints at the fact that Campbell's reconciliation model preferred consultation to facilitating wholesale institutional changes that would necessitate confronting ongoing and systemic colonial beliefs in BC's political paramountcy – and all of this within five years of a referendum that revealed a provincial citizenry's desire to abandon Aboriginal status and self-government. In view of McDonald's efforts in crafting the initial proposal, which drew praise from Aboriginal leaders, this outcome was regrettable (Willcocks 2006).

THE RECOGNITION AND RECONCILIATION ACT

The intervening years following the March 2005 agreement did not appear to lead to the hoped-for New Relationship. As Sto:lo grand chief Doug Kelly noted in 2008, "Here we are three years later and nothing has changed. Of course there is a lot of frustration and anger among first nations' communities" (M. Hume 2008b). For Campbell, who had previously inveigled federal leaders to stop making excuses and to establish proper relationships with First Nations, this was a slippery slope. The promising new provincial model of government–First Nations relations had yet to materialize, and soon the finger pointing began, with Campbell urging caution: "This is a big project and we need to get it right. It will take considerable effort in negotiation and in all of the requisite consultation with our various constituents." He added: "I believe it would be a mistake to commit to a timetable for the introduction of legislation. If we were to do so and not meet it we would appear to fail" (V. Palmer 2008b). For the first time since his ill-advised referendum, Campbell found himself the focus of Aboriginal animosity, and he was clearly taken aback. He had, after all, initiated a process seeking to foster a new relationship. Why was this occurring?

On first blush the proposed legislation sought to attain five primary outcomes. First, it recognized that Aboriginal rights and title exist in BC and throughout each Indigenous Nation's territory, without requirement of proof or strength of claim. Second, it enabled and guided the creation of mechanisms to ensure shared decision making in regard to planning, management, and tenuring decisions over lands and resources. Third, it established a roadmap leading to the successful completion of Indigenous-provincial revenue- and benefit-sharing agreements. Fourth, it offered a vision of rebuilding Indigenous Nations and establishing new procedural institutions. Finally, dispute resolution mechanisms were to be developed to mitigate disagreements arising concerning the interpretation or implementation of the legislation, regulations, or any agreements concluded pursuant to the legislation (UBCIC 2009). In the wake of First Nations and Aboriginal frustration, Campbell did secure the support of the First Nations Leadership Council (FNLC), a coalition of the three key provincial Aboriginal organizations: (1) the First Nations Summit representing First Nations participating in or supportive of the BC treaty negotiation process; (2) the UBCIC, promoting and supporting the affirmation and defence of Aboriginal title and rights; and (3) the British Columbia Assembly of First Nations (BCAFN), a programming advocate for BC First Nations. This support notwithstanding, the proposed act's main weakness was not its intent but, rather, its endemic imprecision related to clarifying complex topics such as Aboriginal title and reconciliation (V. Palmer 2009a).

Upon reviving negotiations in late 2008, several months of uneasy conversations followed, but, on 19 February 2009, the two sides signed off on an outline of the proposed legislation. Unfortunately, after years of working towards this moment, Campbell was unable to convince his own government of its value. Nor could he dampen the fears of industry leaders, who commissioned a legal opinion to determine the legislation's unintended consequences. In response, Aboriginal leaders commissioned a legal opinion as a direct challenge. Unfortunately, as this was unfolding the proposed Recognition and Reconciliation Act was quietly dropped from the legislative agenda (V. Palmer 2009b).

Many individuals, including Jeffrey Rustand, in-house counsel for the Canadian Constitutional Forum, welcomed the move. He believed that each of these issues demanded clarity and that to fail to provide it could compromise reconciliation. On the surface, however, the legislation faced more rudimentary challenges. First, even though Campbell secured Aboriginal buy-in with the original five-page agreement, he failed to pursue ongoing relationship building. As UBCIC grand chief Stewart Phillip would later lament: "I stand guilty as charged, [of] being an individual that was somewhat taken in by the vision and who believed that there was sincerity and commitment on the part of the provincial government to actually turn the page of history" (M. Hume 2008a). Campbell defended his actions, but Aboriginal leaders seeking concrete outcomes remained unconvinced due to the "business-as-usual" approach of provincial government officials, which relied on informal consultations with Aboriginal peoples as opposed to engaging them as partners in policy making and political decision making. UBCIC grand chief Phillip was so disappointed that he publicly endorsed NDP leader Carole James the day before the provincial May 2009 election (Mickleburgh 2009).

Second, Campbell's progressive interpretation of Aboriginal title may have satisfied Aboriginal leaders, but it also seemed to heighten the anxiety of BC's corporate leadership (Simoski 2009). The premier failed to substantially consult these groups, hence their resistance should have been anticipated. Finally, Campbell's attempt to aggregate the more than two hundred provincial First Nations into thirty Indigenous nations based on territorial boundaries was portrayed as a neocolonial attempt to refashion cultural and political complexity in the name of reconciliation. Defending this provision based on the FNLC's support, Campbell ignored the fact that the FNLC was not considered to be the province's First Nations representative as well as the fact that the number of BC First Nations was being reduced by provincial edict.

On 12 May 2009, the Liberal Party under Campbell's leadership achieved electoral history by winning a third consecutive majority government, taking forty-nine seats (three more than the previous election). On 30 August 2009, the BC chiefs pronounced the proposed legislation's demise. One year later, and only seventeen months into his four-year term, Campbell announced his resignation. Three months later he was interviewed for a *Maclean's Magazine* Q&A and was asked to reflect on the New Relationship's demise. He replied simply: "Everyone got a little freaked out – both First Nations and non-First Nations

alike. It was too big a step." He continued: "One thing we're going to regret in years to come is that we weren't able to pass the Recognition
and Reconciliation Act in spring 2009. It would have made a huge difference to First Nations people and the province, and would have laid
the groundwork for future reconciliation and economic development"
(N. Macdonald 2011).

CONCLUSION

This chapter is not an attempt to undo Gordon Campbell's status as
an Aboriginal advocate, and it highlights the bold steps that, after a period of political resistance to Aboriginal self-government and Aboriginal title, he took to reconcile the needs of British Columbians with
those of the Aboriginal people who call BC home. Frequent adversary
and negotiating partner Ed John would describe Campbell in this way:
"He started off fighting us but he ended up as a completely different individual, helping us with quality-of-life issues in our communities"
(Hunter 2011). In this setting, it is vital to probe the policy environment to better comprehend why this occurred – especially given that,
in this so-called "age of reconciliation," so little was accomplished to
improve what to many observers remains a failing BC-Aboriginal relationship. As noted, few substantial systemic changes resulted from
Campbell's reconciliation model, and the reasons for this vary. For one,
I have suggested that the premier lacked clarity on a number of key issues that, in turn, affected his effectiveness as both opponent and advocate. In the growing wake of legal and academic evidence to the
contrary, he consistently refused to acknowledge that Aboriginal self-
government and Aboriginal title preceded BC's emergence, that they
could not be simply ignored or unilaterally legislated out of existence.
Arguably, Campbell understood the impact of his approach and was
engaging in a form of populism that would resonate with voters, thus
ensuring a Liberal electoral victory. This needs to be confirmed, but
similar trends were evident in the post-2003 election after half a dozen
seats were lost to the NDP in ridings sporting high Aboriginal populations. This early stance would nevertheless haunt Campbell and offer
fuel to his critics.

Aboriginal leaders, on the other hand, refused to overlook a sordid
provincial history grounded in their peoples' territorial alienation and
physical removal, and this informed a cautious approach to political
engagement. When coupled with the inter-jurisdictional intricacy in-

fluencing the meaning of Aboriginal title a convoluted roadmap to reconciliation starts to emerge. A host of additional barriers to reconciliation included Aboriginal social, economic, and political heterogeneity, leading to inter- and intra-community power struggles and the desire to engage extra-provincial corporate, municipal, and federal partnerships; growing socio-economic and political divides between urban Aboriginal and reserve communities; corporate pressures to act; and a shifting legal environment demanding provincial leaders consult with Aboriginal leaders. Campbell desired change that would result in the formal integration of First Nations and Aboriginal interests into the everyday business of BC politics and that would simultaneously respect First Nations and Aboriginal confidence in nationhood status. The political, economic, and cultural environments were rife with obstacles that he was unable, or did not know how, to satisfactorily overcome. This, however, did not stop Campbell from making what would become many unfulfilled pledges to Aboriginal leaders. Failure to fully comprehend the scope of those guarantees had the effect of backing him, his office, and the government into a proverbial corner. In either case – as opponent or as proponent – this failure to fully decipher the proposed navigational intricacies led to his undoing.

Campbell's attempts to achieve a "New Relationship" with Aboriginal people in BC were noteworthy. Yet, in the end, these and other types of policy initiatives should be viewed as a cautionary tale of how partiality of political vision can undermine even the most benevolent attempts to draw Aboriginal people in from the political, social, and economic margins. In an age of increasing provincial- and municipal-Aboriginal relations, both premiers and local government leaders alike should take stock of this narrative.

ACKNOWLEDGMENTS

I would like to thank Kate Dekruyf for her excellent research assistance, which led to the timely completion of this chapter; the reviewers, for their helpful comments; and Drs Jason Lacharite and Tracy Summerville for their guidance, all of which greatly improved my argument.

NOTES

1 As an example, he posited the following scenario: "If an aboriginal citizen has land in Vancouver, is it part of the aboriginal land or does it remain in the City of Vancouver?" (Hauka 1992).

2 The Reform Party of Canada merged with the Progressive Conservative Party of Canada in 2003 to become the modern Conservative Party of Canada. Sally Weaver was one of the first to identify the need to clarify in policy and legislation what "Indian government" was, and the need to reconcile these concepts with federal and provincial policy and legislation.

3 Originally found in Trutch to Macdonald, 14 October 1872, LAC, MG 26A, Sir John A. Macdonald Papers, pp. 127650–1.

4 See, generally, LAC, RG 10, vol. 3669, file 10,691.

5 Between fifty-five thousand and sixty thousand votes on each question were rejected.

6 Reid initially anticipated that the questions would "produce affirmative answers in the 90-per-cent-plus range." See Reid (2002).
The eight questions were as follows:
  1 Private property should not be expropriated for treaty settlements. (Yes/No)
  2 The terms and conditions of leases and licences should be respected; fair compensation for unavoidable disruption of commercial interests should be ensured. (Yes/No)
  3 Hunting, fishing and recreational opportunities on Crown land should be ensured for all British Columbians. (Yes/No)
  4 Parks and protected areas should be maintained for the use and benefit of all British Columbians. (Yes/No)
  5 Province-wide standards of resource management and environmental protection should continue to apply. (Yes/No)
  6 Aboriginal self-government should have the characteristics of local government, with powers delegated from Canada and British Columbia. (Yes/No)
  7 Treaties should include mechanisms for harmonizing land use planning between Aboriginal governments and neighbouring local governments. (Yes/No)
  8 The existing tax exemptions for Aboriginal people should be phased out. (Yes/No)
A Yes vote means the government will be bound to adopt the principle in treaty negotiations; a No vote means the government will not be bound to adopt the principle to guide its participation in treaty negotiations.

7   The First Citizen's Fund is a perpetual fund created in 1969 for Aboriginal cultural, educational, and economic development. Interest earned from fund investments supports Aboriginal programs and services. All programs and services are managed and delivered in partnership with provincial Aboriginal organizations.

8   Apologies from federal and provincial governments are not at all common. For example, it would be 2014 before the BC government would once again offer an apology, this time to the Chinese community for the head tax.

9   It included $1.8 billion for education to create school systems, train more Aboriginal teachers, and identify children with special needs; $1.6 billion for housing, including $400 million to address the need for clean water in many remote communities; $1.3 billion for health services; and $200 million for economic development.

4

Riding the Wave
of Available Policy Options
Gordon Campbell and the Rhetoric
of Neoliberalism

TRACY SUMMERVILLE

In this chapter, I argue that Gordon Campbell's leadership may be best understood as "riding the wave" of a form of neoliberalism that had already shaped the post-Keynesian and post-Fordist economic revolution of the 1980s. This time in history was marked by the end of Fordism, which is described as the stable postwar period of "structured national and international systems of governance and production" (Hayter 2003, 708). By the 1980s, the global economy was moving through a period of globalization that was characterized by flexible capital and labour (710). Gordon Campbell swept to power already situated in the context of this global economic shift.

Campbell was not particularly visionary in his approach to economic or social policy, and the contradictions that appeared in his actions over his career as premier were not really contradictions at all. His actions were based on policy options that had emerged earlier in Western democracies and in other provinces in Canada. Moreover, some of his policy choices, particularly in the field of environmental politics, reflected the unique political culture of British Columbia rather than a bold policy agenda.

My intent in this chapter is to demonstrate that Campbell drew from a playbook of policy options that was already being used in other jurisdictions. Neoliberal rhetoric was part of the national and international narrative: big government meant higher taxes and inefficiencies in service delivery, which made it imperative to place greater faith in the market than in the public sector. This attack on the state's role in the economy and society was just one of the dominant lines of argument that spread into politics during the 1980s and beyond – including into the new century, when Campbell took office. In this context, certain policy options came to the fore: public-private partnerships, the veneration of the policy entrepreneur, and the decline of province building in favour of more local and autonomous municipalities/communities. During this long period, which may or may not have come to an end, the dominant storyline has been that efficiencies can be set right if governments simply "get out of the way." In this chapter, I look at how three particular policy approaches came to life in British Columbia under the leadership of Gordon Campbell. I also note that the dominant narrative did hold a particularly interesting contradiction: many people (in BC and elsewhere) were unable to make the connection between cutting taxes and eliminating public services. Campbell's budgets often belied his rhetoric, and his government did invest in areas of education and health, but he was still dependent on policy options that emphasized the state stepping aside so that business could flourish. His budget documents reflect these policy options and the fact that cuts in health and education were a kind of third rail in BC politics (see Beers et al. 2005).

My evidence is drawn from the varying literature on the premier's policy practices over his career. I have consulted the work of various scholars to explain Campbell's approach to public policy in a wide range of areas, including: economic policy, resource development, environmental policy, and his approach to Aboriginal title. I have also drawn upon budget documents that show how Campbell arranged investment through particular policy approaches. It appears that Gordon Campbell was swept into the international and domestic wave of neoliberal policy reform while at the same time being constrained by traditional practices embedded in Canadian institutions and in the psyche of BC voters. The following account outlines the policy options that had been framed in other jurisdictions. British Columbia was already many years behind the reforms that had taken place both in Canada and in other places around the world.

It should be noted that, during the 1980s, BC did flirt with neoconservative policy (see Carroll and Ratner 1989; Resnick 1987). In a compelling article entitled "Neo-Conservatism on the Periphery," Phillip Resnick (1987, 13) describes the early 1980s and the government's move to "themes of privatization, deregulations, and centralization [that] were patently neo-conservative formulae, with direct analogies to practice, both in the UK and in the US." Bill Bennett championed the "New Reality" initiative based on these ideas, and, in many ways, he was successful in branding the message. Resnick notes the significant change in attitude towards public-sector unions and the civil service, and he foreshadows the rhetoric of the private as being better than the public (13–14) and the taxpayers versus the "socialists" (11). Yet, despite the powerful message of the right, leftist elements in BC at the time had not yet begun to relinquish their place, and the Solidarity Movement emerged to rebuff this message. The electorate was clearly split on the need for reforms. Resnick's article leaves off as Bill Vander Zalm came to power, and one wonders, in hindsight, if Vander Zalm may have kept BC on track towards a full-fledged neoliberal agenda if his premiership had not ended with scandal. The period of the 1990s in BC under the NDP held in abeyance the all-out shift that was occurring elsewhere.

To begin this chapter, I briefly outline how neoliberalism came to frame the range of policy choices that were available to governments. Drawing on the work of Daniel Béland, I suggest that neoliberal policy options became the only policy choices during Gordon Campbell's time in office. Clearly, he believed in the tenets of neoliberal philosophy, but he was not a driver of the policy options that would frame his government's policy choices. These were decided in other places and in earlier times, and they were built on ideas that had become a part of restructuring the state's relationship to citizens and interest groups on both the left and the right of the ideological spectrum.

THE GLOBAL CONTEXT AND THE CHANGE IN ATTITUDE REGARDING THE ROLE OF GOVERNMENT

Daniel Béland (2009; 2005) argues that historical institutionalism, which he defines as being "grounded in the assumption that historically constructed institutions (i.e. public policies and formal political institutions) create major constraints and opportunities that affect the behavior of the actors involved in the policy-making process" (Béland 2009, 702), "leaves gaps" in its capacity to explain policy change. He asserts that this is true at three levels: (1) it fails to explain agenda setting; (2) it explains what constraints institutions put on policy options but not how actors bring to the table, and then dismiss, particular policy choices; and (3) it does not do a good job of explaining how policy alternatives emerge outside of institutions when a strong policy entrepreneur convinces the public of the moral or political imperative of a policy alternative. I suggest that this third observation is well illustrated by the rise of neoliberalism and its tenets as a moral and political imperative. Béland suggests that "ideological frames are not policy ideas," but it is easy to demonstrate how the ideology set out the principles, or rather ideas, from which neoliberal policy options emerged. Moreover, this paradigm shift took place over both wings of the political spectrum and reconstituted the shape of policy options, including marginalizing some fairly standard twentieth-century policy choices, like labour's involvement in labour law.

NEOLIBERALISM AS AN IDEOLOGY AND THE RISE OF THE NEOLIBERAL POLICY ENTREPRENEUR

Neoliberalism became the ideological alternative to Keynesianism in the 1980s, and the central components of that ideology, including small government, market-driven economies, privatization, and deregulation, became the ideas that drove policy changes and, ultimately, institutional change. For these ideas to have been successful there had to have been a series of policy entrepreneurs that could consolidate power in order to drive the institutional change required to construct a neoliberal state. Beland (2005, 11) makes this point when he argues that "the framing process [i.e., the public pronouncements of certain policy proposals] is indeed a strategic and deliberate activity aimed at generating public support for specific policy ideas." There had to be a way to sell the public on how these ideas were beneficial to individual liberty – even to those who held a largely communitarian approach to public policy. Beland also makes this case when he says that "ideological framing contributes to the 'social construction' of the need to reform" (ibid.).

I argue that BC was ready to embrace "the social construction of the need for reform" (Beland 2005) by the time Gordon Campbell came to power. Neoliberal governments emerged in the 1980s under Margaret Thatcher in Britain, Ronald Reagan in the United States, and Brian Mulroney (to some extent) in Canada, and all of these leaders were able to frame the neoliberal agenda by defending individual liberty against the creep of "big government." There are obviously sophisticated scholarly arguments about the problems of the decline of the welfare state and the loss of state support for public goods, but this matters little in a world driven by public opinion and the "consumer citizen." Antony and Broad (1999), and now Delacourt (2013), suggest that branding political parties as merely product choices that drive a good deal of electoral politics is now the standard by which voters judge competing policy platforms. The war of words regarding big government has worked well and, as Gregory Albo (2002, 47) argues, "neo-liberalism has been equally practiced by political regimes of the centre-left." He adds that "it is a cold hard fact of contemporary politics that regimes of different political stripes have all endorsed capitalist globalization and implemented policies of deregulation, privatization, and social austerity. We get neoliberalism even when we elect social democratic governments" (ibid.). And he points to the "Third Way social democratic governments of Europe through the 1990s, the Clinton presidency in the United States, the *Parti Québécois* in Québec, and the New Democratic Party (NDP) provincial governments stretching from Ontario, under Premier Bob Rae in the early 1990s, [to] the NDP governments in the prairie provinces of Manitoba and Saskatchewan" in the early to mid-2000s (ibid.). Here, of course, Albo is referring to former premiers Greg Selinger (Manitoba) and Lorne Calvert (Saskatchewan). Thus, the dominant political narrative has shifted towards the imperatives of new policy choices framed to deal with the big government boogeyman. I suggest later in this chapter that the framing of this new policy alternative as the scourge of big government worked in BC's political culture despite the province's rather long relationship with social democracy.

Christopher Kukucha's "The Role of the Provinces in Canadian Foreign Policy" points to the shift in direction that occurred by the 1990s and that essentially entrenched neoliberal ideas and practices in Canada. He notes:

Although there is evidence to suggest that states have maintained some policy autonomy in these matters during the last decade, what Hoberg has labeled the "capacity for choice," there are also indications that neoliberal market forces continue to have a dominant impact on the policy process ... Most provinces willingly and actively dismantled the remnants of the Keynesian system in Canada and justified these actions as a result of neoliberal international policies. In fact, by the end of the decade it was arguable that all provinces, regardless of the party in power, had adopted these principles. This point is often lost on observers that claim international pressures leave Canada with no alternative but to pursue purely market oriented positions. (Kukucha 2004, 129–30)

The construction of the neoliberal narrative reduced policy options, and so this narrative was critical to the way that policy entrepreneurs articulated the new paradigm.

In essence, neoliberal thinkers were able to shape the political context to their advantage by first questioning the role of the state and then redefining the state. The political rhetoric was framed in such a way as to convince citizens that there were few, if any, other choices in a globalizing world but for the state to make way for the market. And, most important, the idea that the state was too big was juxtaposed with the idea that the state's decline would benefit individual liberty. For example, while taxes have always been seen as a burden, there was, at least in part, a view that they existed for some greater public good; however, the tax debate has shifted, and taxes have now been reconstructed as an imposition on liberty and choice. To be fair, this problem was exacerbated by evidence of state overspending and the growth of welfare programs. It is interesting to note as well that, during this period, a significant change occurred in the language used to describe welfare programs. The use of the word "entitlement" replaced the word "welfare," the idea being that changing the word would make the cutting of programs easier to sell to the public. It is easier to cut state-run programs if one believes that the individuals benefiting from them feel "entitled" to them rather than facing the fact that they are crucial to someone's well-being (i.e., "well [fare]").

Policy entrepreneurs had effectively captured the public imagination and made it appear that there was an imperative that required a restructuring of the state to accommodate the interests of the market and to welcome it as a partner in solving expensive public projects. From this desire to create new partnerships, or "new public management," came the commitment to public-private partnerships as a revered policy option.

In 2008, Karen Bridget Murray published an article that demonstrates the changing role of the state by examining how Canada's provinces had "realigned" themselves using the private and non-profit sectors to both limit and expand government reach. In some ways, Murray's argument reflects the theory of "roll-back" and "roll-out" neoliberalism. Roll-back reflects the views of the 1980s, when the call was for the state to get out of the marketplace; however, the displacements caused by the first wave of neoliberal ideology led to a roll-out (Peck and Tickell 2002). The transition is described here by May, Cloke, and Johnsen (2005, 704):

Such changes have resulted in new and more complex relationships between central and local government and their non-statutory
"partners," and the ever deeper insertion of central government personnel in both local government and civil society, that in contrast to
more familiar readings of "hollowing out" signal a re-centralisation
and formalization of central state power.

Murray (2008) demonstrates that this realigning was going on in
many provinces through the 1990s and into the 2000s. I show here that
Campbell picked up on this notion and chose policies to realign
the relationship between the BC government, private partners, and
local governments.

NEOLIBERALISM:
DEFINING THE ROLE OF THE STATE

Public-Private Partnerships as an Idea

Neoliberals essentially redefined the role of the state in the economy.
The move to public-private partnerships (P3s) was one of the core policy options that defined this shift. P3s represent a central commitment
of neoliberalism, which is to reduce the role of the state in the market.
The advancement of the idea of P3s could be reconciled on both sides
of the political spectrum. The left saw the trend as a way to enable communities by promoting the role of the non-governmental organization
(NGO) in the delivery of services determined by those "on the ground"
in communities. Citing a number of scholars, Miraftab (2004, 90)
points out that

> advocates [of community development in developing countries]
> argue that strengthening communities is the only way to achieve a
> sustained market economy. As government resources and responsi-
> bilities are more and more constrained, the arena of the communi-
> ties and their NGOs are looked to instead. There is no coincidence
> in the concomitant trends of increased liberalization of the market,
> the shrinking role of governments, and the growth of NGOs and
> CBOs [community-based organizations] ... The activities of NGOs and
> CBOs find enhanced meaning in the context of the privatization of
> public sector activities.

The lure of power to local communities became part of the invitation of neoliberal ideas. P3s were enabled because communities were advocating for an increase in local control of the distribution of resources and control over their own local development. Neil Bradford (2003, 1005) argues that "no strategy has attracted greater interest than *governance through public-private partnerships*, which effectively devolves authority and responsibility from the state and instead relies on the policy networks found in civil society." Moreover, Bradford shows that this shifting paradigm led the Bob Rae NDP in Ontario to "launch ... [its] own distinctive post-Keynesian project" (1010). In important ways, the "narrative" and the "imperative" that neoliberalism had imposed globally made it appear that "private-public partnership[s]... adopt an ennobling quality, fitting into a narrative that celebrates co-operation between diverse shareholders as a means of achieving more than any one party could on its own" (Siemiatycki 2005, 71–2).

I am not arguing here for the efficiency or effectiveness of P3 projects; rather, I am suggesting that P3s became the policy option of choice in the neoliberalizing period of the 1990s and into the early 2000s. Oddly, there is very little in the way of sufficient data to show the true impact of P3s. Indeed, a report by Deloitte (2015, 1) indicates that "P3s around the world are often developed on budget and with efficiency and innovation gains, [but that] many government still lack [the] key data that would allow them to more accurately compare P3s to traditionally delivered projects." The report recommends that governments develop "a planned approach to collection and analyzing project data" (ibid.). Of course, such data would be welcome for research purposes.

The Restructuring of Governance Models

The call for local control was complemented by the idea of decentralizing government. This idea of decentralization also became part of the lure of neoliberal policy. The term "government" could no longer accurately describe how the state would be governed. The term "governance" better described the diffused model of decision-making bodies that would be involved in the delivery of public goods. One could not say the same about the diffusion of economic resources that may be required to provide all of the services that came with this new decentralization of power, and during the height of the neoliberal experiment many were critical of the failure of the state to provide the concomitant power to raise revenue locally to match the ever-increasing responsibilities of those in local governance positions – such as NGOs. There was an inherent contradiction in the idea of a diffusion of power without the resources to use that power. Yet government was taking on a new structure. "Governance" became the new catch phrase that was meant to represent the diffusion of power among multiple governing actors. In this context, there was promise of greater local control of the institutional mechanisms to provide better, more locally appropriate services.

The Creation of Urban Entrepreneurs

As local autonomy grew, a new role was imposed on local governments. In "From Managerialism to Entrepreneurialism: The Transformation in Urban Governance in Late Capitalism," David Harvey (1989) argues that urban governments have had to become entrepreneurs in order to maintain a competitive advantage over other cities competing in the same market place. Whereas urban governments were once directed towards managing local public services, urban government is now concerned with finding ways to interact in the global marketplace.

In this context, urban governments are expected to drive their own destinies, and this shift is not trivial. It means that urban governments must devise ways, often without the resources or the capacity to raise revenue, to *sell* their assets in the global marketplace. Harvey notes that this results in uneven development and instability across urban centres, in particular, those that seek the *quick fixes* of economic development, such as bids for the Olympic Games or other large sporting contests or festivals (see Brunet-Jailly, chapter 13, this volume). Harvey (1989, 8) argues that

> the new urban entrepreneurialism typically rests, then, on a public-private partnership focusing on investment and economic development with the speculative construction of place rather than amelioration of conditions within a particular territory as its immediate (though by no means exclusive) political and economic goal.

The decentralization of government has meant that local communities are now required to assert themselves in the global marketplace.[1] This new role changes what communities can do and alters their raison d'être in the hierarchy of government.

Harvey (1989, 5) also points out that "the rise of urban entrepreneurialism may have had an important role to play in a general transition in the dynamics of capitalism from a Fordist-Keynesian regime of capital accumulation to a regime of 'flexible accumulation.'" Harvey (1987, 252) defines flexible accumulation as "the new regime [of advanced capitalism] marked by a startling flexibility with respect to labour processes, labour markets, products, and patterns of consumption." Twenty-five years after Harvey made this observation, it is still relevant – even if the language of post-Fordist models has grown to include a large body of literature on the rise of the urban class and "creative" cities (Florida 2002) as well as on the rise of the "knowledge economy."

The narrative of the new economy, the mobility of capital and labour, and the role of the state did, for a time, begin to shift political attitudes. Both the left and the right were able to use the language of big government to their advantage. The right wing supported the removal of restrictive regulations from the marketplace on the assumption that people would behave ethically, and the left supported initiatives that would shift power to local actors who knew better what was needed for their own communities (on the latter point, see Carroll and Ratner 2005). Under these conditions, which took about thirty years to develop, neoliberal ideology and the concomitant range of policy options began to be seen as the only alternative to dealing with globalizing market systems.

ENTER GORDON CAMPBELL:
THE DECLINE OF THE SOCIAL CONTRACT
AND NEOLIBERAL POLICY

Without doubt, Campbell was a right-of-centre thinker – or, as Pilon, citing Yaffe (1994), suggests in chapter 2 (this volume), a "Blue Liberal" with a "flexible ideological profile" (41) – and he campaigned on the neoliberal ideas of expanding trade markets, smaller government, and less regulation. Campbell needed to change the social contract in British Columbia in order to bring provincial policy in line with what was happening both nationally and internationally. Yet, in comparison to other provinces in Canada, BC was rather late to a full-blown neoliberal approach to public policy.

Indeed, it is clear that BC had already moved somewhat in the direction of reducing the state's influence in the postwar province-building project. Since the early 1950s, the government was engaged in province building fuelled by "intensive investment in industrial expansion and community infrastructure" (Markey, Halseth, and Manson 2008, 409), but the post-Fordist model altered the relationship between the state and society. Actually, Markey, Halseth, and Manson point out that this shift had been going on since the 1980s under successive provincial governments "regardless of [their] political orientation" (415).

Certainly, the NDP had held the reins of power in BC during the 1990s, but it was not immune to the shift that was happening in left-wing labour parties in Canada and around the world. It struggled, as do most left-wing parties, with the diversity of its base. This is/was particularly true in BC, where the environmental base and the labour base were/are often opposed on approaches to public policy. The NDP had to make compromises on issues of social justice because the politics of the welfare state was already coming apart. Outside of the Lower Mainland there is a strong anti-government and anti-elite element of society that is built on individual rights and a deep distrust of the state. There is a much deeper connection between the political culture of Alberta and the political culture of BC, particularly across the northern part of the province, than is generally understood or articulated. The connection is not just represented by resource developers and environmentalists, a relationship clearly understood in the scholarship, but also by a narrative that speaks of distrust of the state and any government agents. This element of the society was very open to the idea that government was too big and that the welfare state had grown too large. By the time of the election in 2001, a perfect storm had formed: the neoliberal agenda was shaping both left- and right-wing politics, and the NDP had made some horrendous blunders with particular programs – especially the Fast Ferry debacle, which had now come to define NDP "mismanagement." Whether it was true or not, the Liberals were able to argue that the NDP could not manage the province's finances (for an excellent review of the state of the BC economy at the end of the NDP's reign, see Beers et al. 2005).

When Campbell came to power in 2001 with an overwhelming seventy-seven- to two-seat victory, he moved quickly to bring BC into the new economic order, and he did this through a number of initiatives, including: public-private partnerships, restructuring governance models, and creating the context in which urban entrepreneurs could flourish. These policy initiatives were already held to be tried and true. Hence, Campbell was not reinventing the wheel; instead, he was simply using policies that had been presented as *the only alternatives* to the

Fordist-Keynesian model of economic development. Predictably, he used state-getting-out-of-the-way-of-business language to open up the entrepreneurial drive of the economic elite and to send a signal to local governments (and communities in general) that they would be in control of their own destiny. Simply put, "BC was now open for business."

POLICY CHOICE

Public-Private Partnerships

Over Gordon Campbell's three terms as premier he initiated Partnership BC and later the Capital Asset Management Framework (CAMF), which aimed at developing public-private initiatives and guidelines. His budget speech in 2002 used the P3 acronym directly. In the section entitled "BC Is Back" the speech referred to "encouraging a greater private-sector role in providing public infrastructure and services through P3s and alternative service delivery models" (British Columbia Ministry of Finance 2002). P3s have included school construction, water treatment plants, and transportation, and they have become part of the political rhetoric of neoliberal policy approaches worldwide. BC's decision to follow suit, then, should not have been a surprise. Be that as it may, it was how the Liberal government handled its P3 initiatives that raises some questions, and it is here that the verdict is mixed. In his study, Daniel Cohn (2008) shows that there was a head-long dive into P3 initiatives before there were guidelines to shape which P3s made the most sense. Cohn looks at the Abbotsford Regional Hospital and Centre and the Richmond-Airport-Vancouver line (RAV line) and notes that they came into being before the CAMF guidelines were established. The purpose of the CAMF was to "give answers to the questions of what the government's aims were in embracing P3s and other forms of alternative service delivery, how they related to core values of the public sector, and how public servants should go about evaluating the options available for undertaking any given project" (86). Had these guidelines been available before the hospital and RAV line P3s had started, Cohn wonders whether they "would have proceeded in the same way" (90). He shows that, in the early days of its mandate, the Liberal government had difficulty showing that P3s were not merely an ideologically driven idea but also a sensibly thought out alternate policy approach (74).

Importantly, though, Matti Siemiatycki (2005) argues that the P3 policy choice was mandated by the provincial government. According to

Siemiatycki, "both the institutional and human agency dynamics of the planning process acted to crowd out options other then [sic] neoliberal, marketized solutions" (68). Right up until the end of his time in office, Campbell was touting the P3 policy approach. The final Campbell government throne speech included the line: "British Columbia is recognized as North America's leader in public private partnerships, working with the private sector to build affordable and innovative public infrastructure – housing, hospitals, transit, highways and bridges" (British Columbia 2011).

The Restructuring of Governance Models in the Province

Like most neoliberal governments, the Campbell government moved to reshape the social contract within the province. This section looks at the three imperatives of this process: (1) to create market security for forestry companies by disassociating the companies from their communities; (2) to ensure land certainty in British Columbia; and (3) to shift the province toward a "governance model" in which local communities would take on the responsibility of becoming part of the new post-Fordist economy. These imperatives can be demonstrated by looking at Campbell's approach to forest tenure, Aboriginal politics and policy, and the development of the Community Charter.

In 2001, Campbell created the BC Progress Board, which is an independent board that established benchmarks for economic and social development in the province. In 2002, the Project 250 Regional Economies panel published *British Columbia's Economic Heartland Report* (note that 250 represents the area code outside of the Lower Mainland). In this report the panel suggests a "three-pronged approach to ensuring that challenges currently facing Region 250 are met":

> First, we must restore the wealth generation capacity of the land base, currently hampered by regulatory delays, tenure and access uncertainty, unresolved Aboriginal land claims, and poor international market conditions. Second, renewal will require looking for new ways of generating more value from the province's resources by systematically identifying and nurturing BC's leading innovators and emerging industry clusters, while communicating BC's advantages and the durability of the province's "new" investment climate to other provinces and the world. Third, government must maintain and improve supportive transportation, communications and

education infrastructure that – first and foremost – enhance the prospects for spurring economic growth. (British Columbia Progress Board 2002, 22)

While I am loath to give too much credence to one report, the recommendations of the 250 Panel highlight the direction of policy options that the premier "chose" as he came into office. In the 2003 budget there is an entire section entitled "Opening Up BC's Heartland to Economic Growth" (British Columbia Ministry of Finance 2003). It includes key strategies that replicate the 250 Report's recommendations:

Opening up the province – to all British Columbians and to the world – is a central strategic imperative.
• The government will complete and implement economic development plans across the province, incorporating plans for infrastructure, human capital and marketing.
• In addition, the BC Heartlands Economic Strategy will open up increased opportunities in energy development, new partnerships with First Nations, new investments in transportation infrastructure, new opportunities for tourism, sport and recreation from a successful Olympics bid, and a revitalized forest industry. (British Columbia Ministry of Finance 2003)

First, a key strategy was to ensure that the land base was secure and that forest companies could compete in the global market. In BC, this meant that at least two other critical issues had to be resolved: (1) the regulations and forest tenure that was "hampering" forest companies had to be rethought; and (2) treaty claims had to be reconciled. In 2003, one of the first major policies that ensured a strong social contract between the state and forest-dependent resource communities was broken: the policy of appurtenancy came to an end. Appurtenacy was designed to guarantee that logs had to be milled in the region from which they were taken. It was this policy that was critical to the province-building strategy of postwar BC. The end of appurtenancy marked, at least in part, the close of an era of connecting the resources to the community from which they were taken. This policy opened up the possibility for raw log exports and a decline in the number of local mills.

A second critical piece of the strategy to secure the land base for resource exploration and extraction was to try to deal with the many competing land claims of BC's First Nations peoples. In his "BC as an Intergovernmental Relations Player: Still Punching Below Its Weight?," Hamish Telford argues that Campbell's about-face on Aboriginal issues was likely the result of at least two events. First, "before becoming Premier he was remarkably ignorant of Aboriginal and Canadian constitutional law," and second, he was "almost certainly visited by mining and forestry executives who told him that they would not invest in new developments until land claims were settled" (Telford 2010, 41). Campbell came to power on the promise of holding a referendum on Aboriginal land claims precisely because the unsettled title was "creat[ing] an unstable environment for investment in the province's resource sector" (Rossiter and Wood 2005, 359). This second reason – land uncertainty – was probably a greater driver of Campbell's turnaround than were the constitutional or legal issues. While Campbell was arguing that BC was open for business, investors were shying away from the province because the overarching issue of land tenure was not settled. The 2004 budget speech included reference to "investing in First Nations and *land certainty*" (British Columbia Ministry of Finance 2004, emphasis added).

In light of this, Campbell's decision to move forward on negotiations for Aboriginal self-government makes sense. Indeed, the move to secure self-government for Indigenous people has been linked to neoliberal policy options as a way of restructuring the state. In "Indigenous Peoples and Neoliberal 'Privatization' in Canada," Fiona MacDonald (2011) makes a compelling case that the strategy of providing self-government to Aboriginal communities

> is not simply about meeting the demands of Indigenous peoples but also about meeting the requirements of the contemporary general shift towards "privatization" within liberal democratic states. Touted by the state as enhancing Indigenous autonomy, these policies appear to respond to Indigenous demands but serve a neoliberal welfare state agenda and, as a result, their effects often run in opposition to meaningful autonomy for Indigenous peoples. (257)

In this context, "empowering" local self-governing Indigenous communities was also a way for the state to "devolve ... complex policy areas [like education and child welfare] and the colonial legacies they entail ... [and allows the state to] distance [itself] from these problems while appearing to concede to Indigenous demands" (265) Moreover, in BC, where the land title issue is still very fluid, negotiating self-government serves the second purpose, which is to ensure land security for resource development. As MacDonald argues, "the biggest reason for leaders to defend certain notions of self-government, however[,] comes with the uncertainly that *not* resolving these issues brings" (264). The policy option to advance self-government makes a great deal of sense in this context, and this is precisely what Campbell did. In the end, his work in this regard was largely thwarted. As Burke Wood and Rossiter (2011, 423) argue, Campbell's efforts "were doomed to failure, regardless of his motivation." They suggest that the institutional arrangements of colonialism prevented the provincial government from acting in a meaningful way. Belanger makes a similar point in chapter 3 (this volume).

In many ways, self-government had to stand in for settling treaties, a process that had become, and that still remains, very difficult. The complexity of competing land claims, the establishment of title, and the internal politics of First Nations communities have stalled the treaty process to this day.

The third area in which neoliberal policy choices were evident is in the development and execution of the Community Charter. Campbell, as mayor, had fought hard to get more power to local governments. Thus, his choice to retreat from the Community Charter seems to be a contradiction of the idea of granting self-government or local autonomy. But, as Patrick Smith shows (chapter 11, this volume), Campbell resisted, and even reversed, his pledge to create real local autonomy for self-government for fear that municipalities would make policy choices counter to those of the provincial government, especially where policy choices might be counter to the new ideological reality. In fact, Smith uses the example of the decision by the Provincial Ministry of Transportation "to determine the route/cost/public-private partnership provider for the West Vancouver segment of the Sea-to-Sky 2010 Olympic Highway upgrade – after listening to, then ignoring, local protests including legal action against the province by the municipality" (218–19).

Siemiatycki (2005) also argues that municipalities were being held to certain policy options, particularly the P3s. He writes:

With an institutional structure in place that clearly promoted the neoliberal ideology of private-public partnerships, the provincial government set out to superimpose this agenda on the RAV project … In spite of repeated requests by local officials to examine a more traditional public delivery mechanism during the analysis and tendering phase of the planning process, the provincial government was unyielding in their demand for private-public partnerships. (70)

Ultimately, the Community Charter was a deeply watered-down version of what Gordon Campbell, the mayor, had envisioned, and yet there were certainly new expectations for local governments. The social contract had been rewritten in such a way as to put more responsibility on local/municipal governments to *find their own way* in the new global economy, even if these new responsibilities did not come with concomitant power or financial resources. In this context, local governments became like "urban entrepreneurs" (Peck and Tickell 2002). This new trend has meant that communities (i.e., large cities to small rural and remote towns) must compete in the global market by determining their assets and then marketing their product. This undermines the traditional "comparative advantage" approach to the economy in favour of a "competitive market approach" (see Markey, Halseth, and Manson 2006).

CONCLUSION:
THE PERFECT STORM?

Campbell employed well-known and accepted policies that had become part of the new paradigm of a public policy that got the state out of the way of business, but he did not make this shift in a political vacuum. Even though the broad narrative of the state's role in society had shifted through the 1980s and the 1990s, something else had happened in British Columbia that gave the Liberal government an overwhelming mandate to govern from the right: a decade of the New Democratic Party.

Campbell entered provincial politics in the context of what had been framed as a series of NDP debacles not just in British Columbia but also in Ontario under Bob Rae. The famous Fast Ferry fiasco, as well as the ethical scandal that plagued Glen Clark, came back to haunt the NDP in the 2001 election. BC voters had generally adopted the narrative of neoliberalism. The Liberals were able to attract voters who wanted to "throw the government out," but the party's "Four-Peat" cannot be explained in these terms alone. The two elections after the 2001 victory have also kept the Liberals in power, and the 2013 election was won in another remarkable landslide considering that the NDP held a substantial lead in the polls going into the election.

One possible way to explain the NDP's electoral defeat is to examine the split of ideas that occurred to make it less relevant in the 2013 context. Campbell is touted as having had a crucial shift to the left when he, and he alone, decided to pursue a carbon tax. Yet, if one looks at his "transformation," it is notable that his ally was California governor Arnold Schwarzenegger, who had also taken up the war-cry for climate change solutions/policy. Schwarzenegger was selling the idea as compatible with a right-wing conservative agenda. He argued that climate change mitigation is critical to the US economy. Campbell's speech to the UBCM in 2008 linked economic diversity and stability with environmental responsibility: "It's time for us to take responsibility and to contribute to try and mitigate the challenges that are created by climate change ... So I want to tell you that not just me, my caucus, our government is going to continue to pursue this because *it's right for the economy*, it's right for the environment, it's right for families, it's right for our kids, and it's right for our grandkids" (Campbell 2008, emphasis added). The 2008 budget spoke directly to "overturn[ing] the notion that you have to choose either a strong economy or a healthy environment. [The budget] encourages cleaner choices, invests more than $1 billion in climate action initiatives, lowers taxes to stimulate investment, and increases funding for health care and education to their highest levels ever in British Columbia" (British Columbia Ministry of Finance 2008).

Campbell's conversion is completely consistent with the ideation approach to public policy choice. Indeed, as Rabe and Borick (2012) argue:

> State and provincial governments have a near-infinite number of options in energy and climate policy, if they attempt to do anything at all. They also have strategic choices in framing and labeling these options as they consider adopting them as policies. Issue framing reflects the most common way that a policy issue has come to be understood in a particular political system. For climate change, proposed mitigation policies may either be framed as legitimate responses to an environmental threat, pursuit of an economic development opportunity, or *something to be avoided due to its potential economic threat*. If policies are adopted, they require specific labels. These may seem purely semantic and symbolic but instead give government authorities some latitude in the explicit language that will officially be used in publicly describing the policy. (362, emphasis added)

Premier Campbell chose to label the carbon tax as revenue neutral and vowed to return the benefits to local communities and taxpayers, but he also was able to court environmentalists who had not seen any significant moves on climate change under NDP leadership (Rabe and Borick 2012, 365–6). Moreover, traditionally resource dependent communities in the north had seen economic opportunities linked to resource extraction decline rapidly as a result of the pine beetle epidemic – an epidemic that has been linked to climate change. Campbell's speeches in fact linked the epidemic to climate change. Without doubt, there was still resistance to the carbon tax, but, remarkably, it did not spark the backlash that would hit the Campbell government over the harmonized sales tax.

The HST was different because Campbell had said that he would not bring it in; however, after the 2009 election, he broke that promise. I suggest that Campbell was pilloried because of the broken promise and not necessarily because of the tax itself. Yet, as Lacharite asserts regarding BC's tax system from 2001 to 2011 (chapter 5, this volume), politicians are entitled to change their minds on issues related to fiscal policy when and where they deem it necessary. Regardless, the "broken promise" explanation makes the 2013 Liberal victory more understandable, especially if we consider that Campbell had already been disciplined both by his forced resignation and by the referendum that forced the repeal of the HST. The electorate did not need to "throw the bums out" because they had already been reprimanded.

Another interesting phenomenon was the shift in the opinion about the role of the state in social justice and the decline of the voice and impact of the proponents of social justice. The rhetoric of taxation as essentially an imposition on individual liberty worked in the pockets of the province beyond the Lower Mainland and Vancouver Island. The ideas of social justice were tied directly to the NDP's spending record and the growth in so-called welfare culture. In their article "The NDP Regime in British Columbia, 1991–2001," Carroll and Ratner (2005, 183) cite a civil servant from the BC Ministry of Human Resources: "within the dominant political discourse his ministry's impoverished clientele appeared as 'tax takers,' not 'taxpayers.'" The anti-elite and anti-government rhetoric resonated with BC's consumer citizens, and the NDP became less attractive to individuals who might have traditionally found a home in its labour union membership. This was not only going on in BC but also in other places in Canada, including Ontario.

Finally, it is worth noting that BC is not an island in the Canadian federal state. As Bakvis and Skogstad (2008) demonstrate in their analysis of the changes that came to federalism in Canada during the 1990s, a more "collaborative federalism" arose out of many factors, including the "'*internationalization*' of the Canadian political economy" and the "ascendency of neoliberalism and the companion philosophy known as *new public management*" (10, emphasis in original).

In all, Gordon Campbell's leadership is marked less by his policy choices than by his consistent construction of a particular type of politics. His populism, his construction of the new social contract, his decisions to engage with Aboriginal self-government, and his choices on environmental legislation were not enigmatic. Each decision fit well within the context of the post-Keynesian and the post-Fordist approach to province building, which was led by limited policy options.

NOTE

1   See for example the case of the port and airport developments in Northern British Columbia referenced by Summerville, Wilson, and Young (2013) and Summerville and Wilson (2015).

5

Tax Policy in British Columbia from 2001 to 2011

Too Progressive, Too Regressive, or Just the Right Mix?

J.R. LACHARITE

Discussing taxes and taxation can electrify, enrage, and stupefy citizens all at the same time. Tax policy or, more broadly, fiscal policy ultimately clarifies a government's priorities, purpose, and plans for the future. In essence, tax system design (and the revenue derived from the tax mix) is the wellspring from which many (if not all) social, educational, and health care policy decisions flow. As such, it remains a highly sensitive and contested subject.

Up to this point, we have examined Campbell's "rise to the top," elements of his governance and management styles, and some important institutional reform issues (such as reconciliation with First Nations and more open and transparent government) that have partially defined his legacy as premier of British Columbia from 2001 to 2011. However, tax policy under the Campbell administration was, for lack of a better word, notorious. Indeed, with the benefit of hindsight, it is clear that tax cuts, the issue of tax equity, and the now defunct harmonized sales tax accounted for both his political success and his untimely demise.

To be sure, in 2001 he employed a variant of American populism steeped in the familiar narrative of "low taxes" to persuade provincial voters to reject the "big government" alternative. Of course, as has been well documented, he won a landslide victory that relegated the New Democratic Party to relative obscurity. Premier Campbell played the same hand in the 2005 election, promising more modest (income) tax

cuts and warning voters against the pernicious nature of large and un-
wieldy public institutions – presumably the very sort of thing BC would
confront should the NDP depose the province's fiscal saviours. Again, it
worked to great effect, securing Campbell's Liberals another majority
government. Yet the former premier's tax policy took a rather odd turn
in 2008 with the introduction of the much maligned carbon tax – a so-
called revenue-neutral consumption levy designed to moderate the
province's greenhouse gas emissions. Then, on 23 July 2009, shortly
after winning a third consecutive majority, Premier Campbell, flanked
by Finance Minister Colin Hansen, announced that the province would
be adopting a 12 per cent HST effective July 2010.

It was Campbell's commitment to the HST that precipitated his pre-
mature exit from provincial politics and his party's (short-term) mis-
fortune. Confronted with an abysmal public approval rating and the
possibility of an internal party revolt, Campbell decided to resign as
premier on 3 November 2010. His remaining months as a now moderately influential figure in BC politics were largely uneventful from a
tax policy point of view. The Liberal Party was engaged in a highly anticipated leadership convention that resulted in a victory for Christy
Clark. But the highly contentious HST issue lingered for several months
until it was abolished via a provincial referendum in August 2011.

How are we to appraise Gordon Campbell's tax policy record? Did he
leave us with a system devoid of progressivity? Did tax equity matter to
Premier Campbell? These are difficult questions to answer. They are
difficult to answer because they tend to be cloaked in partisan sub-
terfuge. For example, the pro-tax crowd seems to forget that Premier
Campbell was given a considerable amount of leeway (and public support) to pursue a personal and corporate income tax-cut agenda. Moreover, proponents of increased taxes fail to identify what constitutes
"paying a fair share of tax" (Ivanova and Klein 2013a; Lee, Ivanova, and
Klein 2011). Instead, we are left to assume that the wealthy should pay
substantially more without the benefit of knowing why – simply because they can? Similarly, anti-tax intermediaries tend to overlook the
fact that no such mandate was granted for a harmonized sales tax (Lammam and MacIntyre 2013; Veldhuis, Lammam, and Palacios 2011;
Mintz 2010). As a matter of good faith, governing political parties generally try to fulfill some of their election promises – if only to remain
in power.

The purpose of this chapter is to show that Campbell's "taxing" legacy was neither too progressive nor too regressive. Certainly, mistakes

were made as he attempted to reconfigure the province's tax mix and tax system. Principal among them was the decision to pursue deep and lasting income tax cuts: concerns related to structural deficits, the province's accumulating debt, and educational and health care "affordability" could have been more easily addressed if personal income tax rates had remained intact or moderately adjusted upwards during his decade in power. In part, this, along with his government's legislated commitment to balanced budgets, necessitated an increased dependency on tax source alternatives that were more regressive in orientation. However, if we assess Campbell's tax policy against the backdrop of global taxing trends and take into account the fact that he was utilizing a successful brand of populist politics, then his legacy looks decidedly less predatory, ideological, and/or arbitrary.

I make two broad claims. First, I argue that, while a tax shift has occurred since 2001, Premier Campbell's emphasis on regressive or indirect taxes – to compensate for three rounds of income tax cuts between 2001 and 2011 – was consistent with a broader OECD trend towards greater reliance on social security contributions and value-added, retail, and various other consumption taxes. In this sense, Campbell's tax changes were only "revolutionary" in a very narrow sense – and probably not at all if we consider that former Alberta and Ontario premiers Ralph Klein and Mike Harris executed successful tax-cutting strategies well in advance of Campbell's ascent to power. Second, a high degree of vertical and horizontal tax equity appears to have prevailed under Campbell's watch. One way to interpret the data, then, is to suggest that he may have struck a more reasonable balance between direct and indirect taxes than he is given credit for.[1] Furthermore, it is important to reiterate that his electoral success was due in large part to his promises to cut taxes and control government spending. Simply put, he had a mandate – through three successive terms – to modify the province's tax codes and tax system. Does this mean that he was guilty of conforming to a neoliberal taxing agenda? Perhaps, but the case could also be made that he was simply engaging in a time-honoured and well-practised form of populist politics that had already generated positive results in Ontario, Alberta, the United States, and Australia (Ibbitson 1997; Taft 1997; Kazin 1998; Costar and Economou 1999).

The following chapter is divided into four areas of analysis. Section 1 examines BC's tax system and charts the tax shift that took place under Campbell's stewardship. For the most part, BC remained an income tax-dependent regime from 2001 to 2011, but there were some important changes that bear scrutiny. Section 2 highlights the taxing trends that have taken root in the Organisation for Economic Co-operation and Development (OECD) since 1965. The comparative dimension to this report is crucial insofar as it shows that retail, value-added, and other specialized sales taxes have become an important source of revenue for many well-established and transitional democratic regimes. Section 3 chronicles former premier Campbell's income and corporate tax cuts and passes some judgment on the efficacy of this decision. Finally, section 4 looks into the province's Medical Services Plan (MSP) premiums, carbon tax, and the HST debacle.

BC'S TAX SYSTEM

BC possesses a rather intricate mix of direct and indirect taxes. Since 2001, however, it has relied predominantly on eight main sources of revenue: income taxes (personal and corporate); a social services tax (also known as the provincial sales tax and from 2010 to 2013 as the harmonized sales tax); a motor fuel tax (including dedicated taxes designed to help support transportation projects located across the province); a revenue-neutral carbon tax; property taxes (residential, business, rural, and transfers); natural resource revenues; and income derived from the MSP. In fiscal year 2011–12 – shortly after Premier Campbell's departure from public office – these revenue sources accounted for approximately 55 per cent of the government's total income. The remaining relevant sources of tax revenue include Ottawa's health and social transfers (and other federal contributions for community development and social services programs); income supplied from the province's commercial Crown corporations; and various other fees, investment earnings, and consumer taxes (e.g., tobacco). Figure 5.1 underscores the comparative importance of the province's major revenue sources between 2001 and 2012.[2] It also, albeit casually, details some of British Columbia's more noticeable taxing trends during this time.

The most striking trends highlighted in figure 5.1 are the periodic declines and recovery in income taxes coupled by a simultaneous and gradual increase in sales taxes. For tax analysts and media pundits, this represents one of Campbell's signature trademarks: income tax cuts supplemented by an increasing reliance on value-added or consumption-based fees. Indeed, a diachronic comparison of the province's budgetary data shows that, from 1991 to 2001, income taxes, on average,

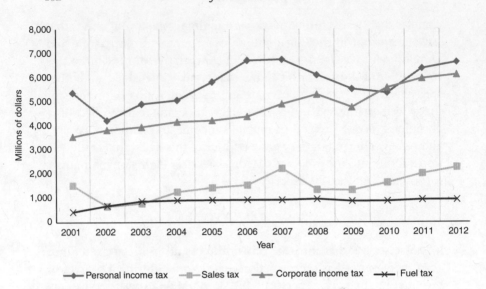

Figure 5.1   Primary and secondary sources of tax revenue for BC, 2001–2012

Source: British Columbia Ministry of Finance, 2001–13.

accounted for close to 25 per cent of all the tax dollars collected in BC (Statistics Canada 2009; Lacharite 2008, 101–3). This level of income tax dependency dropped rather abruptly over the next ten years as personal and corporate income taxes were subjected to several rounds of tax reform. Under Campbell, income taxes, as a percentage of all government-own source revenues, averaged only 21 per cent. Yet it would be misleading to conclude from this that "sales" and other consumption taxes became the go-to revenue source for the governing Liberal Party. Again, a diachronic comparison of sales tax collection from 1991 to 2011 reveals that, under the NDP, sales and overall consumption taxes accounted for approximately 12 per cent and 21 per cent, respectively, of the government's total income. Compared to Campbell's decade in power, the numbers vary only slightly, representing a combined average increase of just 1 per cent. On the basis of this metric, it is difficult to state, unequivocally, that Campbell's tax policy was entirely regressive or even trending in a regressive direction. Reviewing revenue and expenditure data from Statistics Canada shows that his budgets were the principal beneficiary of increases to federally sponsored health and social transfer grants. Ottawa's desire to rectify persistent funding gaps in provincial health and social programs – and likely an attempt to secure voter patronage – made it easier for Campbell to pursue a populist taxing agenda and to counter-balance what he believed to be the overly progressive nature of BC's tax system. Be that as it may, BC remains a fully committed income-tax-dependent regime. It appears to have retained a high degree of tax progressivity as well. Unsurprisingly, income taxes continue to provide the provincial government with over a fifth of its total income – this, despite slower than expected economic growth and a resource sector that has experienced only a modest recovery since the US sub-prime crisis.

Still, BC's tax mix has become far more variegated than it was in the past. The most obvious change concerns the Liberal government's increasing reliance on unconventional consumption taxes. Two of the more arresting developments during Campbell's tenure as premier were a greater emphasis on consumer-oriented MSP premiums and a carbon tax. Typically, these are both denounced as regressive tax measures, but they can also be seen as enterprising and even "progressive" policy instruments.

Over the past ten to fifteen years, provincial expenditures on health care across Canada have grown considerably (Simpson 2012). In BC's case, it now represents approximately 37 per cent of the government's total expenses – a number projected to increase over the next several years (Treff and Ort 2013; British Columbia Ministry of Finance 2001–13). Shifting part of the cost of medical services to consumers, while not novel, is nevertheless a practical way to contain government spending on health-related programs and initiatives. Moreover, it is important to understand that MSP premiums only account for a mere 11 per cent of the province's health care budget.[3] Thus, it remains a highly subsidized public service. I discuss the incremental increases in MSP premiums in more detail in section 4. With regards to BC's carbon tax, the intent was to dissuade fossil fuel consumption. Undoubtedly, there is a regressive hue to the tax, but the province, to its credit, has tempered greenhouse gas emissions since 2008, thereby accomplishing a key and publicly supported policy objective of the Liberal Party (Elgie and McClay 2013a; Sustainable Prosperity 2012).[4]

How, then, might we initially appraise Campbell's tax policy record? First, it would be unreasonable to assert that Campbell abandoned the province's historical commitment to, and preference for, tax progressivity. He was a populist premier who attempted to satisfy a diverse cross-section of societal interests, but he did not "hitch" the province's fortunes to the promises and perils of a regressive tax system. Even so, and this is perhaps the more pressing point, the tax mix in BC did change and we now see a province defined more by consumption and Pigovian taxes than was the case in the 1990s. Campbell's taxing legacy, however, is somewhat reminiscent of the tax changes that have taken root in the OECD since 1965. Hence, the next section attempts to better contextualize BC's rather gentle transition away from income taxes by examining the taxing developments that have marked other liberal democratic entities in the OECD.

OECD TAX TRENDS

OECD tax systems and policies have changed considerably since the 1960s (OECD 2012a, 2012b; Messere et al. 2003). The adoption and rise of broad-based consumption taxes (or taxes on goods and services) has been one of the most important developments in taxation over the last fifty years. On average, taxes on general consumption now account for roughly 20 per cent of all the taxes collected in OECD countries (OECD 2012b). An increase in social security contributions has also marked a significant change in tax policy: social security contributions or payroll taxes have now supplanted personal income taxes as the most important source of tax revenue for the OECD as a whole – both as a percentage of gross domestic product (GDP) and in terms of total taxation (OECD 2012a).[5] In addition, the postwar period saw personal income taxes change from an elite tax to a mass tax. Today, personal income taxes remain a critical source of revenue in the OECD, but its share – of the total taxes collected – has been declining since the 1990s (OECD 2012a; Messere et al. 2003).

Three other trends have developed across the OECD since the mid-1960s. First, there has been a gradual increase in the ratio of tax to GDP – that is, the tax burden. Second, a divergence has occurred within the OECD with regard to the distribution of tax revenue among major taxes. In the European Union and Japan, for example, an increased reliance on social security contributions and consumption taxes has coincided with a decreased reliance on personal income taxes. By contrast, the United States and other Anglo-liberal regimes have continued to pursue a course of income tax dependency. But they too – with the exception of the United States – have turned increasingly to general consumption taxes to finance popular social and health care programs. Finally, "public spending on pensions, poverty alleviation programmes, education, and health care has continued on a clear upward [trajectory] over the past [three] decades in virtually all OECD countries" (OECD 2003, 163).

One way to interpret these trends is to suggest that many high-income states have responded to the demands for equitable public services by increasing the tax burden and expanding the tax base via consumption and payroll taxes. And, for our purposes, the growth in consumption tax dependency among OECD members is notable. In essence, it provides us with a better understanding of global taxing trends and better situates BC's recent experience with tax reform.

Since the mid-1980s, BC's (and Canada's) general tax mix has not evolved to the same extent as have those of other advanced democratic regimes in the OECD. Content to rely predominantly on income taxes, BC (and Canada) has yet to embrace general consumption taxes with the same level of enthusiasm that is found in Europe, Chile, New Zealand, and even Mexico. Tax mix ratios naturally vary from country to country, but "in the vast majority of countries (27 of 34) general consumption taxes account for more than 15 percent of total taxation" (OECD 2012b). There are two essential advantages, relevant to BC, to adopting or relying more heavily on value-added taxes (VATS) or goods and services taxes (GSTS). One is that it is a "particularly efficient tax for raising revenue" (OECD 2012b, 58). It is not unreasonable to suggest – based on tax reform developments in other provinces – that BC's tax structure was due for a fundamental overhaul in 2001 (Kesselman 2002). Cutting personal income taxes by an average of 25 per cent may have been too extreme (McBride and McNutt 2007, 187), but revising the province's consumption tax rates could be seen as both appropriate and necessary given the chronic funding gaps that appeared to afflict BC's health, social, and educational services. In other words, there was certainly some room to manoeuvre in this area of provincial tax policy, and Campbell appeared to be mindful of this opportunity. The other main advantage of general consumption taxes relates to the export-oriented nature of BC's economy. The OECD asserts that shifting the burden away from commercial enterprise "supports greater integration [into] the global market place because it removes taxes on exports through the application of the destination principle" (OECD 2012b, 58). From a provincial perspective, this make good sense considering: (1) BC has been a beneficiary of trade liberalization, but (2) it has therefore had to forgo crucial revenues from custom duties that would have accompanied bilateral and multilateral trade agreements with the US, Japan, China, and others. Importantly, then, the turn to VATS and GSTS reflects a natural (and inevitable) transition designed to accommodate a more open and transparent regional and global trading system.

The Campbell administration, of course, as Brown (2012) has wonderfully expressed – and as Low reiterates in his work on BC's creative economy (chapter 12, this volume) – did not have "social licence" to tinker with the province's social services tax. But tax reform decisions of this kind are never taken lightly precisely because of the potential political fallout that can materialize.

In sum, BC and Canada continue to rank well below the OECD in terms of taxes on general consumption as a percentage of GDP and as a percentage of total taxation (OECD 2012a). This, in itself, is not sufficient justification to radically reform or experiment with the province's tax mix; rather, it illustrates that Campbell was not completely out of line on the issue of tax reform. BC has a raft of welfare services that require immediate and lasting income support, and exploring a flexible and reliable set of taxing options is simply part of a governing party's public services repertoire.

CAMPBELL'S INCOME TAX REGIME: STIMULATING ECONOMIC GROWTH OR POPULIST POLITICS?

One of the crucial issues highlighted by Pilon (chapter 2, this volume) and Smith (chapter 11, this volume) is that Campbell, at times, had some difficulty fulfilling his rather extravagant election campaign promises. Low (chapter 12, this volume) and Belanger (chapter 3, this volume) make similar observations. Provincial tax policy, however, was a different matter. In the Liberal Party's 2001 platform document, *A New Era for British Columbia*, Campbell promised to "introduce a dramatic cut in personal income taxes within 90 days" and to "cut the base personal income tax rate to the lowest rate of any province in Canada for the bottom two tax brackets, on the first $60,000 of income" (British Columbia Liberal Party 2001, 5). This he did with alacrity and a fair degree of swagger. As well, the province's corporate income tax rate (CITR) was scheduled to be reduced by three percentage points by 1 January 2002.

Voters witnessed more of the same in the lead-up to the 17 May 2005 general election. Over the course of this contest, there was more emphasis placed on education, health, culture, and family services, but here, too, modest tax reductions – and other forms of tax relief – were implemented to (ostensibly) stimulate economic activity across the province. Some of the Liberal Party's more notable accomplishments included: (1) eliminating provincial income taxes (entirely) for residents earning less than $15,500 per year; (2) significantly reducing the province's top marginal tax rate; and (3) introducing a series of tax credit initiatives designed to ease the tax burden on low-income earners. A further 1.5 per cent decline in the CITR – from 13.5 per cent to 12 per cent – also featured heavily in the Liberals' 2005 election "playbook."

Despite the risks to natural resource revenues posed by the 2008 recession in the US, the Campbell administration, once again, turned its attention to "reducing taxes on families" and supporting small businesses and corporations through additional tax relief measures. To be sure, they were quick to reminded voters that "British Columbians now [had] the lowest personal income taxes in Canada at every income level up to $116,000" (British Columbia Liberal Party 2009, 10). Another conspicuous development during the 2008 pre-election contest involved tax cuts for the province's small businesses and corporations. The year 2008 actually turned out to be a boon for private enterprise, with a "44 percent reduction in small business income taxes" coupled with a further 2 per cent decline in the general corporate income tax rate scheduled to take effect in 2010 and 2011 – which, at 10 per cent, would bring the province's corporate income taxes down to the lowest rate in Canada (11). As it turned out, this would be the last time the corporate sector would benefit from the Liberal Party's indulgent approach to business taxes.[6]

With the benefit of hindsight, it is probably fair to say that Campbell's long-term income tax reform package possessed both merits and shortcomings. With regard to the latter, it was initially based on the rather narrow and misleading assumption that tax cuts would improve the province's competitiveness, create jobs, and ultimately generate more revenue. This is an appealing public pronouncement and one that often resonates with disgruntled voters. Yet the tax-cutting mantra employed by Premier Campbell – and the BC Liberals more generally – rested upon a very shaky foundation and continues to lack a degree of credibility. A careful review of the evidence actually shows that there are real limits to what income tax reform can accomplish (Tyson and Zidar 2012; Leonhardt 2012; Hungerford 2012; Greenstone et al. 2012; Jackson 2000).[7] Furthermore, a 2012 report issued by the Business Council of British Columbia (2012) found that average GDP and employment growth were higher under the "tax-and-spend" NDP governments of the 1990s – though it did show other areas in which the Campbell government excelled. The report also indicated that both export growth and productivity lagged under Campbell's direction despite the manifold tax relief measures instituted from 2001 to 2010. In BC's case, then, the "positive" link between tax cuts, employment, competitiveness, and revenue growth remains largely unsubstantiated.

However, it is important to consider that Canada's and British Columbia's high-income earners pay a disproportionate amount of the income taxes collected across the country. Could Campbell's tax-cutting agenda then be construed as an exercise in tax equity? Possibly, but, if so, it would likely have been a secondary concern only. Campbell's primary objective was to win elections, and, for good or ill, tax cuts appear to win elections. Still, what is often overlooked – or simply dismissed – in relation to the broader tax equity debate is that high-income earners have contributed an increasing amount of their earned income to state and sub-state taxing agencies since at least the 1990s (Cross 2013; Martineau 2005). In 2010, for example, the top 10 per cent of income earners paid approximately 55 per cent of all the taxes furnished by working Canadians, while the bottom 50 per cent contributed a mere 4 per cent "towards the collective personal tax bill" (Golombek 2013). Taxing the rich has become the clarion call for many cash-strapped governments (particularly in Ontario and Quebec), but it fails to rectify or add anything remotely substantive to the tax-equity debate in BC. Most of the benefits accruing from the income tax cuts introduced under Campbell went to high-income earners, but it is critical to recall that low-income earners also benefited from his government's tax reform efforts. The real issue, however, is the extent to which the province's tax system maintained a degree of progressivity. Did it? As has already been pointed out, the answer, of course, is yes. Campbell remained firmly committed to the principles of vertical and horizontal tax equity, but it would seem that he also recognized that there were other ways to generate tax revenue – to simultaneously remain in the voting public's good graces and balance budgets. Fundamentally, what he failed to do was to account for the demand in, and inflationary pressures attached to, provincial health, social, and educational services. In essence, he overlooked the profound impact that deep and lasting tax cuts can have on distributional politics.

By 2001, Campbell was a well-seasoned populist angling for victory. He discovered a formula that worked, and he deployed it to great effect through his three successive terms as premier. In a sense, he gave British Columbians what they asked for – lower income taxes. At the same time, he managed to maintain the overall progressivity of the province's tax system. His income-tax-cutting agenda could perhaps be judged to have been too aggressive, but he was essentially doing what politicians tend to do – winning the confidence of their constituents to govern. Alas, it was also his tax policy that led to his hasty departure from provincial politics, and it is to this that we now turn.

THE CONTROVERSIAL MEDICAL SERVICES PLAN, CARBON TAX, AND HST

While Campbell's income-tax-cutting agenda has been universally pil-loried by his critics, the more controversial tax measures to come under scrutiny are the increases to MSP premiums, the implementation of a "carbon tax," and the HST. This section examines these tax measures to determine the extent to which they were necessarily punitive, discrim-inatory, or "immoral" additions to the Campbell government's taxing inventory. I hope that the following discussion sheds some light on this particular aspect of Campbell's taxing legacy.

BC's medical services plan "pays for medically required services of physicians and surgeons and for dental or oral surgery – when med-ically required to be performed in a hospital. MSP also provides cover-age for other health benefits" (British Columbia Ministry of Health 2013a). To be eligible for the plan, residents must be Canadian citizens, "make BC their home," and/or be "physically present in the province for at least six months per calendar year." In 2013, basic monthly costs for an individual were set at $66.50, $120.50 for a family of two, and $133 for a family of three or more. On the surface, it seems to be a rea-sonably well-managed health insurance scheme that provides univer-sal medical coverage to most of the province's permanent residents. However, as Ivanova and Klein (2013a); Lee, Ivanova, and Klein (2011); and Murray (2005) indicate, MSP premiums increased at a substantial rate while Campbell was in power.[8]

The MSP has been labelled by its detractors as a regressive tax that generally discriminates against lower- and middle-income earners. By definition it qualifies as a regressive tax – and would therefore be con-sidered unfair by those more inclined to support a hyper-progressive income tax alternative. Yet there are two counterpoints to bear in mind here. First, the MSP could be thought of as (and perhaps *should* be thought of as) a pseudo–social security tax in that it is designed to par-tially subsidize provincial medical care and expenses. Indeed, it is use-ful to point out that Employment Insurance and the Canada Pension

Plan are simply social security mechanisms intended to supplement personal living standards and expenses; they are not wholesale income-replacement guarantees. The expectation is that unemployed Canadians will eventually find a job and/or that eligible citizens will have partially saved for their retirement. Clearly, the Liberal Party's philosophy under Campbell was the same – that residents should bear some of the additional costs of maintaining provincial health care services. This is an observation consistent with Summerville's work (chapter 4, this volume) on Campbell's leadership and governance styles, and it explains, in part, the rationale behind the periodic fee increases. At times, he expressed an uncompromising form of Red toryism (or as Pilon [chapter 2, this volume] suggests, Blue Liberalism) that resonated with his political supporters, and this was just one visible manifestation of his commitment to individual and familial responsibility. In all, Campbell may have been constrained by a particular beliefs system, but there was nothing (obviously) prejudicial in his MSP policy.

The other matter to consider is that the MSP continues to provide "premium assistance" and "temporary premium assistance" to eligible applicants. Moreover, "families receiving full and partial assistance may qualify for additional health care services through the *Healthy Kids* program" (British Columbia Ministry of Health 2013b). When families and/or individuals are confronted with serious financial challenges there are options built into the system to alleviate the burden of paying for MSP premiums. These were proactive measures enacted by the Campbell administration to ensure that families could appeal to government agents should they find themselves in straitened conditions. Are they sound and unassailable? No, but they do demonstrate that Campbell was not the antipathetic ideologue that he is sometimes made out to be. The Liberal Party's carbon tax gambit, in some ways, seems to add weight to this assertion.

BC's carbon tax shift generated a fair degree of controversy before and after its implementation on 1 July 2008. It was originally embraced by several progressive elements in the province, including the David Suzuki Foundation and the Canadian Centre for Policy Alternatives. British Columbians, in general, were also widely supportive of the new tax (Harrison 2012). However, a concerted effort by the Northern Central Municipal Association and the NDP to deride the tax ultimately altered the public's perception of its overall fairness and utility. Predictably, there were also concerns that it would impair the province's economic performance (Elgie and McClay 2013a). Was/is it an "unfair" tax?

Similar to the MSP, BC's carbon tax typically takes a larger percentage from low-income earners than it does from high-income earners. But there is more to this tax initiative than its much maligned regressive character suggests. As was alluded to earlier, Campbell's carbon tax remains a "central component of the province's climate change strategy, as BC aims to reduce its greenhouse gas (GHG) emissions by 33 [per cent] below 2007 levels by 2020" (Sustainable Prosperity 2012, 5). The evidence seems to indicate that, as part of a collective strategy to reduce GHGs, BC has been successful and has actually outperformed all of its provincial counterparts in this area (Elgie and McClay 2013a). Furthermore, over the past five years, the tax does not appear to have had any discernable impact on the province's competitiveness or economic growth (Elgie and McClay 2013a; Sustainable Prosperity 2012). Most important, though, the tax was intended as a revenue-neutral supplement to the government's tax revenue accounts. Fundamentally, it was designed to compensate for tax cuts elsewhere and gave the premier the flexibility to lower business taxes, fund a low-income tax credit, and provide a generous rebate for homeowners in Northern BC (Sustainable Prosperity 2012). Diversifying BC's tax system and combating climate change were priorities for the Campbell government from 2001 to 2011. Again, there was nothing (obviously) deleterious in Campbell's decision to pursue these two mutually compatible policy objectives. Voters – and other societal interests – wanted tax reform (and a plan to ease provincial GHG emissions), and this is what he endeavoured to give them.

The final and most contentious tax reform measure to be pursued by the Campbell administration was the transition to a harmonized sales tax. The government's confidence in the HST appeared to be driven by two factors: (1) the need to better compensate for anticipated revenue shortfalls (as a result of income tax cuts) and (2) the need to ensure that the (legislated) promise to balance budgets would remain feasible. Certainly, it was a regressive tax, but Kesselman (2011, 140) asserts that the entire HST issue, from the outset, was "beset by widespread misconceptions concerning its impact on consumers and taxpayers." Had members of the public been better prepared for the HST, they might have accepted tax harmonization as a suitable alternative to provincial sales tax collection and as an instrument shown to benefit productivity, investment, and employment (Kesselman 2010; Finlayson and Peacock 2010). Instead, they were led to believe that it was merely a "tax grab," that it would have a negative impact on household consumer expenditures, and that all goods and services would now be taxable. According to Kesselman's (2011) superbly crafted review on the "consumer impact of the HST," though, very little of this turned out to be true. For example, with regard to the distributional impact of the tax, Kesselman found that "both single persons and families at the lowest income levels would be net beneficiaries of the HST and that the burden imposed on middle income earners would likely be moderate at best" – this due to the compensatory provisions, credits, rebates, and income tax adjustments related to the tax (152–3). He also observed that "most goods taxed under the HST were already taxed by the RST [retail sales tax], and eliminating their embedded taxes result[ed] in a lower effective tax rate on those goods" (156).

Over the longer term, the HST – including the $1.6 billion transition payment provided by Ottawa – would have improved the province's fiscal position and equipped subsequent governments with a "more stable and robust base for financing provincial public needs" (Kesselman 2011, 156–7). Granted, Campbell could have better prepared the province for the ensuing change, but taxation and tax policy should never be subjected to the emotionally charged process of a public referendum – if only because voters, in general, appear to lack the instrumental competence to connect the dots when it comes to critical tax policy issues of this sort. Truly, one of the more common limitations highlighted by democratic theorists and social psychologists is that citizens tend to lack the political resources, skills, awareness, and incentives to make meaningful and well-informed decisions on complex policy issues, particularly in our now hyper-commercialized and information-abundant social environments (Williams, Kruger, and Dunning 2013; Schlosser et al. 2013; Dunning 2011; Dunning et al. 2003; Dahl 2006; Dahl 1989; Macpherson 1977). Campbell may not have had sufficient "social licence" to pursue an HST taxing agenda, but he certainly seemed to have the right idea and perhaps should have been judged on the benefits that may have accrued from preserving the tax.

CONCLUSION:
"TAX ME, I'M BRITISH COLUMBIAN"
OR A SHIFT TO A REGRESSIVE TAX REGIME?

In 2002, the self-professed anti-tax crusader Mark Milke (2002) made the somewhat dubious allegation that Canadians, in general, were overtaxed.[9] Since the 2008 US financial crisis, many provincial and local governments have supported some form of tax reform – and, in particular, income and property tax increases – to resolve mounting public debts, urban infrastructural decay, health care costs, and so on. The lingering perception now appears to be that certain elements in society are not paying their fair share and should therefore be held to account. So, which is it? Over-taxed or not taxed enough? The position taken in this chapter is that, while Campbell's tax policy was not perfect, he probably struck a better balance than many of his peers and counterparts across the country and in the United States.[10]

BC now has a tax system that can better combat a series of fiscal exigencies, though it would have been stronger had the HST survived the 2011 provincial referendum. There remains a fair and progressive income tax plan that seems to satisfy a diverse cross-section of societal interests and a carbon levy that demonstrates the province's commitment to alleviating the effects of climate change. The MSP too, for all of its faults (perceived or real), continues to provide residents with a taxing instrument designed specifically to address the issue of health financing. Furthermore, BC's Crown corporations continue to generate substantial income for Victoria, and the province's resource sector, while still reeling from lagging demand in the US, is showing some promising signs of recovery.[11]

No government will ever produce a universally acceptable set of tax measures. Former premier Campbell clearly made some crucial tax policy errors over the course of his time in public office. But he also seems to have given the province a tax system that continues to respect a well-establish fiscal tradition of income-tax dependency, while at the same time recognizing the usefulness of other unconventional (and globally adopted) means of generating revenue. Ultimately, he was voted in on his promise(s) to reform the province's tax system, and reform is exactly what he delivered.

NOTES

1 "Horizontal equity requires that people in a similar economic position should pay the same amount of tax" (OECD 2001, 22) – also referred to as tax neutrality. Vertical equity, on the other hand, "requires that people on higher incomes should pay a higher proportion of their income in tax" (ibid.) – also known as tax progressivity. Horizontal and vertical equity are reflected in the consumption and payroll taxes and progressive income tax rates that exist in Canada and its provinces.

2 The year 2012 has been included to account for the overlap that typically characterizes annual budget figures.

3 BC's health budget is financed by multiple revenue sources: the HST, MSP premiums, the tobacco tax, a health special account, Ottawa's Canada Health Transfer, and a "wait times reduction" transfer. In 2013, the BC Liberals' health funding report claimed that the demand for the province's medical services exceeded revenues by a substantial margin. See O'Neill (2013) for more details.

4 Though I acknowledge that this decrease is due to other factors as well – such as a downturn in economic activity from 2008 to 2010.

5 Social security contributions or payroll taxes are taxes that an employer withholds from an employee's wages – also referred to as a "pay-as-you-earn" or "pay-as-you-go" tax. They are normally maintained to provide additional income support to social and health care programs such as the Canada Pension Plan, Employment Insurance, Medicare (in the United States), or even local transportation projects. Taxes of this sort are likely to be itemized on an employee's pay stub.

6 On 27 June 2013, the government under Christy Clark reintroduced legislation to increase the general corporate income tax rate to 11 per cent effective 1 April 2013.

7 In fact, this series of assertions regarding the "positive" relationship between tax cuts, economic growth, employment, and productively have been proven to be unequivocally false.

8 Ivanova and Klein (2013a) estimate that overall premiums have increased by 85 per cent since 2000.

9 According to the OECD's data, Canada ranked seventeenth (out of thirty-four) in terms of comparative "tax burdens" in the early 2000s. By 2011 (provisional), it ranked nineteenth (out of thirty-four). From a comparative perspective, then, Canada appears to have struck a fairly even balance.

10 By any objective measure, Campbell seems to have done a much better job addressing the issues of fiscal management and tax equity than Dalton McGuinty (Ontario), Jean Charest (Quebec), Arnold Schwarzenegger (California), and even Alison Redford (Alberta).

11 It would have to be conceded that natural resource revenue, at times, suffers from rather wild fluctuations. Given its unreliability as a major source of tax revenue, future governments may have to readjust their fiscal projections to account for declines in demand for BC forest products, mining materials, and liquefied natural gas. However, it might also represent a boon to BC's tax collection regime. In any case, the Ministry of Finance will have to be attentive to global trends in resource consumption. See O'Neill (2013) for more information.

6

BC Labour Relations in an Era of Neoliberal Reform

The Campbell Years, 2001–11

GARY TEEPLE

Over the course of former premier Campbell's decade in power, the working class and trade union movement were subjected to an extensive and unambiguous assault on the laws, social programs, and institutions that gave them certain rights to act collectively, some protection from conditions at work, partial compensation for work-related injuries, illness, and death, and some degree of respite from labour market vagaries (Fairey, Sandborn, and Peters 2012). The ten-year-long attack in BC was the continuation of earlier decades of retrenchment, marked by dramatic cuts in 1982–83 (Fawkes 1983; B. Palmer 1987) and interrupted with only modest and ambivalent reversals by NDP governments between 1991 and 2001.

Several lists, surveys, and commentaries already exist on these legislative attacks on workers' rights in BC and Canada (Camfield 2011; Fairey, Sandborn, and Peters 2012; McBride and McNutt 2007; Panitch and Swartz 2003; Sandborn 2010). But there remains room for more analysis of the historical context, the state rationale, and the significance of the cutbacks for workers. In general, the changes in BC, like those around the world, would appear to signal nothing less than the restructuring of the class relations established in the postwar era.

The historical context of these attacks begins after the Second World War, when a certain confluence of circumstances and heightened class struggle gave rise to the Keynesian welfare state, new labour legislation, and the political rights that provided some leverage for the working class over state policies. During this period, it could be said that the working classes in the industrial world gained the greatest degree of material betterment (Albrecht 1995) and highest degree of legislative protection in the history of capitalism.

As long as the effects of these circumstances and the demand for labour remained, the welfare state and legislated protection for workers continued to expand. Trade unions grew in size and number, exacted more favourable labour legislation, and increased their powers. They improved key collective rights, employment standards, industrial accident insurance schemes, and spurred the development of unemployment insurance, state pensions, and public health care. Previously treated largely as "externalities" by employers, these costs of reproduction were increasingly socialized through state redistribution of deductions from high wages and profits.

The achievements partially decommodified the existence of workers. Because labour power is bought and sold as a commodity, its price (wages and salaries), marketability, and the relative freedom of its owner are circumscribed by all the variables that impinge on its value – namely, the labour market, wage rates, employer dictates, and the cost of food, shelter, and clothing, among others. All the legislative and programmatic changes won by workers increased the degree of their freedom as commodities by offsetting the effects of these variables.

This relative freedom was, however, dependent on legislation, policies, and programs that rested on a particular set of historical circumstances. Ironically, it was this freedom and the high wages in the postwar era that allowed the working class to be convinced that capitalism actually had a "human face" and that workers had a place in it as a nonantagonistic "middle-class." But the achievements proved self-defeating in that they, along with other factors, grew to undermine capital accumulation, the raison d'être of the system, necessitating their retrenchment (Glyn 2008, 1–23).

By the late 1970s, the world economy was becoming increasingly global, dominated by transnational corporations, with globe-spanning production and distribution chains, driven by a computer-based mode of production (Pupo and Thomas 2010). Corporations could employ workers in the global labour market without the protections or rights of workers in the industrial world. The age of the relatively integrated national economy was coming to an end, along with its tax regime, welfare state, and labour legislation. They were becoming barriers to accumulation in a world economy in which transnational corporations required and demanded increasingly unfettered access to, and levelling of, national capital and labour markets and standards.

This chapter takes the position that the achievement of a high degree of relative freedom for the worker, as a commodity in the industrial countries in the postwar era, persisted beyond the conditions that made it possible and that it grew to become incompatible with the development of global capitalism. In BC's case (notwithstanding the arguments made by Pilon [chapter 2, this volume]), labour laws, welfare services, and liberal democracy all had to be curtailed so that corporations could assert their freedom as global capital from national and provincial constraints. The retrenchment of labour legislation has been a central part of these cuts.

LABOUR LEGISLATION

The term "labour legislation" is often used as a reference to a labour code that delineates union-management rights. There are, however, two other arenas of labour law that are directly related to work relations. One deals with employment standards, which regulate and define minimum health and safety conditions, hours of work, minimum wage rates, holidays, severance pay, and so on. The other regulates industrial accident insurance, which in the main provides financial reimbursement for job-related injuries, diseases, or death. There are, moreover, many other laws and programs that affect workers, such as unemployment insurance, state pensions, public health care and education, industrial training, foreign worker policies, and pay equity – but these are usually defined as part of the so-called welfare state or human rights policies rather than as labour legislation. And it should be added that many changes prejudicial to unions and workers are not legislated but are brought about by numerous small but significant decisions by the government regarding appointments, budgets, office location, and so on.[1] In this chapter, I restrict the analysis to "labour legislation," referring to the labour code, employment standards, and industrial accident insurance.

The reproduction of all social formations depends on the production and distribution of goods and services. Capitalist society is no different, but central to the way it produces and allocates its resources is a conflict of interests between employers and employees. The regulation of these contradictory demands as "labour relations," then, is of central importance to the system. Because these conflicts potentially threaten it and periodically have done so, they have had to be circumscribed and institutionalized through legal mechanisms to define and restrict the limits of action of both sides. It is a far from equal compromise that casts otherwise potentially violent conflicts into a legal framework that is subject to political, judicial, police, and corporate pressures.

These laws, rights, regulations, and programs are almost always cast as matters of legislation – that is, as statutes that can be changed at will by a party in power. They are rarely defined as constitutional rights because they reflect the ongoing class struggle rather than the legal principles belonging to the dominant class and paraded as universal. If constitutionally defined, they would counter the existing, but veiled, biases in structure and principle in constitutional law – that is, they would become "fundamental" rights instead of contested statutory ones that are only tolerated to the degree that they can be defended.[2]

Labour legislation is central to economic activity, regulating, in large measure, the relations between workers and employers, the role of trade unions, the terms of labour exploitation, aspects of the reproduction of the working class, and capital accumulation. Located at the centre of class relations, then, it is a body of law to which the corporate sector pays considerable attention.

It embodies two conflicting sets of demands. The employer needs to accumulate sufficient capital to reinvest and expand the business, and this process obliges the employer to minimize the costs of production, including wages. And the employee strives to exact what is at least necessary to live with dignity in a "normal" manner.

It follows that, if political parties represent different coalitions of class forces, a change of government can mean a shift in the balance of rights from one side to the other. This is what happened in 2001, when the Campbell Liberals ended ten years of NDP governments in BC.

The BC Labour Relations Code

Unions are, for the most part, the leading edge of the working class – the sector that has the organized power to assert its own demands and those of the class as a whole. The labour code has a special importance in the broad arena of labour legislation because it most directly affects the activities of the unions. It restricts their activities within certain legal limits, in particular, the right to form a union, to bargain collectively, and to strike.

Early in its mandate, the BC Liberals introduced Bill 18 (2001) and Bill 42 (2002), which made many changes to the Labour Relations Code. Of all the changes made, there were two that did not receive much attention but that carried profound implications. One was the introduction of a third party, the individual employee, into the code along with unions and employers. This is the only labour code in Canada with such a provision. Section 2(a) of the code states that those who exercise its powers must recognize "the rights and obligations of employees, employers and trade unions" – "employees" are inserted as a distinct player, separate from unions. This change, promoted by the Coalition of BC Businesses (CBCB) (CBCB 2004; CBCB 2006), has little to do with the rights of individual workers. The same coalition also campaigned to undermine and eliminate the rights of employees under the Employment Standards Act (ESA), with WorkSafe, and later protested the rise in the minimum wage. The rights of employees in those statutes have been dramatically scaled back, and the ability to exercise those rights has been made increasingly difficult.

The most plausible interpretation of this addition is an attempt to weaken union bargaining power by giving its members the right to disassociate from unions, much as the so-called "right-to-work" laws have done for decades in the United States (Fawkes 1983). It undermines the collective force of the union by providing a formal regulatory path for individual dissent and by implying that workers on their own can negotiate as good a contract as can a union. More specifically, it can be used to convince or bribe or otherwise use workers to reject a union certification and to attempt to decertify or partially decertify an existing union,[3] not to mention to contest union dues and activities. The only beneficiaries of the new clause are the employers (CBCB 2004, 3–4). For workers, this "right" translates into weakened unions or non-unionized workplaces that usually afford few if any benefits.

Section 2(b), the other relatively unexamined change, states that the powers and duties of the code "must" be performed "in a manner" that "fosters the employment of workers in economically viable businesses." The Labour Relations Board (LRB) acknowledged this addition as a "statutory recognition of the need to find ways of enhancing productivity, competition, and economic growth." And, according to the CBCB, the board "noted the importance of unions, employers, and government working towards the realization of these economic goals in every labour relations activity and decision" (CBCB 2004, 8).

The "viability" of a business can be construed to mean many things, and it can be used to frustrate or reverse issues of certification, grievance, health and safety, arbitration and mediation, or to assess bargaining units, undermine strikes and picket lines, and justify lock-outs.

There is, moreover, no definition of what constitutes productivity, competition, or growth; all can be taken as code words for speed-ups, longer or flexible hours, lower wages, fewer benefits, and less job security. Management can now argue, and has argued, that certain union demands may undermine the "viability" of a business and so run counter to the principles of the code. To date, the LRB has rejected such arguments, but the principle has been established, and its application is likely a matter of time.

These additions constituted nothing less than a fundamental shift in the nature of labour relations in BC. If the main principle of the Labour Relations Code was to institutionalize collective bargaining between two purportedly equal parties, to reconcile or resolve two ostensibly equal conflicting sets of interests, it was now encumbered by a third strictly individual self-interest and framed by the general interests of one side as the overarching priority.

The Right to Organize

Perhaps the most important right won by trade unions in the nineteenth century, but not fully established until well into the twentieth century with the obligation for employers to bargain, was the right to form a trade union. In order to confront the employer, a collective force of capital, workers too had to organize as a collective force of labour. This right to organize unions was, and continues to be, resisted by employers because those workers who do unionize no longer have to face management as mere individuals with little or no power over their employment terms or conditions.

Many of the changes brought in by the BC Liberals in 2001 and 2002 were intended to circumscribe this right to organize. Section 24 of the Labour Relations Code was amended to make a secret ballot mandatory for certification. In the past, depending on the party in power, the steps to certification shifted from a predominantly card-check system, allowing a union to be certified with a certain percentage of employees signed up, to a mandatory vote system, obliging a majority vote by secret ballot after a required number of cards were signed. In 2001, the BC Liberals eliminated the single card-check certification, adding an obligatory vote in all cases. Under the 2001 code, then, at least two expressions of employee support for unionization are required – the signing of the card (minimum 45 per cent) and then the vote. If the vote is less than 55 per cent, however, a third vote is required.

The necessity for at least two demonstrations of union support in all certification drives places a much greater demand on union time and money than was previously the case. It also creates opportunities for employer intervention (MacDonald 2002). Indeed, a review panel of union and business representatives during the NDP regime in 1992 "unanimously recommended a return to the card-check system" (Dickie 2005, 10) because, they argued: "Since the introduction of secret ballot votes in 1984 the rate of employer unfair labour practices ... has increased by more than 100 percent." They concluded: "The simple reality is that secret ballot votes and their concomitant representational campaigns invite an unacceptable level of unlawful employer interference in the certification process." Another review committee on the Labour Relations Code in 1998 wrote: "Experience demonstrates that employers do seek to affect employees' right to choose. In our view, extending the certification process by introducing a mandatory ... vote would only further invite such illegal activity" (cited in Dickie 2005, 11).

The evidence suggests that the mandatory vote reduces the number of successful certification applications (Dickie 2005, 10). Since the new law was promulgated, the growth rate of newly organized workers has declined significantly to the lowest rate in the last thirty years (six), even though the absolute number of organized workers has modestly continued to rise. Union density, the number of unionized workers as a percentage of all workers, however, is declining (Dickie 2005, app. 4). Its impact will be expressed as an increasingly defenceless working class.

There are other contributory factors to this decline in union density. Most are related to changes in the mode of production and the rise of the global economy, resulting in the growth of many precarious part-time jobs with low wages, which are difficult to organize. The change in the Labour Relations Code, however, is a policy-related factor – that is, a political action that privileges the interests of one party over another, or an intervention by the state intended to favour the interests of one side in an ostensibly neutral regulatory framework.

Unfair Labour Practices

Widely used to frustrate certification drives, unfair labour practices are curbed in all labour relations codes. While they circumscribe and prohibit certain actions by both sides, unions and employers, the evidence before labour relations boards points to the fact that employers are far more likely to engage in illegal labour practices than are unions.

Changes to the 2002 BC Labour Relations Code (specifically sections 6 and 8) expanded the possibilities for employers to interfere in relations between the union and its members. Employers were given increased "freedom to communicate to an employee" during certification drives and the life of the contract. The previous wording restricted this freedom to "statements of fact and opinion reasonably held with respect to the employer's business," while the 2002 wording also permitted the "freedom to express his or her views on any matter, including matters relating to an employer, a trade union or the representation of employees by a trade union, provided that the person does not use intimidation or coercion" (s. 8). While on the surface the wording appears to be neutral, it does not reflect the decidedly non-neutral structural reality of corporate powers over employment. And this is not to mention the practices of the state in partisan appointments to the Labour Relations Board, or the subsequent non-committal interpretations of these sections by the board, allowing employer campaigns that include a great many anti-union communications to workers.

The CBCB was forthright in its praise for these new "freedoms." It noted, among other things, that the LRB now "supported the right of employees to hear employers' views on the impact of unionism on a business and industry" and the LRB's position that "employer communications critical of the union would not constitute an unfair labour practice, even during certification drives, provided that the messages were expressed as a view" (CBCB 2004, 3). Since 2002, there has been an increase in employer-labour practices that violate what used to be defined as unfair.

Not only are these changes prejudicial to unions but also, to address these unfair practices, the LRB has few "effective remedies" and is increasingly reluctant to use those few that it does have. The key remedy is "remedial certification," the power to grant certification, if unfair labour practices are proven, even though a union does not have the required number of votes to be certified. The LRB has used this remedy so infrequently that it is not much of a deterrent to employers engaging in unfair labour practices. The unwillingness of the LRB to take action to address these practices has very likely been a contributory cause in the growing number of unfair labour practices (Dickie 2005, 14–15).

The LRB's "administrative procedures" can also affect the success of certification (Dickie 2005, 16). The time to process certification applications, for example, is now about double what it was during the previous period, thus frustrating unions, costing them money, and allowing time for management to interfere in the application. Employer objections to the application can last for weeks, or months, before they are decided upon. The representation vote after application with the signed cards, to give another example, is not usually carried out until near the end of the requisite ten-day period, again giving employers time to intervene (17–18).

Process and procedure in the LRB were among the first targets of the Campbell government. In 2001, it let go a large number of Industrial Relations Officers (IROs) and "closed most of their offices throughout the province" (Dickie 2005, 18). Because the IROs play such a central part in the certification process, it is difficult to interpret these acts as anything but an attempt to slow down and frustrate the growth of unions in BC.

IROs are the first point of contact with the LRB in applying for certification: they examine the application and write the report that assesses its compliance with the code. Among other duties, they can decide "whether the union has met the required 45 percent level of membership support needed to obtain a representation vote." To do this, they determine how many employees comprise the bargaining unit and how many have signed union cards. Before 2001, IROs would check both the union cards and "payroll records" in order to judge the percentage and determine the legitimacy of the representation vote. After 2001, the size of the bargaining unit was "determined solely on the employer's say so." This ability gave the employer the freedom to make unproven claims about employee numbers, with the intent to have the certification application dismissed for not achieving the necessary 45 per cent quota. As a consequence, an employer is now in a position of considerable control over a union drive and application for certification (Dickie 2005, 19).

As if to confirm the bias in practice that favours employers, IROs "now only inspect payroll records occasionally, when directed to do so by the Labour Relations Board," but they "regularly inspect union membership cards, which are then inspected a second time by the vice-chair hearing the certification application." Not only are the cards checked twice, the LRB "requires a union to demonstrate that an employee list provided by the employer in secret is incorrect before the Board will disclose the employee list portion of the report to the union" (Dickie 2005, 19n). This difference between the treatment of payroll records and membership cards is stark evidence of structural and procedural bias in the LRB.

The Right to Bargain Collectively

If the union has managed to certify a bargaining unit, the code presents more structured obstacles at the next stage: negotiating the contract. In the construction trades, sectoral bargaining made it easier for unions to establish wage rates and benefits across much of the industry, but, in 2002, sectoral bargaining was abolished, to the sole benefit of the contractors.

Another barrier to collective bargaining is the creation of certain exemptions for employees. Optional exclusions for individuals, usually on religious grounds, from union membership and dues payments undermine union solidarity by allowing some employees in a unionized workplace to refuse to join the union or opt out of it and to direct the amount in dues and other fees to a registered charity of their choice (s. 17).

Perhaps the most dramatic example of the violation of collective bargaining by the Campbell Liberals was the reneging on established agreements with the BC Teachers' Federation and the Hospital Employees' Union in 2002. Not only were existing contracts broken, the very principle of collective bargaining was breached.

Bill 29 confronted health care workers with extensive revisions to the terms of their existing agreement. The changes were so dramatic and arbitrary – including thousands of lay-offs, wage roll-backs, privatizations, contracting out, and the elimination of many services – that the government brought the province to the brink of a general strike in 2004. The violations of workers' rights in this bill, moreover, were appealed to the Supreme Court of Canada, where the decision in 2007 found that the government had violated the Charter rights of health care workers to bargain collectively (Camfield 2006; Camfield 2009; Isitt and Moroz 2007).

Bill 28 also, in 2002, stripped the teachers' union of its right to bargain many aspects of teachers' working conditions as well as class size and composition. The BC Teachers' Federation took the government to court over this bill, and, in 2011, the BC Supreme Court ruled that Bill 28 was unconstitutional, infringing on the right to bargain collectively, but it gave the government a year to negotiate the ruling with the BC Teachers' Federation. In 2012, the government returned with Bill 22, new legislation that pointedly used some of the same language previously ruled unconstitutional, along with further restrictions that proved to be even more severe. Among other revisions, it removed many items from possible negotiation; it prohibited strike action and replaced impasse resolution with a mediation process; and it laid out harsh financial penalties against individual teachers, union representatives, and the union, making strike action all but impossible.

Bill 22 was then challenged by the union, and a second decision came from the BC Supreme Court in January 2014, in which the judge ruled that the government had bargained in bad faith with the union and had left much of the unconstitutional language unchanged. It ordered the government to pay $2 million to the union, to cover the court costs, and to uphold the earlier decision. Undeterred, the government appealed this decision, and the appeal was decided in favour of the BC Teachers' Federation in November 2016.

The Right to Strike

In all labour codes the right to strike is well circumscribed by qualifications, requirements, and limitations. After decades of successive legislation to restrict this right, it has been narrowed generally to situations in which negotiations for a new contract or renewal of a contract have failed. Even in these cases, labour codes have curbed this right by obliging the union to move through specified steps over periods of time before striking. Besides the legislative barriers, strikes are also a major financial burden on unions whose strike funds can be quickly diminished and on workers who rarely have the financial resources to forego their wages for any length of time. The paucity of workers' and union resources and the stringent legal regulations mean a strike is nearly always the product of an intolerable situation.

The right to strike can also be limited by the use of an essential services designation. This usually means that a strike can take place, but it is not permitted to shut down all operations or services that are struck. The designation, then, has an impact on the bargaining process given that effective collective bargaining depends on unions having the right to prevent all work in the event of an impasse. Importantly, without the right to strike or to withdraw all workers, the union contract becomes less voluntary and more coercive, framed by the threat of fines and even imprisonment. Firefighters, police, and some health care workers are the public services commonly put into this category, for reasons of public safety.

In 2001, however, the Campbell government placed public education in the "essential service" category and gave the minister in charge discretionary power to decide which aspects of public education would be considered essential. This was an odd change of policy given that education is not usually considered to be an essential service and that the time lost in BC to strike action in this sector has been very limited – as well, BC is the only province in Canada with such a provision in its labour code. The plausible motive for this inclusion is that it is calculated to handicap the bargaining process for the BC Teachers' Federation, a strong and militant public-sector union, allowing the provincial government more power to restrict the final offer (Camfield 2009).

EMPLOYMENT STANDARDS

The progressive expansion of employment standards since the nineteenth century has been an attempt by the state to ameliorate working conditions and the operation of the markets. Employers are guided by few principles beyond capital accumulation, regarding workers merely as a factor in production (i.e., as a form of capital), to be exploited to the maximum degree possible. Treated in this way and without any guarantee of employment, workers are obliged as a matter of self-preservation to resist the lack of standards in employment and the absence of provisions outside of employment. Because their demands for survival impinge on corporate profits, and hence potentially threaten the system, their self-defence appears as subversive social unrest. The state is obliged to act because corporations, as mutually antagonistic competitors, usually lack the ability to act with a single voice and because their profits, in part, are mirrored in their treatment of workers.

As a way to mitigate worker unrest, the state provides a legislated base of minimum standards that is equal for all employers and employees. These are not "fundamental" rights or minimums; the level and extent of the standards are all a matter of struggle that is implicit in the system and that waxes and wanes with the relative strength of the organized working class and the ability of the corporations to stand firm or to push back. The resulting standards usually take the form of regulations that stipulate the lowest possible wages, hours of work, paid holidays, severance conditions, and so on.

BC Employment Standards Act (ESA)

Although generally set as low as possible, employment standards do provide all workers with a baseline for their conditions, rights, and wages. For unionized workers, they present a starting point in negotiations for improvements. Just as important, they protect non-unionized and vulnerable workers, comprising a majority of the labour force in British Columbia, from undue exploitation (Fairey 2005, 10). For corporations, these standards also have positive long-term effects in establishing a level playing field, reducing their competition for workers, and helping to maintain a healthy labour force.

But employers and employees see employment standards differently. Corporations see only their cost (in the shape of higher wages, paid holidays, infrastructure expenditures, severance costs, and the like) and the limits they place on "management rights." They press for lower or fewer or no standards. Workers and unions press for higher standards as a matter of self-preservation. There are then two sets of rights at play: on the one side, the corporation and its right to hire and fire and set the conditions over the use of its private property; and on the other side, the workers and their demands for a living and a life, albeit as an embodiment of private property. As long as both sides have the power to defend their interests, there will be some compromise.

The Campbell Liberal Party revised the Employment Standards Act through three main legislative bills: Bill 48 (2002), Bill 37 (2003), and Bill 56 (2004). They comprised a set of changes that went largely unchallenged, even though they were a significant setback, albeit with a few improvements, for workers and unions, and were enormously beneficial to management, increasing its rights and decreasing its liabilities (Fairey 2005, 17).

Probably the most significant of these changes was the exclusion of unionized workers from some terms of the ESA, whereby a collective agreement covered "any provision" in the act that dealt with issues such as hours of work, statutory holidays, annual vacations, seniority, termination, layoff, and most everything to do with wages. Previously, unionized workers were covered by the ESA, which meant that its minimum standards provided the floor that collective bargaining could assume or improve. Now, however, for unions – representing about 30 per cent of public-sector workers and 18 per cent of private-sector workers in BC – some of these rights and standards were up for negotiation and could end up being lower than the minimum if not negotiated into the agreement.

This one change had a profound effect on union bargaining. It increased the workload for union negotiators, strained the resources of unions, and opened the possibility of losing some minimum standards as a trade-off, thereby lowering the protections for members and undermining the key motives for joining a union. It also meant that the unions would have to spend their time protecting, as best they could, the minimum standards in their own collective agreements and would now have much more difficulty advancing the interests of the class as a whole by raising the floor through collective bargaining.

Furthermore, it opened the door to an expansion of possibilities for wage theft (Bobo 2009). Because all contracts deal with matters of wages, the pertinent clauses covered in the ESA now became open to negotiation and therefore open to manipulation and misuse by employers. It also encouraged the growth of, and competition from, weak or corrupt or otherwise questionable unions (favoured by employers) that were willing to bargain away many minimum standards (Fairey 2005, 18).

Minimum Wage

The minimum wage is part of the safety net for workers, acting as a floor on wages. Its introduction has usually been a response to workers' demands to prevent the drive by employers to reduce wages to as low a level as possible. The level is always established below the value of labour power (i.e., less than what is required for workers to reproduce themselves in a normal manner) and below what are usually considered the thresholds of poverty. As a result, workers earning minimum wage must take on more hours than normal, often leading to physical and mental exhaustion. Or they have to be subsidized by the state, family, cooperative, charity, or medical system – in other words, some redistributive mechanism other than wages. From this perspective, the minimum wage provides an indirect subsidy to employers because the remaining cost to reproduce this labour power is borne in one way or another by the individual and society and not the corporation.

A low minimum wage rate also acts as a drag on the whole wage structure, adversely affecting workers but advantageous to corporations. For employers, it makes demands for increases more difficult because it induces in workers an "economic" discipline based on fear of unemployment and abject poverty, and it also lowers the wage bill, which, from their perspective, can never be too low. For workers, a low rate necessitates more than one job or more working hours, thus preventing a normal life. As well, it can lead to physical exhaustion and mental depression, and a declining incentive to work if there is no life beyond work and no life with work. It also appears to encourage a movement into the informal economy, criminal activities, and a reliance on state subsidies or charities.

Although only a small percentage of the labour force actually earns the minimum wage in BC, a much larger percentage earns only marginally above the minimum. As a baseline, it makes anything above it seem positive, even though it may be below various measures of poverty or a calculated "living wage" (Ivanova and Klein 2013b). From the workers' perspective, then, the higher the minimum wage, the better; from the employers' perspective, the higher the minimum, the greater the wage bill and the less the disciplinary effect on the workers.

The level of the minimum wage is more a class issue than anything else, decided by the relative strength of the two parties and the economic and political conditions of the times. The state "mediates" the conflicting demands to keep the level as low as possible, to blunt any increase if it seriously threatens profitability, and to drive it lower if there is no significant resistance on the part of workers.

When the Campbell government assumed power in 2001, the eight-dollar-an-hour minimum wage was among the highest in Canada. The government, however, did not increase this rate until 2011, which meant that, after a decade of erosion by inflation, it had become one of the lowest by the time the premier left office. By May 2012, after incremental increases, it was raised to $10.25, but it was not indexed in any way, allowing for its subsequent renewed erosion. In 2013, the campaign for a "Living Wage for Families" calculated that, to meet the basic needs of a family of four in Vancouver, the two principal wage earners would have to have two full-time incomes at over nineteen dollars an hour (Ivanova and Klein 2013b).

Not only did the fixed minimum rate rapidly decline in value after 2001, but the Liberal government also introduced "The First Job/Work Entry Minimum Wage," set at six dollars an hour for the first five hundred hours of work. Ostensibly intended to reduce youth unemployment, its effects were never monitored to measure its impact or to prevent arbitrary termination after the five hundred hours (followed by new hires) or the many other abuses to which it was put by employers. This, too, was ended with the resignation of Premier Campbell.

Another change in the ESA (section 34) that affected part-time workers included a cutback to the minimum call-in time for work from four hours to two, meaning that a job could depend on going in for as few as two hours in a day or having a working day broken into two or more two-hour periods. Given that the value of an hourly wage is determined by the assumption of a normal work week of forty hours, a mere two-hour block, indeed any number of hours fewer than a normal full day and week, precludes an income sufficient to sustain oneself. The reality of such short work shifts negatively affects many workers in the food service, recreational, and retail industries.

The vulnerable could also "agree" to give up their statutory right to higher overtime pay rates under a new "hours averaging agreement" that permitted no overtime pay if the hours of work did not exceed an average of forty hours per week over four weeks. This provision opened the door to abuse by employers who might regularly ask for overtime, but who might not as regularly calculate the average four forty-hour weeks. Overtime pay that was double-time, moreover, was reduced to time and a half, under certain circumstances. For many part-time workers, restrictive qualifications for statutory holidays with pay were introduced that, in effect, eliminated the extra pay. Other conditions were introduced preventing many part-timers from ever qualifying for these paid holidays.

Even the period of employers' liability for violations of wage payments was cut back from two years to six months, a reduction that greatly lessened the obligation to pay back wages and widened the door to employer meddling with unpaid wages. Corporate officers and directors were also relieved of their personal liability for wages owing in the case of bankruptcy or receivership. However difficult it was for workers to extract these owed wages before 2002, several hundred thousands of dollars were collected, but after that date it became even more difficult. In other cases of failure to pay wages, the changes to the ESA reduced employer obligations (Fairey 2005, 22).

Even the very process for a worker to make a complaint about violations of the ESA was radically revised. Now, the employee must fill out many pages of a "self-help kit" and make the initial complaint to the employer; if there is no resolution at this stage, the worker has to initiate a long process with the Employment Standards Branch (ESB), at considerable cost in time and money. And, instead of an investigation of the complaint by branch officers, there is a "mediation" process aimed at a "settlement agreement." These new regulations have led to a dramatic reduction in complaints, rendering violations very difficult to address.

As if mocking what was left of the complaints process, the Campbell government reduced the staff at the ESB by about one-third and enforcement officers by almost one-half. Further to this it closed about one-half of the branch offices across the province. And as though this were not enough, the random auditing of businesses as an enforcement mechanism was ended in sectors in which non-compliance was common. Even for appeals about a decision by the director of employment standards, there was now a fee to be paid, strict restrictions to the grounds for appeal, and new powers for the Employment Standards Tribunal to reject the appeal (Fairey 2005, 23; Fairey, Sandborn, and Peters 2012, 111–12).

Child Labour

Since the rise of industrial capitalism in the late eighteenth century, opposition to child labour has been a central issue in the demand for employment standards. Without regulation, corporations have had no hesitation to exploit labour in whatever form. Children are more vulnerable, impressionable, malleable, and easily intimidated than adults, and their employment allows for the expansion of the labour supply through the use of docile and cheap workers. Although often pushed to work by their parents or guardians in order to expand family income, they undermine the employment of adults. As employed minors, they represent an obvious violation of the principle of private property, not being fully "persons" under the law and therefore not responsible for their actions. They stand as clear examples of unfree labour.

In the early years of the Campbell government, Bill 48 (2002) and Bill 37 (2003) made many changes to the ESA concerning child labour. Prior to 2002, no employer could hire a child under fifteen without obtaining a permit from the director of the ESB, who, in turn, required the consent of both a parent or guardian and school officials. The director also had the power and obligation to investigate the workplace and put restrictions on the type and hours of work.

After the bills were passed, children from the age of twelve could be hired, now with simply the consent of one parent or guardian. And the responsibility for assessing the conditions of employment shifted to the parent or guardian; school approval was no longer required. Moreover, a child under twelve could be hired with the permission of the director of the ESB. Any child worker could now work for up to four hours on a school day and up to twenty hours in a five-day school week. If the school week was fewer than five days, seven hours on a non-school day was allowed, up to thirty-five hours a week. These changes meant that a child in the usual five-day school week could be occupied with school and employment for up to fifty hours: in a four-day school week, a child could be similarly occupied for over sixty hours.

It is worth pointing out that there is effectively no longer any age limit – except that to employ a child under twelve, the director of ESB must issue a permit, for which there are no criteria. In other words, the minimum age and other criteria for child labour have become merely discretionary matters for an unelected government official.

The shift in responsibility from the ESB and school officials to the parent in reality meant that there would be little or no oversight of the child's work environment or experience because parents do not have the authority or power or ability to assess either the health and safety of a worksite or the integrity of an employer. The parental letter of permission, moreover, has to be produced by the employer only in the case of a complaint; otherwise there is no need to demonstrate that it exists.

Other than a ban on working during school hours, there are few other prohibitions on child labour. There is no prohibition on night work (and no provision for transport to or from work at night), and there are very few excluded occupations. Even previously prohibited activities have been deleted (e.g., the use of power-equipment like power hammers, forklifts, and other warehouse vehicles; work close to grills or deep-fryers; work with chemicals; or work at heights) (Luke and Moore 2004).

What little evidence that exists regarding the effects these changes to the ESA reveals a decidedly negative impact on school success and points to high rates of accidents due to burns, cuts, falls, and the operation of machinery. But because government statistics relating to the labour of children under fifteen are not gathered, there is little or no objective information on these effects. Undocumented, they are almost impossible to assess, making for fewer objections (Montani and Perry 2013).

Farm Labour

Farm workers have always been among the most poorly paid, and there are many reasons for this. Generally, these workers are unskilled, and poor wages, in part, reflect this lack of human capital. They are also difficult to organize because the jobs are seasonal or temporary and the majority are migrant or immigrant workers and so are handicapped by a range of uncertainties – not to mention language and cultural barriers. Finally, they are usually subject to specific restrictive state regulations because low food costs are so important to restraining wage levels in the non-farm strata of the working class.

In British Columbia, farm workers face other complicating structural factors. Much farm labour, for instance, is first sold to labour contractors, leading to a deduction of wages for their "services," and presenting ambiguities about the actual employer – the farmer or the contractor? The divided jurisdictions – between the federal government's Seasonal Agricultural Workers Program, under which many thousands of workers are hired seasonally every year, and the provincial government's powers over employment standards, the labour code, and workers' compensation – also present workers with significant dilemmas about their status and rights.

Notwithstanding these existing disadvantages for farm workers, in 2001 the new Liberal government set about to systematically undermine their rights and wage schemes. First, it abolished the proactive enforcement program that had ended many of the deceitful practices of labour contractors and employers, and established direct relations between farm workers, agency staffers, and other players – replacing it with a system of complaint-driven compliance, opening up the possibility of the unprincipled practices of the past.

In 2002, the Campbell government, among other things, eased employers' liability for unpaid wages and removed the requirement to keep records of wages paid to workers provided by contractors. And, in 2003, it reduced the minimums on piece rates and overtime payments, changed the entitlements to holiday pay and vacations, and made other changes to the ESA negatively affecting farm workers with respect to overtime, sick leave, maternity benefits, and pensions (Fairey et al. 2008; Otero and Preibisch 2009).

Farm workers in BC comprise the lowest-paid sector of the labour force and are the least protected by legislation or unions. They are subjected to wage theft by employers and contractors, and left largely unprotected against occupational hazards, job insecurity, and overwork.

In general, changes to the ESA made these standards more abstract than real. If the state does not enforce them, or monitor their application, or even issue minimal penalties, and the employer refuses to acknowledge or respect them or, worse, consciously ignores them, then they cease to be of any real value. Similarly, if workers do not know about them, or are too fearful to demand that they be respected, then, for practical purposes, they do not exist.

WORKERS' COMPENSATION

Workers' compensation systems are publicly administered socialized corporate insurance schemes intended, by and large, to cover employer liability for reparations to workers in the case of injury, illness, or death at their place of work. These systems were established because the growth of industrial capitalism in the nineteenth century spawned a commensurate rise in industrial accidents, taking an ever larger toll over many decades. Workers were hard pressed to obtain compensation of any sort, except inadequately through their own organizations or infrequently from a lawsuit against a company. That corporations could evade legal responsibility for the growing number of accidents provided the emerging working class with stark evidence of a class-divided society and its lack of justice for workers.

Once the working class had a certain degree of organization and consciousness of itself, its social demands and critical awareness provided the unspoken rationale for governments to legislate these insurance schemes. They are clearly an advantage to workers, providing a right to compensation that otherwise does not exist. But to realize this right depends largely on the level of financing, inspection of workplaces, and medical assessments, all of which can be manipulated to make the right more abstract than real. The underlying "bargain" is that, in the event of an accident, workers forego the right to sue the corporation for damages in exchange for a workplace insured against accidents. As with all such "bargains" in a class society, it is constantly contested; and the entitlements to reimbursement for loss of income, medical treatment, and rehabilitation have been in constant dispute between workers and employers. It has always been an uneasy compromise, but now it appears increasingly as a contract that locks one side in while exempting the other.

The general decline of workers' rights under these schemes in recent years has nothing to do with a decline in the number of deaths, injuries, and diseases experienced at the workplace. These numbers continue to rise around the world (International Labour Organization 2013).[4] The explanation for the decline in entitlements is likely due to the growth of global labour arbitrage, now extending into labour markets in which no such protection exists, and the relative fall in union membership everywhere, hence the decline in the ability to resist.

WorkSafe BC

Not to be left behind in the retrenchment of these schemes, the Campbell Liberals amended the Workers' Compensation Act (WCA) in 2002 and 2003 in Bill 49 and Bill 63, respectively, and also changed the Workers' Compensation Amendment Act (no. 1 and no. 2) in a major overhaul of the system that seriously damaged workers' rights. The changes to preventive regulations, medical treatment, financial compensation, and vocational rehabilitation were so extensive as to create a relatively inaccessible system that denies workers many of the rights they once had. They have been described by legal observers as shifting the point of the system from workers' compensation to employers' cost reduction and evasion of responsibility (Guenther, Patterson, and O'Leary 2008).

Among the many changes to the WCA were reductions to the benefits for injured workers, to the indexing of pensions, and to the calculation of workers' wage rates, along with the near elimination of pensions for long-term loss of earnings. These cutbacks to workers were justified on the grounds of making the system financially sustainable. Yet, in the years since 2003, there have been substantial surpluses collected by the Workers' Compensation Board (WCB), amounting to hundreds of millions of dollars. And these have grown despite the decline in employers' assessment rates, which are now among the lowest in the country (Guenther, Patterson, and O'Leary 2008).

Besides these cutbacks, there has been a large increase in waiting times: the average wait for the first compensation payment in BC is now 19.7 days. At the time of the Royal Commission on Workers' Compensation in BC in 1998, employers argued that a waiting time of three days would provide "an incentive to stay at work and eliminate questionable and minor or nuisance claims" (Royal Commission on Workers' Compensation in British Columbia 1998, 15). The longer wait times in other jurisdictions, they maintained, resulted in a reduction in claims, especially minor ones, and in administrative costs. For injured workers, the longer wait time serves as a gratuitous punishment.

The longer wait time, however, has a number of employer-friendly consequences. It constitutes a form of deductible for workers on accident insurance – that is, a means to shift some costs from employers to workers. For individual employers, it reduces potential penalty increases in compensation assessment; it is a disincentive for workers to stay off the job and seek treatment; and it allows for the under-reporting and suppression of claims. For workers, the long wait times in BC can quickly become a financial disaster, especially when the initial days of wage loss are not compensated. The loss of income for a worker who has been injured or diseased or killed can be financially devastating in a matter of a week or two.

Compensation, it must be added, has never been the full amount of wages. WorkSafe does not compensate the non-wage portion of income, which can range from 15 to 30 per cent of wages. The loss of non-waged income and the various ceilings placed on compensation are ways of defrauding the vulnerable – the injured or diseased workers and their families – from their assumed insured income. These many forms of reduced compensation income can be interpreted as a regulated theft of wages and reduced liability for the insurers via the workers' compensation system. They translate into benefits to the employer in the form of smaller premiums and assessments as well as lower capital costs for workplace health and safety, and they translate into benefits to the WCB in the form of a larger pool of unexpended funds that are available for investment.

In 2002, the changes to the WCA effectively eliminated the budget for vocational rehabilitation or retraining. The amount spent in 2002 was over $130 million, and it was reduced to about $1.5 million in 2005 – a reduction of almost 99 per cent (Guenther, Patterson, and O'Leary 2008, 10). There is a distinction between vocational rehabilitation and medical and/or physical rehabilitation. In BC, the main goal has not been vocational rehabilitation but simply to get the worker back to work, and at the earliest possible time, placing the emphasis on medical rehabilitation. These cutbacks, however, represent significant reductions in compensation benefits to injured or ill workers. It also suggests a certain analysis of the projected labour market in BC that increasingly needs part-time and relatively unskilled workers.

With WorkSafe, like most workers' compensation systems, not all workers are covered and not all conditions are accepted for compensation. In general, the processes are bureaucratic and the medical personnel are trained with a "return-to-work" philosophy as their priority. Since 2003, there have been many limitations placed on the medical conditions of workers that are open to compensation. Workers suffering from permanent chronic pain and work-induced psychological conditions, for instance, have seen increased restrictions placed on the definition of their state of health.

Workers' compensation boards are often structured as independent corporations, sometimes not responsible to a government minister, with broad policy established at the government level but with specific policies, operations, and interpretation established at the board level. Although governed under administrative law, the board's decisions often seem arbitrary, and its final decisions are open only to limited review by the courts. Notwithstanding important reversals, these decisions often appear as violations of natural justice, due process, and the rule of law.

Workers, for instance, have to endure an appeal process that is technical, confusing, and complex. They often have to prove that they are not at fault for the injury, disease, or death, even though the compensation system is cast as no-fault. They are confronted by bureaucrats, lawyers, and physicians, all from a different class and alien to the worker. The boards themselves are usually tripartite bodies, with the union or worker representative outnumbered. Throughout the history of workers' compensation schemes, workers have complained of arbitrariness, insufficient compensation, paternalism, and indifference to the worker's life (besides the ability to work) – and these complaints remain (Bittle 2012; Barnetson 2010).

Part of the mandate of the BC Labour Relations Board is to oversee the province's occupational health and safety regulations. Its role is to promote and enforce policy, but given the shift in focus of WorkSafe, enforcement and promotion activities declined after 2003. The site visits are fewer, the penalties are not sufficient to be an effective deterrent, and the research into work-related ill-health and accidents is very limited. Under the Campbell regime, changes to the WCA have decreased benefits to workers, restricted access to benefits, initiated cutbacks on inspections and preventive measures, more or less abolished vocational rehabilitation, and reduced premiums to employers, among other amendments.

CONCLUSION

The retrenchment of workers' rights and wages briefly outlined here are merely part of a much wider and deeper set of restrictions, exclusions, and cutbacks that the BC Liberals imposed on the province's working class. In general, they have undermined the relative freedom from commodification provided by the welfare state and labour legislation for all workers.

These growing restraints are confronting the unions in BC with the same dilemma faced by organized working classes throughout many industrial nations. National governments are increasingly unable and unwilling to allow the safeguards for workers they once did in labour law and broad social reform. They increasingly disrespect the will of the citizens with arbitrary rulings and actions – here with stealth, there with undisguised zeal. Corporations commit a range of illegal acts with relative impunity, as is reported daily. And, as Summerville alludes to in chapter 4 (this volume), policies of the labour parties of the past are now almost indistinguishable from those of their conservative counterparts. With the disappearance of postwar circumstances, the political leverage once commanded by the working class and trade unions has progressively dissipated.

The main arena of capital accumulation has shifted to the global level, undermining national interests and political structures, and creating a new playing field for capital and labour markets. A new mode of production has brought new occupations and demands for "flexibility" and, for many strata of workers, stagnant or lower wages. The rights of workers, however, remain defined by national legal frameworks and the state-distributed social programs dependent on disappearing high wages.

For the working class in BC, as in all liberal democratic capitalist regimes, labour law and the welfare state have always been paradoxical. They appear to provide workers a legitimate role and place in the system, yet their advantages for workers have always been minimized or opposed. They allow for degrees of working-class freedom, yet the state uses them as instruments of social control and employers continuously contest their extent and even their very existence.

The conditions allowing for this paradox are in obvious decline, making workers' rights and the welfare state more difficult to defend. Workers become increasingly "unfree" – that is, more subject to the discipline of the labour market, the dictates of employers, repressive laws, and state threats of fines and imprisonment. The "human face" begins to appear as merely a mask. The legitimacy of liberal democracies declines when they can no longer offer the leverage, or promise the benefits, they once did to the working class, and postwar rights cannot be defended or expanded at the national level. The new economy is global and will increasingly oblige the working class to define and defend itself at that level.

NOTES

1 Thanks to Leo McGrady for this important point and critical review of the paper.

2 Since 2002, court intervention in labour issues in Canada has begun to change this situation. For a catalogue of some of these changes see McGrady and Sabet-Rasekh (2016).

3 Partial decertification refers to decertifying one or more bargaining units from a multiple location collective agreement or excluding certain employees from a bargaining unit.

4 According to the International Labour Organization in 2013: "An estimated 2.34 million people die each year from work-related accidents and diseases. Of these, the vast majority – an estimated 2.02 million – die from a wide range of work-related diseases." Moreover, "an estimated 160 million people suffer from work-related diseases, and there are an estimated 270 million fatal and non-fatal accidents per year" (International Labour Organization 2013).

7

Putting Preservation First

Assessing the Legacy of the Campbell Government's Approach to Health Policy

NEIL T. HANLON

The Campbell government took office at a time when calls for major reforms to health care were resonating from all corners of the political spectrum in British Columbia. At the risk of reductionism, the many and varied targets of reform can be organized in four broad categories: rationalizing, preserving, expanding, and personalizing. Those concerned with health care rationalizing were preoccupied with containing the inflationary tendencies of publicly funded health care programs, which includes allowing a greater role for privatization. Preservationists were concerned to protect the key principles of the Canadian medical and hospital care insurance plan (or Medicare), which were seen to be under threat from fiscal conservatives and the vested self-interest of health professionals. Expansionists wished to add new services and programs to the list of those covered by provincial plans, moving Canadian Medicare beyond the confines of hospitals and doctors' offices to include things such as prescription drugs and home care. Finally, people across the political spectrum were concerned that health care was too impersonal and unresponsive to the needs of patients, leading to calls for a wide range of reforms, including primary health care development, chronic disease management, evidence-based practice, more consumer choice, and greater attention to patient satisfaction.

The BC Liberals faced pressure from all four of these reform groups from inside as well as outside its core base of support. Interest in, and concerns about, health care are so ubiquitous that any government is wise to wade carefully into health policy reform. For their part, provincial governments in the early 2000s were still reeling from the fiscal shocks of the Canada Health and Social Transfer (CHST), which brought about drastic reductions in direct federal transfers and greater responsibilities of provincial governments to contain health care costs. The cost of hospital and medical insurance to both levels of government had risen well above rates of inflation and population change for decades, and in many ways the CHST succeeded in forcing provincial governments to impose systems of rationalization and cost containment on Medicare. While the Campbell Liberals knew they needed to be seen to be doing something about persistent health care concerns, whatever that "something" was had to take into consideration a wide range of political and economic factors that might easily undermine the government's intentions.

Upon taking office in autumn 2001 with an overwhelming majority government (seventy-seven of seventy-nine seats), Gordon Campbell appointed a record number of cabinet ministers in his first session of the provincial legislature, an odd decision for a politician who espoused core conservative values of streamlined and small government. In any case, the health sector was apparently a priority for the incoming government, receiving a total of four ministerial appointments. Rather than appoint one minister of health, Campbell created the Ministry of Health Services to tend to the operation of the health sector and the Ministry of Health Planning to look after long-term policy and planning. In addition, two ministers of state were appointed with health-focused portfolios (i.e., continuing and home care, and mental health and addictions). It was clear that Campbell had ambitious plans for health care.

In November 2001, the Honourable Sindi Hawkins, minister of health planning, released *Putting Patients First*, which promised to "modernize" health care in BC. *Putting Patients First* outlined a host of planned initiatives, including Pharmacare reform, a major reorganization of health care governance, the creation of a more positive environment for health care practice, primary health care reform, and the development of a new health accord with First Nations. Elements of rationalization, preservation, and personalization are recognizable in the document, but the Liberals were careful not to raise expectations that they would take on new health care commitments.

Putting Patients First was intended to offer a ten-year blueprint, perhaps reflecting the hubris of an incoming government that swept office with a near total majority. As it turns out, the BC Liberal government under Gordon Campbell would remain in office the full ten years and more, and, in that time, its intentions and actions in the area of health policy stayed remarkably faithful to this blueprint, with one exception.

As the BC Liberals began their second term in office (with a much reduced majority government), Premier Campbell sent a very clear signal
that he wished to embark on major reforms to health care financing
and delivery. Under the rubric of "sustainability," his ideas for reform,
inspired by initiatives under way at the time in Western Europe and
New Zealand, would invite direct private-sector provision of medically necessary services (in direct contradiction of the Canada Health Act)
and greater scope for publicly administered programs and facilities to
contract out for services offered by private-sector interests. Here, for the
first time, Campbell explicitly stated a preference for rationalization
and personalization (i.e., at least those aspects appealing to greater patient choice) at the expense of preserving, never mind expanding, the
status quo in Canadian Medicare.

True to his commitment to public consultation, but also surely in deference to the contentiousness of health care politics, Campbell chose
not to embark on reform without first garnering widespread popular
support. To this end, he initiated a provincewide consultation process in
September 2006, A Conversation on Health, which took eight months
to complete (British Columbia Ministry of Health 2007). In spite of appearing to engineer the process to garner support for greater health care
marketization (e.g., controlling who was allowed to participate, asking
leading questions), participants expressed resounding support for maintaining and enhancing (i.e., preserving and expanding) the provincial
government's commitment to the principles of the Canada Health Act
(Davidson 2008; White and Nanan 2009). As a result, Campbell's government retreated from its commitment to greater marketization and instead stayed the course on the more balanced and less contentious
activities spelled out in *Putting Patients First*.

The intentions of the Campbell Liberals are one thing, but health care
is a complex field in which institutional change is difficult to achieve
(Moran 1999; Tuoy 1999). To address the legacy of the Campbell government's approach to health policy, this chapter examines four aspects
of his government's actions in health care. These aspects are funding,
governance, health and human resources development, and discretionary program delivery. Each of these areas is illustrative of the means
by which the Campbell government navigated institutional pressures
(especially the influence of health care professionals, public expectations, and relations with the federal and other provincial governments)
in order to operationalize its blueprint for health care reform.

FUNDING

Health care funding is a major and going concern for all levels of government in Canada. Even accounting for population growth and demographic aging, government spending on health care programs rose well above inflation and per capita growth in gross domestic product. During the 1970s and 1980s, hospitals and physician billings were the main drivers of health care inflationary spending. In recent years, pharmaceuticals and medical technology have become the most inflationary areas, although apparently no component of health care spending is immune.

Data on BC provincial government spending on health from 2001 to 2011 are provided in table 7.1 (appended). The figures are presented in constant per capita Canadian dollars for more meaningful analysis of trends. Corresponding national data are provided for the purposes of context and comparison. The data reveal that provincial health spending grew over the eleven years the Campbell government was in office but that this growth was relatively modest in comparison to the rest of Canada. Meanwhile, other provincial governments struggled to contain spending, and BC moved from the second highest provincial government commitment (and higher than national average spending) in 2001 to the seventh highest level of provincial spending (and virtually on par with the national level) in the final three years of this time period.

The figures tell a story of the influence of public opinion and the broad popularity of Canadian Medicare. The Campbell government took office with an injection of health spending (an additional $1 billion), even as it set about to rationalize acute care and renege on the contracts its NDP predecessors had negotiated with the Health Employees Union. In fact, the Campbell government did not impose overall fiscal austerity on its health programs and services until after it secured re-election in 2005.

A common expectation of the incoming Campbell government was that it would be ideologically predisposed to enable a greater role for the private sector in the delivery of health care. Indeed, the manner in which the BC Liberal government framed its Conversation on Health appears to confirm this predilection for marketization (Davidson 2008). The data in table 7.2 (appended), however, suggest that private spending on a per capita basis was stagnant and that its share of overall spending in BC was lower by the end of Campbell's term as premier than it was at the beginning. Apart from a jump in per capita private spending in 2006 (not coincidentally the same year the provincial government reduced its financial commitment to health care and embarked on the Conversation on Health) and again in 2008, growth in private health care spending was fairly modest over the entire time period and certainly not out of line with what was happening elsewhere in Canada. Indeed, at no time under the Campbell government was the level of private funding higher than the national per capita level.

All of this is not to say that the Campbell government did not impose measures of fiscal constraint on particular health care sectors and programs, as is discussed below. But the fiscal austerity measures taken were typically offset by reinvestments elsewhere (again, as is outlined below). The BC Liberals under Gordon Campbell were committed to a balanced budget approach and they put in place legislation to this end. Other ministries and program sectors (e.g., environment, social services, etc.) experienced declines in absolute and relative terms over the ten plus years that Campbell was premier. During this time period, health care spending went from 38 per cent of provincial government spending (not including debt servicing) in 2001 to 42 per cent in 2010, the latter figure being higher than national levels (Canadian Institute for Health Information 2011a). All of which tends to reinforce the notion that the health sector in general enjoyed a comparative degree of priority and protection under the Campbell government.

HEALTH CARE GOVERNANCE

At the time the Campbell government assumed office, BC was one of nine provinces that had introduced some form of regional health care governance as a step towards "modernizing" their respective health care systems by providing a platform to rationalize acute care and to reallocate resources according to changing population needs. In BC, the initial implementation of regional health governance under the NDP in the early 1990s was tumultuous, creating considerable tension between provincial authorities and key health professionals – especially physicians and nurses – who were prohibited from serving on health boards. A second wave of regionalization in the late 1990s changed the focus from lay participation to a greater emphasis on population health principles. While this went some way to appease health professionals and to provide more clarity of direction for health boards, it still left in place a patchwork of two-tiered local authorities (i.e., boards for districts served by larger urban centres, and councils for districts serving rural and small towns). The Campbell government promised that, if elected, it would overhaul the system of health governance implemented by the NDP. In November 2001, the Honourable Colin Hansen, minister of health services, announced that the then existing fifty-two health boards and councils would be consolidated into five regional health authorities and one provincial health services authority to oversee highly specialized care.

In the context of Canadian health care, regionalization involves the transfer of responsibility for the delivery of health services to a geographically delineated board or organization. Health care regionalization offers the potential to reduce geographical disparities in program function and service availability, enable greater integration of services by removing bureaucratic barriers to cooperation, and bring decision making closer to home to better serve local needs and preferences (Lomas 1997; Touati et al. 2007; Trottier et al. 1999). At the same time, regionalization in the Canadian context also entails a certain degree of centralization of control over health programs and facilities, as numerous local voluntary health boards and committees are consolidated into a considerably smaller number of boards overseeing entire districts or regions (Andrews and Martin 2007; Lewis and Kouri 2004; Peckham et al. 2005). This rebalancing of local and central control, while potentially a source of political tension, is seen as an important step in supporting health care reorganization to better meet the needs and preferences of health care users (Casebeer 2004; Casebeer, Scott, and Hannah 2000). In practice, however, very little decision making has been truly "devolved" from central governments to regional authorities, especially as the former retains final authority over funding and regulation. While regional health authorities set priorities for health service delivery and have some discretion to pursue their own initiatives (e.g., primary health care reform), they are ultimately accountable to the provincial government.

Some critics question the extent to which most regional boards in Canada are able to achieve more patient-focused (i.e., personalized) health care delivery, citing concerns over the recalcitrance of curative-focused models of health care and the tendency for professional interests to capture the agenda of regional boards (Davidson 2004; Moran 1999). On a more cynical note, other critics regard regional health authorities as a vehicle by which provincial governments impose unpopular decisions while deflecting criticism away from themselves (Church and Barker 1998; Church and Noseworthy 1999). These concerns notwithstanding, the consolidation of governance achieved by the Campbell government, and the fact that the BC Liberals did not tinker fundamentally with regional boundaries and responsibilities once established, enabled the redirection of resources from traditionally privileged services and sectors (e.g., acute care) to those that have been traditionally neglected or marginalized, such as public health and primary care (Lewis and Kouri 2004).

At the same time, the Campbell government does appear to have used regional governance as a way to diffuse opposition to cuts to core services. Health authorities were given specific performance targets for acute care rationalization. While this led to some discontent among some members of the public and health care profession, this exercise in rationalization did not encounter widespread opposition. No doubt the Campbell government benefitted from the fact that it was spared the more politically contentious exercise of closing hospitals, as many of its counterparts in other provinces experienced in the 1990s (Hanlon and Rosenberg 1998; Hanlon 2001; James 1999).

The Campbell government embarked on one other major change to health governance in BC. In its second term, it followed through on a promise to establish a First Nations health plan as a key part of its *Transformative Change Accord* (First Nations Leadership Council and Government of BC 2006). This was a critical step in the development of the Tripartite Health Partnership Accord involving the BC First Nations Health Council, the BC government, and the Government of Canada (First Nations Health Council, Government of Canada, and BC Ministry of Health Services 2012). The stated long-term objectives of the *First Nations Health Accord* are to eliminate the health gap between the First Nations and non-First Nations populations of BC by enhancing access to culturally sensitive health services and to equip individual First Nations to take more control over health care planning and governance. In the short term, the Campbell government charged regional health authorities with the task of integrating their service plans with those of First Nations groups. To accomplish this, an Aboriginal lead was positioned in each regional health authority, with individuals assigned in each local health area, reporting to an Aboriginal lead, and tasked with developing community-based health services and assisting in the development of Aboriginal health services plans (First Nations Health Council, Government of Canada, and Government of BC 2007). It remains to be seen if BC's regional health authorities were given adequate time and resources to enable more responsive and culturally sensitive health planning to begin to meet the lofty goals of the *First Nations Health Accord*.

HEALTH HUMAN RESOURCES

Beyond the areas of health funding and governance, there were major health human resource challenges facing the BC Liberals as they took office. In fact, the Campbell government waded straight into labour conflict immediately following its electoral victory in May 2001. The BC Liberals' first order of business was to introduce legislation that would signal an end to work stoppages and job action on the part of the Health Sciences Association (representing a wide range of health professionals such as psychologists, speech language pathologists, social workers, and others). The Health Care Services Continuation Act legislated a "cooling off period" of sixty days and forced the government and unions back to the bargaining table. Many saw this measure as evidence of the Campbell government's willingness to play hardball with health-sector unions and professional associations in order to contain health care costs. The government's relationship with health-sector unions and professional associations, however, turned out to be a little more complicated than this. While its bargaining with these particular groups of health personnel continued to be tough, the BC Liberals made generous concessions for registered nurses and physicians, who together account for the lion's share of provincial government expenditures on health human resources. In fact, in its first budget, the Campbell government committed an extra $1 billion in funding for health care, much of which was earmarked for additional health personnel in the areas of mental health and addictions programs and continuing care.

In 2001, concerns about health human resource shortages were nationwide. As the two largest groups of health professionals, physicians and nurses were singled out for attention. The BC government was particularly sensitive to the recruitment practices of its neighbours in the east (Alberta) and south (sunbelt and northwestern states in the United States). As a result, competitive wage and fee increases were a priority for the incoming Campbell government. For its part, the BC Medical Association (BCMA) was unhappy with the fee schedule under the NDP, with threats of a general strike and concerns that general practitioners (or medical doctors) would leave the province and practise elsewhere. As a means to improve the environment of practice, the Liberal government brought in fairly hefty increases in fee schedules that averaged approximately 20 per cent in revenue for physicians. Admittedly, the BCMA and Ministry of Health Services did not agree on the extent of the increase, and the matter had to be settled through arbitration. Nevertheless, in bringing about this settlement with physicians, the BC Liberal government made clear its intention to appease rather than to challenge the medical community.

Beyond the matter of funding for medical services, there remained more persistent issues with the physician workforce in need of policy attention. One issue was the balance between specialists and general practitioners. Historically, more than half of physicians worked in general practice, but the balance had steadily shifted over the 1980s and 1990s towards an even share between specialist and general medicine, and there were fears that the shift would continue in favour of specialists. In addition to being a cost driver, this situation was typically seen as a threat to primary care access and gatekeeping, which would ultimately have a negative impact on the allocation of health care resources. A second issue was the fee-for-service arrangement by which most physicians were, and continue to be, paid under provincially administered Medicare. Such a system is seen to hinder the quality of patient visits and create built-in inflationary incentives. A third problem was the geographic maldistribution of physicians. Even though the ratio of physicians to population in the province was higher than the national ratio, there remained great geographical inequalities in physician distribution, with shortages evident in rural, northern, and inner-city locations.

The Campbell government made small strides to address all three of these areas of concern. In terms of maldistribution, the Liberals treaded a fine line between mere expansion of medical seats and the need to recruit and train more students for rural and small town practice. After two decades of policy constraint on the number of medical education seats, there was growing concern about physician shortages, both for general practice and for various specialties. The number of seats in BC was capped at 250 per year, the same level it had been since the early 1980s. In 2001, the minister of health Services and the minister of advanced education announced that the provincial government was funding the expansion of the UBC Medical Program by nearly 100 per cent and that the new seats would go entirely to distributed campuses in Victoria and Prince George (Kelowna has since been added). Considerable investments in technology, capital infrastructure, and operations occurred at the distributed sites. While it remains too early to judge the success of the distributed educational model in recruiting and retaining physicians in rural and remote locations in the province, this policy has nevertheless attracted much interest and positive attention elsewhere, and did much to cement support for the Liberals in the provincial hinterland.

The BC Liberals made some progress in promoting alternate funding plans for physicians as well. The most common of these was a salary based on past billings and population data. Nearly one-quarter of all practising physicians and an equivalent share of BC government funding of physician services fall under a method other than fee for service (Canadian Institute for Health Information 2011b). These figures were less than 15 per cent in 2000–01 (Canadian Institute for Health Information 2008). Nevertheless, BC was the third lowest ranked province in terms of the share of alternative remuneration schemes in 2000, and it remained at this rank during Gordon Campbell's time as premier.

The other key focus of the Campbell government was to stabilize the nursing workforce and ensure that there were sufficient new graduates to fill vacancies as nurses retired, moved elsewhere, or else left nursing for other opportunities. The rates of wage increases that nurses enjoyed surpassed the rates of increase in medical fees, and this at a time when considerably more modest wage increases were the norm for most public servants. In addition, the Liberals greatly expanded the number of nursing education seats, again by adding rural programs in places like Prince George, Kamloops, and Kelowna. This tended to bring about some stability in the provincial nursing workforce. Under the BC Liberals, the registered nurse (RN) workforce grew in absolute terms, but this growth did not keep pace with overall population growth, let alone with the increased demands of an aging population (Canadian Institute for Health Information 2011c). On the other hand, the number and percentage of the regulated nursing workforce comprised of licensed practical nurses (LPNs) grew throughout the decade that Premier Campbell was in power (e.g., from 103 LPNs per 100,000 population in 2002 to 186 LPNs per 100,000 people in 2011). In addition, the number of nurse practitioners (NPs) in the province nearly doubled from 2006 to 2011, and new legislation was drawn to expand the scope of practice of NPs (e.g., ability to prescribe and refer patients directly to specialists). Many of these NPs are now located in rural and remote parts of the province, which has done much to stabilize and enhance primary health care in these traditionally underserviced locations.

In spite of the tough stance they took in collective bargaining with some health service personnel, at least early in their first term of office, the BC Liberals under Gordon Campbell seemed to prefer a strategy of appeasement to one of confrontation and hard bargaining. Nurses and physicians, in particular, enjoyed relatively generous salary increases at a time when other public-sector employees were offered much more modest contracts. The Campbell government also invested in expanded educational seats for both medicine and nursing, and opened distributed medical and nursing education programs geared towards primary health care and rural practice. At the same time, the budgetary constraints imposed on regional health authorities resulted in a diminishing share of regulated nurses who are trained as RNs at the expense of LPNs and, to a lesser extent, NPs. A case could be made here that the conditions set in place by the BC Liberals achieved a form of labour substitution that went largely unnoticed by most of the general public, while the new training programs and expanded roles for NPs received generally favourable attention.

DISCRETIONARY PROGRAMS

Provincial governments are solely responsible for any programs or services beyond the limited scope of medically necessary and hospital-based activities (i.e., Medicare). As a result, there is tremendous variation in things like publicly administered home care, occupational and physical therapy, and prescription costs. Without federal cost sharing, however, there is also greater discretion on the part of provincial governments to introduce reforms. These "provincial" plans and offerings, therefore, offer a window into a government's unadulterated preferences for health policy, at least with respect to relations with the federal government. This section offers an analysis of reforms in two areas of discretionary programming: pharmaceutical drug benefits and continuing care for the frail elderly and persons with disabilities. These also happen to be the two programs of greatest interest to those interested in expanding Canadian Medicare.

When the Campbell government first assumed office, the BC Pharma-Care plan was predominantly an aged-based drugs benefit plan that offered 100 per cent coverage for prescription drugs, although seniors were responsible for dispensing fees up to a combined annual total of $200. Those on social assistance also received 100 per cent coverage, including dispensing fees, while low-income non-seniors had 100 per cent coverage after an $800 deductible, and other non-seniors had 70 per cent coverage after the first $1,000 in costs incurred and up to a maximum of $2,000 per annum. This program was a costly one for the provincial government, which had incurred double-digit rates of growth through the 1990s.

The Campbell government introduced reform of BC PharmaCare in two stages (Fuller 2003). In 2002, co-payments were introduced for seniors. Low-income seniors had to pay the first ten dollars of the cost of each prescription, up to a total of two hundred dollars in total expenses per year, after which they received 100 per cent coverage. Other seniors paid the first twenty-five dollars of each prescription up to a total of $275. In 2003, the new seniors' plan was combined with the catastrophic plan under the title of the Fair PharmaCare BC Program. This program introduced a pure income-based benefit, although those born before 1940 were "grandfathered" under the older plan.

The crux of the reforms to BC PharmaCare were that the provincial government was able to lower its financial commitment to drug coverage without unduly affecting access to prescriptions (Morgan and Coombes 2006; Morgan et al. 2006). The emphasis on "fairness" enabled it to achieve cost savings to provincial coffers (thus pleasing its core voter base) without damaging its popularity with softer supporters. The government could also appear to be doing something to reform health care without taking on new responsibilities for health insurance. In fact, many touted the BC Fair PharmaCare reforms as a potential model for other provinces to follow (Morgan, Barer, and Agnew 2003).

Turning attention to the area of continuing care reveals a similarly nuanced effort to advance a rationalization agenda in spite of widespread public support in favour of expanding provincial government commitments. In the BC case, continuing care refers to a broad suite of programs and services meant to improve or maintain the health and functioning of the frail elderly and persons with disabilities, such as home support, home care, assisted living, and long-term care (Hanlon and Halseth 2005). Early in its first term, and in reference to objectives set out in *Putting Patients First*, the Campbell government introduced changes to continuing care under the rubric of "renewal" rather than rationalization. The underlying premise for reform was that too many individuals were occupying acute and residential care beds because of inadequacies of community-based services (e.g., assisted living, home support). The provincial government promised to "renew" continuing care by building new residential and assisted-living beds as well as investing in home care and home support services. They also insisted that

Table 7.1
Per capita government expenditure on health, 2000–2011 (constant 1997 CDN$)

	British Columbia	% annual increase	Canada	% annual increase	BC rank*	Ratio (BC/Canada)
2000	2,135.80		1,935.65		2	1.10
2001	2,276.80	6.60	2,025.58	4.65	2	1.12
2002	2,329.73	2.32	2,076.63	2.52	2	1.12
2003	2,361.07	1.34	2,157.07	3.87	3	1.09
2004	2,352.71	-0.35	2,238.86	3.79	3	1.05
2005	2,433.21	3.42	2,296.61	2.58	4	1.06
2006	2,412.88	-0.84	2,357.34	2.64	7	1.02
2007	2,474.71	2.56	2,420.64	2.69	6	1.02
2008	2,568.85	3.80	2,499.65	3.26	6	1.03
2009	2,568.51	-0.01	2,558.48	2.35	6	1.00
2010	2,605.14	1.43	2,613.35	2.14	7	1.00
2011	2,621.65	0.63	2,600.25	-0.50	7	1.01

* Not including the Yukon, Northwest Territories, and Nunavut.

Source: CIHI 2011a, series B.4.7

they would more than match the number of acute and residential care beds removed from the system with new resources in the community-based sector (e.g., assisted-living units, home care).

Analysis of the reforms, however, suggests that many of the reinvestments in community-based care never fully materialized (Cohen et al. 2005). At best, the Campbell government replaced a similar number of residential care beds (which receive round-the-clock supervision by registered nurses) with less resource intensive, and hence lower-cost, assisted-living units (Cohen et al. 2005; Hanlon and Halseth 2005). Without explicitly stating so, therefore, the BC Liberals managed to impose rationalizations in particular aspects of seniors' care while claiming to be expanding other areas and offering more personalized continuing care services across a broader continuum of needs.

CONCLUSION

Analysis of actions of the BC Liberal government suggests that it tempered its preference for reducing health care spending (i.e., rationalization) in deference to public demands to preserve Medicare. The Campbell government did manage to rein in, or at least maintain reasonable control of, its health spending without upsetting key en-

Table 7.2

Per capita private expenditure on health, 2000–2011 (constant 1997 CDN$)

	British Columbia	% annual increase	Canada	BC rank*	% annual increase	Ratio (BC/Canada)
2000	821.11		893.44	6		0.92
2001	848.33	3.31	945.30	7	5.81	0.90
2002	891.44	5.08	1,001.02	7	5.89	0.89
2003	916.39	2.80	1,025.65	8	2.46	0.89
2004	976.05	6.51	1,063.93	6	3.73	0.92
2005	979.95	0.40	1,091.16	7	2.56	0.90
2006	1,109.54	13.22	1,154.02	6	5.76	0.96
2007	1,073.37	-3.26	1,171.30	7	1.50	0.92
2008	1,152.64	7.39	1,204.95	5	2.87	0.96
2009	1,114.20	-3.33	1,210.97	7	0.50	0.92
2010	1,103.48	-0.96	1,238.25	10	2.25	0.89
2011	1,126.55	2.09	1,282.52	10	3.58	0.88

* Not including the Yukon, Northwest Territories, and Nunavut.
Source: CIHI 2011a, series B.2.5

trenched interests (especially health professionals and community groups). It held the line with other provinces in not taking the bait to expand its commitments to include universal home care and pharmaceutical coverage. It established health authorities to tackle potentially contentious issues such as acute hospital bed cuts that proved useful in taking the sting out of rationalization, all the while claiming its directives were useful in achieving more patient-focused health care (i.e., personalization) and necessary to preserve publicly funded health care.

In spite of an apparent predilection for market solutions to health care problems, the Campbell legacy can hardly be held up as an exemplar of privatization. The outcomes of the Conversation on Health reaffirmed that BC residents, like their counterparts elsewhere in Canada, had little appetite for ideas such as medical savings plans, user fees, and two-tiered access. As the Campbell government appears to have conceded, there was never sufficient popular support to pursue a "neoliberal" approach to health care reform under Gordon Campbell's premiership. Instead, the Campbell government's record on health reform suggests that it put "preservation" first, even if it did so reluctantly.

Whatever reform objectives the BC Liberals under Gordon Campbell would have preferred, their performance is best described as one that did much more to stabilize the infrastructure of Medicare than to dismantle it. Changes to systems of governance and accountability, health human resource management, and discretionary program eligibility kept a reasonably tight lid on health care spending. Campbell's approach to health policy was driven by a concern to avoid confrontations with powerful interests, to appease popular sentiment, and not to rock the boat on Medicare. The Campbell government carefully picked its fights with some groups (hospital employees and allied health professionals) while preferring to appease others (First Nations leaders, registered nurses, physicians). And, above all else, it was careful to frame its actions as those best poised to "modernize" and "sustain," rather than to undermine, Medicare.

8

Downsizing Equality, 2001–11
The Best Place on Earth for Whom?

GILLIAN CREESE AND VERONICA STRONG-BOAG

As has been suggested in several chapters in this volume, the financial crisis that sparked the global economic recession in 2008 has highlighted central problems with neoliberal economics. Years of state deregulation, the growing power of the stock market and the "paper" economy, the corresponding decline of the "real" economy,[1] and the weakening of effective state oversight have plunged the world into a serious and prolonged economic downturn. In British Columbia, Liberal premier Gordon Campbell prepared the way and presided over one province's particular expression of neoliberal restructuring. Greater social inequality resulted. While provincial advertising lays claim to British Columbia as the "best place on earth," we should ask: Best for whom? If, as the Liberal Party likes to proclaim, the first decade of the twenty-first century has been "golden," only a minority has reaped its rewards. In bleak contrast, most citizens have faced compromised living standards and restricted opportunities.

Although Canada is one of the most affluent societies in the world, twenty-first-century BC, where "the level of inequality ratcheted up" (Fortin et al. 2012, 123), reveals deepening disparity. Gender stands at the heart of much disadvantage. Even in good times, it interacts with cleavages of race, class, age, (dis)ability, and region to determine well-being. In the 2011 *World Economic Forum Global Gender Gap Report*, Canada ranked eighteenth on the gender gap index, a significant drop from its overall sixth place on the Human Development Index and an apt reflection of how neoliberal policies regularly disadvantage women and girls (United Nations 2011; World Economic Forum 2011).

As the global economy went into a tailspin in 2008, Gordon Campbell embraced recovery budgets that invoked a decade of priorities privileging men and the powerful. Indeed, $14 billion invested in "shovel-ready" initiatives (Hansen 2009), a vision that invokes gender differences in the paid work done by women and men, paved the promised road to economic salvation. Funded by tax-paying women and men, these ventures involved jobs (and profits) in construction, trades, and transportation (93 per cent male jobs), engineering (78 per cent male jobs), manufacturing (69 per cent male jobs), and primary industries (79 per cent male jobs) (Lahey 2009). Notably absent was equivalent funding in areas employing large numbers of women, including social services, health care, and education, or the creation of a much needed provincial child care program. Similarly invisible were commitments to strengthen and broaden social support programs already brutally pared down through neoliberal reforms that had further feminized poverty.[2] The "shovel-ready" agenda, in combination with familiar neoliberal policies of tax cuts and downsizing the public sector, was never neutral. It always disproportionately benefited men, more affluent citizens, and corporate interests, while it injured women and the more disadvantaged in general (Lahey 2009; Hunter 2009).

The stage for the promotion of inequality had been set much earlier. By the time Campbell became premier in 2001, neoliberalism had become "the defining political economic paradigm of our time" (McChesney 1999, 7). Neoliberalism refers to a series of economic and social policies that prioritize private capital accumulation, limit state involvement in the economy, pare back entitlements and services in the welfare state, and create a more flexible low-wage labour force. Though the Social Credit government of Bill Bennett first introduced neoliberal policies in 1983, and subsequent NDP administrations sometimes flirted with its doctrines (as Summerville points out in chapter 4, this volume), Campbell significantly extended the core tenets of tax reduction, market liberalization, social service cuts, and privatization of the public sector (Graham et al. 2009; Magnusson et al. 1984; McBride and McNutt 2007).

The result increased social and economic inequality. In *Where Are the Women? Gender Equity, Budgets, and Canadian Public Policy*, Janine Brodie and Isabella Bakker (2008) document the systematic elimination of gender justice from the public policy process and its critical impact in increasing inequality in the last two decades. They identify three strands of a process of "de-gendering": (1) delegitimization (feminist scholars and activists are discredited as "special interests" who do not represent "real" women); (2) dismantling (institutional structures established to monitor and advocate for women's equality are cut back or eliminated); and (3) disappearance (women cease to be an analytic category in social policy development). The combined outcome of the "3Ds'"is the intentional and systematic removal of gender equality from much of the Canadian policy landscape. Much like the ruling Conservatives under Mike Harris (1995–2002) in Ontario (Bezanson 2006), BC's Liberal Party under Campbell engaged in a process of de-gendering public policy.[3]

This chapter rejects the disembodied rhetoric of neoliberalism; instead, it directs attention to the "winners and losers" over the course of Campbell's decade in power – that is, it sheds light on who is privileged and who is injured by the political choices that were made by the Campbell government from 2001 to 2011. Neoliberal policies have generally increased inequalities among British Columbians and deepened cleavages of gender, race, class, age, (dis)ability, and region. The following discussion is organized in three parts. In the first, we outline how the Campbell government reduced government revenues and redistributed tax relief to upper-income British Columbians; in the second, we examine policies designed to create a more flexible and precarious labour force; and in the third we review how these policies have increased inequality in British Columbia.

THE AUSTERITY STATE

Gordon Campbell identified his government's primary objectives as encouraging investment, competition, entrepreneurship, a flexible labour market, and nominal state intervention (McBride and McNutt 2007, 187). A widespread restructuring of labour and social policies was required, but his first order of business was dramatically reducing provincial taxation and redistributing the tax burden away from corporations and affluent citizens to middle- and lower-working-class families. A 25 per cent cut in personal income tax instituted in 2001 was followed by a $1.5 billion tax cut in 2007 (Murray 2005; Murray 2007a). Their combined effect profited the most affluent: those earning $100,000 or more annually received an average of $864 a year, those earning between $15,000 and $20,000 received only $82, and those earning less than $15,000 received nothing (Murray 2007a). Represented as a percentage of taxable income, the regressive effect of these policies is startling: those with incomes of $150,000 got a rebate of 4.27 per cent. A $50,000 income translated into 2.55 per cent, and a $15,000 income received only a 0.37 per cent rebate (2). Alongside tax assistance for the most privileged, Campbell increased the sales tax, medical service premiums, postsecondary tuition fees, and car insurance premiums, all hitting the majority of less affluent citizens the hardest (McBride and McNutt 2007, 191).

Liberal tax favouritism deepened long-standing divides between the haves and the have-nots. Most women continue to stand close to the bottom of BC's economic pyramid. In part thanks to the Liberal government's policies, women in BC earned only 61 per cent of men's incomes in 2008, compared to 65 per cent in Ontario and 64 per cent nationally (Statistics Canada 2011).[4] Aboriginal Canadians, racialized minorities, new immigrants, the elderly, and citizens with disabilities are similarly concentrated among low-income populations disadvantaged by tax breaks. Furthermore, the concentration of wealth in Vancouver and Victoria ensures regional disparities and, ultimately, maximizes the wealth of a tiny urban elite (Lee, Murray, and Parfitt 2005).

Even as they contributed to the income gap between rich and poor that grew faster in Canada than in the United States in the 2000s (Grant 2011), the Liberal approach to fiscal management depleted government income to the tune of billions of lost tax dollars. Lost revenue, in combination with continuing reductions to federal transfer payments to the provinces (McBride and McNutt 2007), generated an "austerity state" with the perpetual spectre of state insolvency. An empty public treasury was employed to justify cutting social programs, generally scaling back entitlements in the welfare state, and shrinking the public sector, all disproportionately hitting women and other disadvantaged citizens.[5] Campbell's deliberate creation of the austerity state established a precondition for the rest of the neoliberal agenda.

FLEXIBLE LABOUR AND PRECARIOUS WORKERS

The creation of a more flexible, or a more vulnerable, labour force is a central tenet of the neoliberal agenda. During his tenure as premier, Campbell introduced legislation covering employment standards, labour relations (see Teeple, chapter 6, this volume), minimum wages, and privatization of public-sector jobs, which set out to make labour cheaper, more pliable, and more defenceless. Predictably, Premier Campbell's Liberals gave BC "the lowest employment standards in

Canada" (Fairey 2006). They allowed children as young as twelve to work for pay with only a parent's approval, reduced minimum shifts from four hours to two, repealed double-time premiums for overtime, introduced "overtime averaging" resulting in less predictable working hours, and shifted enforcement from the Employment Standards Branch to individual workers (Fairey 2006; McBride and McNutt 2007). Unionized workers were denied even these weakened protections as they were removed from Employment Standards altogether (Fairey and McCallum 2007). The inauguration of a six-dollar-an-hour "training wage" for the first five hundred hours worked was a full two dollars below the meagre provincial minimum wage of eight dollars an hour (Murray 2007b). Throughout most of Campbell's time as premier, BC, with its escalating housing costs, had the lowest minimum wage in Canada.[6] "Policy-induced" casualization helps explain why one-quarter of BC's female workforce and one-tenth of its male labourers were in casual employment in 2004, an increase from the late 1990s of 50 per cent and 25 per cent, respectively (MacPhail and Bowles 2007).[7] The proliferation of "McJobs" helped fuel the "Poverty Olympics" – that is, protests organized by social movement activists ahead of the tax-payer-funded Olympics that occurred in Vancouver and Whistler in February 2010 (Poverty Olympics 2010).

The Campbell administration also set about to undermine opposition. As Teeple shows in chapter 6 (this volume), the Labour Relations Code was revised to make it harder to unionize and included modifications such as raising the percentage of signed-up members needed for certification, mandating secret ballots for certification votes, and inserting employers' "right to communicate" (see also McBride and McNutt 2007). Settlements and back-to-work orders were imposed throughout much of the public sector, but the most dramatic intervention occurred in the health care sector. In 2002, the misleadingly named Health and Social Services Delivery Improvement Act unilaterally stripped "no-contracting-out" language from union agreements in hospitals and long-term care facilities and initiated massive contracting-out in housekeeping, laundry, security, and food services (Cohen 2004). Wages dropped by more than 40 per cent and "more than 30 years of pay equity gains for women in health support occupations" disappeared (Cohen 2004, 4). Although Canada's Supreme Court struck down much of the bill in 2007, worsened wages, job security, and public services persist (Sandborn 2007; Lee and Cohen 2005). During its first term, the Campbell government

eliminated close to twenty thousand public-sector jobs. Three-quarters
of the casualties of contracting-out and other cutbacks were women,
an especially brutal outcome of "cost-cutting" since women earned
an equity dividend in public-sector jobs – which was the product of
greater public unionization and accountability (Fuller 2005; Fuller
and Stephens 2004).

With the same aim of generating a cheaper and less assertive labour
force, the governing BC Liberal Party undermined the social safety net.
For instance, 30 per cent of the budget of the Ministry of Human Resources was cut: ministry offices were closed, staff was laid off, social
assistance benefits were reduced for most categories of recipients (including single-parent families), and modest exemptions for spousal support and earned income were eliminated (Klein and Smith 2006;
Pulkingham 2006). More restrictive criteria for social assistance included a three-week job search and a two-year independence test,
redefining single mothers as "employable" when their youngest child
turned three (instead of seven) years of age, restricting eligibility for
disability support, eliminating back-to-work benefits, cutting child-care
subsidies, and excluding full-time students (Brodsky et al. 2005). As a result, the number of social assistance recipients declined by 25 per cent,
while those who still qualified fell further below the poverty line (Wallace, Klein, and Reitsma-Street 2006). "With no rate increases between
the early 1990s and 2007, families on income assistance ... [lost] purchasing power each year" (Graham et al. 2009, 5). In the middle of
Campbell's reign an international study of support for single-parent
families on social assistance ranked BC fifteenth out of sixteen OECD
countries – only the United States was worse (Kershaw 2007).

The carefully constructed "austerity state" also justified reduced
public access to, and increased charges for, public services – from
provincial parks and ferries to medicare and homecare. Despite the
2001 election pledge to "increase child care choices for parents by encouraging the expansion of safe, affordable child care spaces" (British
Columbia Liberal Party 2001, 24), Campbell's Liberals removed $24
million from this program during their first term and eliminated
monthly subsidies for many low-income earners (Fuller and Stephens
2004). In 2004, BC had just over eighty thousand supervised child care
spaces, while Quebec, with twice the population, had four times that
number (Roy 2006). The initiation of the feeble StrongStart program
for pre-schoolers in 2007 only highlighted the Liberals' inadequate attention to child welfare. In 2017, British Columbians anxious for paid

work and better life chances for their sons and daughters still wait for a provincial child care program.

Early childhood education fared only slightly better. A commitment to (but not the realization of) full-day kindergarten, a perennial promise from Victoria, only came as Campbell resigned as premier in 2010. For older students in the K-12 system, resources for the most vulnerable were pared back significantly. Special needs youngsters joined the line-up of targeted losers in calculations that reckoned austerity ahead of well-being (Beresford and Fussell 2009; British Columbia Teachers' Federation 2007). Older learners paid a similar price. Female postsecondary students and those from low-income households took on higher debt loads (Andres and Adamuit-Trache 2008). Between 1999 and 2005, as tuition fees nearly doubled, university students became increasingly reliant on loans but found grant portions eliminated (Dehaas 2008). Many British Columbians encountered still another narrowed path to opportunity when the province's Adult Basic Education Program ended tuition-free upgrading. Combined with welfare regulations denying assistance to full-time students, this change compromised many hopes for educational upgrading. In effect, citizens were directed to minimum-wage jobs if they couldn't enter or complete postsecondary programs and, otherwise, to whatever employments they could find to subsidize education and repay student loans (Butterwick and White 2006).

While the list of other programs and services eliminated or reduced in the name of austerity touched most aspects of social life, space allows no more than brief reminders of the Liberals' determined side-stepping of the wealth-well-being link so clearly spelled out by the Canadian Medical Association's 2012 *Annual Report Card on Health Care in Canada*.[8] The desperate plight of "kids in care," and that of so many mothers and foster mothers, confirms indifference to the connection between poverty and poor outcomes (Strong-Boag 2011). The damage to women was similarly clear when Campbell eliminated the Women's Health Bureau and the Advisory Council on Women's Health and cut funding for sexual assault centres, women's centres, and shelters for victims of domestic abuse. As BC's recent Missing Women Commission of Inquiry has highlighted, however inadequately, Indigenous women bear the brunt of official disregard for violence against women, but few entirely escaped the consequences.

Calculating the Campbell government's disinvestment from equality should also include attention to strategies of promoting public ignorance. The purging of watchdogs, protection, and assistance makes the collection of relevant data increasingly difficult, and the public became more dependent on "spin doctors" and other partisan commentaries. Accessing knowledge about (and resistance to) policies was made all the harder when many community-based victim services, the Human Rights Commission, and the Ministry of Women's Equality were discontinued. Cutting legal aid, closing courthouses, and dismantling the Public Sector Employer's Council Pay Equity Policy Framework produced the same result.

EMBODIED WINNERS AND LOSERS
IN THE NEOLIBERAL POLICY AGENDA

The "face" of the poor offers powerful reminders of how real citizens have experienced neoliberalism under the Campbell administration. For years, BC has had the highest provincial rate of poverty in the country (defined as those living below Statistics Canada's low-income cut-off rate) (Collin and Jensen 2009). In 2009, for the eighth year in a row, it reported the highest level of child poverty, at 16.4 per cent, or 137,000 children (British Columbia Campaign 2000 2011).⁹ For those under age six the poverty rate was 20.2 per cent, a key influence on the escalating numbers of youngsters, nearly one-third (31 per cent) of all entering kindergarten, who are deemed to be "at risk" (BC Campaign 2000 2011, 4). By the middle of Campbell's tenure, BC was "the only province where the child poverty rate was actually higher in 2005 than in 1997 despite increases in [federal] child benefits" (BC Campaign 2000 2007).

Neoliberalism's precarious employment helps explain why three-quarters (74 per cent) of all children in poverty live in two-parent families (British Columbia Campaign 2000 2011). Children in households composed of recent immigrants (42 per cent), Aboriginal families (36 per cent), racialized minorities (33 per cent), lone-mother families (33 per cent), and those with disabilities (27 per cent) were especially disadvantaged. In Vancouver, poverty's toll typically included 50 per cent of all lone-mother households, but this became 60 per cent when such mothers were persons of colour or Aboriginal, and 70 per cent when they were recent immigrants (Vancouver Foundation 2007). Campbell's policies ensured that average government transfers to lone mothers declined by $2,300 between 2001 and 2004. As a result, "poverty among lone mothers rose an astounding 15.8 percentage points between 2000 and 2004; Vancouver was still worse at 24 percentage points" (Pulkingham 2006, 26).

Poverty differs by region, with particularly high rates on many First Nations reserves and in the Lower Mainland.[10] As the Vancouver Foundation (2007) observed, "the gap between the rich and poor [individuals] increased by 8.7% between 2001 and 2005 in Metro Vancouver."[11] By 2010, it concluded that "the richest residents earn 10 times more than the poorest and the gap is growing faster than in Toronto and Montreal" (Vancouver Foundation 2010, 15). The overall depth of disadvantage was conveyed by the fact that the average British Columbian in poverty in 2006 struggled with an annual income $7,700 below the Statistics Canada's low-income cut-off line (Klein et al. 2008). In the "austerity province," that abysmal record was directly linked to another ranking: first in Canada for millionaires per capita (ibid.).

Another development worth highlighting is that holding a full-time, full-year job offered no guarantee of economic security. In 2009, BC had the highest proportion of "working poor" families, while 48 per cent of poor children lived in households where at least one adult held a full-time full-year job (British Columbia Campaign 2000 2011). In 2005, a full-time job at ten dollars an hour (two dollars per hour more than Campbell's minimum wage of eight dollars, and four dollars an hour more than the training wage of six dollars), working for forty hours a week for fifty-two weeks, was only enough to bring a single person to the poverty line in Vancouver (ibid.). In 2007, nearly one in every six workers in BC (16 per cent), two-thirds of whom were women, earned less than ten dollars an hour (Klein et al. 2008). Full-time earnings for minimum wage (eight dollars an hour) workers amounted to only $16,640 a year, more than five thousand dollars below the Statistics Canada poverty line for someone in a large urban centre in 2007. Poverty was further exacerbated by the increased "casualization" that saw one-quarter of female and 10 per cent of male workers in temporary, short-term, and part-time jobs (MacPhail and Bowles 2007). A "living wage" based on two parents working full time all year at thirty-five hours a week requires $18.81 an hour in Metro Vancouver, $18.03 in Victoria, and $16.98 in Kelowna (British Columbia Campaign 2000 2011).

One outcome of inadequate incomes is compromised nutrition. In 2009–10, Health Canada reported that "8.4 percent of all households were food insecure" in BC, with 5.2 per cent "moderately" so and 3.2 per cent "severely" so (Health Canada 2012). The Dieticians of Canada (2012) calculated that it cost $868 a month for "a nutritious food basket" to feed a BC family of four. Including only housing and food costs, a household on income assistance falls short by

$124 every month, while a low-income family (earning eleven dollars an hour) has just $867 left over to meet all other needs. Not surprisingly, food banks became a growth industry. At the beginning of Gordon Campbell's mandate, in March 2001, 67,237 British Columbians used a food bank. In March 2010, their numbers had reached 94,359 (Food Banks of Canada 2011). In 2010, nearly half (46 per cent) of food bank recipients in BC were single, 22 per cent were single-parent families, 20 per cent were two-person families, and one-third (32 per cent) were children.

Policies of precarious and low-wage employment collided with gentrification and a sky-high real estate market to put affordable accommodation increasingly out of reach. Growing homelessness was the starkest outcome. In March 2002, the homeless count in Metro Vancouver identified 1,121 people as homeless. Four years later homelessness had increased to 2,174, increasing again to 2,660 in 2008 before levelling off at 2,650 in 2011 (Regional Steering Committee on Homelessness 2012). More than one-quarter of the homeless count (27 per cent) are Aboriginal, 20 per cent are youth, 12 per cent are over fifty-five years of age, 30 per cent are female, and 52 per cent are on income assistance. The 2011 homeless numbers included fifty-six families with children. Understandably, the Poverty Olympics named housing as a major "hurdle" in the "race" to the bottom of BC's economic pyramid (Poverty Olympics 2010).

CONCLUSION

Gordon Campbell's ultimate legacy left British Columbia more polarized between the affluent and the struggling; deepened inequalities of gender, racialization, age, (dis)ability, and region; and weakened the social solidarity upon which welfare state programs were built. As the departing developer-turned-politician confronted opinion polls naming him Canada's "most unpopular premier" in 2010 (Ward 2010), even the momentary lift of the budget-busting Winter Olympics could not obscure the many personal tragedies that unfolded during his administration. There was nothing random about such outcomes. They were predictable. Much more than merely policies to enhance private profit for global capitalism and local entrepreneurialism, neoliberalism is a political movement to curtail citizenship entitlements in the welfare state. This contest over citizenship rights underlies diverse social movements that oppose increasing globalization and corporate power, envi-

ronmental degradation, and human rights abuses, including the recent
Occupy Movement with its evocative claims to represent the interests
of the 99 per cent of citizens whose quality of life is imperiled by neoliberal policies (Klein et al. 2008; Rebick 2012). BC is likely to remain
an important political arena for these contestations over the meanings
of democracy, another outcome of Gordon Campbell's decade-long
legacy of downsizing equality.

ACKNOWLEDGMENTS

An earlier version of this chapter appeared as *Still Waiting for Justice:
Update 2009. Provincial Policies and Gender Inequality in BC*, a report prepared for the BC Federation of Labour and the Centre for Women's and
Gender Studies, 8 March 2009. We very much appreciate the support of
the BC Federation of Labour for our work. We also wish to thank the
many people who have contributed to our ongoing assessment of BC social policy, including Lesley Andres, Benita Bunjun, Shauna Butterwick,
Sylvia Fuller, Preston Guno, Paul Kershaw, Sarah Leamon, Emilia Niel-
son, Amy Parent, Jane Pulkingham, Jane Staschuk, Katherine Teight-
soonian, and Margot Young.

NOTES

1 Jim Stanford (2008) makes a useful distinction between the "real economy," which produces concrete goods and services to meet people's needs,
and the "paper" economy, which involves complex financial transactions
that do not produce any actual goods or services.
2 The feminization of poverty refers to the overrepresentation of women
and girls among those living in poverty, a trend found in Canada and
around the world.
3 "Re-gendering" is perhaps more accurate than "de-gendering" because social policies enacted by neoliberal governments are always gendered, reinforcing male advantage and female disadvantage.
4 In 2008, BC women earned an average of $29,100, while men earned
$47,600; in Ontario, the numbers were $31,600 versus $48,600; and na-
tionally they were $30,100 and $47,000 (Statistics Canada 2011, Income
Table 1: Average total income of women and men by province, 2008).
5 Of course, the Liberal government managed to find money when doing
so coincided with its priorities, such as funding for the lavish 2010 Winter Olympics.

6 The minimum wage was not raised until May 2011, when Christy Clark announced the first of three increases to bring it to $10.25 in May 2012 – see British Columbia Government News (2012).

7 MacPhail and Bowles (2007) adopt a narrow definition of casual employment that includes temporary jobs (on contract for fewer than six months) and permanent part-time employment.

8 According to the Canadian Medical Association (2012, 22), "Those earning $30,000 or less are 29 percentage points less likely than those earning $60,000 or more to describe their health as excellent or good (39% vs. 68%)."

9 After taxes the rate of child poverty is reduced to 12 per cent (or 100,000 children), still the highest in the country (see British Columbia Campaign 2000 2011).

10 Exact numbers are unknown since neither BC nor Statistics Canada properly monitors reserve communities.

11 The Vancouver Foundation's Metro Vancouver's Vital Signs 2007 is a web document with no page numbers. The quote is found in the section of the document entitled "Gap between Rich and Poor."

9

Ambition without Capacity

Environmental and Natural Resource Policy in the Campbell Era

GEORGE HOBERG

Environmental and natural resource policy has been one of the most dynamic areas of policy development during the Campbell era. This chapter provides an overview of the most significant policy changes during Campbell's tenure, focusing in particular on climate policy, land use, forest policy, and species protection. It also examines three major changes in environmental governance: the efforts to forge a new relationship with First Nations, attempts to reorganize government to more effectively integrate resource management in the province, and the downsizing of resource agencies. This overview is not intended as an evaluation of the merits of the changes but, rather, as a review of the most consequential developments.

From its inception as a province, the political economy of natural resource development has played a pivotal role in British Columbia. With the emergence of the modern environmental movement in the 1970s, conflicts over the environmental impacts of resource development, especially forestry, have played a significant role in politics and policy controversies in the province. As a tenuous coalition of labour and environmental interests, the New Democratic Party reshaped the landscape of environmental policy during its decade in power in the 1990s. Gordon Campbell's BC Liberals represented a "free enterprise" ideology, and with the strong support of the business community, were intent on rolling back what they considered to be the NDP's overregulation and unwarranted government intrusion in the marketplace. For example, their *New Era* platform called for "reducing the regulatory burden by one-third." However, the extent of deregulation was ultimately constrained by the enduring political power of the province's environmental movement and by First Nations flexing court-sanctioned power.

CLIMATE POLICY:
GORDON CAMPBELL'S POWERFUL LEGACY

The signature environmental initiative of Gordon Campbell's time as premier was climate policy, introduced in 2007 and 2008. The policy has three core components: (1) ambitious legislated greenhouse gas reduction targets (33 per cent reduction by 2020 over 2007 levels), (2) a revenue-neutral carbon tax, and (3) a carbon-neutral government supported by regulated carbon offsets. These initiatives made the province a North American leader in climate action and won Campbell praise from the environmental community. The carbon tax became a divisive political issue, especially when the NDP made "axe the tax" the centrepiece of its 2009 election campaign (for more detail on BC tax policy, see Lacharite, chapter 5, this volume). With Campbell's election to a third term as premier that year, the NDP reversed its position and the carbon tax is now widely accepted.

Campbell's dramatic climate policy initiatives reflected a marked change in position for the premier. He showed little interest in climate policy during his first term, and the Campbell government actually expressed opposition to Prime Minister Chretien's ratification of the Kyoto Protocol – the treaty requiring Canada to reduce its greenhouse gases by 6 per cent below 1990 levels by 2012. Campbell's conversion has been attributed to a combination of factors. First, there was a surge in public attention to climate change in Canada and the US in 2006, and the premier saw a political opportunity in promoting an initiative on the topic. He was impressed by California governor Arnold Schwarzenegger's policy leadership on the issue as well, and he saw an opportunity to give BC, within Canada, a reputation for being a policy innovator on an increasingly important issue. The mountain pine beetle epidemic that was ravaging the province's interior forests also gave the premier direct experience with palpable climate impacts – something rare for politicians at the time. Finally, as a person, Gordon Campbell seems to have become convinced of the gravity of the issue and the need to provide leadership. Personal influences included a visit to heavily polluted China in 2006 and the birth of his first grandchild that same year (Harrison 2012, 389). The premier-centred institutions of

Canadian governments (Ruff 2010b) empowered Campbell to act on his own personal commitments, and this was facilitated by political and environmental conditions.

The policy shift was announced in the 2007 Speech from the Throne, the rhetoric of which was very forceful:

> The science is clear. It leaves no room for procrastination. Global warming is real.
>
> We will act to stem its growth and minimize the impacts already unleashed. The more timid our response is, the harsher the consequences will be.
>
> If we fail to act aggressively and shoulder our responsibility, we know what our children can expect – shrinking glaciers and snow packs, drying lakes and streams, and changes in the ocean's chemistry.
>
> Our wildlife, plant life, and ocean life will all be hurt in ways we cannot know and dare not imagine.
>
> We do know this – what each of us does matters. What everyone does matters.
>
> Things we take for granted and that have taken millennia to evolve could be at risk and lost in the lifetimes of our children. (Government of British Columbia 2007a)

The Throne Speech committed the government to set ambitious greenhouse gas reduction targets – 33 per cent by 2020 and 80 per cent by 2050 – and to explore actions to make it carbon neutral. It did not mention the carbon tax. The legislature passed the Greenhouse Gas Reductions Targets Act later in 2007.

The carbon tax emerged from the budget process and was introduced with the 2008 budget. It imposed a tax of ten dollars per tonne of carbon dioxide produced through fuel use, an amount that was designed to increase by five dollars per year through 2012, when it would reach thirty dollars per tonne. The tax was explicitly designed to be revenue neutral; that is, as Lacharite explains (chapter 5, this volume), other taxes were reduced so that the overall, or net, tax burden in BC did not increase.

These and other policies were consolidated in the June 2008 Climate Action Plan (Government of British Columbia 2008), which also introduced the third component of the province's climate policy: carbon-neutral government. All provincial government operations in British Columbia, including universities, hospitals, and schools, were required to become carbon neutral by 2010, meaning that they had to measure their carbon emissions and offset them by purchasing carbon offsets. The government required that the carbon offset be purchased from a new Crown organization established for this purpose, the Pacific Carbon Trust, for a set price of twenty-five dollars per tonne. While the public sector is only a small share of provincial emissions, the Campbell government emphasized the importance of this policy in showing government leadership on greenhouse gas reduction. The Campbell government repeatedly claimed it was the first government in North America to be carbon neutral.

The cornerstone of Campbell's climate policy was the carbon tax, and it took centre stage in provincial politics when the NDP, under leader Carol James, chose to make "axe the tax" the centrepiece of their 2009 election campaign. This decision caused a major split in the NDP coalition, with several notable environmental leaders publicly denouncing the NDP stance and expressing support for Campbell's climate policies. While there's no reason to believe the carbon tax helped Campbell win, the major lesson climate advocates have taken from the 2009 BC Liberal victory is that a government can introduce a carbon tax and survive. After the election, the NDP reversed course and embraced the carbon tax, and the tax now has broad (if grudging) political support within the province (Harrison 2012). The Clark government conducted a carbon tax review, which endorsed maintaining the tax, and Clark's 2013 election platform committed to maintaining the carbon tax (but not increasing it for five years).

BC's climate policies have resulted in greenhouse gas reductions without negative impacts on the economy. A report by Sustainable Prosperity, an Ottawa think tank, shows that, over its first four years, greenhouse gas emissions in BC's economy declined by 10 per cent, compared to only 1 per cent in the remainder of Canada. Over the first five years, consumption of fossil fuels subject to the carbon tax in BC declined by 17.4 per cent, compared to an increase of 1.5 per cent in the rest of Canada. The one fuel that bucks the trend, jet fuel, is not covered by the tax. While these data provide strong evidence the carbon tax is having a positive environmental impact, the study also argues that there is no evidence the carbon tax has had a negative economic impact on the province. Between 2008 and 2011, BC's economy actually outperformed (by a very small margin) the rest of Canada (Elgie and McClay 2013b).

Certainly, BC is making progress in reducing greenhouse gases, but it has a long way to go to meet the challenging legal requirement to reduce emissions by 33 per cent below 2005 levels by 2020. Even the government's own modelling shows that current policies won't meet the target. In addition, even though the Clark government continues to express commitment to the legislated target, the emphasis on massive development of liquefied natural gas seems to be patently inconsistent with meeting the province's targets.

THE GREAT BEAR RAINFOREST
AND LAND USE PLANNING

Aside from climate policy, the greatest environmental achievement of the Campbell government was the Great Bear Rainforest land use decision in 2006. In 1996, when environmentalists launched an aggressive marketing campaign against logging in the central and north coasts of BC, NDP premier Glen Clark denounced them as "enemies of BC." In February 2006, Gordon Campbell shared a stage with First Nations leaders, industry CEOs, and representatives of the Sierra Club of BC, Greenpeace Canada, and ForestEthics. After announcing the terms of the new plan, Premier Campbell reached over and shook the hands of the environmental representatives on stage. The next day, the websites of Greenpeace Canada and ForestEthics both boldly proclaimed "victory in the Great Bear Rainforest."

This extraordinary turnaround resulted from two very important shifts in power in the forest sector (Smith and Stewart 2007). The first power shift came about due to environmental groups successfully adopting the strategy of pressuring large consumers of BC forest products to avoid those products that came from "endangered forests." Indeed, as evinced by the Clayoquot Sound conflict in 1993, such market campaigns empowered environmentalists by allowing them to go beyond the soft and fickle support they found in public opinion. Now, they had a form of economic power that forced industry and government to address their concerns (Pralle 2003; Shaw 2004). The second power shift came about due to the court-sanctioned assertion of the right of First Nations to be consulted and accommodated before the Crown infringed upon their rights and title. As discussed further below, this power shift forced the government to more directly involve First Nations in land use decision making.

One of the NDP government's most significant accomplishments in the 1990s was moving beyond valley-by-valley resource conflicts to integrated, collaborative land use planning and thus meeting their target of increasing protected areas in the province from 6 per cent to 12 per cent (Cashore et al. 2001). When the Campbell government swept into office in 2001, it was not keen on continuing strategic land use planning, but it was committed to completing the intensely controversial land use planning process in the north and central coast regions, which environmentalists had reframed as the "Great Bear Rainforest." Just before leaving office, the New Democrats had forged an interim agreement between First Nations, industry, and environmentalists that established a four-part framework for completing the land use plans. It included the following:

1 Protecting 20 per cent of the region and deferring logging in an additional 11 per cent while studies and consultations proceeded;
2 Committing to managing the remainder of the region according to a new paradigm of ecosystem-based management;
3 Creating an independent science team to identify additional areas to protect and to define ecosystem-based management; and
4 Committing to engage in consultation with First Nations in the region on land use plans on a "government-to-government" basis. (Howlett, Rayner, and Tollefson 2009; Shaw 2004; Price, Roburn, and MacKinnon 2009)

The Campbell government gave priority to the completion of this agreement. The multi-stakeholder consultation process was completed, with agreement, in 2004. The government then engaged in unprecedented government-to-government negotiations with First Nations in the area, which culminated in the 2006 agreement. This agreement set aside one-third of the region as protected areas, and the remaining two-thirds was to be subject to new ecosystem-based management principles.

While environmentalists declared victory, the details of the agreement showed that ecosystem-based management principles had yet to be fully developed. The best way to understand the challenge of defining ecosystem-based management in the region is to look at how it addresses conserving the spectacular coastal old-growth forests that were at the core of the conflict. The independent science team that reported in 2004 stated that 70 per cent of "natural" old growth should be retained. Environmentalists supported this objective. But when the multi-stakeholder land use planning tables were reported, they could only agree on 30 per cent old growth retention, with a vague commitment to "full implementation" of ecosystem management in the future. When Campbell announced the 2006 agreement, the government committed itself to full implementation by March 2009.

In March 2009, the government announced that it had established, and had set in law, land use objectives for retention of old-growth forests in the region. The preamble to the cabinet order said that the objective was to conserve 50 per cent of the old-growth forests across the region. But, as with many such rules, the "devil is in the detail," and a close examination of the text shows that forest companies could potentially opt out of the 50 per cent retention with easily satisfied exemptions (Hoberg 2009). These provisions left the "default" retention level at 30 per cent, well below the 70 per cent "full implementation" recommended by the independent science team and supported by environmentalists. This difference is fundamental to the political economy of environmental policy in the region. Thirty per cent is only modestly above the status quo under the Forest Range and Practices Act, and it does not reflect the paradigm shift implied by the concept of ecosystem-based management. Seventy per cent is more consistent with that paradigm shift, but it is apparently inconsistent with the ability of industrial forest operations to turn a profit in the region. Whether or not environmentalists can justifiably claim victory in the Great Bear Rainforest conflict hinges on the outcome of how ecosystem-based management is defined. They did not get there by the end of the Campbell government. The agreement was finalized in January 2016, a full ten years after the initial land use order (Government of British Columbia 2016).

While the Great Bear Rainforest agreement was a major accomplishment for the Campbell government, in late 2006 the government quietly made a major change in land use planning. The document entitled *A New Direction for Strategic Land Use Planning in BC* indicated that the era of comprehensive land use planning would be brought to a close. All ongoing strategic plans were to be concluded by March 2010. Any new planning would be undertaken only under a specific set of conditions, including: new legislative directives, accommodating First Nations interests, and/or a major environmental change. Despite the havoc wrought on the forest land base by the mountain pine beetle epidemic, the government has not yet reopened any of the existing land use plans. The innovative collaborative planning model introduced by the New Democrats in the 1990s would also be abandoned. The planning that did occur would be led by the government, and, where appropriate, it would engage First Nations on a government-to-government basis. Other stakeholders would advise the process, but the consensus-oriented multistakeholder roundtables would no longer be used (Integrated Land Management Bureau 2006).

By 2008, land use plans had been completed for 86 per cent of the province. The new protected areas in the Great Bear Rainforest, along with other areas of the province, increased the amount of protected areas in BC to 14 per cent of the land area. The plans completed during the Campbell era increased protected forest land by one-third (Ministry of Forests, Lands, and Natural Resource Operations 2010, 208).

FOREST POLICY:
REGULATORY RELIEF WITHOUT
UNDULY REDUCING ENVIRONMENTAL PROTECTION

Forest policy reform was a major part of the Campbell government's first term as the party came into power with a twelve-point plan for a "New Era of Sustainable Forestry" oriented towards reducing the regulatory burden and creating a more competitive industry (British Columbia Liberal Party 2001). The centrepiece of the reforms was the Forest Revitalization Plan, unveiled in 2003, during what Campbell called the "year of forestry." The plan was designed to increase the role of market forces in industry decision making, both because this was more consistent with the ideology of the Campbell government and because it would help address concerns raised by the United States in the long-running softwood lumber dispute. The plan created a new system of market-based pricing for stumpage by taking back 20 per cent of the harvesting rights of major forest companies and reallocating part of the allowable cut to competitive timber sales. The plan also removed a number of regulations that constrained market transactions. It eliminated the obligation of tenure holders to maintain manufacturing facilities and made it easier for companies to exchange tenures. This economic deregulation unleashed a wave of corporate consolidations that reshaped the sector (Hoberg 2010).

The forest policy change with the greatest environmental implication was the introduction of a so-called "results-based" framework for forest policy regulation. The 1994 Forest Practices Code was a signature initiative of the New Democratic Party, but the forest industry considered it unduly burdensome and costly. The BC Liberals' 2001 platform explicitly called for "streamlining the Forest Practices Code to establish a workable, results-based Code, with tough penalties for non-compliance." The Campbell government enacted the Forest Range and Practices Act (FRPA) in 2002, and then brought it into force with a series of regulations in 2004.

FRPA simplified the planning process by eliminating the requirement for submission and approval of site-level plans. The original proposal was for the government to specify "result-based standards" that would reorient regulation away from process-oriented planning requirements to measurable objectives designed to address environmental values like protection of fish and wildlife habitat. However, the government was unable to develop results-based standards for most values and, instead, established vague and unmeasurable objectives in regulation (Hoberg and Malkinson 2013). For example, the objective for river and stream protection in Section 8 of the *Forest Planning and Practices Regulation* (Government of British Columbia 2004) states: "The objective set by government for water, fish, wildlife and biodiversity within riparian areas is, without unduly reducing the supply of timber from British Columbia's forests, to conserve, at the landscape level, the water quality, fish habitat, wildlife habitat and biodiversity associated with those riparian areas."

Instead of specifying results-based regulations, FRPA left it up to forest companies to propose "results and strategies" to meet the vague government objectives in their forest stewardship plans. If they preferred, forest companies could use government-specified "default rules," which were the old, much maligned rules embodied in the NDP's Forest Practices Code. In fact, when the first round of plans was approved, the overwhelming majority of them simply relied on the default standards of the Forest Practices Code (Hoberg, Malkinson, and Kozack 2016). By eliminating approval requirement for site-level plans, FRPA has reduced the planning burden on industry and produced cost-savings by increasing operational flexibility. But because, for the most part, the "old code" standards remained in place, it has not resulted in as significant a reduction in the protection of environmental values. The changes to forest practices produced neither the extent of relief that industry hoped for nor the extent of rollbacks that environmentalists feared.

While the Campbell government achieved several of its platform commitments by reforming the Forest Practices Code and implementing the Forest Revitalization Plan, it failed spectacularly on another major forest policy commitment. The number one priority in its 2001 "New Era" forestry agenda was the establishment of a "working forest" to promote commercial investment in forestry by increasing the certainty of a working forest zone. This commitment was seen as the free-market party's compensation for the NDP's successful commitment to

double protected areas during its decade in power. After struggling for
several years to design a proposal that would free up more land for industrial forest use without undermining environmental commitments
or jeopardizing already strained relations with First Nations, the proposal was quietly dropped before the 2005 election (Hoberg 2010).
Struggling for policy initiatives to address the mountain pine beetle
epidemic, the idea was reborn as the Commercial Forestry Reserve as a
result of the Working Forestry Roundtable in 2009. But, since being re-
juvenated, it has gone nowhere.

By ensuring that the clause "without unduly reducing the supply of
timber from British Columbia's forests" was contained in each government objective in the *Forest Planning and Practices Regulation*, the Campbell government clearly demarcated how far the province was willing
to go to protect environmental values. At the same time, respect for the
political power of environmental interests, both at home and internationally, constrained how far the Campbell government could go in reducing the regulatory protection of environmental values. It seems that
the unspoken rule for reform was: "provide regulatory relief without
unduly reducing environmental values."

Despite concentrated efforts to improve the competitiveness of the
forest sector, employment took a beating during Campbell's tenure.
Forest-sector employment decreased 40 per cent, from 88,000 jobs
in 2001 to 53,000 jobs in 2011 (see figure 9.1). The change has been
wrenching for forest-dependent communities throughout the province.

SPECIES AT RISK: LIMITED PROGRESS?

Environmentalists have criticized the BC government for having no
endangered species legislation. For example, a Wilderness Committee
report profiles the fact that "BC and Alberta are the only provinces in
Canada with no endangered species legislation" (Wilderness Committee 2012). The Campbell government's muted response to this enduring
criticism was to create a Species at Risk Task Force in 2009 to consider,
among other things, the adequacy of the province's regulatory framework for protecting endangered species. The task force report was published in January 2011, and it contained an elliptical recommendation
with respect to legislation: "establish a government legislative writing
team to prepare legislation to consolidate the acts, regulations, and policies that are related to the conservation of species and ecosystems"
(British Columbia Task Force on Species at Risk 2011, 21).

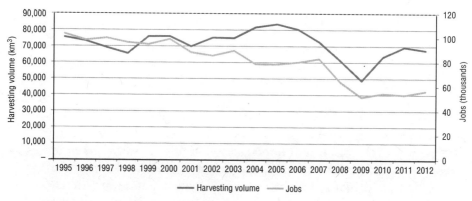

Figure 9.1   BC forest harvesting and jobs

Source: BC Ministry of Business, Industry, and Trade,
http://www.bcstats.gov.bc.ca/StatisticsbySubject/BusinessIndustry/BusinessCountsEmploymentBy
Industry.aspx

While BC does not have a stand-alone species at risk act, it does have the legislative authority to protect species and their habitats through the Wildlife Act and the Forest Range and Practices Act. The problem is that while these acts provide enabling authority, they don't force the government to act when species are in peril. In addition, in some cases they are designed to be carefully limited in their economic impact. For example, wildlife protection under FRPA is not permitted to exceed a 1 per cent impact on the timber supply. As a result, the record of implementation of species protection, and broader biodiversity measures, in BC is poor. A recent report by the auditor general provides an overview of BC's progress and notes some significant shortcomings: "Despite the BC government's decades-long objective to conserve biodiversity, and commitments made on the national and international stage, the biological diversity of our province is in decline. This audit found that government is not doing enough to address this loss of biodiversity" (Auditor General 2013, 1).

FIRST NATIONS RELATIONS: FROM CONFLICT TO ACCOMMODATION

Climate policy was not Gordon Campbell's only about-face. The magnitude of change in Campbell's approach to dealing with First Nations was comparable (for more insight into this matter, see Belanger, chapter 4, this volume). Gordon Campbell entered government as an opponent of Aboriginal rights. When the Campbell government was elected, the premier and two of his senior ministers were part of a lawsuit challenging the constitutionality of the only modern-day treaty, the Nisga'a Final Agreement. They dropped the suit when they became government. In 2002, Campbell pushed through a treaty referendum that antagonized First Nations throughout the province. In 2005, however, he changed course completely and forged a "new relationship" with First Nations that promised shared decision making on resource projects. He became a champion of reconciliation. While the effort to provide a legislative foundation for the new relationship ultimately failed, there was real progress in power sharing through specific reconciliation agreements between the BC government and First Nations along BC's coast (Forsyth, Hoberg, and Bird 2013).

There were two major (and related) reasons for this turnaround, in addition to whatever personal change of heart Gordon Campbell might have had. First, court cases were increasingly critical of BC's approach to addressing (or failing to address) First Nations concerns during decisions concerning resource development. The most important case in this regard involved the Haida and the transfer of a tree farm licence from one forest company to another. The Haida claimed they were not adequately consulted. The BC Court of Appeal agreed and, in a 2002 decision, denounced the BC government's position in very strong terms. When the Supreme Court ratified both the substance and the tone of that decision in its famous 2004 ruling, the Campbell government was forced to accept that the modest tokenism it had offered First Nations up to that point was not going to satisfy the courts. Second, the persistent uncertainty about who owned the land was a serious risk to investor confidence. Once the Campbell government realized the courts were not supportive of its position, a business logic emerged to transform its approach.

The new approach to reconciliation was not reflected in success at the treaty table. Despite Campbell's 2005 conversion to being a champion of Aboriginal reconciliation, during his ten years in office, only one treaty had been finalized (with the Tsawwassen First Nation). The real progress came in the form of specific non-treaty agreements with First Nations, the most path-breaking of which are with coastal First Nations. The Haida have actually achieved a form of joint jurisdiction over Haida Gwaii – an arrangement unprecedented in BC history. A joint management board, consisting of an equal number of Haida and Crown government representatives, is responsible for resource management decisions (Forsyth,

Hoberg, and Bird 2013). Much work clearly remains to be done on reconciliation, but the change in the government's approach to dealing with
First Nations that occurred in the second half of Campbell's mandate is
one of his most important legacies.

ORGANIZATIONAL TURMOIL

The organization of environment and natural resource agencies during
the Campbell years was quite fluid. Campbell twice flirted with creating a "super-agency" that would have combined functions within
one large ministry, but both times the challenge proved too daunting
and the result was a significant amount of organizational turmoil and
confusion. The first stage occurred in 2001 with the first set of cabinet
assignments. The Ministry of Environment was awkwardly renamed
the Ministry of Water, Land, and Air Protection, and many of its functions and staff were shifted over to the newly created Ministry of Sustainable Resource Management. The Ministry of Forests also lost some
of its staff and authority to the new ministry. The purpose of the new
ministry was to facilitate the integration of environment with multiple resource industries. What the sector quickly learned, however, was
that the Ministry of Water, Land, and Air and the Ministry of Forests
retained sufficient authority over approvals to frustrate integration. As
a result, the reorganization ended up increasing transaction costs, not
reducing them. When Campbell was re-elected in 2005, the new
agency was dismantled and its function redistributed back to the Ministry of Forests and the Ministry of Environment – renamed yet again.

The Campbell government tried a more ambitious reorganization in
the fall of 2010. This time, the new super-agency was called the Ministry
of Natural Resource Operations. The philosophy behind the reorganization was "one land base, one land manager," and its purpose was to
promote integrated resource management of a land base for which multiple users were increasingly competing for resource development
rights (Ministry of Forests, Lands, and Natural Resource Operations
2011, 6–7). But the approach it took to doing this was awkward: the reorganization separated the policy and operational functions of five ministries and consolidated operations into the new Ministry of Natural
Resource Operations. The extent of organizational change caused a significant amount of confusion for many units and public servants.

The rationale for consolidating functions in one ministry seemed
strong, and it had two main drivers. The first driver was the dramatic re-

duction in budget. Resources agencies needed to find ways to deliver their mandates with substantially fewer resources, and consolidating some functions, like resource permit approvals for different resources in the same regional office, would enable them to do that. The second driver was the fact that, with increased pressure on the land base (most critically the rapid expansion of the natural gas sector in the northeast of the province), there was a great need to bring the chimerical goal of integrated resource management closer to reality.

However, the rationale for separating policy and operations was neither clear nor well-articulated (Hoberg and Taylor 2010). Why would the government, so intent on creating strong integrated land management, choose to maintain resource-specific policy-focused ministries? Understanding this requires delving into the politics of cabinet formation in just such a resource-dependent economy. The major resource sectors were concerned about the loss of direct access to cabinet ministers should forests, energy, and mines all consolidate under one minister. So a decision was made to keep ministries and ministers with those resources in their names, but to limit their role to policy and to consolidate all operational functions into one agency. This triumph of politics over administrative logic, while commonplace in any governance structure, contributed to the confusion and instability of the new organization of natural resource agencies.

Probably no other function experienced as much instability and confusion as land use planning, arguably one of the most important natural resource management functions. When the New Democrats began comprehensive land management planning in the early 1990s, they integrated decision making into a special cabinet agency, the Land Use Coordinating Office (Cashore et al. 2001). Land use planning was, sensibly, housed within Campbell's first mega-agency, Sustainable Resource Management. But after barely four years, that organization was dismantled and the new Integrated Land Management Bureau (ILMB) was created in 2005 and housed within the Ministry of Agriculture and Lands. In 2009, ILMB was moved over to the Ministry of Forests and Range. When the 2010 reorganization came, land use planning got caught in the ill-considered efforts to separate policy and operations. ILMB, as such, disappeared, its remnants scattered to a variety of agencies, including the new Ministry of Regional Economic and Skills Development. It was very difficult to see how that move improved the coordination of natural resource management in the province.

When Christy Clark took control in 2011, some of the biggest tensions were reduced by reuniting forests with natural resource opera-

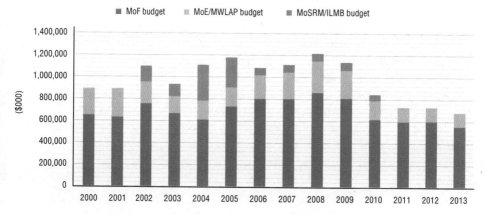

Figure 9.2   Resource ministry budget estimates, constant 2012 dollars

Source: Bank of Canada Inflation Calculator.

tions in the new Ministry of Forests and Natural Resource Operations. But the idea of creating an organization to house the variety of values and resources involved in natural resource management under one umbrella organization remained unrealized. Environment still had a separate ministry, as did energy and mines. After the 2013 election, Clark actually magnified the multiplicity of resource agencies once again by creating the new Ministry of Natural Gas Development, outside of energy and mines.

DOWNSIZING NATURAL RESOURCE AGENCIES

Despite the palpable increase in demands on resource agencies for approvals and integrated resource management, the "free enterprise" element of the Campbell government was concerned with reducing the government's role in the resource sector, and it has certainly succeeded in terms of the decreased capacity of provincial resource agencies. The budget of all the major resource agencies in 2011 was 40 per cent below the 2008 peak, and 18 per cent below the last NDP budget in 2000 (constant 2012 dollars; see figure 9.2).

An analysis conducted by a group of ex–senior public servants shows disturbing trends in human and financial capacity for resource management. There has been a significant decline in the number of government staff responsible for resource management: in 2010, there were 27 per cent fewer staff working in renewable resource ministries than there were in 2002 (Archibald et al. 2012) – after 2010, the government stopped reporting agency breakdowns for full-time equivalents, making it impossible to monitor the trend going forward. According to the group's analysis, the total budget for renewable resource ministries has "been lower since 2003 than it was at any time in the 13 years prior to that" (8). The declines in budgets and staff have occurred despite a greater increased burden on resource management agencies and dramatically increased spending by the rest of the BC government. Archibald et al. concluded that "decreased funding is jeopardizing key functions both inside and outside of government" (12).

CONCLUSION

For a business-oriented government swept into power with promises of restoring business confidence, Gordon Campbell's environmental legacy is complex and somewhat surprising. His transformation of the province into an innovative champion of climate policy is certainly his most powerful contribution to environmental policy. Whether or not it endures the LNG boom promised by his successor is far less certain. The fiscal changes – carbon pricing – are likely to be more durable than the challenging legislative greenhouse gas reduction targets. The Great Bear Rainforest agreement is widely acknowledged to be both an environmental advancement and an exemplar of collaborative governance.

Climate policy and the Great Bear Rainforest are clear examples of environmental policy advancement. Forestry regulations were targeted for regulatory relief. The Forest Revitalization Plan succeeded in removing the hand of government from many economic transactions in the forest sector. The Campbell government was intent on reducing the extent to which forestry regulations were used as a tool for economic and regional policy, although it embraced forest policy as a tool to accommodate First Nations. Campbell also attempted a major reform of environmental rules in the forest sector that resulted in a simplified planning process but that did not accomplish the degree of regulatory relief that the industry had hoped for – or the degree of regulatory retrenchment that environmentalists had feared. Environmentalists used their new-found powers in the marketplace to constrain efforts at environmental deregulation.

Campbell's most significant legacy in governance may be found in his efforts at reconciliation with First Nations. When court decisions rejected his government's early defiant approach to Aboriginal rights, he reversed course and pursued reconciliation through sharing with First Nations government decision making over resource management. His government took two cracks at reorganizing resource agencies to improve integrated resource management. The first attempt was a demonstrable failure and was quickly reversed. The second has been partially reversed by the Clark government and is struggling to cope with increasing demands and declining resources. The defunding of resource management agencies poses major risks to responsible environmental and resource management in the province. In the end, Gordon Campbell's environmental legacy is a mixture of remarkable policy advancement, constrained regulatory reform, and dramatically reduced government capacity for sustainable resource management.

10

Privatizing Electricity in British Columbia

Incremental Steps

MARJORIE GRIFFIN COHEN

The privatization of electricity generation in BC did not involve the massive sell-off of public assets, as was typical of the Margaret Thatcher–type privatization of electricity in the United Kingdom and Australia (Beder 2003; Spoehr 2003). This would not have been popular in BC because people appreciated the advantages of its public utility, BC Hydro. Unlike the UK, where electricity prices were extraordinarily high and the fuel source very dirty, BC had one of the best electricity systems in the world. It was clean because it was almost totally hydro-based; it was inexpensive, and this contributed to industrial development in the province; and it was consistently one of the most efficient and reliable public utilities on the continent. Despite the advantages of this public-sector system, the election of Gordon Campbell's Liberal government in 2001 radically changed the way electricity was treated in the province. This occurred through a deliberate and incremental program of electricity privatization.

Breaking up BC Hydro had long been promoted by the private sector and its champions (e.g., the Fraser Institute). The first step in this direction was taken through the actions of a Social Credit government in the late 1980s, when BC Gas was hived off from BC Hydro. At the same time as BC Gas was privatized, the government directed BC Hydro to begin acquiring energy from private power producers. While this was small initially, and continued in a minor way throughout the NDP governments of the 1990s, it provided a springboard for the private sector to demand a larger role in electricity generation in the province.

The justification for privatizing electricity production changed over time and shifted from initial arguments promising greater efficiency and lower costs to consumers to later justifications that primarily centred on stressing both the benefits to the province of increasing private power exports (as a result of market changes in the US) and the way that private power would be "clean power" and, therefore, better for the environment.

In this chapter, I analyze the government's policy directions regarding electricity privatization, the consequences this has had for the cost of electricity in BC, and the environmental implications of increasing private power generation. My main point is that the various directives of Gordon Campbell's government (that have been upheld by his successor Christy Clark) successfully undermined the advantages that BC Hydro, as a Crown corporation, was able to provide to the province. As a result of the privatization initiatives, the very high cost of acquiring private power has weakened the financial health of BC Hydro, while, at the same time, the increased generation of power in private hands through the various types of so-called "clean energy" projects has led to increased environmental degradation. The changes in the regime of acquiring power has led to enormous increases in costs for BC Hydro – costs that invariably will be passed on to the consumer.

JUSTIFICATIONS FOR PRIVATIZATION IN BC

In Canada, electricity generation, distribution, and transmission has developed through large-scale monopolies that have been overwhelmingly supplied by public-sector entities.[1] This occurred mainly because large electric utilities were a natural monopoly, and the capital costs involved in providing large amounts of electricity were much bigger than private corporations wanted to risk. In BC over the last fifty years an extensive infrastructure, consisting of reservoirs, generating stations, transmission lines, and local distribution and service systems, was built in the public sector by BC Hydro to provide electricity to serve most businesses and residences in the province. This infrastructure did not come easily or without enormous costs. Creating large reservoirs and transmission systems required a great deal of money and, just as significantly, caused damage to wildlife habitat, local communities, and the way of life of many Aboriginal peoples.[2] But however problematic the construction of these systems, once in place they provided a secure

and reliable supply of inexpensive and clean energy that was paid for by
the people of the province.

The restructuring of electricity systems in both Europe and North
America was a major feature of neoliberal governmental policy
changes, and the very successful nature of BC Hydro made it a target for
private-sector attention. Serious debates about a greater role for the
private sector began in BC in the mid-1990s, with the most radical proposals for change coming from the Fraser Institute and its supporters.
The Fraser Institute advocated outright privatization of the utility
through dismantling its various major functions and selling them to
private companies. The purpose of this privatization approach, according to the Fraser Institute, was to reduce the government's debt by
$12.2 billion and to "enhance efficiency, effectiveness, client relations,
and cost control" (Howe and Klassen 1996). The Fraser Institute's argument hinged on the assumption that large-scale hydro-electric projects would no longer be wanted or needed and that this, in turn, would
pave the way for smaller-scale electricity generation through privately
owned natural gas plants. To accomplish privatization, the Fraser Institute recommended breaking up BC Hydro into a variety of different
companies, including three separate private companies for electricity
generation on the Peace, Columbia, and other smaller hydro systems.
These companies would sell power to a pool and be transmitted by a
common regulated private monopoly. Four regional distribution companies that would also be regulated private monopolies would undertake distribution. BC Hydro would retain ownership and management
of the large reservoirs on the Peace and Columbia systems and, after
full privatization, would retain only these reservoir assets and about
one hundred employees.

Other voices advocating a shift towards private power production
had a powerful political impact in that they were more incremental
and, therefore, more palatable for governments that did not want to be
seen to privatize a BC "Crown jewel" through an outright sale of assets.
Foremost among these was Marc Jaccard, who had been appointed by
the NDP government under Mike Harcourt to chair the BC Utilities
Commission (BCUC). The government asked Jaccard to chair the Task
Force on Electricity Market Reform, but, since this task force failed to
achieve its mandate of coming to a consensus, Jaccard issued his own
report, which he characterized as representing "the middle ground" between the participants of the task force (Jaccard 1998). Jaccard's report
focused on increasing competition in generation, stating that, in order

to facilitate this process, the government would permit private electricity producers to have access to BC Hydro's transmission and distribution systems. Jaccard argued that the economic fundamentals of the electricity market had changed and that vertically integrated monopolies were no longer in the public interest:

> Today, competition in generation is widely recognized as offering several benefits from both a consumer and societal perspective. The benefits for consumers include greater choice, customer responsiveness, lower prices and less risk. The broader social benefits include the economic development and job creation resulting from lower prices and greater returns to publically owned assets, and the potential for regionally dispersed resource development as environmental and social considerations are combined with market reform. (Jaccard 1998, i)

Under the task force's terms of reference, Jaccard was not able to deal with issues related to the outright selling of BC Hydro's assets. However, he did feel that it was still possible to achieve competitive prices (rather than the cost-of-production-related pricing under which BC Hydro operated) by allowing industrial customers to buy directly from private power producers. He also advocated separating BC Hydro's transmission function from its generation and distribution functions (to facilitate private access to transmission) and establishing a grid oversight committee to ensure the grid's independence from BC Hydro's interests. The major intent of his recommendations was to institute private competition in electricity generation and to ensure that private power companies would have direct access to customers.

The enormous problems that were encountered in California due to its botched attempts at electricity deregulation, and particularly the ability of a private power trader, Enron, to "game" the system, made the NDP government wary of implementing many of Jaccard's recommendations.[3] Nevertheless, the pressures from the US to adopt a competitive market-oriented system to allow BC to retain its ability to export electricity, in addition to the demands by private power producers that they have access to both the US and domestic markets, led to enormous changes when Gordon Campbell was elected in 2001.[4]

The arguments that privatization would be more efficient and less costly shifted as the privatization initiatives began. The shift occurred as it became clear through restructuring and deregulation exercises elsewhere, especially in California and Alberta, that the competitive market model greatly increased prices for customers and too often also resulted in an insecure supply of power. As the Campbell government rolled out its energy plans, the justifications changed and the reference to lower prices was abandoned; instead, arguments for relying on increased private generation of power for becoming "self-sufficient" in electricity and for providing "clean" power became more prominent.

In each of the Campbell government's major energy initiatives it became clear that the sale of public assets would not be necessary to undermine the dominant role of the public-sector utility in the provision of electricity (along with the benefits that would derive from it). The path to privatization was more carefully crafted and proceeded incrementally. Ultimately, however, it was extraordinarily successful in changing the nature of the electricity sector in BC.

CAMPBELL GOVERNMENT'S INSTRUMENTS OF PRIVATIZATION

Gordon Campbell's government promoted privatization through three main directives that were designed to greatly increase the proportion of private power produced in BC. The first major document was *Energy for Our Future: A Plan for BC*, which came out in November 2002. This document outlines the policy directions that were to be undertaken by the whole energy sector. Its electricity designs are largely based on the recommendations of Marc Jaccard and were reviewed by a task force on energy that had issued its report in March 2002. The introduction by Minister of Energy and Mines Richard Neufeld stresses four "cornerstone objectives" that would guide the government's energy policy: (1) low electricity prices and public ownership of BC Hydro; (2) a secure, reliable supply of energy; (3) more private-sector opportunities; and (4) environmental responsibility with a guarantee of no nuclear generation in BC (Government of British Columbia 2002).

Despite the reassuring tone of these objectives, there were serious contradictions between them and the specific policy initiatives. One of the most glaring of these was the pledge that BC Hydro would remain within the public sector. While this was literally true, other aspects of the policy greatly reduced the scope of BC Hydro's activities and expanded the scale of private-sector activity, the most significant being the limits that were put on BC Hydro's ability to generate electricity. Rather than allowing BC Hydro to pursue new generation projects in expanding areas of "green" energy outside that produced by the major dams (e.g., run-of-river hydro, wind, tidal, and biomass), BC Hydro's new generation was restricted to only what could be achieved from upgrades to existing generating facilities. The door was also left open to permit BC Hydro to develop Site C on the Peace River.[5] BC Hydro would need to buy all other increases in electricity needs from private power producers.

Three other actions were instrumental in promoting private power. One was separating transmission from BC Hydro and making it into a separate company – the BC Transmission Corporation. In essence, this involved adopting a version of US market rules to allow private energy access to the transmission system and to encourage exports. The plan specifically stated: "BC will need to adopt evolving market rules in the United States, if we want to continue earning export revenues that contribute to our low power rates" (Government of British Columbia 2002, 6). The government gave the impression that this was essential in order to continue exporting. I argue elsewhere (Cohen 2003) that the BC government's notion that markets needed to be identical in order to export was faulty and that the North American Free Trade Agreement did not make "reciprocity" a condition of trade. Even within the US there was considerable opposition to these new market rules, and many states simply did not adopt them. But, in this case, it served the interest of the government, which was to further privatization. Ultimately, making transmission into a separate company was extremely inefficient and expensive, so the company was eventually reabsorbed by BC Hydro. The second initiative to boost private power concerns the calculated need for large amounts of energy in the future. As was seen in later directives, this exaggeration of energy demands had serious consequences for BC Hydro's finances. But, at this point, restricting the activities of BC Hydro and excluding the use of power under the Columbia River Treaty had the effect of greatly encouraging rapid development of private power generation within the province. The third major boost to private power producers involved allowing them to sell directly to customers in the US and to large industrial customers in Canada rather than relying on selling directly to BC Hydro.

Another major contradiction in *Energy for Our Future* is its stated environmental objectives and the specifics for future electricity generation. Because the province was hoping to expand all types of energy production and it specifically wanted to encourage coal mining, it promoted electricity derived from coal through private power generation.

Coal had not been used to generate electricity through BC Hydro, so this would clearly be a regressive step, and one that was rescinded in the 2007 BC *Energy Plan: A Vision for Clean Energy Leadership* document (Cohen and Calvert 2012). At the same time, BC Hydro's generation was clearly not considered green, while many private types of generation were, even though they caused considerable environmental damage.[6]

Aside from privatization initiatives associated with the generation of electricity, *Energy for Our Future* directed BC Hydro to outsource (or privatize) the delivery of services when cost savings could be found. This resulted in contracting out its major administrative and financial functions to Accenture, a private firm. The operations contracted out included all of BC Hydro's billing activities, IT services, human resources, purchasing, building services, customer service, and other finance activities (Gurstein and Murray 2007).

The privatization initiatives of the Campbell government were strongly supported by potential private power producers, including large industrial corporations that hoped to get into the business, but others were worried by the likelihood of a rapid increase in prices for electricity. While the NDP was in power a BC Hydro rate freeze was in effect, one that was rescinded after the Liberals' election victory in 2001. The spectre of rising costs for ratepayers was very real. All new electricity from new facilities cost more than the electricity that was generated from public assets that had been paid off over time. With virtually all this new electricity to come from the private sector, BC Hydro would not be acquiring new assets that could mitigate the costs over time. Furthermore, it was highly likely that the new smaller private power producers would be less efficient because they would lack the economies of scale that BC Hydro had, so the unit cost of electricity was likely to soar. To cope with the expected negative impact of privatization on customers the government instituted a "Heritage Contract," which ensured that the low rates associated with BC Hydro assets would be maintained for at least ten years. By the time the ten years was up, BC Hydro had incurred problems because of the huge increased costs of buying private power. At the same time, the Heritage Contract was extended in perpetuity, primarily for the benefit of industrial customers (Calvert 2007, 31). The results, which necessitated the blending of the new costs with the "heritage" costs, meant much more costly power and a political nightmare for Gordon Campbell's successor Christy Clark – a nightmare that, in fact, remains unresolved.

Energy for Our Future was a policy document that initiated a radical change in BC's electricity system. But it was a change that involved little in the way of public debate or discussion. Establishing the British Columbia Transmission Commission (BCTC) and the Heritage Contract were the only legislative initiatives that were subject to debate. The other privatization initiatives were directives to BC Hydro that did not undergo a review through the BCUT and had no other venue for evaluating the assumptions of the benefits of privatization or its costs.

THE 2007 BC ENERGY PLAN: A VISION FOR CLEAN ENERGY LEADERSHIP

The justification for privatization shifted between 2002 and 2007, with "self-sufficiency" and concern for the environment and climate change being prominent in the messages associated with the need for additional changes in the electricity sector. Also mentioned was the need to deal with the higher prices that accompanied electricity market changes. At the same time, ramping up electricity generation through private sources was presented as important for BC clean exports to the US. Gordon Campbell, in a preface to the BC *Energy Plan: A Vision for Clean Energy Leadership*, explained that the plan

> sets out a strategy for reducing our greenhouse gas emissions and commits to unprecedented investments in alternative technology ... We are looking at how we can use clean alternative energy sources, including bioenergy, geothermal, fuel cells, water-powered electricity, solar and wind to meet our province's energy needs. The combination of renewable alternative energy sources and conservation will allow us to pursue our potential to become a net exporter of clean, renewable energy to our Pacific neighbours. (Government of British Columbia 2007b, 1)

The biggest boon to the private sector was the requirement that BC be self-sufficient in electricity by 2016 and that, by 2026, an additional three thousand GWH of "insurance" be acquired.[7] While this undoubtedly sounded reasonable to the general public (who probably thought BC was self-sufficient in electricity), the government's definition of self-sufficiency was very specific and out of character with the operations of a hydro-based system. Hydro systems with large storage dams are very efficient, but the amount of water behind the dams fluctuates quite a bit between wet and dry years. Over the course of any year, but especially in dry years, the utility would buy power on the open market when it was relatively inexpensive – something BC Hydro regularly did in its purchase of power from Alberta when it was cheap. But the directive in the energy plan would require BC Hydro to buy enough power so that, even in rare extremely dry years, it would not need to buy power from outside the province. The requirement that there even be a large additional amount for "insurance" meant that BC Hydro would need to very rapidly ramp up its acquisition of private power. This was because, in the earlier 2002 directive, it had been mandated mainly to buy private power rather than to generate it itself.

Since both the directive for "self-sufficiency" and the directive for "insurance" were clearly unnecessary as security of supply measures, they appear designed solely to support the private generation of electricity in the hopes that the huge excess supply this would provide could be exported to the US as "green" energy.[8] BCTC was also directed to ensure that there was sufficient transmission capacity to support any new private power projects.

One other significant measure that would contribute to the rapid increase of private power was the instruction to BC Hydro to accept any small hydro project through a "standing offer" program at prices based on the most recent BC Hydro call for power. Any project less than ten MW (later fifteen MW) would have to be accepted, as would any excess power produced through a net metering program (Government of British Columbia 2007b, 10).[9]

The BC Energy Plan: A Vision for Clean Energy Leadership was carefully crafted to use "clean" initiatives as its major selling point and as the main justification for the rapid increase in expensive and inefficient private power. The power that was being acquired through "run-of-river" hydro and wind projects was not "firm" power. That is, it was not constant and, therefore, could only be relied on at specific times – mainly in spring runoff (when it was not needed) in the case of run-of-river power, and only when the wind was blowing. This meant that BC Hydro was buying extremely expensive power from private sources within the province when it could have been buying much more cheaply outside the province.

Several other measures in the BC Energy Plan were designed to emphasize its clean nature. One was the requirement for zero greenhouse gas emissions from coal-fired electricity generation. The tremendous opposition to coal-fired electricity generation that was attempted through the initiatives announced in 2002 was undoubtedly behind the government's reversal on coal. By requiring zero greenhouse gas emissions from coal generation, the province was effectively shutting down the possibility of any being developed since no known technology that was remotely affordable could provide this. Other directives had clean objectives as well. These included the requirement that 50 per cent of BC Hydro's new energy needs come from conservation, that there be zero greenhouse emissions from existing thermal generation plants by 2016, and that the use of BC Hydro's main thermal plant, Burrard Thermal, be discontinued by 2014.

2010 CLEAN ENERGY ACT

The press release that accompanied the BC government's Bill 17 – the Clean Energy Act – stressed three primary objectives: (1) ensuring electricity self-sufficiency at low rates, (2) harnessing BC's clean power potential to create jobs in every region, and (3) strengthening environmental stewardship and reducing greenhouse gases (Ministry of Energy, Mines, and Petroleum Resources 2010). The major effect of the act was to rapidly increase the demands on BC Hydro to acquire private power. This occurred due to various aspects of the act, but one significant change concerned the acceleration of the extra "insurance" of three thousand GWH of electricity above the "self-sufficient" requirement that now needed to be met by 2020 rather than 2026, as had been indicated in the 2007 energy plan (Government of British Columbia 2010). Meeting this requirement would mean that BC Hydro would need to buy more private power since it was limited in the amount that it could generate itself. But also, since the "insurance" would probably never be used for the domestic market, this would potentially provide considerable surplus power for export.

Major changes also occurred in the oversight that BCUC would have over new electricity projects in BC. In particular, some very expensive projects that were to be undertaken to support private power producers were not to undergo review by the BCUC, as would normally have happened whenever BC Hydro undertook a new project. BCUC's normal role was to undertake a public review of BC Hydro's proposal to ensure that the costs were reasonable and that the project was in the public interest. Through this review, various sectors in BC (including industrial, labour, and other members of civil society) would be able to examine and comment on the proposal. Under the Clean Energy Act 2010 the projects exempted from BCUC oversight included the 287 kV Northwest Transmission Line and most acquisitions of private power (such as those acquired through pulp and paper companies), calls for electricity from clean or renewable resources, a bio-energy acquisition call, the standing offer program, and the feed-in tariff program. It also exempted from review the extraordinarily expensive and unpopular Smart Meter Program, the equally divisive Site C dam, and new generating facilities through BC Hydro at the Mica and Revelstoke dams. The other major exclusion was any oversight over exports of electricity. These were all very expensive for BC Hydro, and therefore the ratepayer, yet they would not undergo review either for their efficiency or for their necessity.

Another major feature of the Clean Energy Act was the reintegration of the BCTC into BC Hydro. As many critics had anticipated, the functional separation of the transmission system into a separate company was both expensive and inefficient. People within the organizations knew that the operations between transmission and generation were so integral that a great deal of duplication of effort would need to occur when BCTC was separated from BC Hydro. Interestingly, bringing BCTC back into BC Hydro was not explained by referring to the earlier government analysis, which held that these two entities would need to be separated in order to meet US requirements. These supposed "requirements" from the Federal Energy Regulatory Commission in the US were hotly contested by various jurisdictions in that country, and, ultimately, the common market design that they were attempting to achieve did not occur. It was clear that the Campbell government was much too hasty in bowing to what it perceived to be US demands for the restructuring of the electricity sector in BC. Nonetheless, major changes in market structures that had been put in motion because it was assumed that they were essential to BC's being able to continue to export to the US continued long after it was clear that this was not the case.

CONSEQUENCES OF THE PRIVATIZATION INITIATIVES

The major consequences of the Campbell government's electricity policies were a massive increase in the damming of rivers by private power corporations, an increased use of gas in electricity generation, and a dramatic increase in costs for BC Hydro (due to the requirement that its new electricity supplies come from the private sector).

The environmental damage wrought by the run-of-river hydro projects initially became apparent to the public through one project close to Vancouver. This was the Ledcor development of the Ashlu Creek in the Squamish-Lillooet Regional District (SLRD) (Calvert 2007, 165–80). Environmentalists, whitewater kayakers, labour and community groups, and, especially, the SLRD itself objected to the damage to the river system. Since the SLRD had some say in what would be happening in its district, the Campbell government passed legislation to override the ability of any local government to object to any power development within its boundaries (Government of British Columbia 2003). Throughout the province local groups tried to prevent their river systems from being developed for electricity generation. However, because of the very lax environmental review, which treated each project on a river system as independent, the impact of many projects on one river system was not examined. In almost all cases the projects passed the environmental reviews. Sometimes these projects were massive, such as those on the Toba River system, and the resulting degradation of the river systems, especially for fish habitat, were severe (Forest Practices Board 2011). In labelling the energy from the private exploitation of the river systems "clean energy," the Campbell government stressed that these projects produced no greenhouse gas emissions. This was certainly true; however, Campbell did not point out that they produced other forms of environmental damage.

Ultimately, the government's desire to export massive amounts of electricity at high prices by generating it from the province's rivers was not realized. Partially, this was because the US fixed its own problems, which had erupted in the initial phases of electricity deregulation, but it was also because California recognized that run-of-river generation was very hard on the environment. Given this, it would appear that the calculations of the Campbell government were both inaccurate and costly.

While initially the environmental issue was the most prominent problem associated with private electricity generation, late in Campbell's premiership, costs also became a very visible and public problem. Even by 2010 the very high cost of the power that BC Hydro was forced to buy became a political nightmare. In November 2010, BC Hydro asked the BCUC for a rate increase of 55 per cent to go into effect between 2011 and 2015 (BCUC 2010). While, in the month Gordon Camp-

bell stepped down, this was revised downward to 32 per cent for three
years and, later in 2011, to 15.8 per cent, BC Hydro's cost problems were
serious and were not going away. Public opposition to dramatic rate increases was considerable, and a review of BC Hydro was undertaken to
examine the reasons for them (Government of British Columbia 2011).
As John Calvert and I have pointed out, the review did not identify government policies on privatization as a major cost driver since the mandate did not include this, but it did include recommendations to
eliminate the "self-sufficient" requirement, one of the major drivers of
the proliferation of private power producers (Cohen and Calvert 2012).
This, in itself, appears to indicate that the government recognized that
its earlier directives had resulted in power that was both unnecessary
and too expensive.

   According to the BC Hydro Revenue Requirement Applications, private power acquisitions account for 20 per cent of its supply. The annual
cost of this power has increased from about $300 million in 2003 to an
estimated $1.1 billion in 2014.[10] While most of this acquisition is
through long-term power contracts with a large long-term financial
commitment, the auditor general of BC, John Doyle, was very concerned
about the lack of transparency in these contracts, and he was especially concerned that they were did not appear directly shown in the corporation's books but, rather, were hidden in "deferred" accounts
(Auditor General 2011).

CONCLUSION

The magnitude of change in the electricity system instituted under
Gordon Campbell was not initially apparent, nor were the cost impacts immediately felt. This was primarily because the costs of restructuring were delayed. Fundamentally changing a public system
that was one of the healthiest on the continent and that contributed
significantly to the government's revenue was not easy to do. People
had great confidence in BC Hydro, not only in its ability to deliver secure power but also in its ability to do so at low prices. By using various arguments at different times, the Campbell government was able
to circumvent the popularity of the Crown corporation to promote
the development of privately supplied electricity. But most significantly, little public debate was allowed on the major initiatives that
began the privatization process, and over time even the scrutiny of the
regulator, BCUC, was removed.

The private power projects came into effect gradually, but once they were built and began delivering power to BC Hydro, they had a huge effect on the costs of acquiring power. To be sure, building any new generation facilities would have made the cost of new power much more expensive than that derived from the "heritage" assets. However, if this were to be undertaken through the public utility, the public would own the assets and, as happened with BC Hydro's assets over time, the costs would be reduced and, ultimately, the assets would be owned outright. Rather than the resources within BC being owned by the people for the benefit of the province, they have been turned over to private power corporations, most of which are not BC-based.[11]

Although the review of BC Hydro undertaken in 2011 did delay for customers the impact of the huge cost increases – at least beyond the period of the 2013 election – ultimately, the large costs of acquiring private power will need to be confronted. By that time, the origins of the problem will be too detached from Gordon Campbell to be blamed on him; rather, BC Hydro will undoubtedly be presented as inefficient and as unable to control prices. This was the basic message of the 2011 review, and it was something that was designed to serve the Liberal government well into the future.

APPENDIX: ABBREVIATIONS AND UNITS

Volt	Measures the pressure under which electricity flows. Transmission and distribution lines are measured in volts. BC Hydro's high-voltage transmission system has 18,286 kilometres of lines, from 60 kV to 500 kV. The 500 kV lines are the bulk transmission from the interior to the lower mainland.	
kV	kilovolt	1,000 volts
watt	Measures the power at which energy is generated. The capacity of generating stations is measured in watts. The largest generating station in the BC Hydro system is the Shrum at 2,730,000 kW. BC Hydro has a total of installed generating capacity of over 11,000 MW.	
kW	kilowatt	1,000 watts
MW	megawatt	1,000,000 watts
GW	gigawatt	1,000,000,000 or 1,000,000 kilowatts
TW	terawatts	1,000,000,000,000 watts

NOTES

1 Electricity generation was always in the private sector in Alberta, although it was highly regulated until 1996. Nova Scotia completely privatized its public utility, Nova Scotia Power Corporation, in 1992. Other than these instances of provincial private electricity, all of the major provincial electricity utilities are in the public sector.

2 As I argue elsewhere, the terrible environmental damage that was done in the name of utilities in the public domain cannot be ignored, and planning for clean energy in the future should be the focus of all energy planning. See Cohen (2006).

3 Power traders like Enron took advantage of the deregulated market in California to make enormous profits. A report by California's electricity grid managers concluded that 98 per cent of the trading bids between May and November of 2000 were driven up by non-competitive behaviour. According to one attorney involved in the class-action suit against the traders (including BC's Power Ex): "The whole trading thing is just a front that lets them game the market. They can get away with it because no one (outside the industry) can figure out what they are doing" (Liedtke 2001).

4 For a discussion of the pressures from the US, see Cohen (2002a), Cohen (2002b), and Cohen (2003).

5 That this would occur, or occur under the auspices of BC Hydro, was certainly not clear, and the possibility that this would be done by the private sector was left open. Developing Site C was highly controversial and would require the approval of the provincial cabinet before it would go ahead.

6 For a discussion of environmental concerns associated with electricity restructuring, see Cohen (2006).

7 This is a huge amount of power, equivalent to about 65 per cent of what would be expected from Site C, the proposed dam on the Peace River. For a list of abbreviations for voltage and wattage, see appendix.

8 For a critique of this strategy, see Sheaffer (2007).

9 The net metering program was for customers with small generating capability who sometimes produced excess power that would be sold to BC Hydro.

10 This has been calculated from BC Hydro Revenue Requirement Applications 2004–05 to 2012–14. For a graph of this, see Cohen and Calvert (2012, 22).

11 Examples of some of the largest projects that are under the auspices of
     owners outside the province or country are Ashlu Creek Investments,
     Rio Tinto Alcan, Roba Montrose, Domtar, Innergex Renewables. For a
     list of current IPPs, see "Independent Power Producers Currently Supply-
     ing to BC Hydro," http://www.bchydro.com/content/dam/BCHydro/
     customer-portal/documents/corporate/independent-power-producers-
     calls-for-power/independent-power-producers/independent-power-
     producers-currently-supplying-power-to-bc-hydro.pdf.

Local Government Legislative Reform in British Columbia

The Gordon Campbell Decade, 2001–11

PATRICK J. SMITH

In an early first-term review of Gordon Campbell's legacy on local governing legislative reform in British Columbia, Smith and Stewart (2007) conclude that the best descriptor of Campbell's early approach to this issue is "one oar in the water" – a lot of activity that produced very little by way of actual progress with regard to having much impact on local democracy, participation, and accountability. Still, it is fair to say that Gordon Campbell and his governments of 2001–05, 2005–09, and 2009–11 did undertake a good deal of legislative activity related to local governing: a new community charter, a major restructuring of the Vancouver city-region transportation authority, a significant projects streamlining act, completion of a third rapid transit line (the Richmond Airport–Vancouver Canada Line), work to get a fourth (Evergreen) line under way, a local government elections task force, and other transportation undertakings such as the twinning/bridging of the Trans-Canada Highway, expansion of the Sea-to-Sky Highway link between Vancouver and Whistler, and other activities.

But where are we now after the Campbell decade? In strangely similar local governing legislative topography it would seem. This says something about lessons from the Campbell decade in BC regarding municipal reform. This chapter offers reflections on the Gordon Campbell "municipal" legacy – a decade of legislative activity, but one in which any major reform of BC's local and regional governments and democracy is still largely pending.

When compared with the NDP administrations of the 1990s, Gordon Campbell's Liberal administrations were essentially consistent, with an average of around 20 per cent of all provincial legislative actions annually affecting local governing – some centrally, others more peripherally. What follows is an examination of each of Premier Gordon Campbell's three terms in office.

GORDON CAMPBELL'S FIRST TERM, 2001–05: THE NEW ERA DOCUMENT, THE COMMUNITY CHARTER, AND OTHER LEGISLATIVE REFORMS

In the BC Liberal Party's New Era Document (NED) for the 2001 BC general election, one of the campaign commitments was that, during the "first ninety days" in government, action would be taken to create new municipal legislation – a community charter would be completed. However, despite an overwhelming victory (77 of 79 legislative seats), at the end of those first ninety days, instead of new legislation, British Columbians got process, or more correctly the promise of process. To manage the numerous local reactions and objections to initial local governing legislative ideas, Campbell appointed an eleven-member community charter council made up of current and past municipal/regional officials and provincial appointees. Four members were selected by the Union of British Columbia Municipalities (UCBCM), four members-at-large were selected by the provincial cabinet on the recommendation of the UCBM, and the provincial government appointed three members to represent provincial interests. This "council" reported to a new minister of state for the community charter, Ted Nebbeling, former mayor of Whistler, BC. The community charter minister of state's task was to consult and develop draft legislation; in October 2001, the Charter Council published *The Community Charter: A Discussion Paper*. Much preliminary work on its key ideas had already been completed during the 1990s, while the Campbell Liberals waited their turn to govern BC. Some were ideas Campbell had then posed to the Federation of Canadian Municipalities.

Initially, public input into the Charter Council was limited to a small number of municipal officials and representatives from the UBCM, but after considerable criticism – media and otherwise – the process was broadened to include input from elected officials from various parts of the province (K. Vance, UBCM staff member, interview with author, 25 July 2002). In May 2002, a year after the general election, the Ministry of Community, Aboriginal, and Women's Services (MCAWS – which had "replaced" the Ministry of Municipal Affairs) released *The Community Charter: A New Legislative Framework for Local Government*. According to Minister of State Nebbeling, the new legislation had several goals. It would:

replace a provincial tradition of rigid rules and paternalism with flexibility and co-operation ...

encourage municipalities to be more self-reliant ...

present simple, concise legislation that balances broad municipal abilities with public accountability. And

ensure protection of province-wide interests in key areas like the economy, environment and public health. (Ministry of Community, Aboriginal, and Women's Services 2002, 3)

Structurally and functionally, little changed under the Community Charter (Smith and Stewart 2009), but the legislation did bring about a number of financial and jurisdictional reforms – all aimed at freeing the hands of local government – a process that began with the NDP in its new Local Government Act of the late 1990s.

BC's Community Charter did iterate a number of values in support of this goal:

"Natural person" powers. Under legislation prior to the Community Charter BC municipalities were corporate entities, meaning that their powers were subject to some limitations on the making of agreements and providing assistance. "Natural person" powers do away with itemized corporate powers and increase the corporate capacity of the municipality in relation to already delegated powers.
Service powers. Under the Charter, municipal councils may now provide any service they consider necessary and bylaws are no longer required to establish or abolish services.
Agreements. In terms of public-private partnerships, municipalities gain a simplified authority to grant an exclusive or limited franchise for transportation, water, or energy systems, and the requirement of provincial approval for agreements between a municipality and a public authority in another province is eliminated.
Additional revenue sources. The Community Charter "puts forward for discussion," but does not yet commit the province to, a number

of potential municipal revenue sources outside of property taxes, including: fuel tax, resort tax, local entertainment tax, parking stall tax, hotel room revenue tax, and road tolls – in the case of Greater Vancouver's transportation authority, some of these tax powers had already been transferred; though provincial oversight continued. (Government of British Columbia 2003b)

In addition, the Community Charter went to some lengths to clarify local-provincial relations by recognizing municipalities as "an order to government" and promising the following:

Consultation. The provincial government committed to consult with the UBCM before changing local government enactments or reducing revenue transfers.
No forced amalgamations. Amalgamations between two or more municipalities will not occur unless electors within the affected communities approve the merger.
Reduction of provincial approvals. Under the Community Charter the number of routine provincial government approvals will be reduced. As well, the Community Charter allows the province to reduce approvals further over time through regulations. (Government of British Columbia 2003b)

These commitments indicated that the Campbell Liberals wished to increase administrative flexibility and, as much as possible, free local authorities from time-consuming provincial interference – a move underscored by the shift from corporate to "natural person" powers, reduced provincial oversight, and promises of consultation and increased revenue-generating capacity. Thus, this initial Liberal round of municipal legislative reform in British Columbia can be seen as an attempt to increase efficiency through decentralization based on limited financial and jurisdictional tinkering and no major structural or functional reforms (Smith and Stewart 2009).

However, despite this policy promise, BC local governments appeared wary of such assurances. For example, after the 2001 provincial general election, local BC school boards were dealt with in ways entirely opposite to the sentiments expressed in the Community Charter. Not long after being elected, the Campbell Liberals imposed a three-year provincewide teachers' pay settlement, then announced that local school boards would be responsible for the pay increases for years two and three without any additional compensation; this occurred despite the Campbell government's earlier electoral promise not to cut education funding. As a result of this de facto cut, most school boards had to lay off teachers and close schools. Even when some of the funding was later restored, local school boards were left significantly disadvantaged and having to deal with the political fallout from local cuts. Similarly, restructured health boards (now just six for BC) found that many decisions on costs and closures were left to them, after health budgets were limited, despite the provincial government's promise that there would be "no cuts to health-care funding." Again, the rubber-meets-the-road work of provincial cutbacks fell on "local" authorities. While not an entirely unusual event, this continuing practice spoke to, and about, the early Gordon Campbell local governing legacy.

In terms of improving local accountability, the Liberals argued that they were shifting responsibility for monitoring local councils from provincial ministries to local communities: "The Charter is founded on a principle that municipalities are accountable to the public, not the province. Therefore, the ... Charter does not call for reporting to the province but rather to citizens" (Ministry of Community, Aboriginal, and Women's Services 2002, 14). The Liberals appeared to recognize that municipal policy decisions should/would more likely reflect the will of the local community only if local accountability was improved. However, by adding only an "annual reporting" requirement and very minor changes on conflict of interest to the legislation, the Liberals ran the early risk of freeing the hands of under-accountable local governmental bodies. The BC Community Charter legislation was given royal assent on 29 May 2003. It came into effect on 1 January 2004.

When asked about the possibility of including substantive accountability (e.g., electoral) reforms in what was initially termed the Phase 1 version of the Community Charter, officials at MCAWS, the Ministry of State for the Community Charter, and the Community Charter Council conceded that such democratic reforms were problematic and "would have to wait at least until 2004–2005" – *and past the next municipal electoral cycle* window. MCAWS officials and BC politicians concluded that, after several years of "reforms" during the first term, no new initiatives were planned prior to the 2005 BC general election (BC government interviews, February, March, and August 2004; Campbell 2001; Bill 14, Community Charter Act, proclaimed 29 May 2003 and in effect from 1 January 2004; Bill 14, the Community Charter, "Principles of the Provincial-Municipal Relationship," pt. 1, sec. 2). In fact, as subsequent BC provincial government thinking attested, no such reforms on accountability occurred before the 17 May 2005 provincial general election, leaving such initiatives as key second-term challenges.

After much delay to its Community Charter legislative reform package, the BC Liberal government had intended to meet just once more with the UBCM at its annual conference in Whistler, BC, in September 2002. The government then planned to introduce its Community Charter bill to the BC legislature in autumn 2002 for approval. However, the more UBCM members considered the draft charter, the more concerns they expressed. For example, they found that, while the Community Charter promised no provincial "downloading" to municipalities without consultation and equivalent fiscal compensation, no such consideration was made when the province simply "off-loaded" a responsibility or service. "Off-loading," they discovered, occurred when the senior provincial authority simply abandoned a service – often leaving local citizens pressuring their local municipalities to restore it. Without provincial dollars, this meant that municipalities often had to buy their community hospitals (as Kimberley did after provincial cuts forced its closure) or hold a referendum (as Delta did in the November 2002 municipal election to get voter approval for a local tax increase to fund its hospital emergency ward on a twenty-four-hour basis).

The mid-first-term concerns raised by local governments meant another delay – until spring 2003 – and a new timetable for Community Charter legislative reform. That decision, and the time and energy devoted to the related "transitionals" and "consequentials" act (Bill 76), pushed back any planned Phase 2 Community Charter regional district reforms until well after the already announced May 2005 provincial general election (G. Paget, executive director, Governance and Structure Division, BC Ministry of Community, Aboriginal, and Women's Services, interview, 13 February 2004). It also meant that serious local accountability reforms (Phase 3) were not even anticipated going into a second mandate (2005–09) for the BC Liberals (B. Walisser, Local Government Section, Ministry for Community, Aboriginal, and Women's Services, discussion, 2002, 2003, and 2004). The reality was that only so much legislative time could be devoted to local governing reform matters. The key legacy test for the Campbell Liberals was whether accountability was a sufficient priority not only to be on the government's 2001–05 agenda but also, if necessary, to be carried through as unfinished business to its second term. With Phase 2 and Phase 3 reforms of the Community Charter falling off the provincial government's to-do list, it appeared

likely to be a long incubation before real regional district and local governmental accountability reforms returned to active policy consideration in British Columbia. There were a number of assessments of why
Gordon Campbell's initial local reform energy waned as his second term
got under way.

For example, (1) for a "policy wonk" the premier was sometimes criticized for "flitting" from one area to another; (2) the policy window
available from pre-2001 commitments on local government reform was
closed by other, newer priorities – most importantly the focus shifted to
being prepared for the 2010 Winter Olympics; and (3) as Cobb and
Elder (1971) remind us, the range of issues that can be considered by
any polity is restricted. Campbell's second-term agenda was quickly fill-
ing up with alternative agenda items. Campbell's agenda did include a
commitment to undertake a review of *provincial* electoral matters – a
process centred on a citizens' assembly and proposals to initiate a referendum on electoral reform across the province. Those recommendations
– for a single transferable vote (STV) voting system – even if successful,
would not have brought provincewide electoral reform prior to the 2009
general election. In the end, despite 57 per cent plus support, it failed to
meet a self-imposed provincial "super-majority" 60 per cent requirement.

Like previous NDP governments throughout the 1990s, the Liberals
were certainly aware that if they were bringing local efficiency through
decentralization they also needed to empower local citizens with the
appropriate tools to help them hold local officials responsible for their
actions. Although Community Charter provisions for annual reports
and revised conflict of interest legislation were a start down this road,
these efficiency measures could be effective only if barriers to electoral
participation were lowered, local elector organizations were helped to
mature, local elections finance rules were dramatically reformed, and
council seats were distributed more fairly. Such reform ideas were clearly raised but only resonated with the City of Vancouver; the city undertook a commission study (Berger Report) and held a referendum
during the November 2005 civic election.

BC's biggest local democratic problem has been that the larger the
municipality, the lower the voter turnout. Municipalities under ten
thousand residents generally had more than 50 per cent electoral
turnout. Most of the biggest of the province's local governments fell
between 20 and 30 per cent. Some, like Vancouver, with well-established
local political parties, managed a little above 30 per cent turnout (Stewart 2003).

Thus, the local government reform picture at the end of the first Campbell mandate had gone from promising to uncertain. The Community Charter (Bill 14), in place since 1 January 2004, set out its purpose in clear language, which was most evident in its purposes:

> The purposes of this Act are to provide municipalities and their councils with
> (a) a legal framework for the powers, duties and functions that are necessary to fulfill their purposes,
> (b) the authority and discretion to address existing and future community needs, and
> (c) the flexibility to determine the public interest of their communities and to respond to the different needs and changing circumstances of their communities.

The principles of the act sound close to the views of advocates for more local autonomy. They reflected a stated desire to clarify both municipal and provincial components of the provincial-municipal relationship in British Columbia and, potentially, to add to local autonomy, with municipalities recognized as a democratically elected, autonomous, and accountable "Order of Government," exercising adequate powers and discretion and with adequate financing. Meanwhile, beyond the province's acknowledgment of local jurisdiction, it promised more cooperative approaches.

However, this legislative language was not always reflected in provincial actions. For example, despite talk of limiting interference by senior provincial authority, should local governments (under BC's Community Charter) decide to raise local taxes, rather than opt for user fees or introduce other tax measures (particularly those affecting local business), the province reserved the right to impose limits on property tax rates, in direct contradiction of the Community Charter's expressed intent to empower local autonomy. And, under a redefined provincial-municipal relationship, the Community Charter reminded local governments that, apart from acknowledging and respecting each other's jurisdictions, the legislative intent was, and continues to be, "[working] towards harmonization of provincial and municipal enactments, policies, and programs." This may work in many instances, but not where a local government wishes to take a divergent policy tack. Here, the intergovernmental game becomes more perilous for local authorities.

This was the case before Gordon Campbell, and it remained the case during his second and third terms in government.

The earlier 1980s Social Credit government's dismissal of school boards and its "over-a-weekend" elimination by Order-in-Council of the Greater Vancouver Regional District's authority over the region's watershed (when it tried to block provincial implementation of a natural gas pipeline through that watershed to Vancouver Island) serve as historical reminders of such senior provincial powers (Smith and Oberlander 1998). The more recent (Campbell Liberal) provincial overturning of a local governmental (Delta) bylaw to limit the negative impacts of large greenhouses on air quality by requiring them to use cleaner-burning natural gas or propane as opposed to wood waste is another arresting example (see Penner 2003). In this case, the Municipality of Delta passed a bylaw to provide some local controls of large (e.g., in this case eighteen-acre) greenhouse operations and, in particular, their use of less-clean fuel sources for heating. The BC government intervened when a grower challenged the bylaw, citing right-to-farm legislation over the right of a municipality to legislate on local businesses. The province also argued that the local bylaw contradicted the provincial Waste Management Act, which exempts agricultural operations. Urban-rural issues of this sort are not new to Delta. In the late 1980s and 1990s, Delta held the longest land-use dispute hearing in Canadian history over efforts to develop farmland for urban use. The debates over the so-called Spetifore (and South) lands near the Tsawwassen ferry terminal initially led to Bill Bennett's Social Credit government abolishing regional planning in 1983 when the GVRD initially prevented the development plans of a Delta Social Credit supporter (Magnusson et al. 1984).

Subsequently, a Campbell minister of agriculture/fisheries precluded use of local bylaws to prevent/regulate coastal fish farms in BC as well as the use of similar provincial powers (right-to-farm legislation) to prevent local coastal municipalities from using their bylaw powers to limit possible negative environmental impacts from fish farms (on such fish farms issues, see, for example, Anderson 2004). And the provincial "return" of fines to those same fish farm operators continued to serve as reminders that constitutional authority did matter when significant policy differences arose between local and provincial players. In the summer of 2004, the provincial Ministry of Transportation's decision to determine the route/cost/public-private partnership provider for the West Vancouver segment of the Sea-to-Sky 2010 Olympic Highway upgrade – after listening to, then ignoring, local protests including legal action against the province by the municipality – reiterated this point. This senior pressure continued throughout 2004–05 and intensified during the 2005–09 build-up to the 2010 Olympics. Consider, for example, the West Vancouver dispute with the province regarding the Sea-to-Sky Highway. In this, the municipality indicated that it was extremely disappointed with the province's decision.

One of the best indicators of the first-term Campbell Liberals' shift away from establishing local accountability markers was demonstrated in changes to the Community Charter's counter-petition provisions: under the Local Government Act, there was a 5 per cent threshold for local voters to force a referendum on bylaws. Under the Community Charter, local councils were made less accountable as opposition now required 10 per cent of the local electorate. Robert Bish (2002) summarizes this well:

> In effect, a 5% turnout of all voters is likely to mean 10% to 15% of actual voters, and a 10% ... is likely to mean 20% to 30% of all voters in the last election. What the increased requirement does is limit the likelihood of a successful petition to only those decisions opposed by very well organized interest groups, not just a ... group of citizens ... I believe local governments would be more accountable if referenda were required for major capital projects ... In summary, upping the counter-petition requirements for decisions that should be considered in a referendum is a move away from, not toward, accountability to citizens. Anyone concerned with the visibility of local governments and low voter turnout at municipal elections should be strongly in favour of increasing the visibility and interest in local government created by referenda, not trying to suppress them.

And beyond provisions on counter-petitions, perhaps the most stunning legislative statement, eroding the Community Charter promise, was BC's Bill 75 – the Significant Projects Streamlining Act. Introduced and passed in just three weeks in November 2003, the act allowed the provincial government to override any local governmental opposition to any project deemed by the province to be of significant provincial interest. Then minister of state for deregulation, and subsequently for transportation, Kevin Falcon noted that the intent of the act was to "cut red tape," to "remove unnecessary and costly delays," and to "create new

economic activities." The significant projects legislative initiative produced an official and highly critical response from the UBCM, with over
half of its member municipalities passing motions condemning Bill
75. According to a UBCM press release:

> the UBCM Executive is shocked by the degree of intrusion of this
> legislation into local affairs. It allows *any* Minister ... to replace *any*
> local government bylaw, plan, regulation, policy, etc. to facilitate
> the approval or development of a "provincially significant project."
> Cabinet can make that determination without *any prior* notice to
> the local government or the community. The *Community Charter* ...
> promised us recognition as an independent, accountable and re-
> sponsible order of government ... The *Community Charter* touted
> public accountability and openness but Bill 75 replaces local, pub-
> licly developed plans (including those developed through public
> hearing processes) with fiats from the provincial Minister. We rec-
> ognize there is a need to balance local and provincial interests ...
> This is just not the way to achieve it. The Executive is calling on the
> provincial government to remove local government from Bill 75.
> (Union of British Columbia Municipalities 2003)

Thus, in British Columbia, the year 2004 started much the same way
as 2003 had ended: with the province again showing a large degree of
disregard for local decision making. In a small but telling example of
provincial interference in local affairs, on 30 December 2003, local police forces found out that, beginning on New Year's Eve 2003, all bars
and restaurants in BC would henceforth be allowed to stay open until
4:00 a.m. The new provincial rules did allow municipalities to be part
of the decision making on how they would be applied locally. The
provincial Liquor Control and Licensing Act had been amended in late
2002 allowing for this change, but it was not implemented, nor was notice sent to local authorities. Local police forces first learned of the
change fewer than forty-eight hours before its impact, resulting in expensive overtime/shift changes, with all costs borne by the municipalities – who naturally expressed considerable displeasure.

   At the end of Gordon Campbell's first term, the provincial-municipal relationship was still more top-down than locally led. That was not
what had been anticipated given Campbell's early first-term positions
on local government reform. The lead-up to the 2010 Winter Olympics
and criticism of the premier's policy style (he was sometimes accused

of skipping from one policy focus to another) came more to the fore as the second term started following a clear election victory in 2005.

GORDON CAMPBELL'S SECOND TERM (2005–09): FORGOTTEN REFORM PRIORITIES, NEW PROJECTS, AND CHANGED AGENDAS

As others in this volume note, Gordon Campbell's second-term agenda was focused on a new and different set of priorities. On matters local/municipal, the 2005 legislative list was mainly focused on housekeeping rather than on reform. With both a spring and an autumn legislative sitting, and the general election in between, local legislative change was limited to miscellaneous amendments and a provision requiring municipalities to collect a parking site tax for the Greater Vancouver Transportation Authority. The provincial inclination to underscore its superior jurisdictional authority also continued. In 2006, slipped into Bill 30 (Miscellaneous Statute Amendment Act [2]), the province modified the Utilities Commission Act to protect independent power producer proposals from obstruction by local governments – in effect to ensure that, on such matters, the province, not local or regional authorities, would be "the decider."

By 2006, Vancouver's successful bid for the 2010 Winter Olympics came to be the biggest driver of provincial policy and intergovernmental initiatives. This focus and the timetable, requirements, and infrastructure needs posed by the International Olympic Committee (IOC) meant that, when provincial interests potentially clashed with local-regional ones, the provincial government insisted – at times in legislated form – on prevailing. While not a terribly surprising outcome (given the Constitution Act, 1867, sec. 92.8), local and regional matters are still affected by some of these early Gordon Campbell legislative changes and, significantly, by failures to complete promised reforms.

In 2007, local governing legislative changes were also fairly limited: they allowed for the creation of resort regions/resort municipalities – and additional designation for the financing, development, and governance of resort municipalities (Bill 11). The Miscellaneous Statutes Amendment Act (Bill 35) on some new taxation rules also materialized. Other minor amendments (e.g., on tobacco in public places, legislation to allow the province to collect up to 50 per cent of local policing costs from small municipalities, and provincial ratification of the Tsawwassen First Nation treaty [Bill 40]) were also part of the 2007 legislative calendar.

The major change – and the one still resonating following the May 2013 general election victory of Campbell's successor, Christy Clark – was the Campbell government's legislative reaction to Greater Vancouver/Metro Vancouver/Translink's frustration over BC's Olympic rapid transit/transportation plans. Bill 43 – the Greater Vancouver Transportation Authority Amendment Act – largely stripped the local-regional role out of transportation planning, created an appointed corporate board structure, and limited local input into decision making at Translink to more circumscribed overview powers exercised by a mayors' council. It also renamed Translink the South Coast British Columbia Transportation Authority (Smith 2008). The resulting accountability disjuncture between who should pay and who, legitimately, should control, and be held accountable for, transportation planning in BC's largest metropolitan region represented one of the major failures of the Gordon Campbell decade regarding municipal-regional matters.

BC's regional district system was created in the mid-1960s (Smith and Oberlander 1993; Smith 2009) as a consensus-based regional decision-making platform. This was particularly the case in Greater Vancouver because finding regional solutions to major service delivery challenges such as water, sewage/drainage, flood control, and so on had been locally inspired since before the First World War. By 1948, the Lower Mainland Regional Planning Board was functioning, and it produced a regional plan in the early 1960s. This relatively high degree of local consensus on regional issues generally found provincial blessing, where needed, in a form Tennant and Zirnhelt (1973) have refer to as "gentle imposition."

In the mid-1970s, Greater Vancouver (since the mid-1960s a province-wide regional district system) agreed to a "new" Livable Region Plan. This was followed in the early 1980s by some disagreements between the province and region over preservation of farmlands. As a result of this conflict, Bill 9, introduced in the Bill Bennett/Social Credit Restraint Program of 1983, saw the province strip all regional districts of regional planning responsibilities (Magnusson et al. 1984).

The regional planning ethos, in the Vancouver region at least, was strong enough that it continued under alternative forms, such as "Development Services." In the early 1990s, the Harcourt NDP government restored regional planning. As in the 1980s, however, the eventual linking of transportation planning to land-use planning on the part of regional decision makers did not occur until near the end of the NDP decade (1991–2001), at which time a regional transportation authority was established under a soon-to-be-defeated NDP government. This was institutionally separated from the traditional regional district. To be fair to the Campbell Liberals, each recent previous government – whether Social Credit, NDP, or Liberal – has made its own decisions on rapid transit technology, on financing transportation improvements, and, most fundamentally, on transportation governance with relatively little local input.

When they are left to their own devices, BC's regional authorities have proven remarkably capable of achieving consensus regarding "planning" in their regions. In the mid- to late 2000s, Gordon Campbell's Olympic dreams presented a challenge to the promises of the Community Charter. The IOC and Ottawa emphasized rapid transit connections between Vancouver's international airport and downtown Vancouver as well as an upgraded Vancouver–Whistler Sea-to-Sky Highway connection. On the former, the region had already planned and promised that three northeast-area municipalities (Port Moody/Coquitlam/Port Coquitlam) would get the next major investment in rapid transit – the Evergreen Line. This extension of rapid transit was the "reward" for these local-area municipalities agreeing to add new growth from the 1996 Livable Region Strategic Plan to their current share of the population. The Olympics brought federal funds to match provincial contributions to such infrastructure, and this brought a provincial/federal priority shift to the RAV airport–downtown line from the already regionally agreed-upon Evergreen Line. Local mayors balked. Additional pressure was applied by the minister of transportation; again the mayors balked. Evergreen was their promised regional priority, and there were misgivings about RAV's P3 aspects and financing.

The Campbell government's reaction to this regional frustration of the province's priority was to set up a "study," with the minister of transportation branding the locally controlled Translink Board as dysfunctional and as incapable of making a decision. In fact, the regional transport authority was entirely capable of making a decision; it was just not the decision preferred by the province. As a result of this regional push-back, the government introduced Bill 43, which created a very different, less locally controlled, Translink governance structure in the form of the South Coast British Columbia Transportation Authority. Day-to-day operations were under an appointed corporate board. A mayors' council with limited powers kept some overall budgetary decision-making authority, and a regional transportation commission had various responsibilities, including setting fares. Three board seats were held by provincial MLAs, appointed by the government. At the end of the NDP era these MLAs did not attend meetings, and this remained the custom under the Campbell Liberals.

Gordon Campbell's revised Translink was not a complete failure; some saw the new structure as more efficient. But it left the region (and the province) with more unresolved issues than answers – something far removed from what the premier indicated were his initial local reform intentions. Little that transpired over the rest of Campbell's terms, and into successor Christy Clark's administrations, reflected much of the local autonomy commitments of Campbell's first term. By late summer 2014 – and the November 2014 BC local elections – Translink/provincial and local/regional remained hot and mostly unresolved matters (see, for example, Smith 2017). The province had tried to push more costs back to local mayors/municipalities, including through a forced referendum on local tax increases for Translink. However, local mayors successfully pushed back, using the seemingly limited powers of the Mayors' Council to force a temporary provincial climb-down in the lead-up to the 2015 transit referendum.

With Olympic and other matters top of mind, the 2008 and 2009 local governing agendas were mostly housekeeping versus substantial reform: this included an amendment to require financial agents for local elections "to improve the transparency of local elections finance," encouraging local reductions in GHG's, and miscellaneous amendments on housing, small business, public health, and forest and range. By 2009, the local governing legislative agenda was even lighter: one bill allowing additional anti-graffiti and regulation of IOC-related signage powers to Vancouver, Richmond, and Whistler. There were also thirteen "minor amendments" (two before the May 2009 election and the rest after) on items like assistance for local homeless shelters as well as on police discipline, wills and estates, public safety, and workers' compensation.

Two things stand out in this second Campbell term. First, the province's insistence on the routing for the West Vancouver end of the Olympic Sea-to-Sky Highway. Despite strenuous, even judicial, objections on the part of the municipality of West Vancouver, the minister of transportation insisted that the province's more environmentally invasive, but cheaper, plan prevail. It did, at a cost of $1 billion – plus an estimated $2.5 billion in P3 maintenance costs over the twenty-five-year lifespan of the contract. The second thing that stands out is how the government took some of the local control over transportation governance out of the hands of locals and placed day-to-day decisions in the hands of a corporate board.

In all, Gordon Campbell's second term ended with a different, rather narrower, local governing focus than had been indicated by his initial/ first-term New Era Document (NED) reform agenda and the Community Charter. Simply stated, the early first-term promises of local democratic reforms were overshadowed by the Olympic mega-project.

GORDON CAMPBELL'S THIRD (HALF) TERM (2009–11): OLYMPIC LEGACIES, TALK OF A FOURTH TERM, AND SUCCESSORS

Local democratic reform did return to the Campbell agenda in his third term, albeit briefly. BC has the least regulated ("wild west") local election finance regulation in Canada. Anyone can contribute any amount, and no voter would hear of it until months after an election; and there is no local lobbying registration, despite significant sums of money floating through BC's local elections. In a minor genuflection to making local elections finance more transparent, in 2010, the premier announced at the annual UBCM meeting that he was appointing a task force on local elections. Rather than an "all-party" legislative committee, however, this committee was an odd reform duck: it was co-chaired by the community's minister and by the head of the UBCM, and with backbench Liberal MLAs and UBCM-selected municipal councillors. In other words, it had no Opposition members. Given the odd nature of its genetics, it was perhaps not surprising that this committee had a rather limited impact on local governing reform. Ultimately, it produced no significant local democratic reform measures (Smith and Stewart 2010), though it did start a much needed conversation on reform.

Other than the foregoing rather limited electoral reform effort, 2009–10 was essentially focused on the Vancouver Winter Olympics. Part of the legacy for Gordon Campbell's third term is an enduring picture of the premier in red Olympic mittens. Juxtaposed with this was a post-Olympic letdown: fiscal accounting in 2010–11 – Gordon Campbell's last year as premier – meant that the premier and his minister of finance found themselves pressured to say "okay" to an offer from Ottawa for $1.5 billion in transitional funding if BC would abandon its

long-standing provincial sales tax and adopt a harmonized sales tax
(HST) with the federal government.

During the 2009 election, both the premier and finance minister had
given clear electoral commitments that no such federal-BC plan would
be forthcoming. However, immediately following the 2009 election, a
new HST was announced by the BC government. Had that decision involved a little more democratic background and civic engagement, Gordon Campbell might have gone on to serve a forth term. Instead, the
outcome was a late 2010 announcement that Campbell was "stepping
down" due to negative political reactions. Campbell was replaced in
March 2011 by former deputy premier/colleague and talk radio host
Christy Clark.

Premier Clark's first main local governing initiative was the creation
of an auditor general for local government, not something sought by
BC's municipalities but lobbied for by its chambers of commerce. Clark
won the May 2013 BC general election, despite polls indicating that she
would not. Local governing accountability reforms remained low on
the Clark agenda. Pipelines – for LNG rather than tar sands bitumen –
and First Nations title issues have come to dominate the BC agenda. Indeed, the Supreme Court of Canada's Tsilhqot'in decision of July 2014
represents a "game-changer."

LOCAL GOVERNMENTAL REFORM:
COMPARING CONCLUSIONS – THE NDP DECADE (1991–
2001) AND THE GORDON CAMPBELL LIBERAL DECADE
(2001–11)

It is surprising to think that, although a significant amount of local-
related legislation was posed, formulated, consulted on, debated,
passed, and implemented over the two decades comprising 1991–2001
and 2001–11, BC local (and regional) governments continue to closely resemble those of the late 1980s and early 1990s. Of the one hun-
dred-odd acts affecting local governments in major ways passed in
each of the NDP and Campbell decades since 1991, few have affected
the structure or function of local government in British Columbia.
Successive BC governments have seemed rather satisfied with the basic
components of the municipal system and content to make smaller financial and jurisdictional alterations rather than to engage in more
fundamental structural, functional, or democratic reforms. The only
major *structural* reform involved the changes made to regional transit

in Greater Vancouver. This involved legislation that was of limited general consequence to municipal authorities in the province's largest city-region and of no significance to those located in the rest of the province. The Greater Vancouver Transportation Authority Act of 1998 (and the creation of the South Coast British Columbia Transportation Authority [SCBCTA] in 2007) represented the only major *functional* change over the last twenty years. Whereas Harcourt's reforms were administrative in nature, all significant changes since 1996 have affected the *financial* and *jurisdictional* capacities of municipal governments in BC. These changes include NDP and Liberal efforts to reduce oversight by the provincial government and NDP/Liberal promises to allow more taxation powers and to transform municipalities from corporations into "natural persons." Looking at the various electoral terms over these two decades, the Harcourt era (1991–96) can be seen as having introduced the most balanced municipal reforms, with the Clark/Miller/Dosanjh and Campbell (including the Campbell-Clark) governments focusing more on efficiency and leaving accountability reform for another term (which meant reforms that never came to be). Under Municipal Affairs Minister Darlene Marzari, the Harcourt New Democrats showed insight in partially devolving power to create a more cooperative municipal/provincial relationship and in achieving widespread agreement on the Growth Strategies Act and regional-local planning. On the accountability side, allowing local parties to be identified on local election ballots and forcing candidates to disclose their funding sources helped speed the development of municipal political parties and increased election transparency in BC's larger municipalities. As strong and active local political parties often represent one of the most significant challenges to long-entrenched urban regimes – and the imperatives of an "at-large" electoral system in large municipalities – Harcourt's "minor" administrative changes (i.e., encouraging municipal political party formation) represent the single largest accountability reform of the past twenty years in British Columbia.

While New Democratic premiers Clark, Miller, and Dosanjh and their respective "local government" ministers were aware that an efficiency/accountability balance needed to be struck, not only did they fail to implement accountability reforms but they also threatened the atmosphere of cooperation cultivated by Harcourt. Minister Mike Farnworth's reforms, embodied in Bill 31, the Local Government Act, began a process of empowering local governments. The task of

strengthening the power of local citizens to control municipal officials was left to Jenny Kwan – Farnworth's successor in the municipal
affairs portfolio. However, her cabinet colleagues were not up to the
challenge, and her Bill 88 changes were largely ineffective, as were
those of her NDP successors. Community Charter reforms under Liberal premier Gordon Campbell – a former Vancouver mayor and GVRD
chair – suggested an overemphasis on efficiency versus accountability.
Despite strong language in the Community Charter about "a new deal
for BC's municipalities," unless substantive electoral and non-electoral
accountability reforms were included in subsequent legislation, all that
could occur was a potential empowering of under-accountable local
governments in BC.

If anything, over his remaining time in office, from 2006 to 2010–11,
the Campbell-inspired regional transportation governance structure
(part of his major local-regional legacy) proved no more successful than
its local-regional predecessor. As with other Campbell changes, efficiency was the predominant policy driver, but a lack of essential accountability proved the central point made in the 1979 federal Lambert
Royal Commission on Financial Management and Accountability: for
Lambert and his commission colleagues, "in a democracy, you cannot
have efficiency without accountability" (Royal Commission on Financial Management and Accountability 1979).

Immediately prior to the 14 May 2013 general election, BC's then
minister of transportation called for an eighteen-month study on
funding and other challenges, including a forced referendum in
Metro Vancouver on regional transit funding. This locally unpopular
referendum – seen by Metro municipalities as a provincial attempt to
force more transit costs onto local ratepayers – was to coincide with
the November 2014 civic elections. The Opposition NDP leader made
the simple electoral note that what was needed was "more local
democracy." In sum, Gordon Campbell's revised Translink was not a
complete failure; it was also far less than a success. And it left the region (and the province) with more unresolved issues than answers –
something far removed from what Premier Campbell indicated were
his intentions. BC's 2014 transportation minister seemed ready to compromise on timing but not on the province's wish to have the region
pay more for its transportation system – whether on road tolls or
vehicle/mileage levies.

Among other things, this BC legislative experience supports several
conclusions. First, local governmental issues command significant at-

tention from provincial governments in British Columbia. This was clearly the case during the Campbell decade. Second, legislative reform increasingly allows municipal governments more decision-making capacity – though still with limited fiscal capacity. This did not shift in any meaningful way under Gordon Campbell. And, finally, each reform plan included the promise of concomitant democratic reforms (on the accountability side), but in almost every case such promises have remained unfulfilled, particularly during the Campbell decade.

The point here is not to disparage the empowerment of local governments – this notion has been part of the policy discourse in Canada since Lord Durham noted that the Rebellions of 1837–38 were partly caused by the fact that colonial powers had not used the development of local government "as a training ground for democracy" (Smith 1998; Craig 1982). Decentralization has been on the agendas of the Canadian Federation of Mayors and Municipalities and the Federation of Canadian Municipalities at least since the 1976 report entitled *Puppets on a Shoestring*. Rather, the point is that if substantive decision-making capacity is to shift from provincial to local hands, then the local citizenry must be given the tools to hold their elected officials to account. Otherwise, local citizens may have less say than would have been the case had power remained centralized.

As it stands, British Columbia's largest municipalities (and regions) have a continuing accountability deficit. Although useful as part of an overall package, tinkering with conflict of interest laws, open meetings, and annual reports, while necessary, is simply not sufficient. Avoiding the central questions of electoral accountability, the role of unregulated money in local elections, and local democratic disengagement will not solve the problem. In other words, floating about with one oar in the water will not get BC to the accountability shore. Thus, adding accountability to local government reforms remained the major incomplete task of the Campbell Liberal decade. This does not make Gordon Campbell unique, but it does speak to his local governing legacy. Indeed, the Campbell legacy on local government democratic reform strongly suggests this lesson: "LESS is simply LESS!"

Provincial governments in BC continue to try to steer *and* row. The turnout in larger municipalities for civic elections has mostly been under 30 per cent, which is substantially less than for either provincial or federal elections in the province. There is perhaps no more telling evidence of the continued municipal disengagement of British

Columbians, even after more than two decades of continuous local legislative reform efforts. Only real democratic reforms will begin to alter
this local democratic deficit. To date, no BC government has seemed
prepared to grasp the political reform nettle. Until one does, real local
democracy will remain an ideal rather than a reality.

The May 2017 BC general election saw Campbell's successor, Christy
Clark, narrowly defeated (44 seats to 43) by an NDP-Green alliance, thus
ending sixteen years and two months of Liberal rule. The challenge of
democratic reform of British Columbia's local governing and dealing
with Gordon Campbell's legacy now fell to Premier John Horgan and
the NDP.

12

British Columbia's Arts, Cultural, and Creative Sector under Premier Campbell

DUNCAN LOW

The BC Liberals' 2001 election platform document, entitled *A New Era for British Columbia*, spoke of BC's "new economy" and contained both implicit and explicit promises for the province's arts, cultural, and creative sector. The document stated that a BC Liberal government would ensure that music, arts, and physical education curricula would be fully funded in BC's public schools. It also indicated support for Vancouver's Olympic bid, "[increased] funding for [the British Columbia Arts Council] (BCAC) – to promote and support BC arts, music, artists and culture," and pledged to "stimulate tourism" (British Columbia Liberal Party 2001). The "new economy" references reflected the changing political status assigned to the arts, cultural, and creative industries in the province's ever-growing service sector. As highlighted in an interview with a former chair of the BCAC:

> Gordon [Campbell] had a very keen interest in the arts ... He saw how the arts would form the basis of the creative economy ... He was very interested in how you would change BC's economy from a resource driven economy into something that would position us better for the future ... He was a big reader of Richard Florida and saw the arts as a catalyst for a new economy. (Shumka 2012)

In this chapter I examine how British Columbia's arts, cultural, and creative sector fared under Premier Campbell's administration. To provide an assessment of Campbell's approach to the arts, I survey a number of the sectors that fashioned BC's ever-changing cultural landscape.

I examine how the national debate regarding the shifting role of the arts, cultural, and creative industries in a modern twenty-first-century economy manifested itself in British Columbia.

I also scrutinize the 2010 Vancouver Olympics and examine the influence they had on the government's cultural policy. In 2002, Gordon Campbell replaced the original bid society with the Vancouver 2010 Bid Corporation and enthusiastically embraced the Olympic Games, which became a fundamental part of his government's arts program.[1]

I also review the role of the "creative class" theory (Florida 2002) and its impact on BC's cultural policy as it was a core component of the cultural policy debate surrounding the role of public subsidies for the arts and what constituted a creative city.

Finally, I look at some of the component parts of BC's arts, cultural, and creative industries and pass some judgment on how they performed up until Campbell's resignation in November 2010. Specifically, I focus on those areas that fell under the remit of BC government funding agencies such as the BCAC, BC Film + Media, and Gaming and Tourism BC.

In essence, I ask in what way this period redefined BC's artistic and cultural landscape and to what extent the promises contained in the BC Liberals' 2001 *New Era* document were realized. By reviewing individual sectors, I aim to critically appraise Gordon Campbell's perceived success or failure in the realm of BC's arts, cultural, and creative sector from 2001 to 2011.

BC'S TRANSITIONING ECONOMY

Historically, BC's economy has relied a great deal on natural resources. This reliance had changed by the time Gordon Campbell ascended to the position of premier in 2001. More specifically, from 2001 to 2008 the province saw increased numbers of people (four out of five) employed in the service sector.

By the end of the twentieth century, fishing, forestry, and mining continued to decline as a percentage of total employment, and by 2008 they represented a mere 2 per cent of total employment in BC's goods sector (BC Statistics 2010, 224). Moreover, the goods sector's share of total GDP also continued to fall between the 1990s NDP and the 2000s Liberal governments, dropping from about 29 per cent in 1990 to less than 24 per cent in 2008.[2]

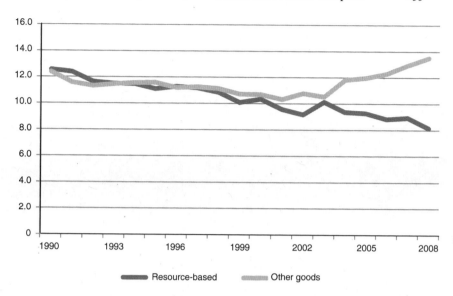

Figure 12.1   The declining role of natural resources in BC's economy (% of total employment)

Source: BC Statistics 2010

As BC's economy was transitioning from a resource-based economy to a more "services"-oriented one, there was a concurrent shift in the role of Canada's professional arts sector. Increasingly, the professional arts and cultural sectors were viewed as instruments of economic development. For example, in his keynote address at the Heritage Conservation 20/20 Round Table in Montreal in March 2012, David A. Walden (secretary-general of the Canadian Commission for UNESCO) suggested: "It is clear that federal policy sought to develop an environment where distinctly Canadian cultural products could both be created (supply) and be consumed (demand)" (Walden 2012).

Walden discussed how law of supply and demand is based upon four principles: (1) when the supply of a product increases the price decreases; (2) when the supply of a product decreases then the price increases; (3) when the price increases producers are motivated to produce more but the customer tends to buy less; and (4) when the price decreases, consumers are motivated to buy more, but producers tend to provide less. Plainly put, his point is that these principles oper-

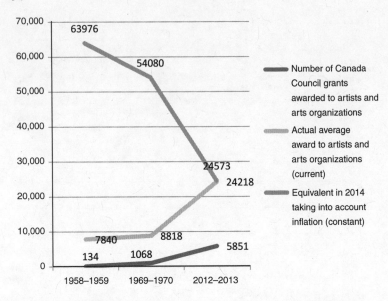

Figure 12.2   Number of grants versus average award (current/constant)

Source: Canada Council for the Arts

ate on the basis of a natural equilibrium. Hence, a balance is established and maintained between supply and demand.

When Canada's not-for-profit public-funding arts model is examined under the economic principles of supply and demand, it quickly becomes apparent that a subsidy system centred upon these principles is flawed. Figure 12.2 demonstrates that, as the supply of Canada's arts products increases (shown by the rapid increase in the number of grants awarded to artists), the average financial award to arts organizations tends to decrease. The reasons for this are highlighted below, and it is hoped that they bring a bit more clarity to how public arts funding is, or ought to be, managed.

Demand-Side Argument(s)

The demand-side argument focuses on the concept of externalities (positive and negative) and public and merit goods. According to Samuelson (1954), the term "public good" has two distinguishing characteristics: (1) non-exclusivity, whereby no one person has exclusive rights to its consumption, and (2) non-rivalry, whereby the consumption of a good by one person does not affect its consumption by another.

Two examples of public goods are the air we breathe and national defence: they are non-rival since consumption by one person does not affect the level of consumption by another, and non-exclusive, since it is impossible to exclude specific persons from the benefits of the good even if they refuse to pay for it (Snowball 2008; Creigh-Tyte 2001).

Are the professional arts a public good? It can be argued that the non-profit arts sector does not fit the concept of a public good because artistic performances are exclusive through limited ticketing and variable pricing. A fact demonstrated by a number of studies that show that arts attendees are often well-educated, employed, and well-paid (Snowball 2005; Snowball and Antrobus 2002; Fullerton 1991), leading one to ask: Why would any government offer to subsidize something that displays the characteristics of a "private good"? The same argument could be made in relation to pursuing a university education in that, like the arts, it is both "rival and excludable." However, the alternative position is that a university education encompasses the characteristics of a public good as society is improved by or benefits from an educated workforce. The arts, it could be said, also falls within this quasi-public goods line of reasoning because of the positive externalities, or merit goods, being conveyed (Creigh-Tyte 2001).

There are a number of varying definitions of the term "merit good." The one I use for this chapter is: "goods which some persons believe ought to be available and whose consumption and allocation are felt to be too important to be left to the private market" (Cwi 1980, 39). The arts, as a merit good, are used in defence of public funding – largely because the arts can be perceived intrinsically as a good thing and the externalities that flow from them possess indirect benefits that cannot be sold or used up. In other words, they provide positive externalities in that the benefits spill over to non-purchasers (Baumol and Bowen 1966).

Still, there are a number of counter-arguments to the position that a merit good deserves public support. The arts can be a source of national pride – in the same way that a well-built automobile or smartphone can be a source of pride. For example, Hyundai and Samsung are both revered in South Korea, but this, in and of itself, does not necessarily mean that they should be subsidized indefinitely – though I do recognize the value of supporting "strategic" industries in an incipient stage of development. Indeed, government support for domestic industrial development can generate immediate and long-term political benefits. Similarly, forward-looking city councils can use arts or cultural activities to attract tourists, elevate the city's profile, and stimulate economic growth. Yet, depending on the level of inter-city competitiveness, there is the possibility that some municipalities will simply be overlooked because they lack sufficient capacity and/or the resources to keep up. In these instances, an investment, and the concomitant return on the investment, in an arts or cultural initiative could be seen as wasteful or difficult to justify.

The debate surrounding the concept of merit goods is often centred on the concept of an intangible asset, or requiring a value judgment, and, as a result, opinions regarding its usefulness can vary. Two prominent theorists in this regard are David Throsby and Don Fullerton. Throsby (1994) argues that the arts do constitute a merit good and are deserving of public funding. Yet at the other end of the spectrum Fullerton suggests (1991) that while the arts may be regarded as a merit good, this is not enough to justify public funding (see Snowball 2008, 15).

Supply-Side Argument(s)

One of the original supply-side arguments relates to the notion of a "cost disease," and this occurs when "the technology of live performances leaves little room for labour-saving innovations, since the end product is the labour of the performer" (Baumol 1966, 390). This can result in an income gap of sorts. Put differently, while the labour costs to produce a car may decrease because of technological developments over time, the labour costs of producing a piece of music will increase due to the fact that there is no productivity offset to the rising costs.

Over the years, the validity of the cost disease theory has been questioned by a number of scholars (Peacock 1969; Cwi 1980; Fullerton 1991; Abbing 2004). In 1987, Baumol made an important addition to the debate, recognizing that a cost disease for the arts does indeed exist and that this, by itself, could undermine public support. In general, public funding will only be forthcoming if the members of a society feel that the arts possess merit goods and that the benefit that flows to society is greater than the money spent to keep the artefact in business. In 1995, Baumol reiterated his position by saying that "without public support the arts will decline, both in quantity and quality" (Snowball 2008, 17). The arguments made against the cost disease theory centre around increased revenue potential through merchandising and corporate sponsorship, and the technological developments in manufacturing that accompanied cultural industries' development resulting in the potential for increased revenues to cover the income gap (Throsby 1994; Tiongson 1997).

An important adaptation of the cost disease dilemma came from Baumol himself when he acknowledged that "the new economy brings both the disease and the means that enable society to deal with it. In other words, the 'cost disease' is, and yet need not be, a primary concern for funding of the arts" (Baumol 2006, 347). The demand-side part of this problem has been at the centre of the cultural value and public subsidization debate for over thirty years. One reason presented for this ongoing debate is that the cultural economic model during this period lacked the necessary framework to truly assess the value of culture.

A Canadian Perspective

In a Canadian context, this debate has focused predominantly on supply-side issues. The Massey Commission's 1951 report highlighted a perceived American threat to Canadian identity. The solution presented was the creation and support of several national and provincial institutions to "pump prime" the supply of artistic products to better develop cultural items that were unable to operate within the principles of the economics stated above and so created conditions for a supply-side approach to Canadian arts that would persist for almost fifty years (Walden 2012).

These institutions included the Canada Council for the Arts and the BC Arts Council, whose role was to nurture Canadian artistic creation, support its presentation to the public, and protect artistic creations from foreign market forces. Thirty years after Massey, the 1982 Applebaum and Hébert Report stated that, in order to thrive, the Canada Council's annual budget allocation would need to be augmented to ensure that its "purpose and value remain[ed] viable," otherwise there would be a serious threat to Canada's artistic future (Applebaum and Hébert 1982). The committee reported that, "in order to flourish, the arts require daring experimentation and risk." It then referenced the Canada Council's submission to the committee, which stated: "because of several years of budgetary restraints and even cutbacks at the Council, support to new companies, to younger artists, to those inventive spirits on the frontiers of art, is simply not possible unless we rob Peter to sponsor Paul" (56).

In 2012, David Walden suggested that "Canadian supply was not a response to consumer demand, but an artificial creation of content regulators" (Walden 2012). Taking this argument to its (il)logical conclusion, Canadians were forced to consume inferior cultural products that were not commercially practicable or competitive. This very troubling assessment of the supply versus demand relationship has resulted in a new focus that examines the need to recalibrate the arts agenda from supply to demand (see Walden 2012).

This shift from supply to demand has had an impact on BC's transition from a resource-based to a service-based economy, but it has also provided a framework for how the BC arts and cultural sector fits within this changing model. The shift from intrinsic to instrumental focus on the arts took place over a thirty-year period, between 1970 and 2000, and set the stage for Gordon Campbell's decade as premier of British Columbia. But there is some additional historically relevant material that should be emphasized, if only to add a layer of context to our understanding of this subject.

The 1968 Trudeau government met with political instability in the form of Quebec separatism. To counter this threat and to strengthen the principle of federalism, the government radically altered the relationship between the state and cultural activity in Canada. Ottawa embarked on a process described as "cultural industrialism," whereby cultural activity was to be promoted as the glue that would hold the "two founding nations" together and whereby cultural devices were initiated for the promotion of the state. This "was not arts for art's sake or even art for a nation's sake, but art for federalism's sake, designed to forge a sense of allegiance and unity in times of political threat" (Edwardson 2012, 95).

The federal cultural bureaucracy was expanded and placed under the authority of the secretary of state. A new arts and culture branch was created and integrated into the federal bureaucracy under the secretary of state. The expanded federal cultural bureaucracy initiated programs of direct investment and earmarked funding aimed at pro-federalist artistic products and events, while excluding Quebec separatist activities. The government's targeted use of arts funding to serve political objectives clearly demonstrated the shift to instrumentalism upon which Gordon Campbell would heavily draw during his time in Victoria.

The new policy of cultural industrialism brought the much-enlarged federal cultural bureaucracy and the primary delivery mechanism of "arm's-length" arts funding – the Canada Council for the Arts – into conflict. The chair of the council actually stated: "it is not our role to exert any kind of control or censorship over those artists or arts organizations that benefit from the Canada Council in any other area than their qualifications as arts and scholastic organizations, so long as they do not actually break the law" (as cited in Edwardson 2012, 1975). Be that as it may, direct intervention is a trait that would appear during the Campbell reign, and it is one that would eventually play a role in the resignation of the chair of the BC Arts Council.

The newly empowered federal cultural bureaucracy was expounding the benefits of the arts and cultural sector as part of the new economic model and touting its benefits by pointing to increased employment and revenue through cultural tourism. This philosophy was embraced by the Canadian Conference of the Arts, and it prompted it to ask the Trudeau government to recognize and reward the role of the arts in economic development.

During the 1970s, Ottawa expanded the cultural bureaucracy, created new direct investment, and actively mobilized the arts in its efforts to strengthen federalism. Simultaneously, it cut arts funding and negatively affected the pseudo-autonomous funding relationship between the council and government. The federal administration, which had up until this point been a cultural observer, now found itself in a position to dictate the future direction of arts activity and funding. This federal shift in responsibility sparked a debate that continues to this day: What are the state's regulatory and funding responsibilities, and might they be distinguished from other policy areas such as infrastructure and jobs growth?

Gordon Campbell's election as premier of BC on 16 May 2001 neatly coincided with the thirty-year transition of Canada's artistic landscape from an intrinsic to an instrumental focus. In May 2001, the Liberal government's minister of Canadian heritage, Sheila Copps, announced a collection of cultural policy programs under the banner of the Tomorrow Starts Today initiative. The Tomorrow Starts Today announcement captured the conflicting aspects of cultural policy development: the struggle between professional arts and centralized authority; the arts as a localized entity servicing local audiences but having to also contend with the challenges and onslaught of "Americanized" cultural globalization; and the perceived roles of the creative and cultural industries in national promotion on the world stage.

The Government in Canada is demonstrating, in the most concrete
way possible, its support for Canadian arts and culture. We are giving our creative people, we are giving Canadians the tools they
need to bring Canadian arts and culture into the 21st century ... To
foster a diverse, inclusive and enriching society, we need not only
the buildings and bridges, and doctors and soldiers, we need also
words and images, song and dance, artists and creators ... In today's
increasingly borderless world, it's more important than ever we
make sure our children have the opportunity to see reflections of
their lives, their realities, and their stories, when they open a book,
switch on the television, buy a CD, or surf the internet ... The cultural sector contributes over 22 billion to our Gross Domestic product. It employs over 640,000 Canadians ... I am proud to be a
member of a government that recognizes the critical role arts and
culture plays in our lives, and in our society. And that realizes that
if our own culture is to flourish, it must be cultivated. (Edwardson
2012, 261)

Tomorrow Starts Today represents a conundrum insofar as it ex-
pounded the benefits of the arts to the well-being of a modern society but, at the same time, had to place exceptional emphasis on its
contribution to jobs creation and the country's gross domestic product. This transition appears to have occurred at the provincial level as
well. When Gordon Campbell became premier he picked up the reins
of cultural industrialism.

As Snowball (2008, 1) states: "the interesting thing about culture, and
its expression, the arts, is that it is nearly always contested and a site of
struggle." In all, this observation reflects the ongoing discussion related
to the cultural and creative industries' place in the new, or creative,
economy and the role of the professional performing artist in the
twenty-first century. However, the more important point to be made
here is that, as BC has continued to transition away from being a traditional "goods" provider to being a service-sector-dependent economy,
more time and energy has been devoted to cultivating cultural tourism
and recreation, the arts, and the creative and cultural sectors.

ARTS FUNDING IN BRITISH COLUMBIA

When the BC Liberals came to power, they faced an arts sector that had-
n't fared well under the previous government. To be fair, the NDP had

introduced legislation that changed the BC Arts Board, as it was then, into an independent arm's-length arts council. Legislation was passed in 1996 and an inaugural council was appointed. The new council received an additional $4 million. However, within months the organization had returned to previous BC Arts Board (1991) funding levels: "The financial squeeze was very difficult, we had to cut grants and institute third party delivery because we didn't have the staff" (N. Baird, chair, BC Arts Council, interview, 3 December 2012).

When the BC Liberals took office, the principal levers of cultural funding remained the same as they were during the previous administration: grants were delivered through the BCAC, the BC Film Commission, and BC Film + Media. Community gaming grants were administered through the BC Gaming Policy and Enforcement Branch. Other areas of support came through tax credits, direct support from the then Ministry of Tourism, Culture and the Arts, and one-off funding initiatives.

THE CREATIVE CITY AND THE CREATIVE CLASS

The persistent decline and volatility in BC's resource sector had resulted in a search for new industries to fill both the economic and community void. Premier Campbell's creation of a new "business advisory council," within weeks of taking office, is an arresting illustration of the reprioritization that was taking root in the province (Chow 2001).

Richard Florida's (2002, 6) assertion that creativity was now the most "highly prized commodity in our economy" marked an important junction for the professional arts sector in BC. This intersection saw the convergence of two ideologies – globalization and neoliberalism. Cultural neoliberalism is often characterized by increased corporate sponsorship, a diminishing role for public subsidy, and a focus on the economic rather than on the artistic return. Furthermore, cultural neoliberalism represents the shift discussed earlier from the "Keynesian" rationale for cultural policy of art for everyone towards the economic goals of urban competitiveness and regeneration (McGuigan 2005). With increased cultural neoliberalism, a funding agency's decision to fund artistic style and content becomes more politically influenced.

Florida's thesis advocating economic development based on the knowledge economy has become one of the most popular and influential policy outlines adopted by municipal, provincial, and federal governments throughout Canada. However, it also represents one of the most debated economic development and cultural policy strategies

of our time. It can be argued that unsuspecting accomplices in this policy initiative were the not-for-profit artists, arts organizations, and urban
arts festivals that were reliant upon public funding for their existence.
These not-for-profit organizations have not fared well under the neoliberal governments that dominated the political landscape of the late
twentieth century. As a result, these arts organizations were particularly susceptible to the new political doctrine of art and creativity, unaware
that the new creativity movement and public arts funding were not
necessarily bedfellows.

In order to assess how Florida's creative class theory became so influential among BC policy makers and to gauge the impact that its implementation had on the equilibrium of local arts and cultural
communities, we must look more closely at the relationship between
economic development and the creative class. There is general agreement that creativity is a core component of the knowledge economy,
and it is recognized as a principal driver of modern economic growth.
From a publicly funded arts perspective this debate as to the relationship between creativity and urban economic growth is important because the arts play a central role in the creative class economic policy
argument. The question at the core of the debate is simple: Do people
follow jobs or do jobs follow people (Leslie and Rantisi 2012)? Richard
Florida's creative class theory is founded upon the principle that jobs
follow people. A city or urban centre that can attract creative human
capital will be more successful in diffusing an atmosphere of creativity
and innovation that, in turn, attracts financial investment in the new
economy resulting in economic growth. To successfully attract the creative class requires direct political action. Florida argues that the creative class is a limited resource for which cities and regions must
compete. Simply stated, the argument is that the creative classes are attracted to cities that have invested in public amenities: public art, bike
paths, festivals, cultural precincts, arts galleries, museums, stadia, and
other examples of starchitecture. The alternate method is not to attract
human capital but, rather, to develop home-grown human capital
through investment in education and training. Rooted in this perspective is the concept that a skilled workforce requires jobs, therefore the
responsibility of a government is to create an economic environment
that supports employment opportunities through channels such as
business start-up grants and tax incentives (Leslie and Rantisi 2012).

Looking at the twenty Canadian cities, large and small, listed in
Richard Florida's Canadian Creativity Index,[3] it is easy to see which of

these two theories prevailed: politicians, public officials, and policy makers across the country have been actively engaged in investing public resources in municipal amenities to attract the creative class (Moretti 2012). Gordon Campbell and the Province of British Columbia embraced the creative class approach to economic development. It could be said that Gordon Campbell's decade in power is an example of direct political action through government investment that used the arts as an instrument of economic development.

One could spend a considerable amount of time examining the creative class debate, but for the purpose of this chapter it is important to recognize the influence this international theory has had throughout British Columbia. A survey of public policy documents produced by three BC municipalities historically rooted in the natural resource sector demonstrates the wide-ranging influence of Florida's theory, of which Premier Campbell was a powerful advocate.

Powell River (pop. 13,000)
The creative economy can be thought of as all that which encompasses traditional arts and culture industries (visual and performing arts, music, writing and literature, etc.) but also extending to those industries where creativity plays a role – architecture and design, information technology etc. The concept of the "creative economy" was largely developed by Richard Florida. (Powell River 2012)

Campbell River (pop. 36,095)
A community with strong cultural institutions attracts a more highly educated and diverse workforce, which is essential as Campbell River's economy evolves from a resource base to a broader, service-oriented base. A "creative economy" leads to economic advancement, diverse development and competitive growth in communities. (Campbell River 2007)

City of Nanaimo (pop. 83,810)
Investing in arts and culture will strengthen our economic base, improve quality of life for residents and visitors and enhance community identity and reputation. (Nanaimo 2008)

These examples reinforce the Campbell government's belief that the arts, cultural, and creative sector(s) are all symbiotic within the new economy, while also providing examples of the definitional debate surrounding the terms "cultural industry" and "creative industry."

CREATIVE INDUSTRY VERSUS CULTURAL INDUSTRY

Much has been written on the cultural industry versus creative industry debate (Throsby 2010; Flew 2012; Potts 2011; Hesmondhalgh 2012). For the purpose of this chapter it is necessary to not only recognize this debate but also to clearly state that, from a performing, visual, and media arts perspective, the current lack of definitional clarity surrounding creative/cultural terminology, added to documented regional and artistic variations (Comunian 2009), makes blanket comparison challenging, if not meaningless.

This definitional debate was illustrated during an interview for this chapter regarding the printing of BC Film's 2000–01 annual report:

> We literally stopped the presses – everywhere where it said "culture" we changed it to "creative" because one of the shifts that happened between the former government (NDP) and the new government (Gordon Campbell's BC Liberals) was that the cultural argument did not resonate in the same way. It was a turning point as to how we started to talk about the industry as part of the creative economy in more economic terms rather than cultural terms. (L. Shorten, managing vice-president, Operations and Member Services, Canadian Media Production Association, BC Producers' Branch, interview with author, 15 January 2013)

Across the province, arts organizations were redefining their terminology, prioritizing the economic value rather than the artistic, social, educational, and cultural value of the arts.

BRITISH COLUMBIA'S CULTURAL LANDSCAPE, 2001–2011

> When the world arrives here in 2010, we want visitors to
> discover that a world of arts and culture is already here.
> (*Record New Westminster* 2004)

During his first ninety days as premier, Campbell had "already begun to shovel money into the Olympic adventure – $22 million for sport

[and] $5 million for an arts fund" (Palmer 2001a), providing an indication of what lay ahead. As the former chair of the BCAC stated: "The focus of many things, not just the arts, became the Olympics ... [I]n that decade it took over the priority, and that is why I say, I don't think there was a huge lasting benefit to the arts" (D. Shumka, former chair of the BC Arts Council [2003–09], inteview with author, 10 December 2012).

The analysis below details several of the areas that Campbell and others deemed worthy of significant financial support. It also highlights the funding mechanisms behind the Campbell government's support for the arts.

Performing and Visual Arts: "One-Off" and Infrastructure Funding

Gordon Campbell's implementation of cultural infrastructure support was delivered through a series of well-documented funding announcements that illustrate his ideological preference for a "market-driven" rather than an institutionally based "public-subsidy" approach. It became progressively more advantageous to frame the value of arts and culture in economic terms.

This method of advancing the agenda for creative change continues to be delivered through mega-events and tourism initiatives. Hosting the Olympic Games is often considered the "ultimate prize" in creative opportunity. We see this reflected in many of the Campbell government's initiatives that fell into the special one-off funding category, many of which supported the 2010 Olympic Games.

Olympic-related initiatives included the creation (in 2004) of the Arts-Now Program, which delivered "non-operational" funding to various arts initiatives through a selection of programs, all of which were phased out on or around the 2010 Olympics. In 2006, the Campbell government invested $5 million in a "cooperative planning process to create a cultural precinct in downtown Vancouver" (Office of the Premier 2006). The precinct concept outline included visions of a new Asia-Pacific museum of trade and culture and a new national gallery of Aboriginal art.

In 2008, to mark the province's 150th anniversary, Gordon Campbell announced a one-off investment of $209 million to support the arts through the creation of a new provincial endowment fund, the BC 150 Fund,[4] a new Vancouver art gallery as a component part of the new cultural precinct ($50 million), and support for the refurbishment of the Vancouver East Cultural Centre ($9 million).[5] Other examples of the premier's one-off payments occurred in 2003 to create the BC Achievement Foundation ($6 million) and in 2005 to create the Renaissance Fund ($25 million).

Several of the above initiatives were geared towards the 2010 Olympic experience, while others were for the long-term potential benefit of the BC arts sector. Yet even initiatives such as the BC 150 fund were discretionary budget items subject to the vagaries of market fluctuations.

Performing and Visual Arts: Operational Support

The BC arts community received funding via the BCAC and BC Gaming receipts through annual "budget" allocations. An illustration of the ideological shift that accompanied the Campbell decade was the BC 150 Fund. The BC Liberal government reduced operational public funding to the BCAC believing that the difference would be made up by returns on market investments from the BC 150 endowment fund. When the market collapsed in 2008, the income from the BC 150 investment was 60 per cent below original projections, which, as we will see, was to have a tremendous impact.

The 2010 Olympics played a central role in the premier's relationship with the cultural sector. Figure 12.3 gathers data from thirty-five arts organizations to provide a funding trend snapshot over Campbell's decade in power. The organizations' funding trends are grouped by: (1) total government funding for eleven arts organizations situated within the Lower Mainland, including federal, municipal, BCAC, and Olympiad funding;[6] (2) BCAC funding for twenty-four theatre, dance, music, visual arts, and festival organizations located throughout the province but outside of the Lower Mainland; (3) gaming funding (bingo and direct access) for twenty-two theatre, dance, music, visual arts, and festival organizations located throughout the province outside of the Lower Mainland; and (4) BCAC and gaming funding combined for twenty-four arts organizations located throughout the province outside of the Lower Mainland.[7]

In order to properly gauge how the performing and visual arts sector fared, the first issue to consider is the impact the games had on the professional cultural community within the Lower Mainland (Low 2010, Low 2012). Then, by widening the scope, one can examine whether Metro Vancouver's experience was reflected across the province.[8]

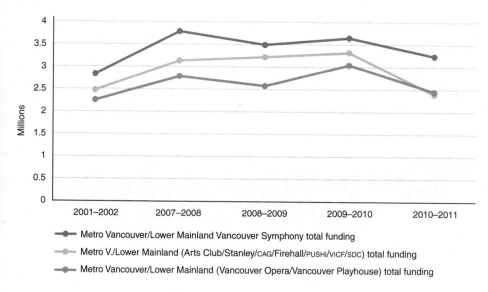

Figure 12.3   BC Arts funding trends, 2001–2011 (Metro Vancouver)

The *2010 Cultural Olympiad Impact Study* recruited a number of Vancouver-based arts organizations as case studies and tracked aspects of their operational activities from 2003 to 2010. These organizations represented major arts producing/presenting organizations in the Metro Vancouver area. All the Lower Mainland case studies that participated in the Cultural Olympiad experienced an increase in funding in 2007–08 (see figure 12.3). But the funding trend reveals an across-the-board fall in funding from 2009–10 onwards as a result of a number of factors, including cuts to gaming and BCAC grants, and the loss of Cultural Olympiad funding. In some cases the trend reverts the funding total to levels experienced a decade earlier.

Widening the circle to examine provincial groups outside the Lower Mainland leads to similar conclusions. One could expend considerable space examining each sector in depth. However, the significance of this chart can be found in the trend lines that emerge from the Campbell decade.

Essentially, BCAC funding levels for clients based outside the Lower Mainland declined dramatically in the lead-up to the Olympics. While the BCAC's funding did recover in 2010–11, the funding trend shows that overall funding levels did not attain previous levels.

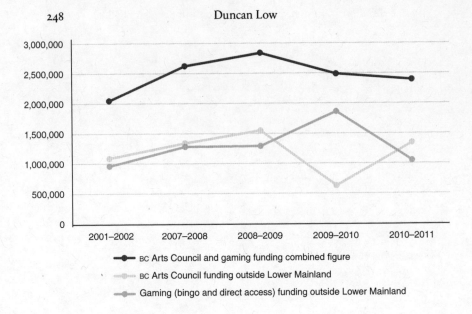

Figure 12.4   BC arts funding trends, 2001–2011

Sources: 2010 Cultural Olympiad Impact Study; BC Arts Council Annual Reports; BC Government Community Gaming Recipients 2001–2011.

Community gaming data provide further insight into the Campbell experience. In 2009, the government took the decision to cut direct access gaming funding by $20 million to arts groups, with a further review of bingo licence gaming grants – a decision that resulted in artists' protests in Victoria and Vancouver.[9]

The gaming trend shows that gaming funds were used as a stopgap to help the BCAC weather the dramatic decline in 2009–10 funding. However, looking at the combined BCAC and gaming trends, we see that the funding peaked in 2008–09 and declined thereafter. Ultimately, the trend lines reveal a great deal about Campbell's legacy, leaving no doubt that the "New Era" promises of increased support for the BC arts and cultural sector, although reasonably consistent in the early years, were to fall woefully short of expectations as the Olympic costs affected other areas of government activity, thus leaving many arts organizations in a similar or worse off financial position than what they occupied a decade earlier.

One of the more telling indicators of the province's gradual divestment in arts and culture over this period relates to the organizations that were entirely dependent upon community gaming revenue – that is, the ones ineligible for BCAC funding. This group of organizations predominantly represented smaller, more rural communities like the Pacific Rim Arts Society at Ucluelet or the Terrace Arts Association, whose funding guarantees appeared to fluctuate from year to year.

Some observers have commented that the funding cutbacks were the result of the world economic crisis of 2008. However, when looking at Canadian provincial and territorial arts budgets over the period from 2007 to 2010, we find that BC was the only province that posted a continuous decline in per capita spending on arts and culture (Canadian Conference of the Arts 2013, 8).

BC's Film and Media Sectors

In November 2001, Campbell was in California as part of a Jean Chretien–led Team Canada mission to promote the BC film industry, among other things. The trade delegation was met by protest calls to end illegal Canadian government film subsidies. In response, Campbell stated: "we are going to continue to compete and we are going to continue to be successful in the competition" (*Kamloops Daily News* 2001).

In May 2003, Premier Campbell introduced the Digital Animation and Visual Effects tax credit.[10] A member of the BC Film Commission recently stated that this tax credit had achieved its aim of bolstering that side of the industry. Yet, approximately one year after the 2003 tax credit announcement, the Campbell government decided not to extend the NDP's BC Feature Film Fund (BCFFF), which had been established in April 2001. The BCFFF's $4 million three-year commitment was managed by BC Film. BC Film's core budget, excluding the BCFFF, had also declined from $4.85 million in 1998 to $2.28 million in 2003–04 (Deveau 2004).

Noticing a reversal of fortunes in the industry, the BC government stepped in to save the ailing BC film and TV sector in January 2005. By raising rates to 18 per cent they matched Ontario's tax credit and averted a threatened exodus by BC-based film companies. At the time, Peter Leitch, chairman of the Motion Picture Production Industry Association, said: "The Premier is very supportive of the industry in the long term, but they're not going to solve our problem with tax credits ... we have to deal with the new reality of the higher dollar and aggressive competition [from other regions]" (Andrews 2005).

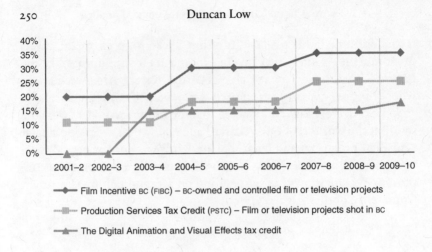

Figure 12.5   BC film tax credit incentives

Source: BC Film and Media annual reports, 2001–2010.

In 2007, the premier announced a five-year extension of the BC Film Tax Credit Program. And, again in 2010, the Campbell government reformed the provincial tax code to encourage film production in the province and to match Ontario and Quebec.

The fact that Premier Campbell was a supporter of the BC film and TV industry, recognizing the important economic impact of the industry, is clearly demonstrated in figure 12.5. That said, while raising tax incentives for the industry, the government was cutting direct subsidies to the BC Film Commission by 23 per cent from $1.2 million in 2009–10 to $948,000 in 2010–11, once again highlighting Campbell's market-driven mindset and perhaps even his pragmatic approach to program funding.

As the 2013 BC election has shown, the BC film industry continues to be an important issue and industry for the province. But it will be the task of future premiers and prime ministers to overcome the fundamental problem that tax credits are unable to solve. That is, they must address the following two questions: "[1] Should the BC government follow suit and increase the available tax credits? [and] (2) When does it stop making sense to continue upping the ante in order to attract Hollywood productions to BC?" (BC Statistics 2006, 3). They must also direct attention towards developing both a home-grown film production sector and a sustainable audience for that market.

BC Books

The book publishing industry in British Columbia represents all genres: scholarly, general trade, children's, poetry, drama, and education. The Association of Book Publishers of British Columbia (ABPBC) works to support the long-term health and success of the Canadian-owned book industry. They believe a healthy BC book industry is essential to the educational, social, cultural, and economic life of the province.

Book publishers have experienced some considerable changes over the last decade and are continuously developing new business models that incorporate changing methods of sales and delivery, including digital publications and e-books. In addition, they are in constant competition with American publishers.

The BC book publishing industry fell into the cultural/creative divide with publishers being "for profit" but also eligible for public support from various funding agencies, including the BCAC. The following statement issued by the ABPBC encapsulates the BC book industry's tenuous position:

> [We] operate in an environment where it is not feasible to be a Canadian publisher without receiving grants. We could not function. It's an environmental issue, the market is not big enough, the distribution is incredibly challenging. Because we have to get across the country – our cost of production is really high. (M. Reynolds, executive director, ABPBC, interview with author, 10 January 2013)

Prior to the 2001 election, BC book publishers had been lobbying for a BC book tax credit. The Campbell government obliged and introduced the credit in 2003. "It has been their [ABPBC] biggest success of the decade" (Reynolds, interview, 2013). "It was huge, worth between $2 to 2.5 million" (S. McIntyre, CEO Douglas and McIntyre, interview with author, 26 February 2013). Apart from the BC tax credit, the Campbell years essentially bypassed the BC book industry, as can be seen by the BCAC block funding figures and the number of BC book publishers that remained constant throughout the decade.

Two evaluations of the book publishing tax credit (BPTC) were carried out in 2006 and 2010. The evaluations confirmed that the BPTC was both efficient and effective and that the system was financially beneficial to the industry. However, the 2010 assessment also claimed that "the

Canadian book publishing industry continues to struggle with limited profitability and issues of competitiveness and stability" (Association of Book Publishers of British Columbia 2011). It is interesting to note that, forty years earlier, at the first meeting of the Independent Publishers Association, some of the same concerns were raised (Independent Publishers Association Meeting 1971).

BC Libraries

Gordon Campbell's commitment to the new economy can also be seen through his support of BC libraries. Soon after taking office, directives from the premier's office appeared asking for a new library plan. That plan, entitled "Libraries without Walls," appeared in 2005, along with a new investment of $12 million, and talked of broadband, online journals, and reference services.[11] One commentator claimed that this plan "resulted in quite a substantial increase through incentive grants to accomplish library projects of a provincial nature" (J. Looney, provincial library services [retired], interview with author, 15 February 2013).

When the US financial crisis hit the province in 2008, many of the new initiatives contained in the "Libraries without Walls" document dried up. For example, child identification cards, electronic access through core databases, books for babies, toddle to the library, and the teen reading club programs were all cancelled.

However, the province's libraries, an apparent policy priority for Campbell since his tenure as mayor of Vancouver, fared much better than did many other sectors that have been examined thus far. When looking at BC Public Libraries' statistics, we see that per capita spending rose from under forty dollars in 2007 to forty-six dollars in 2011.

Cultural Tourism

No examination of British Columbia's new economy would be complete without looking at cultural tourism policy. Premier Campbell launched the Community Tourism Program (CTP) at the UBCM conference in 2004. The CTP was an initiative to support local communities in their efforts to increase tourism as part of Premier Campbell's Olympic initiative to double BC tourism by 2015. The process was simple: local municipalities could apply to the provincial program to support initiatives that included festivals, art shows, music festivals, and other cultural activities. In Phase 1 of the CTP, 548 tourism projects were supported across the province, forty-seven of which were designated festivals and events.[12]

However, Campbell's tourism projections were unattainable. Indeed, a recent report states: "After a brief respite in 2010, the number of entries to Canada via British Columbia was down 4.3 per cent in 2011, continuing a downward trend that began in 2001. Since 2001, the volume of travellers to the province has shrunk by roughly 33 percent" (BC Statistics 2012, 1). The same document shows that, prior to 2001, the province's tourism figures had increased, year on year, since 1987.

Gordon Campbell's "red mitten Olympic boosterism" and promised tourism increases had fallen by the wayside at the time of his resignation. In the fall of 2011, however, Campbell's successor, Christy Clark, launched BC's new tourism strategy, "Gaining the Edge," and "acknowledged that it was time to ditch the pre-Olympic predictions of her predecessor" (Mickleburgh 2011).

Music BC

Cultural policy is often confusing and hard to disentangle. Music BC's funding pattern over this period represents a good example of this declaration as it fell on the cusp of the many definitional idiosyncrasies (e.g., "creative" versus "cultural," "not for profit" versus "for profit"). Music BC's membership includes artists, managers, agents, producers, and recording studios from across the province. The music industry, like many industries, consists of a number of constituent parts, from the independent local musician to the world's largest record producers/entertainment industries and everything in between. While BC does play host to some big names in the Canadian music industry, such as Sarah McLachlan, Bruce Allen, and Nettwerk Records, most of the industry giants and record labels are based in Ontario. In the words of Music BC's director, British Columbia's membership is "more artists, less industry" (B. D'Eith, executive director of Music BC, interview with author, 24 January 2013), meaning that the work of Music BC is predominantly aimed at artists' development, the business aspects of music, trying to get artists seen through trade shows, and touring networks.

Music BC's funding from 2001 to 2011 provides some insight into the cultural policy system in operation. At the beginning of the decade, Music BC received $100,000 per annum to support musicians touring throughout the province. In 2008, this sub-agency's funding was cut to $50,000.[13]

Music BC also received operating funds of $45,000 per year direct from the Ministry of Tourism, Culture and the Arts. In 2008, these operating funds were cut to zero. This funding has, at the time of writing, not been replaced. While other organizations, such as the ABPBC, were able to apply to the BCAC for funds, this avenue was, and remained, inaccessible to Music BC. Yet there have been some minor developments. In 2009, the Juno awards came to British Columbia. Music BC received a one-off $650,000 in direct funding from the ministry to bid for, and host, these national awards.

Similar to the actions of the ABPBC, Music BC embarked on a period of discussion (2001–04) with the provincial government to support the development of the BC music industry through the creation of a tax credit system – similar to those granted to the BC film and publishing sectors. After some debate it was agreed that, due to the make-up of the BC music industry, the introduction of a BC tax credit system wouldn't necessarily be the best way to support BC musicians. All parties agreed that what was needed was more development funding. Music BC, and others, lobbied for the creation of a BC organization similar to the Ontario Media Development Corporation.[14]

In the run-up to the 2013 election, the BC Liberals supported the creation of a development corporation. Minister Bennet, with $1 million in additional funding, announced the creation of "Creative BC, an independent agency that will help BC's creative industries seek new opportunities" (Cassidy 2013).

CONCLUSION

Summarizing Gordon Campbell's decade in government from the arts, cultural, and creative perspective is complicated. Given the itemized examination of several aspects of the arts in British Columbia from 2001 to 2011, one might conclude that his real commitment to the sector and his attempt to diversify funding models based on increased market-driven investment returns was, for the most part, mixed. Indeed, on the one hand, his government's efforts could be judged to have been largely unsuccessful. But how does one define "unsuccessful"? To answer this question we must return to the original election manifesto, which promised to "increase funding for the British Columbia Arts Council to promote and support BC arts, music, artists and culture" (British Columbia Liberal Party 2001, 10).

A series of cultural policy decisions by the Campbell government, both before and after the 2010 Olympics, created the "perfect storm," which not only destabilized but also highlighted the political vulnerabilities of BC's arts community.

First, BCAC funding was reduced by nearly 50 per cent (from $14 million to $8 million). Second, the government rejected the recommendation of its own Standing Committee on Finance and Government Services, which said that arts funding should be restored to 2008–09 levels. Third, the government eliminated gaming grants to adult arts programs. Finally, and perhaps most revealing, came the announcement that a new $10 million arts legacy fund would not be administered by the BCAC and that these funds would only be distributed to arts groups meeting the needs of Spirit Festivals to be held as a tribute to the 2010 Winter Olympics.

On 16 August 2010, Jane Danzo responded by resigning as chair of the BCAC, stating that, "instead of restoring the funding to the BCAC, the government announced the establishment of an Arts Legacy Fund, a surprise as much to the board as to the arts community," once again illustrating the preference for one-off projects as opposed to sustained public funding (Danzo 2010).

This series of decisions illustrated the Campbell government's disdain for the long-held Canadian practice of arts and cultural policy being arm's length from the day-to-day operation of government. This confirmed Danzo's (2010) opinion that the BCAC board did not have a voice independent of government. In her resignation, Danzo said: "In my opinion the work of the BCAC board has not been supported by government on a number of different levels." Further: "the devastating impact of that decision [the decision to reduce both BCAC and gaming funding] is now being felt by artists and arts organizations throughout the province as they receive notification of substantial cuts to their core funding."

The response came from communities spread across the province, confirming the position voiced by the director of the Alliance for Arts and Culture: "the arts community is in crisis." It would be two years before, in 2012, Kevin Falcon, a senior cabinet member during the Campbell decade, confirmed the government's failure to support the arts: "arts and cultural groups got the short end of the stick when the government tried to exert fiscal discipline three years ago."[15]

Something else that must be looked at when defining Gordon Campbell's level of success is tourism in general and cultural tourism in particular. The "New Era" document promised to stimulate tourism in the province, an undertaking that, as we have already seen, was "unsuccessful" while Campbell was premier.

On a more positive note, the Campbell government's use of tax credits to support the creative industries of film, TV, and book publishing enabled BC's industry to maintain a leading position across the continent. Unfortunately, the economic sustainability of this model (according to which separate provincial governments compete by progressively raising their tax credit rates to support their film industry by attracting international productions) remains tentative (and contingent) at best.

Another success that can be attributed to the Campbell government is that of the Knowledge Network. During his decade in power, BC's public broadcaster was transformed from an organization with an uncertain future into an important component of BC's creative economy.

Gordon Campbell will be remembered for his "presidential" use of one-off funding awards. Here, some examples of success include the Renaissance Fund, where the original $25 million investment generated matching funds of $52 million, and the $6 million endowment to establish the British Columbia Achievement Foundation. While recognizing this success, one must also be cautious when evaluating its strategic implications for the cultural sector overall. Historically, groups that disproportionately benefit from "matching programs" are often the larger, more prestigious groups that already have a higher fundraising profile than their smaller community group counterparts – a position that was well articulated in an interview with the director of Vancouver's Bill Reid Gallery over the proposed relocation of the Vancouver Art Gallery (again, a project energized by Campbell's one-off investment of $50 million towards a new building) (Lederman 2013, S3). The Vancouver Art Gallery's new site, part of the proposed cultural precinct, has been confirmed, although the land was conditional upon the gallery's raising $150 million by 2015 (a target not yet achieved). As of March 2017, the city has extended the land availability to allow the gallery more time to achieve its original funding target, and only time will tell whether it is another Guggenheim in Bilbao.

In his recent book, Martyn Brown, Gordon Campbell's chief of staff for thirteen years, talked of the relationship between social licence and political power, claiming that "social license is what legitimizes the use of power for desired outcomes. Power used without social license is just blunt force. The power to act with authority is only as good as the social license that supports it" (Brown 2012). From an arts and cultural perspective, it could be argued that the Campbell government's decision to cut arts funding in the run-up to the Olympics fell into the category of using power without social licence. This was clearly demonstrated by the headline that appeared in the *Vancouver Sun* on 29 May 2010, stating: "Arts Festivals Cut Off from Gambling Funds; Social Development Minister Defends Decision to End Funding for Music and Arts Events He Says Should Pay Their Own Way." The minister, Rich Coleman (a Campbell stalwart), went on to say: "it's not the government's job to decide whether a festival is commercially viable by subsidizing it." An extraordinary statement, considering that the Campbell government had only very recently discharged its duties under the Olympic Charter to host one of the most heavily subsidized arts events on the planet – an Olympic Games and accompanying Cultural Olympiad – both of which were at the centre of Campbell's 2001 "New Era" vision.

I noted at the beginning of this chapter that the arts sector hadn't fared well under the previous NDP government. Reflecting upon Gordon Campbell's ten years in office, it would be fair to say that BC's arts and cultural community's position had not improved. And, in many instances, organizations were worse off in 2011 than they were in 2001. Perhaps the most important conclusion to be drawn from this analysis of cultural policy over the Campbell decade is that the promised "arts legacy" that precedes the hosting of any expensive mega-events has, once again, proved to be a fallacy.

NOTES

1 See News 1130, "History of the Vancouver Olympic Bid," http://www
   .news1130.com/2010/02/05/history-of-the-vancouver-olympic-bid/.
2 The goods sector includes industries with which most people are familiar: agriculture, fishing, forestry, mining, manufacturing, construction, and utilities (BC Statistics 2010, 16).
3 See Martin Prosperity Institute, "Insight – Rise Revisited: Creativity Index," http://martinprosperity.org/tag/creativity-index/.
4 $150 million was allotted to the BC150 Cultural Fund, a permanent endowment.
5 See British Columbia, "$209 Million to Enhance B.C.'s Arts and Culture," news release, 6 March 2008, http://www2.news.gov.bc.ca/news_releases_ 2005-2009/2008OTP0050-000305.htm.
6 Vancouver Symphony and Opera; Vancouver Playhouse; Stanley Theatre;

Arts Club Theatre; Firehall Centre; Dance and Children's Festival; Scotia-Bank Dance Centre and Contemporary Art Gallery; Theatre Northwest; Western Canada Theatre; Belfry Theatre, Victoria; Bill Miner Society, Armstrong; Story Theatre; Kamloops, Vancouver Island, Okanagan, and Prince George symphony orchestras; Prince George, Kamloops, Victoria, Campbell River, and Nanaimo art galleries; Sunshine Coast Written Arts; Victoria Jazz Festival; Mission Folk Festival; Harrison Festival; Uno Festival, Victoria; Crimson Coast Dance, Nanaimo; Suddenly Dance, Victoria; Canadian Alliance of Dance Arts.

7 Theatre Northwest; Western Canada Theatre; Belfry Theatre, Victoria; Bill Miner Society, Armstrong; Story Theatre; Kamloops, Vancouver Island, Okanagan, and Prince George Symphony; Prince George, Kamloops, Victoria, Campbell River, and Nanaimo art galleries; Sunshine Coast Written Arts; Victoria Jazz Festival; Mission Folk Festival; Harrison Festival; Uno Festival, Victoria; Crimson Coast Dance, Nanaimo; Suddenly Dance, Victoria; Canadian Alliance of Dance Arts.

8 Metro Vancouver is a political body and corporate entity operating under provincial legislation as a "regional district" and "greater boards" that deliver regional services, policy, and political leadership on behalf of twenty-four local authorities.

9 See British Columbia, "Updated Community Gaming Grant Documents and Forms," 31 March 2010, http://www.gaming.gov.bc.ca/news/docs/2010-03-31.htm.

10 See British Columbia Ministry of Finance, "British Columbia Digital Animation or Visual Effects (DAVE) Tax Credit," tax bulletin, revised February 2011, http://www.sbr.gov.bc.ca/documents_library/bulletins/cit_011.pdf.

11 See British Columbia, "Public Libraries," http://www.bced.gov.bc.ca/pls/library_strategic_plan.pdf.

12 See Union of BC Municipalities, "Community Tourism," 2012, http://www.ubcm.ca/EN/main/funding/tourism-marketing/community-tourism.html.

13 The Ministry of Tourism, Culture and the Arts is now renamed the Ministry of Community, Sport and Cultural Development.

14 See OMDC, "About Us," http://www.omdc.on.ca/about_us.htm. Ontario Media Development Corporation, an agency of the Ministry of Tourism, Culture and Sport, is the central catalyst for the province's cultural media cluster, including book publishing, film and television, interactive digital media, magazine publishing, and music industries.

15 See Tamsyn Burgmann, "BC Finance Minister Calls Arts Funding Cuts 'A Mistake,'" CTV News, 11 January 2012, http://bc.ctvnews.ca/b-c-finance-minister-calls-arts-funding-cuts-a-mistake-1.752059#ixzz2TyE5PHB0.

13

Vancouver's 2010 Olympic Games
The Mitigated Success of Premier Campbell

EMMANUEL BRUNET-JAILLY

Olympic Games symbolize an important challenge that many modern metropolitan centres face in the twenty-first century. In essence, cities have now become sites where social and economic compromises clash (Shaw 2008). Harvard professor Gerald Frug has been noted for asking "whose city is this?" in his attempt to illustrate and underline the difficulty with which residents of our "brave new urban era" are faced, particularly when they are asked to decide on complex policy issues (Frug 2005). The Vancouver/Whistler/British Columbia/Canadian Winter Olympic Games of 21–28 February 2010 are an excellent example of how difficult compromises are carved out of local, provincial, federal, and international forces.

I begin this chapter by providing an overview of urban growth and entertainment machines and then turn to the link between Olympic Games and the influence of local and global actors. I also address the 2010 Vancouver Olympic Games' history, the role of the Vancouver Olympic Committee (VANOC), BC's and Ottawa's respective responsibilities, the part played by the private sector, and how the games' development was monitored. The material presented here suggests that, although the business and provincial elites of British Columbia, and in particular Premier Gordon Campbell, originally viewed the 2010 Olympic Games as a way to further enhance Vancouver's economic growth, from about 2002 onward both Whistler and Vancouver were sites of debates and controversies that ended up affecting the implementation of the Olympic Games.

In the end, the strategy underlying the implementation of the games was neither uniquely market oriented nor socially oriented but, rather, resulted from a tug-of-war between civic groups and city leaders engaging with provincial and business leaders. In retrospect, the games left little impact on British Columbia outside of Greater Vancouver and did not really benefit Premier Campbell, who remained entangled in the controversy surrounding provincial tax reform, which was later withdrawn from the Liberal Party's agenda.

URBAN GROWTH AND ENTERTAINMENT MACHINES

Students of urban phenomena have argued for a number of years that North American and Western European cities, in particular, are faced with social, economic, and ultimately cultural problems due to, on the one hand, de-industrialization and, on the other, the information-communication revolution. In our post-industrial/digital era, the displacement of economic activities from cities' centres to their peripheries and increased unemployment are the visible parts of a phenomenon that has been deeply transforming the social, economic, and cultural nature of our more modern urban environments.

Terry Nichols Clark argues that urban growth is not primarily driven by production but by consumption and entertainment through the provision of amenities and that it generally results from postmodern values (Clark 2004; Clark et al. 2003). In the same vein, Saskia (2000) proposes that in an international system defined by competition, only *global* cities hosting advanced services and telecommunication industries will manage to win. Castells shows that new technologies of information and communication, instead of diffusing development gains, reinforce processes of concentration into fewer places. These are what Castells (1992) refers to as new "informational cities." Dreier, Mollenkopf, and Swanstrom (2001, 136) suggest that cities' resources are decreasing while demands for expanded municipal services are increasing. According to Savitch and Kantor (2002), what is central to cities' governance success is their ability to set up winning-bargaining coalitions that limit their constraints while increasing their clout in relation to both public- and private-sector actors. Indeed, cities do not systematically lose when businesses win. And cities do not systematically choose either a market or a socially driven governance strategy: most of them choose intermediate governance paths. Hence, cities compete and bargain for amenities, infrastructures, and skills internationally across both intergovernmental and business networks.

Nichols Clark argues that the current "entertainment machine" goes "beyond the growth machine" (Clark 2004, 295; also see Burbank, Heying, and Andranovich 2001) because local economic bases are now dominated by high-technology developments and finance so that land-use intensification does not steer growth to the same extent as it did in the past. It is human capital – that is, an educated and mobile work-force – that leads cities to be "places with talented people [that] both grow faster and ... attract other talented people" (Florida and Gates 2003, 200). Communities, Clark (2004, 297) argues, have embarked on entertainment strategies, and have moved towards a political culture that organizes a "shift from pure economic growth to a (slightly) more managed growth," whereby "production concerns have been increasingly supplanted by consumption and aesthetic issues."

In the same vein, for Richard Florida (2002, 297), cities are entertainment machines where a newly identified creative class contributes to the rise of "the individual citizen-consumer." This translates into greater individualization and volatility of tastes. Florida measures the existence of this "creative class" with a "bohemian" index, which is a composite diversity index suggesting that "social, cultural, and ethnic diversity are strong indicators of a metropolitan area's high-technology success" (200–11). Thus, while city officials used to focus on attracting investments and job-creating factories, now they attempt to provide an attractive environment in which to live, work, and play. The Olympics, for instance, which tend to supersize cities with sports and recreation amenities, are an element of such a strategy (see Judd and Fainstein 1999).

Entertainment strategies are not straightforward approaches that can be easily typified as market-driven or socially driven strategies; these are finely crafted bargaining strategies used to develop critical sets of amenities among which infrastructures play a foundational role, and in which public intergovernmental and private networks intersect more or less successfully. The "Nobel prize" of entertainment – an Olympic Games – is the most complex of all because of its scale: it presents a city with an opportunity to reinvent itself, yet within the BC/Canadian context it also presented some challenges to civic leaders in Vancouver/Whistler in that the Canadian Constitution allows provincial governments to create/terminate local governments. And Canadian municipal-provincial relations remain characterized as quasi-subordinate where provincial governments are able to dictate policy decisions.

HISTORY: TWO CITIES FOR ONE SUCCESSFUL BID

The 2010 Vancouver Olympics ended up costing approximately $7 billion – a third of which was spent on new infrastructure projects. These investments certainly transformed both Vancouver and Whistler, but they gave very little in the way of benefits to the rest of the province. We also know that the federal and provincial governments carried most of these costs and that the revenue derived from the games' ticket sales, merchandise, and so on accounted for only a fraction of its expense. All in all, for every twelve dollars spent by the federal and provincial governments, Vancouver and Whistler residents spent one dollar. At the same time, the Olympic Games did not provide any boost in tourism, nor did it affect, either positively or negatively, the international image of Vancouver and Whistler or of British Columbia as a whole (Van Wynsberghe 2013, 29 and 217–18). The business or real estate attractiveness of both host cities was not impacted either (Van Wynsberghe 2013, 16 and 34–46). The Olympic Games supersized entertainment amenities, and stimulated some investment in public transportation and residential infrastructures in Vancouver (Richmond) and Whistler but, as a whole, had a very limited short-term economic impact when measured in terms of jobs, or per capita economic increase for the province (Van Wynsberghe 2013, 20 and 99–100).

Originally, the idea to make a bid for the Olympics came from Whistler. Specifically, it was the result of the activism of a group of businesspeople that, since the 1960s, had hoped to see Whistler host the Winter Olympic Games. The development of the city of Whistler is, in part, the result of that Olympic dream: in the 1960s, Franz Wilhelmsen had created the Garibaldi Olympic Development Association, with the purpose of hosting the games in 1968. But in 1968, 1976, and 1988, Whistler's bids were unsuccessful. These failed attempts to host the Winter Olympic had "snowballed," however, into to the building of several winter sports amenities, the growth of tourism, and the transformation of Whistler into a very successful internationally visible and established resort. As a result of early bids, not only had Whistler developed outstanding winter sports facilities and major mega-events hosting capacity, but it had also acquired real expertise in bidding for major events. For decades, it had yearly welcomed a World Cup, festivals, and conferences.

Vancouver had also been involved in the mega-event business for a long time. It had hosted the World's Fair Expo '86. At the time, the province's Social Credit Party had taken leadership. Expo '86 changed the city. As Punter (2003, 192) suggests: "Expo '86 is widely credited with marketing Vancouver to the rest of the world and reviving the city's economic fortunes. It has generated a series of public works during an economic recession and left the city with some important tourist and cultural facilities." Above all, Expo '86 triggered and accelerated real estate redevelopment in the industrial brownfield of the False Creek area, the southern part of the core city. The provincial government had bought False Creek North land for Expo '86 and had sold it afterwards to Hong Kong developer Li Ka-shing's corporation Concord-Pacific. The waterfront had then been developed into an integrated mixed-use-high-density residential area made up of high-rises and walkways. This development had also encouraged the migration of Asian families to downtown Vancouver.

Both Whistler and Vancouver had had positive and profitable experiences hosting mega-events, and it is in this context that Tourism Whistler and Tourism Vancouver partnered and approached Vancouver's City Council with an Olympic bid project in 1998. At this time, it is important to note that the bid itself actually originated and was advanced by a provincial NDP government. Indeed, it is easy to forget, through the brouhaha of provincial and local politics (detailed below), that prior to its collapse in 2001, the NDP and its premier at the time, Glen Clark, supported the pan-Canadian bid that allowed Vancouver to compete internationally. It is the NDP that was responsible for this first success: Vancouver won over Calgary and Quebec City, thanks to that leadership. At the time, Premier Clark gave $50,000 to the bid leaders, Antonson of Tourism Vancouver and Griffiths of Whistler, and also admitted: "It galvanizes everyone to host an event like this, and we thought we could use this as a catalyst for very serious investment." In November of 1998, Premier Clark went to Toronto to defend the bid in front of the Olympics committee in person. By August 1999, the NDP and Clark, in particular, were entangled in a casino-related scandal and lost their political credibility (Bula 2009).

Once Vancouver City Council approved the idea of bidding for the 2010 Olympic Games, Vancouver and Whistler jointly established the Vancouver 2010 Bid Corporation. And, once the bid was successful, this partnership became known as the Vancouver Olympic Committee. One of the first steps was the signing of a multiparty agreement, which raised a number of questions in both Vancouver and Whistler. In Whistler, for instance, the city ended up adding to the Multiparty Agreement that "all work necessary for the organization of the 2010 games within Whistler is required to comply with Whistler bylaws and regulations," hence empowering the claims of Whistlerites (Multi-Party Agreement 2002). Indeed, at the time of negotiations,

Whistler's council realized that less than 60 per cent of its residents supported the Olympics bid. When public suspicions and hesitations regarding a new Olympic bid became real, Whistler's city council organized a public consultation that led to the drafting of five guiding principles, which, throughout the bid and implementation of the Olympics, protected the city's priorities and ensured that the Olympic benefited the resort and its community (Interview 2, Whistler Municipal Office, 9 March 2006).[1] These five principles were: (1) the province had to provide new financial tools to the municipality; (2) the province had to provide a community land bank of three hundred acres to develop housing for Whistler residents; (3) Victoria had to approve Whistler's boundary expansion to ensure better control over the use of the land and prevent business development at the edge of the municipal boundaries; (4) the Olympic Games had to respect Whistler's official development plan, notably its growth cap; and (5) the Olympic Games had to be financially sustainable – it should not trigger any budget overruns or increases in local taxes. In sum, in Whistler, the Olympic bid did not just target more visitors, more tourism, and more business development; rather it was tailored to answer Whistler's community, economic, environmental, and social sustainability concerns.

In Vancouver, the Olympic bid also took a progressive turn in the fall of 2002 when a new municipal government was elected. A new civic organization, a progressive and left-wing civic group called the Coalition of Progressive Electors (COPE), came to power along with a new mayor, Larry Campbell; and, despite being split over the issue of the Olympics, COPE was effective in bringing it forward.

Newly elected mayor Larry Campbell had laid out his commitment to public consultation, participation, and approval of the games during the campaign. He had actually linked his mayoral mandate to a thorough consultation on the games. And, despite both the disapproval of the provincial government and of Premier Gordon Campbell, he decided a referendum should be held in the municipality of Vancouver in February 2003. His view was that, in order to overcome his own party's (COPE's) divisions and to increase citizens' input in the decision-making process leading to the Olympic bid (and during the possible implementation of the games), a referendum was necessary. Prior to the staging of the referendum, the mayor set in motion a wide consultation process about the Olympic Games, notably in the Downtown Eastside, the most vulnerable and poorest part of the city.

In November 2002, the Bid Corporation also issued a "2010 Winter Games Inner-City Inclusive Commitment Statement," which was a pledge of social inclusiveness for downtown residents during the implementation of the Olympics. It promised to "[maximize] the opportunities and [mitigate] potential impacts in Vancouver's inner-city neighborhoods from hosting the 2010 Olympics" (Ference Weicker and Company 2003). The principles put forward were the following: accessible games for disabled people, affordable games and recreation, business development and opportunities for the downtown core, protection of civil liberties and public safety, social and environmental sustainability, housing guarantees, and public input in decision making.

In the end, the referendum was successful, with the yes side garnering 64 per cent of the votes. Notable here is that voter turnout was much higher than it had been during the most recent municipal election (about 46 per cent of Vancouverites went to the polls for the referendum). The city immediately ordered a social assessment of the Olympic Games to identify the potential risks and opportunities for inner-city neighbourhoods. A report by Ference Weicker and Company was published in 2003. Also, the Impact on Community Coalition (IOCC), which called itself the "Olympic watchdog," was included along with all other city partners to examine the substance of the bid. IOCC's goals were to identify and address issues of concern for the citizens of Vancouver. It was not opposed to Vancouver hosting the games, in principle, but it wanted to ensure that community issues were addressed. IOCC was the Vancouver umbrella of a number of watchdog and neighbourhood associations that covered a broad array of issues and questions, such as housing, environment, transportation, community economic development, accountability and transparency, security and safety, and civil liberties.

In terms of public involvement and input in the games across the city, the chair of the IOCC drew positive conclusions: "In early 2003, there was a referendum on the Olympics. What happened with that? There were a number of community forums hosted by the City related to the Olympics. It was about economic development, environment, transportation, and housing. These forums were well attended. I think the citizens were well informed. And there was a huge turnout. And 64% of people voted in favor of the games. It was overwhelmingly accepted by the citizens" (Interview 4, IOCC, 15 June 2009).

In other words, following the election of Larry Campbell, and the referendum results, the bid took a much more socially sustainable pathway in Vancouver, and this steered the city's earlier commitment and influenced the Olympic Committee as well as the federal, provincial, and local governments. This, in all likelihood, sealed the feasibility of the bid (Ference Weicker and Company 2003). Not only had the bid and the Olympic Games, on the surface at least, become more inclusive, but they had also become more visible, involving the interests and participation of many Vancouverites and Whistlerites.

The bid had shifted from a relatively elitist beginning to a much more socially and environmentally oriented endeavour that was very much in the public eye. It had evolved into more than an elitist "growth machine" to become a "social contract" between the Bid Corporation and Vancouver and Whistler. Although the Vancouver Olympic bid originated from a cluster of tourism, business, and provincial interests, in the end it seemed more aligned with Vancouver's and Whistler's priorities and seemed to address environmental and social impact issues that were important to each of those communities.

The monitoring of the Olympic Games, discussed in the next section, details the relationships of both Whistler and Vancouver with the province, Premier Campbell, the federal government, the private sector, and VANOC.

GAMES, STEWARDSHIP, AND MONITORING

At the core of a broad Olympics partnership is the coordinating role of the Olympic Committee. Typically, it sets the balance of power between local, provincial, and federal levels of government, on the one hand, and the private sector, on the other. Issues of control of expenditures, direct and indirect costs, the financial structure, and the accountability of Olympic Games are crucial. In Vancouver, these relations shed light on the leadership role of Premier Campbell. Also, because sporting events of this kind have proven to be financially profitable, they can result from the exclusive involvement of the private sector. In the literature, Olympic Games are often discussed as private enterprises. The 1984 Los Angeles Games and/or the 2000 Sydney Games exemplify the implementation of such a private-growth-machine enterprise that restrains community participation. To assess the stewardship of Olympic Games, Lenskyj (1996), therefore, compared the structure of the Olympic organizational committees of Sydney and Toronto, and pointed out that the latter was more democratic because it was accountable to the city council whereas the former was a private-sector corporation. The Toronto Olympic Committee was also more representative in its composition, while Sydney's committee essentially represented business interests. Furthermore, French and Disher (1997) show that the fragmentation of the organizational team of the 1996 Atlanta Olympics acted as a deterrent to community involvement because power was diluted, and, in the end, it was especially difficult to understand who was in charge. French and Disher (1997) argue that, thanks to the limited role of the city government, the games' organization in Atlanta and their exclusively private funding precluded a "truly open and public process in preparing plans and projects" (391). The next section reviews the Vancouver Organizing Committee.

The Vancouver Olympic Committee

A first multiparty agreement, including the Canadian federal government, the province of British Columbia, the city of Vancouver, the resort municipality of Whistler, and the Vancouver 2010 Bid Corporation, was signed on 14 November 2002. It created the organizing committee for the Olympic Games – a not-for-profit organization in charge of planning, organizing, staging, and financing the games.

The organizational committee, later called the Vancouver Olympic Committee, or VANOC, was made up of twenty members appointed by the Canadian Olympic Committee, the Government of Canada, the province of British Columbia, the city of Vancouver, the resort municipality of Whistler, the Canadian Paralympic Committee, and the band councils of the Lil'wat Nation and the Squamish Nation. VANOC was expected to be representative of each party involved politically, locally, and financially.

The role of VANOC was at the core of the partnership. It had to find new partners, to promote the Olympic Games, to manage the budget, to provide information (reports, media release, analyses, etc.), and to gather the different partners involved in this mega-event. Its role was also to campaign and to protect the Olympic Games, its logo, and the Olympic brand. In addition, VANOC played an important role in fundraising for the Olympics. For instance, the 2010 Vancouver Olympics was the first Olympic Games to be promoted through social media, with 1.1 million Facebook friends, and to offer audio and video podcasts on iTunes, with 1 million videos downloaded in about fifty countries around the world (Menzies 2012). John Furlong, VANOC's

chief officer, lobbied the provincial and federal governments as well as
the private sector for resources. VANOC was also in charge of ticketing
and merchandising. All in all, VANOC raised as much as it spent and balanced its $1.8 billion budget. Most of its resources came from corporate
sponsorships, $480 million came from the IOC, $174 million from IOC
sponsorship revenues, $270 million from Olympic ticket sales (about 97
per cent of all of the 1.5 million tickets sold), and $55 million from
Olympic merchandising.

VANOC, however, had very limited influence on Olympic venues,
particularly those that were not directly linked to the games. The development plans and the choice of developers was the responsibility
of each municipality. VANOC was responsible for operating a few sites
and, in most instances, cooperated with each municipality and the
province (Interview 5, Vancouver City Manager's Office, 6 March
2006). VANOC's development responsibilities were limited to Cypress
Mountain, where the snowboarding, aerials, moguls, and ski cross
events were held, and the Vancouver Olympic/Paralympic Centre in
Hillcrest Park. VANOC spent a fraction of its overall budget on those
sites – about $56 millions.

In addition, VANOC had nearly no freedom to act with regards to social issues, as social policies are the responsibility of the province and
each municipality (Interview 5, Vancouver City Manager's Office, 6
March 2006). In brief, VANOC had very restricted powers, whereas the
city of Vancouver, the resort municipality of Whistler, the province, and,
to an extent, the federal government were in charge. Indeed, in the end,
VANOC spent about $470 million exclusively on partnered venue devel-
opment, and those resources came from both the provincial and the
federal governments.

In brief, not all Olympic partnerships are premised on an understanding that every partner involved in the games should be treated on
an equal footing. In this case, both Vancouver and Whistler were to be
associated as much as possible in the monitoring of the games. The
multi-level partnership provided a mechanism to sort out issues before
they could become problematic; therefore, the partnership was perceived as a good problem-solving process. As illustrated in the next section, nearly all the facilities involving VANOC, both cities, and First
Nations are known to have been a success. However, some issues were
never meant to be part of VANOC's mandate.

CITY OF VANCOUVER
AND RESORT MUNICIPALITY OF WHISTLER

Vancouver's city manager was a member of VANOC's Board of Directors and supervised the city's games secretariat, whose goal was to coordinate all city services and to ensure that the city's priorities were taken into account in the monitoring of the games. A wide range of city services were involved, including engineering-related tasks (e.g., transportation, public cleaning, urban planning, etc.), security, communications, and environmental monitoring.

Similarly, in Whistler, the town manager was responsible for all Olympic operations. He was also a member of VANOC's Board of Directors and Tourism Whistler and helped to set up the Whistler Information Centre to advertise the games across the resort.

Both Vancouver and Whistler partnered with the provincial and federal governments and, with VANOC, spent about $900 million to renovate or develop new Olympic venues across their respective communities. Across Metro Vancouver, the following facilities were established, renovated, or redeveloped: Richmond's Olympic Oval, the University of British Columbia's Thunderbird Sports Centre, Vancouver's Hillcrest Community Centre, the Vancouver Olympic Village, West Vancouver-Cypress Mountain ski resort, and the Whistler Olympic Park and Sliding Centre.

In sum, the participatory bent of both Vancouver and Whistler paid off enormously. Indeed, what is striking is that most of the amenities built for the Olympics remain and have been successfully transformed into municipal-neighbourhood housing, recreation, and sporting facilities. With the exception of Vancouver's Olympic Village, none of these ever became seriously controversial. These are exemplary because they emerged from one of Canada's most complex urban regional and intergovernmental environments and involved cities engaging and cooperating with multiple governments and First Nations (see below).

FIRST NATIONS

Early in the Olympic bid, there were media reports that First Nations were reluctant to engage with it. In the end, however, their involvement was critical not only to the success of the bid but also to the overall success of the games. One example of initial concern may be found in the views of Gord Hill, of the Kwakwaka'wakw Nation, who argued that

the implementation of the Olympics would adversely affect traditional First Nations ways of life and hurt their territories. Others, like Leah
Wilson-George of the Tsleil-Waututh Nation, defended the First Nations relationship with VANOC, describing it as "exemplary."

The involvement of First Nations in the planning and development
of the Olympic Games is well documented. For instance, one of VANOC's
media releases underscores the fact that First Nations businesses were
deemed to have benefited from contracts to the tune of about $45 mil-
lion. Others, like hereditary Squamish Nation chief Bill Williams, saw
opportunities for his people in terms of jobs related to developing the
games. All in all, however, post-games assessments highlight the limited nature of the impact of the games on First Nations well-being.
VANOC's success with the private sector and the provincial/federal governments, however, was much less obvious.

FEDERAL AND PROVINCIAL GOVERNMENTS

The federal and provincial governments funded most of the indirect
costs of the Olympic Games. These were expenditures either planned or
in discussion prior to the Olympic bid and whose implementation
timeline was shortened thanks to the success of the bid. The most expensive infrastructure undertakings were the SkyTrain Canada Line,
which cost $2.1 billion; the expansion of the Vancouver Convention
Centre, which cost $900 million; and the Sea-to-Sky Highway linking
Vancouver to Whistler, which cost $600 million. Indeed, both the Cana-
da Line SkyTrain and the Sea-to-Sky Highway ended up being extremely controversial and led to provincewide political tensions. At one
point, Victoria stepped in and stripped Vancouver's transportation
agency, Translink, of any power to implement the Canada Line – a move
that frustrated concerned municipalities in the Greater Vancouver area.
Similarly, regarding the Sea-to-Sky Highway, the provincial government
ignored environmental concerns and superior railway transportation
proposals (Cornwall 2004). In all, the province spent about $3 billion
on the Olympics, $2 billion on indirect infrastructure costs, and $1 billion on sports venues, organizing the Olympic Games, and security.
Ottawa paid about one-third of those indirect infrastructure, and most
security-related, costs.

To monitor its contribution, the federal government set up the
Olympic and Paralympic 2010 Federal Secretariat, originally committing $497 million, and then kept a keen interest in raising sponsorship

and business opportunities through its "Canada 2010 Marketplace" forum. Also, it was responsible for delivering essential government services for the games, such as security, customs, and immigration.

The province, as had been the case for Expo '86, provided the 2010 Olympic Games with extremely strong support in the form of funding, expertise, and leadership. It is notable that, once the bid phase was successful, the province's commitment to the games became decisive. But, as early as 1998, Campbell's Liberal government had entered into a participation agreement with Vancouver to address cost issues arising from the bid for the 2010 Olympic and Paralympic Games. The province had agreed to fund overruns of the Olympic project through the creation of a contingency fund. As well, it set up a special "secretariat" under the Ministry of Economic Development to monitor its contribution to the games. Originally, it was primarily responsible for overseeing a $600 million commitment, and budget overruns, which affected most areas of expenditures due to rising costs in the construction industry – indeed, between 2003 and 2008 economic growth led to major development cost increases. Those tumbled when the most dramatic economic crisis since 1929 hit in the fall of 2008 and then rolled across the Western world, sinking a large number of economies and financial-sector icons. In the end, the direct costs of the Olympics to the provincial government ended up being closer to about $1 billion, with indirect costs reaching $2 billion (Interview 6, Olympics Planning Team, 16 June 2008). Because of this very high level of financial and organizational involvement the province managed its financial support closely.

As early as 2002, the minister of state for Community Charter and 2010 Olympic Bid published initial estimates in *The Economic Impact of the 2010 Winter Olympic and Paralympic Games*, a report that had been prepared by the Ministry of Competition, Science, and Enterprise the year before (Ministry of Competition, Science, and Enterprise 2002). It is interesting to note that, at this early stage of the bid and partnership, the report already acknowledged representatives of the BC business community – Jock Finlayson, then vice-president of policy at the British Columbia Business Council, figured prominently. The report forecasted 59,000 to 106,000 new jobs, an economic contribution to the provincial economy of between $5.7 and $10 billion, and, in the best estimate, federal, provincial, and local taxes would increase by $535, $496, and $100 million, respectively (8). Particularly interesting is the fact that these positive outcomes were all premised on an increased number of foreign visitors, which would contribute to a 43.5 per cent increase in tourism (29).

The Olympic Games were also promoted on the assumption that provincial businesses would benefit, in particular tourism, construction, and development. On several occasions, Premier Gordon Campbell voiced his strong commitment to the games. His leadership position could not have been clearer than during his 2 July 2002 keynote address to the Vancouver Board of Trade. It is probably one of his most visible and quoted addresses. He said: "The Olympics can help make us better in BC. The Olympics can help take us out beyond the mundane to something bigger than all of us, something that is stronger than we can imagine" (British Columbia Olympic and Paralympic Winter Games Secretariat 2004). Furthermore, when Ted Nebbeling, a former city councillor and mayor of Whistler, was re-elected as a member of the Legislative Assembly of British Columbia in 2001, he was made minister of state for the Community Charter and for the 2010 Winter Olympics – a clear indication that Premier Campbell's Liberal cabinet was behind the Olympic bid. His position, however, was that a referendum on the Olympics was not a good idea. Yet both the mayor of Vancouver, Larry Campbell (GamesBids.com 2002a), and the mayor of Whistler, Hugh O'Reilly, and a large number of activists pushed for the referendum (GamesBids.com 2002b). Also, on 29 November 2005, Premier Campbell gave a press conference regarding the management of cost overruns at which he stated that the games represented an opportunity for local businesses to grow and prosper and create more jobs for British Columbians (Vancouver Board of Trade 2005).

Because the provincial government had become the Olympic Games' main financial partner it also promoted the games aggressively to BC businesses. In addition, it put forward the business opportunities the games represented for British Columbians. *Striving for Excellence: Your Guide to Business Opportunities for the 2010 Winter Games* was published to entice sponsors and to maximize economic benefits (Royal Bank n.d.). In the guide, the province points out: "The 2010 Winter games will offer outstanding opportunities for Canadian companies to expand, diversify and reach new markets across the country and around the world. It's both a market place and display window of world-scale proportions" (2). The province insisted that there were substantial economic benefits: it supplied, for instance, yearly reports on the likely economic impact from January 2002 to 2010 (British Columbia Reports 2003). Most of these studies highlighted the potential economic benefits of the Olympic Games. They also highlighted the positive impact of new Olympic facilities, the contribution to the development and real estate industries, the importance of broadcasting rights/ revenues, the likely increase in tourism, and the increased visibility of Whistler, Vancouver, and British Columbia on the world stage. In all, the leadership role of Campbell, the provincial government's resources, and a tourism/business-driven coalition worked in concert to promote the event.

It is notable that the provincial government promoted the Olympic Games across British Columbia through a provincial program, "2010 Legacies Now," which marketed the event and created sports and cultural opportunities across BC communities. This was promotion, not development. What emerges clearly is that the largest investments took place at the very core of the Lower Mainland across the greater Vancouver region. These developments, however, remained at the periphery of the Olympic partnership. For financial and planning reasons, they ended up being imposed by the provincial government and its partners, the federal government, and the private sector on local and regional governments and their communities.

PRIVATE SECTOR

VANOC signed major corporate sponsorship deals with the Royal Bank of Canada, Rona, Bell Canada, the Hudson's Bay Company, Air Canada, Petro Canada, and General Motors worth $790 million. These institutions were referred to as premier national partners (Lee 2005). Yet public-private partnerships were found to be unsuccessful due to their inadequate numbers.

But this situation should not be confused with the importance and the influence of the province's business community views on the Olympics, which can be illustrated by the extremely close political and personal relationship between Jack Poole and Premier Gordon Campbell. Poole was chairman of the bid campaign, and one of the Olympic sites, the Jack Poole Plaza (where the 2010 Olympic cauldron stood), was named after him.

In 2002, when he accepted a leadership role in the Olympic bid, Poole was semi-retired from a boom-and-bust real-estate career. Born in a small rural community in Saskatchewan, he graduated with a civil engineering degree in the 1940s and moved to Vancouver in the 1960s to manage a business and then start his own in development. In the 1980s, he was known to be worth $100 million when the 1982 recession nearly destroyed Daon Development Corporation. After a few difficult years, during which he flirted with the idea of running for the Liberal Party but stepped back in favour of Gordon Campbell, he founded the Vancouver Land Corporation (VLC), which subsequently became Greystone Properties and then, finally, Concert Properties, a development business that in the 1990s had about $1.5 billion in assets.

As a teenager Campbell got his first job (as a labourer) when he was hired by Poole – Poole actually made note of this at one point (BC *Business* 2009). Poole accepted the position of chair of the bid committee for one dollar per year and offered to pay for his own expenses. He ultimately shared the work with Furlong, an old friend and business partner, who co-chaired the bid committee. Furlong took charge of VANOC's day-to-day activities as chief administrative officer, while Poole chaired the preparation committee.

Some media reports indicate that, early on, Poole (through Concert Properties) probably had ambitions to bid on some of the Olympic infrastructural projects (Lee 2005) but that, due to negative media coverage, Concert Properties abandoned its Olympic ambitions.

In the end, Jack Poole left an important legacy not only as a prominent member of the Vancouver business community but also as an avid supporter of Gordon Campbell as mayor and as premier. The media documented their relationship at length, and while many admitted they admired Poole, some also saw the Poole-Campbell relationship as one that really benefited the province's business elite (Shaw 2008). But according to Shaw, for instance, the tight Vancouverite political community of both the left and the right actually extended to all, and the feeling was that the Olympics would make Vancouver a "world-class" city. This can be vouchsafed by Poole's close personal relationship with Campbell as well as by the presence of labour union representatives, Ken Georgetti and Tony Tennessy, on the board of directors of Concert Properties. As Shaw argues, this relationship goes back to a time when, in its early development, VLC had secured city land from both the city of Vancouver's mayor Gordon Campbell and New Democrat premier Mike Harcourt (6).

Poole died of cancer at seventy-six on the day the Olympic torch was lit in Olympia, Greece. His presence at the side of Gordon Campbell's business and political career, and his leadership as co-chairman (with Furlong) of the Vancouver Olympic Bid team from July 2001 to his death, clearly illuminates not only a very important link between the two leaders but also the extent to which the business and political communities of Vancouver are intertwined.

Also, critics argued that Premier Campbell used the games to advance his agenda of privatization, service cuts, and union busting. In his address to the Vancouver Board of Trade, Campbell indicated that the Olympic Games bid and implementation had to take into consideration a strong public-private partnership: "the 2010 games are the largest single public-private initiative going in Canada right now" (C. Smith 2004). Olympic sponsors participated through the Olympic Partners Program as worldwide partners. Critic David Whitson (2004, 1228), for instance, suggested in "Bringing the World to Canada":

> We are living through a reprise of the 1980s, with a neoliberal government firmly committed to the Olympics while also slashing taxes and "rationalizing" public services. It is noteworthy that Olympic infrastructure (and hence Olympic investment) will be concentrated in what is already the wealthiest corner of the province – Vancouver and the ski resort of Whistler – while schools and hospitals are being closed in rural communities in the interior. It is also not surprising that the biggest boosters of the Vancouver Olympic bid was the Vancouver corporate sector, precisely the group that stands to get most of the public money that will be spent on construction and promotion, as well as to benefit personally from the rises in property values that are already enriching homeowners from Whistler to Point Grey. For these people and their allies in the government of Premier Gordon Campbell it may not be going too far to say that the Vancouver Olympics are envisaged as a showcase for a decade of neoliberalism.

Two of the most expensive infrastructure projects, Vancouver's Olympic Village ($700 million) and the Canada Line ($2.1 billion) between Vancouver's Richmond Airport and downtown Vancouver, sum up the tug-of-war that brought city communities and Campbell's provincial government together to work with the private sector for the implementation of Olympics during the 2003–10 period. These infrastructures, because of their location and their cost and size, were highly visible. The construction of the two athletes' villages in Vancouver's False Creek and Whistler were described as resulting from a strong public and private partnership for the planning and development of new neighbourhoods. Whistler, for example, founded the Whistler 2020 Corporation to manage and evaluate the development of its athletes' village. Local elected officials, public officers, and developers sat on the

Whistler 2020 board. Erik Martin, a developer, chaired the board, and
Jim Mudy, a development consultant, served as advisor. In doing this,
Whistler "wanted to use the corporation to engage the Development
Community to support an expertise" (Interview 1, Whistler Housing
Centre, 10 March 2006). Similarly, Vancouver's athletes' village neighbourhood, built on the southeast side of False Creek, was planned with
a stewardship group made up of "project managers, businesses, environmental group professionals, housing advocates, and architects" (Interview 5, Vancouver City Manager's Office, 6 March 2006). Today the
village is city property.

From about 2006 onward, VANOC and both Vancouver and Whistler
had apparently ended up on the wrong side of the bargaining table
when faced with increasing development costs. Developers became less
and less willing to undertake Olympic contracts because of the tight financial conditions associated with specific venues, the complexity of
the projects, and regulatory/sustainable guidelines. Working with contractors became more and more difficult thanks to tensions around regulations attached to bid competitions. After some highly publicized
and difficult decisions, it had become clear that, for instance, the Vancouver Olympic Village saga gave many opportunities to the city of Vancouver to reappropriate the urban redevelopment project and to take
nearly full responsibility for the southeast False Creek Village. The turning point may have come in 2009, when the city agreed to back up the
Millennium Corporation – the developer that built the Vancouver
Olympic Village – including $600 million in debts. The city's "Olympic
Hangover," however, turned to opportunity when, in the spring of
2011, the city decided to seize Millennium's assets, thirty-two properties
(including the site of the Olympic Village and other assets for about
$60 million), and sold much of the village's eleven hundred units to
the highest bidders rather than as affordable housing (as originally
planned) (Markle 2011).

In sum, while the corporate sector was seduced into complex partnerships with VANOC, the provincial and federal governments, and city
of Vancouver, and the resource municipality of Whistler, the outcomes
of these relationships varied greatly. After much tergiversation, the city
of Vancouver owns its Olympic Village. And, despite being a user-
friendly success, the implementation of the Canada Line remains an
issue of contention between a number of southern Metro Vancouver
municipalities, Translink, and the provincial government. Indeed, the
Canada Line was legislated in opposition to residents and municipali-

ties because it served provincial goals. In a way, the implementation of the Canada Line encapsulates Gordon Campbell's legacy.

ACCOUNTABILITY MONITORING

The Olympic Games construction process was monitored closely: the Bid Corporation released a first assessment in the bid book and provided the expected costs and revenues incurred by the staging of the games. Then three economic impact studies followed in 2002 and 2003: one by the provincial government; one by a private consultant, Inter-VISTAS Consulting Inc.; and one by the auditor general of British Columbia. Vancouver mayor Larry Campbell had ordered a social assessment of the games as well (Ference Weiker and Company 2003). VANOC worked closely with community organizers and advocacy groups to develop monitoring indicators (Olympic Games Global Indicators), which were used to make a total impact analysis of the games.

Also, following the guidelines of the International Olympic Committee, each venue had to be assessed against the Agenda 21 environmental standard. Several reports were issued regarding Vancouver's Olympic Village, for instance, looking at issues that included urban agriculture, energy, water and waste, and transportation options as well as questioning the development against the LEED standards, which are the highest sustainable standards. In 2011, the village won the platinum certification for being the greenest, most environmentally friendly, and largest urban neighbourhood in the world (Robertson 2010). Also, planning of each venue included citizen participation in the form of open houses, public workshops, and being observed by Vancouver's Planning Advisory Commission.

Ken Melamed, then mayor of Whistler, nonetheless regretted that there was no "third member" monitoring the Olympic Games. Even so, he noted: "I know there is at least one group in Vancouver that saw itself as an Olympic watchdog. I always believed that there was a place in all process for advocacy groups and it kept everybody on their toes and it's a healthy way to do business" (K. Melamed, interview with author, 9 March 2006). He was referring to the Vancouver advocacy group called the Impact on Community Coalition founded in 2001. IOCC was an umbrella organization grouping watchdog associations focused on a number of policy issues: housing, environment, transportation, community economic development, accountability and transparency, security and safety, and civil liberties. It worked with Olympic organizers at an early stage of the bid to "to ensure that community issues [were] addressed." The collaboration between IOCC and VANOC was peaceful and worked relatively well. IOCC convinced VANOC to incorporate fourteen recommendations related to housing in the Downtown Eastside in the Inner-City Inclusive Statement (Frankish, Kwan, and VanWynsberghe 2010).

Overall, wide public participation, high levels of accountability, and strong public stewardship characterized the monitoring of the Olympic Games, which in turn, were managed in a highly entrepreneurial environment. During the early stages of the games bid and implementation, all four central actors were satisfied with the multi-level partnership and admitted that their views were taken into account (Interview 3, Whistler Mayor's Office, 9 March 2006). All acknowledged the strength resulting from the multi-level process. Thus, for Whistler Olympic manager Jim Godfrey: "The planning of VANOC, together with the plan required at the local level, is a significant undertaking. And we are going to meet our commitment to provide extraordinary games, it requires a partnership beyond belief" (Godfrey, interview with author, 9 March 2009).

CONCLUSION

The bid book, the Multi-Party Agreement, and VANOC all suggest that the partnership-oriented thrust of the Olympic Games was "non-partisan" and would remain non-political. Yet, in 2005, VANOC chief officer John Furlong had to argue that critics should focus on "sport and athletics," thus calling all Olympic partners to unite. Furlong also criticized the politicization of the games by labour unions and university professors, who disrupted, he argued, the peaceful development of the Olympic plan even though they had so much to gain by it (Vancouver Sun 2005).

There is some interesting evidence that the Olympic enterprise amounted to more than a commitment to neoliberalism or to Gordon Campbell's personal ambitions: First, the bid was launched and approved in 1998 by then premier Glen Clark, the leader of the left-wing New Democratic Party. Second, when the city of Vancouver agreed to partner with Whistler to put together the Olympic bid, its mayor was Philip Owen, who, although on his third mandate, had succeeded Gordon Campbell and was the leader of the Non-Partisan Association, a liberal-civic outfit. When Larry Campbell became mayor in 2002, he was the candidate of the left-green Coalition of Progressive Electors, which had conflicting views regarding the Olympics, including relating to infrastructure and the role of citizens. Yet it was Larry Campbell's referendum proposal that ended up being critical to the games' bid for international success.

Leadership transitions and public opinion in Vancouver and Whistler, however, seemed unimportant in Vancouver when the NPA's Sam Sullivan won the mayoralty in 2005. His inaugural address on 5 December 2005 provided a sense of emergency. His view was that the Olympics were apolitical: "It is time to end the endless debates. It is time to put aside ideology and get down to doing the people's business ... we have an Olympics to host" (Sullivan 2005). Similarly, in the resort municipality of Whistler there were also important leadership changes between 2002 and 2005. Indeed, in 2005, Whistlerites, rather than re-electing their former mayor (and minister of state for the Community Charter and the 2010 Winter Olympics) Ted Nebbeling, elected Ken Melamed, an environmentalist, who had opposed the Olympics because of the lack of provincial financial transfers and his concerns that it might compromise the future sustainability of Whistler. By and large, these events show us that the desire to bring the Winter Olympic Games to British Columbia was widely shared by the political and economic elite.

Scholars of the Olympic Games portray Olympic organizations, notably during the bid phase, as active growth machines (Burbank, Heying, and Andranovich 2001). Olympic Games are described as elitist initiatives driven by business. And, indeed, from the bid phase onward, Vancouver's and Whistler's private-sector actors and business representatives, along with provincial premiers Clark and Campbell, prevailed in the organization and promotion of most activities. Both Vancouver and Whistler launched the games' bid as a growth-oriented coalition with activities directed at business-developer-tourism coalitions.

It is interesting to underscore, however, that in the case of the Vancouver-Whistler bid, although the goals of the Olympic enterprise were formulated and progressively reformulated to fit business ambitions and priorities and provincial and federal government goals, ultimately they were such that they also suited the ambitions and priorities of both Vancouver and Whistler. This success should be attributed to the egalitarian partnership established within, and managed by, VANOC. What made those games a little more controversial were indirect infrastructure projects involving a committed provincial government.

Olympic Games are among the most complex of entertainment strategies, and, in the case of the 2010 Vancouver Olympics, the political and economic impact of the games is still at play. Indeed, the 2010 Olympics may have been the first to use social media, and it was inclusive of and accountable to the communities of Vancouver and Whistler; however, there is no evidence that it served the province at large. As has been documented in this chapter, all new infrastructure was built at the core of the southern part of British Columbia and across Metro Vancouver.

Terry Nichols Clark (2003) describes cities as entertainment machines led by a new political culture that cannot be clearly attributed to right- or left-wing politics. In Vancouver's case, there did not appear to be a straightforward approach – whether market-driven or socially driven – to the 2010 Winter Olympics; however, the resulting development of amenities and infrastructure only benefited two very specific urban populations. The Vancouver 2010 Olympic Games served the Metro Vancouver region well, while at the same time giving the provincial government the pretext it needed to cut resources to health and education sectors across the province.

NOTE

1   The University of Victoria's ethics code strictly prohits interviewee identification. I have complied with the university's ethics standards in protecting interviewees' anonymity.

Conclusion

Campbell's Legacy?

J.R. LACHARITE AND TRACY SUMMERVILLE

Revolutionary or impersonator? Pragmatist or ideologue? As we have maintained from the outset, Gordon Campbell's legacy is complicated and could thus best be described as mixed. One of the themes addressed in this volume suggests that he was driven by a set of neoliberal principles and was determined to implement a neoliberal reform package that would fundamentally alter the province's political, economic, social, and cultural landscape(s). In some ways, he pursued this agenda with a fair degree of ebullience. Summerville's, Teeple's, Creese and Strong-Boag's, and Cohen's chapters reflect the pseudo–laissez faire approach that Campbell adopted from 2001 to 2011. In these areas in particular, he conformed remarkably well to Harvey's (2005) description of what constitutes a shift to neoliberal ideals. Cultivating a program of "individual entrepreneurial freedom," institutional reform, and minimal government intervention were clearly important to Campbell. But instituting "fresh" political economic practices that affirmed the utility of unencumbered market transactions was also part of the Bennett, Harcourt, and (Glen) Clark regimes. In this regard, Campbell's legacy was to add a measure of inevitability to this evolution in policy development in BC, and, as one would expect, this policy evolution has had implications for the province's government-funded health, social, and educational services. As Teeple and Cohen explain, this new political settlement has also critically transformed relations between workers and the state and the way collectively owned assets are managed, seen, and delivered.

Unsurprisingly, then, Campbell's "neoliberalism" bore a striking resemblance to the "third way/new public management" paradigm that was taking hold of Western Europe, Australia, New Zealand, the United States, and various parts of Canada in the decades that preceded his ascent to power (Giddens 1998, 2014; Lund 2008; Clark 2004; Singer 2000; Gray 2009).[1] In our introductory remarks, we made a point of highlighting Campbell's reliance on an already well-established form of populism that emphasized government modernization (in the form of smaller government and lower taxes) and exercising more individual responsibility (in the form of empowering civil society) to convince voters that his Liberal Party was the better alternative. He did not have the luxury or "social licence" to completely dismantle the province's welfare provisions. Nevertheless, he utilized a characteristically sugar-coated social justice refrain to ensure that British Columbians remained confident in his government's ability to "right" past NDP "wrongs." One of the ways he did this was to create the impression that his government would "reinvigorate community, reinvest in skills development, and reform welfare to promote opportunity rather than dependence" (Clark 2004, 497).

However, he failed to deliver on many of these promises. Instead, as we proposed in our introduction, he simply pursued a policy agenda that – perhaps unintentionally – contributed to an "undermining of the collective sense of identity that had previously underpinned most social policy initiatives" (10). We think that this theme was suitably addressed in the chapters supplied by Pilon, Smith, and Belanger, and it is here that we get a better sense of a more obvious legacy. Despite his best intentions, Campbell was ultimately reluctant to cede power to the varied and competing operators in civil society – or what he likely perceived to be subordinate institutions and actors. Pilon, Smith, and Belanger chronicle his change of heart in terms of what would have amounted to a significant devolution of power to voters, municipalities, and First Nations.

Yet, in 2001 the idea and electoral strategy of promising to diffuse power was not new. Preston Manning's federal Reform Party, Tony Blair's "new labour movement" in the UK, and Mike Harris's "Common Sense Revolution," with varying degrees of success, all attempted to persuade voters of the merits of less intrusive government and more autonomous and market-driven individuals and communities. However, what we have actually witnessed is an ever greater concentration of power in executive institutions across several liberal democratic states (Savoie 1999; Wolin 2010; Dye 2014; Jeffery 2015; Bower 2016). In the BC context, Campbell seemed to confront a dose of reality that made it difficult for him to follow through on his campaign pledges. The catch, of course, is that this has now become normalized – that is, executive power and privilege – and will almost certainly serve as an instructive template for future premiers.

Turning to our third theme, contributors such as Low, Lacharite, Brunet-Jailly, Hanlon, Ginnell, and Hoberg show convincingly the economic conservatism that underscored many of Campbell's most significant policy decisions/outcomes. As Lacharite suggests, Campbell's income tax-cutting record was "notorious," but this forced him into a tenable position whereby he could justifiably claim that crucial government services were too expensive and needed to be reconfigured. Low, Hanlon, and Hoberg provide some crucial insight(s) into how choking off revenue limited the government's capacity to protect forests, provide health care, and/or deliver cultural products, while parts of Ginnell's contribution accentuates Campbell's desire to forcefully modify what he believed to be overly capitalized municipal services. Much of what is examined in these chapters is consistent with: (1) the third way politics that had already been adopted in many Anglo-liberal regimes in the 1980s and 1990s, (2) neoliberalism, and (3) the fiscal austerity employed by antecedent governments in the US, the UK, Alberta, and Ontario.

Importantly, though, their chapters also demonstrate that Campbell was probably more pragmatic than doctrinaire – within the limited policy context/framework/options that were available to him during his time in Victoria (recall that this is something that Summerville places a great deal of importance on in her chapter). The case could be made that he was simply trying to satisfy the myriad competing interests – both public and private – that customarily look to government(s) for more money, power, and influence. Here it could be argued that his legacy is that he was a reasonably competent manager of the various domestic policy actors and stakeholders that shape BC's complex policy environment. BC's nurses, doctors, logging firms, taxpayers, the arts and cultural community, and so on all wanted, and got, something from Campbell. He adapted and overcame numerous objections to his overarching plans for the province without alienating his core base of support. Certainly, and again like his progenitors, he was not unique in this regard, but it is easy to forget, given the media's focus on controversy, that governance is an arduous and convoluted undertaking. On this matter, Lacharite's and Hanlon's chapters on tax and health care policy are both striking illustrations of how demanding the act of governance can be. In addition, it is probably fair to say that Campbell had to operate within a more contextually complex political atmosphere than did his predecessors – and one that was certainly more regional and global in scope.

Finally, Belanger's, Smith's, and Pilon's chapters provide us with a better understanding of the rather ambitious institutional changes that Campbell had hoped to instill into the province's public psyche. Yet, despite his efforts to implant a more robust and inclusive form of participatory politics and more local government autonomy, his impact turned out to be largely inconsequential. And, as we have already asserted, many of his institutional reform projects lacked substance. What he appears to have done reasonably well, however, is to institute a sophisticated marketing scheme for other future premiers to follow. Campbell's communications strategy was not always successful, but he quickly seemed to recover from fairly (politically) damaging and scandalous incidents – with the exception of the HST. One could even infer that Christy Clark's entirely insipid approach to public relations – consisting mostly of gratuitous photo opportunities – has drawn lessons from Campbell's periodic lapses in judgment to better insulate the premier from any potentially negative press. Campbell's legacy here could very well be not only that he refined and bolstered executive-oriented public relations but also that his experiences – good and bad – proved to be wholly instructive.

But surely there is more to the former premier's legacy than the so-called neoliberalism and economic conservatism that have been presented in this book. What about all of his personal and political scandals? It is useful to point out that British Columbia's political history is filled with interesting characters, dynamic personalities, and leaders who, at times, have behaved eccentrically and/or who have appeared to be ensnared in some sort of public imbroglio. For Bill Bennett it was the "Restraint Program" that refashioned social services and weakened provincial labour laws, and the Coquihalla Highway/ Kerkhoff Construction Company affair that cost provincial taxpayers millions in subsidies to support what turned out to be an egregiously expensive infrastructure project that appeared to only really benefit a non-union contractor. Other notable examples include Bill Vander Zalm's close association with Peter Toigo and the sale of his Fantasy Garden's theme park to Tan Yu – something for which he was charged with criminal breach of trust – and Glen Clark "fudge-it budget" debacle. It could be argued that Campbell actually descends from a proud line of venal and/or egocentric premiers. Understandably, there may be a number of readers who are unhappy that we did not deal with his improprieties in a more thoughtful and reflective manner.

In the absence of a systematic appraisal of his policy accomplishments and failures it would be tempting to focus merely on his foibles and/or policy missteps. *The Campbell Revolution?*, however, is intended to be much more than a reductionist assessment of his decade in power. Our hope is that we have produced an account of his policy record that delves more deeply into the proximate and contextual factors that influenced his policy initiatives and final decisions. Focusing exclusively or even predominantly on his "cult of personality" would likely have failed to shed any light on what he achieved and/or failed to achieve over his ten years as Liberal Party leader and premier of British Columbia.

Looking forward, there is perhaps one other unresolved question that warrants some additional commentary. Has Campbell's legacy permanently altered BC's otherwise dynamic political environment? This is a difficult question to answer. We would argue that a high degree of polarization still prevails in BC politics. At the same time, however, we also feel that a neoliberal ascendency has crept into the province's myriad policy subsystems and that eligible voters have become more or less unconcerned about it – as can be evidenced by BC's appallingly low voter turnout rates for elections and referenda.[2] We think that Christy Clark's improbable election victory in 2013, voters' lingering objections to big government and taxes, hostility to unions, and general political disengagement currently point to a province that has been subjected to a fair dose of ideological indoctrination. We accept that political and policy preferences are cyclical, and we are not asserting that BC's political culture has now shifted permanently right. Rather, we believe that Campbell helped to ensconce a reasonably acceptable alternative political discourse into the province's public consciousness. And this, for all intents and purposes, is what has allowed BC's neoliberal-inspired policy regime to thrive.

Be that as it may, we are not prepared to speculate further on this issue – mostly because we do not know for sure that this is what has happened. Hence, we think that there is considerable room to bolster scholarship in this specific area of inquiry. It will require more concrete quantitative data to get a better fix on the current state of BC's political culture, but, as academics committed to establishing a better understanding of what makes BC tick, we are excited by the idea of delving into this mystery. Surveying the province's voters' desires, motivations, and ideological orientation, to our mind, is long overdue. In the meantime, we anticipate that BC politics and government will continue to provide us with peculiar characters, wildly contested policy alternatives, and a fruitful environment in which to debate and examine government action and inaction.

NOTES

1   Anthony Giddens and others describe "third way politics" as an attempt
    by centrist-leaning political parties to fashion free market capitalism and
    state socialism into a more unified and practical alternative to the classic
    "right" and "left" politics that defined Cold War–oriented democracies
    from the 1940s to the late 1980s. In essence, it is meant to represent an
    equitable synthesis of the very best of capitalism and socialism. In some
    quarters it has even been called a "warmed-over" form of neoliberalism.
    Gordon Campbell appeared to adopt a version of this third way politics
    during his ten years in power.

2   The alarming number of disinterested or disengaged voters in BC aligns
    nicely with the notion that the province's eligible voting population has
    adopted a less deferential and obligatory stance towards civic participa-
    tion because it reflects a greater attachment to individual expression, au-
    tonomy, and agency. Incidentally, these are the qualities upon which
    Campbell placed a great deal of emphasis and are expressed overtly in a
    number of critical policy areas, such as health, education, and social wel-
    fare. The simple, but effective, message was/is that we have been given the
    gift and right of choice and we should exercise it in all that we do. With-
    drawing from, or ignoring, the electoral process is a calculated choice that
    embodies the exalted individualism that Campbell so dearly cherished.

References

Abbing, H. 2004. "Let's Forget about the Cost Disease." Paper presented at the 13th Conference Association of Cultural Economics International, 2–5 June, Chicago.

Albo, Gregory. 2002. "Neoliberalism, the State, and the Left: A Canadian Perspective." *Monthly Review* 54 (1): 46–55.

Albrecht, D. ed. 1995. *World War II and the American Dream: How Wartime Building Changed the Nation*. Cambridge, MA: MIT Press.

Alcantara, C. 2007. "To Treaty or Not to Treaty? Aboriginal Peoples and Comprehensive Lands Claims Negotiations in Canada." *Publius: The Journal of Federalism* 38 (2): 343–69.

Anderson, Charlie. 2004. "Auditor-General to Look into Return of (Fish-) Farm Fines after a Complaint by the Sierra Legal Defence Fund." *Province*, 15 February, A6.

Anderson, James D. 1972. "Nonpartisan Urban Traditions in Canada." In *Emerging Party Politics in Urban Canada*, edited by J.K. Masson and J.D. Anderson, 5–21. Toronto: McClelland and Stewart.

Andres, L., and M. Adamuit-Trache. 2008. "University Attainment, Student Loans, and Adult Course Activities: A Fifteen-Year Portrait of Young Adults in British Columbia." In *Who Goes? Who Stays? What Matters? Accessing and Persisting in Post-Secondary Education in Canada*, edited by R. Finnie, R.E. Mueller, and A. Usher, 1–37. Montreal and Kingston: McGill-Queen's University Press.

Andrews, M. 2005. "Province to Announce 'Interim' Film Industry Plan," *Vancouver Sun*, 19 January.

Andrews, R., and S. Martin. 2007. "Has Devolution Improved Public Services?" *Public Money and Management* 27 (2): 149–56.

Antony, W., and D. Broad. 1999. *Citizens or Consumers? Social Policy in a Market Society*. Winnipeg: Fernwood.

Applebaum, L., and J. Hébert. 1982. *Federal Cultural Policy Review*. Ottawa: Government of Canada.

Archibald, R., D. Eastman, R. Ellis, and B. Nyberg. 2012. "Trends in Resource Management in BC." http://bcforestconversation.com/wp-content/uploads/TrendsinRR.pdf.

Association of Book Publishers of British Columbia. 2011. *2011 Program Evaluation: BC Book Publishing Tax Credit*. Vancouver: BC Book Publishers.

Auditor General. 2006. *Treaty Negotiations in British Columbia: An Assessment of the Effectiveness of British Columbia's Management and Administrative Process*. Victoria: Office of the Auditor General of British Columbia.

– 2011. *Report 6: Observations on Financial Reporting: Summary Financial Statements 2010-11*. Victoria: Office of the Auditor General of British Columbia. http://www.bcauditor.com/pubs/2011/report6/observations-financial-reporting-sfs-2010-2011.

– 2013. *An Audit of Biodiversity in BC: Assessing the Effectiveness of Key Tools*. Victoria: Office of the Auditor General of British Columbia. http://www.bcauditor.com/pubs/2013/report10/audit-biodiversity-bc-assessing-effectiveness-key-tools.

Austin, Ian. 1990. "Mayors on Warpath: Meeting to Discuss Call for Return of Rentalsman." *Vancouver Province*, 17 January.

Bailey, I. 2001a. "BC Native Leaders Will Tone Down Protests." *National Post*, 22 September.

– 2001b. "BC Premier Promises Candid Cabinet: TV Cameras Invited: Campbell Dismisses Fears Open Meetings Will Close Ministers' Mouths." *National Post*, 25 June.

– 2003a. "Campbell Says Sorry to Natives." *National Post*, 12 February.

– 2003b. "Opponents Drop Attempt to Oust BC Premier: Recall Legislation." *National Post*, 6 May

Bakvis, H., and G. Skogstad. 2008. "Canadian Federalism: Performance, Effectiveness, and Legitimacy." In *Canadian Federalism: Performance, Effectiveness, and Legitimacy*, edited by H. Bakvis and G. Skogstad, 3–23. Toronto: Oxford University Press.

Balcom, S. 1989. "New Development Fee Awaiting Approval." *Vancouver Sun*, 3 July.

Barnetson, B. 2010. *The Political Economy of Workplace Injury in Canada*. Edmonton: Athabasca University Press.

Barney, D.D., and D. Laycock. 1999. "Right Wing Populists and Plebiscitary Politics In Canada." *Party Politics* 5 (3): 317–39.

Barrett, T. 1996. "Anti-Right-Wing Liberals Quit Party." *Vancouver Sun*, 30 April.

– 2001. "When Delgamuukw Speaks, the Premier Listens." *Vancouver Sun*, 10 May.

Baumol, W.J. 2006. "The Arts in the 'New Economy.'" In *Handbook of the Economics of Art and Culture*, edited by V. Ginsburgh and D. Throsby, 339–58. Elsevier. doi:10.1016/S1574-0676(06)01011-8.

Baumol, W.J., and W.G. Bowen. 1966. *Performing Arts, the Economic Dilemma: A Study of Problems Common to Theatre, Opera, Music and Dance*. New York: Twentieth Century Fund.

BC *Business*. 2009. "Life and Times of VANOC Chairman Jack Poole." 2 July. Accessed 26 May 2017. https://www.bcbusiness.ca/life-and-times-of-vanoc-chairman-jack-poole.

BC Hydro. 2014. "Independent Power Producers Currently Supplying to BC Hydro." http://www.bchydro.com/content/dam/bcHydro/customer-portal/documents/corporate/independent-power-producers-calls-for-power/independent-power-producers/independent-power-producers-currently-supplying-power-to-bc-hydro.pdf.

BC Statistics. 2006. *Business Indicators: Roll the Credits for BC's Film and TV Sector*. Victoria: BC Government.

– 2010. *A Guide to the BC Economy and Labour Market*. Victoria: BC Government.

– 2012. *Visitor Entries in 2011: A Year in Review*. http://www.bcstats.gov.bc.ca/StatisticsBySubject/BusinessIndustry/Tourism.aspx.

BC Treaty Commission. 2003. "Update." Accessed 3 November 2014. http://www.bctreaty.net/negotiation-update.

BCUC. 2010. Order G-180-10-2. http://www.bcuc.com/Documents/Proceedings/2010/DOC_26531_G-180-10_BCH-F2011-Revenue-Requirements-Reasons-WEB.pdf.

Beatty, J. 1999. "Campbell Lays Out Plan to Restructure Government." *Vancouver Sun*, 19 April.

– 2001. "Liberals Fulfill List of Election Promises: 90-Day Agenda Expected to Be Completed Today with Appointment of Ferries Inquiry." *Vancouver Sun*, 28 August.

– 2002a. "Staff Must Support Our Goals, Premier Says: Critic Dubs New Communications Setup 'Spin Headquarters.'" *Vancouver Sun*, 28 June.

– 2002b. "Premier Hopes COPE Will Scrap Plan for Referendum on Olympics: Gordon Campbell Says the Vote Would Be Bad for BC and for Canada Series." *Vancouver Sun*, 18 November.

Beder, S. 2003. *Power Play: The Fight for Control of the World's Electricity*. New York: The New Press.

Beers, D. 2001a. "Get Ready for the Big Teach-In: Can Anything Worthwhile

Come from the Referendum on Treaty Negotiations?" *Vancouver Sun*, 29 September.

– 2001b. "Treaty Referendum: 'Way of Chaos.'" *Vancouver Sun*, 3 May.

Beers, D., with R. Francis, B. McLintock, W. McMartin, A. Smith, C. Tenove, et al. 2005. *Liberalized: The Tyee Report on British Columbia under Gordon Campbell's Liberals*. Vancouver: New Star Books.

Béland, D. 2005. "Ideas and Social Policy: An Institutionalist Perspective." *Social Policy and Administration* 39 (1): 1–18.

– 2009. "Ideas, Institutions, and Policy Change." *Journal of European Public Policy* 16 (5): 701–18.

Belanger, Yale D., and David R. Newhouse. 2008. "Reconciling Solitudes: A Critical Analysis of the Self-Government Ideal." In *Aboriginal Self-Government in Canada: Current Trends and Issues*, edited by Y.D. Belanger, 1–19. Saskatoon: Purich.

Belanger, Yale D., David R. Newhouse, and Heather H. Shpuniarsky. 2008. "The Evolution of Native Reserves." In *Handbook of North American Indians: Indians in Contemporary Indian Society*, vol. 2, edited by G. Bailey, 197–207. Washington, DC: Smithsonian Institution, 2008.

Beresford, C., and H. Fussell. 2009. *When More Is Less: Education Funding in BC*. Vancouver: Centre for Civic Governance, Columbia Institute. http://www.columbiainstitute.ca/sites/default/files/resources/When MoreisLess.pdf.

Berger, T. 2002a. "Why I Won't Be Voting: The BC Treaty Referendum Raises Serious Legal Issues for a Former Judge." *Vancouver Sun*, 15 April.

– 2002b. *One Man's Justice: A Life in the Law*. Toronto: Douglas and McIntyre.

Bezanson, K. 2006. *Gender, the State, and Social Reproduction: Household Insecurity in Neoliberal Times*. Toronto: University of Toronto Press.

Bish, R.L. 2002. "The Draft Community Charter: Comments." Paper prepared for the workshop on the Community Charter sponsored by the Local Government Institute and the School of Public Administration, University of Victoria, 14 June.

Bittle, S. 2012. *Still Dying for a Living: Corporate Criminal Liability after the Westray Mine Disaster*. Vancouver: UBC Press.

Blake, D.E., and R.K. Carty. 1995–96. "Partisan Realignment in British Columbia: The Case of the Provincial Liberal Party." *BC Studies* 108: 61–74.

Bobo, Kim. 2009. *Wage Theft in America*. New York: The New Press.

Bohn, G. 2001. "'Natives' Plan for BC: Blockades, Protests.'" *Vancouver Sun*, 9 March.

Bolan, K., and K. Baldrey. 1987. "Premier's Sex Education Plans Lauded." *Vancouver Sun*, 29 January.

Bolan, K., and G. Mason. 1988. "Premier Welcomes Debate on Abortion." *Vancouver Sun*, 29 February.

Bower, T. 2016. *Broken Vows: Tony Blair and the Tragedy of Power*. London, UK: Faber and Faber.

Bradford, N. 2003. "Public-Private Partnership? Shifting Paradigms of Economic Governance in Ontario." *Canadian Journal of Political Science* 36 (5): 1005–33.

Bramham, D. 1989a. "Poole's Closing of Land Deal Fails to Silence Opponents." *Vancouver Sun*, 3 October.

– 1989b. "No Quick Housing Fix for City, Mayor Says." *Vancouver Sun*, 20 October.

– 1990. "Green Set to Take on Campbell." *Vancouver Sun*, 29 September.

Bramham, D., and J. Buttle. 1989. "Housing Scheme Faces Hurdles." *Vancouver Sun*, 12 August.

British Columbia. 2011. Speech From the Throne. Delivered 14 February 2011, https://www.leg.bc.ca/content/legacy/web/39th4th/Speech%20from%20Throne_Oct%202011_WEB.pdf.

British Columbia Campaign 2000. 2007. *2007 Poverty Report Card*, "Fact Sheet # 3."

– 2011. *2011 Child Poverty Report Card*. Vancouver (First Call): BC Child and Youth Advocacy Coalition.

British Columbia Government News. 2012. "BC Workers Benefit from Minimum Wage Increase." Technology Innovation and Citizen Services. 1 May. https://news.gov.bc.ca/stories/bc-workers-benefit-from-minimum-wage-increase-1.

British Columbia Liberal Party. 1996. *The Courage to Change*. N.p.: n.p.

– 2001. *A New Era for British Columbia: A Vision for Hope and Prosperity for the Next Decade and Beyond*. Gordon Campbell and the BC Liberals (BC Liberal 2001 Platform). http://www.scribd.com/doc/48388741/BC-Liberal-2001-Platform-complete.

– 2009. *Keep BC Strong: Proven Leadership for BC's Economy*. https://www.poltext.org/sites/poltext.org/files/plateformes/bc2009lib_plt._12062009_161400.pdf.

British Columbia Ministry of Finance. 2001–2013. British Columbia Budgets. http://www.bcbudget.gov.bc.ca/default.htm. Accessed 12 April 2017.

– 2002. "Budget 2002 in Brief." http://www.bcbudget.gov.bc.ca/2002/BudgetInBrief/default.htm.

– 2003. "Budget 2003 in Brief." http://bcbudget.gov.bc.ca/2003/inbrief/bgt2003_inbrief.pdf.

- 2004. "Budget 2004 in Brief." http://www.bcbudget.gov.bc.ca/2004/
  highlights/BudgetHighlights.pdf.
- 2008. "Budget 2008 in Brief." http://www.bcbudget.gov.bc.ca/2008/
  highlights/2008_Highlights.pdf.
British Columbia Ministry of Health. 2007. "Index for Summary of Input on
  the Conversation on Health." Health and Human Services Library.
  http://www.health.gov.bc.ca/library/publications/year/2007/conversation
  _on_health/.
- 2013a. "General Interest Publications: Information Brochures (MSP)." MSP
  Publications. http://www2.gov.bc.ca/gov/content/health/health-drug-
  coverage/msp/bc-residents.
- 2013b. "MSP Premiums." http://www2.gov.bc.ca/gov/content/health/health-
  drug-coverage/msp/bc-residents/premiums.
British Columbia Olympic and Paralympic Winter Games Secretariat. 2004.
  "Progress Report."
  http://www.fin.gov.bc.ca/reports/GamesSec_AR2004.pdf.
British Columbia Progress Board. 2002. "Restoring British Columbia's Economic Heartland Report of the Project 250 Regional Economies Panel."
  Accessed online 21 May 2004 (archived).
British Columbia Reports. 2003.
  http://www.2010commercecentre.gov.bc.ca/StaticContent/documents/BIK
  /Section%202%20BC%20Secretariat.pdf.
British Columbia Task Force on Species at Risk. 2011. *Report of the British Co-
  lumbia Task Force on Species at Risk*. http://www2.gov.bc.ca/assets/gov/
  environment/plants-animals-and-ecosystems/species-ecosystems-at-
  risk/species-at-risk-documents/speciesatrisk_report.pdf.
British Columbia Teachers' Federation. 2007. "Education Funding: A Brief to
  the Select Standing Committee on Finance and Government Services."
  Vancouver: BCTF.
Brodsky, G., M. Budkley, S. Day, and M. Young. 2005. *Human Rights Denied:
  Single Mothers on Social Assistance in British Columbia*. Vancouver: Poverty
  and Human Rights Centre.
Brodie, Janine, and I. Bakker. 2008. *Where Are the Women? Gender Equity,
  Budgets and Canadian Public Policy*. Ottawa: Canadian Centre for Policy
  Alternatives.
Brown, M. 2012. *Towards a New Government in British Columbia* (e-book).
  Vancouver: Martyn Brown.
Bula, F. 2001a. "The Long Way Home: Gordon Campbell Is Days Away from
  What Appears to Be His Destiny but the Path from There to Here Has
  Been Anything but Straight." *Vancouver Sun*, 29 April.

– 2001b. "Natives Promise Trouble for Liberals." *Vancouver Sun*, 9 March.
– 2009. *How the Olympics Came to Vancouver*, News and Features Vancouver, 1 December. http://www.vanmag.com/News_and_Features/How_the_Olympics_Came_to_Vancouver?page=0%2C1.

Burbank, M., C. Heying, and G. Andranovich. 2001. *Olympic Dreams: The Impact of Mega-Events on Local Politics*. Boulder, CO: Lynne Rienner.

Burgess, Steve. 2010. "Nine Per Cent Gordo." *The Tyee*, 19 October. http://thetyee.ca/Opinion/2010/10/19/NinePerCentGordo/.

Burke Wood, P., and D.A. Rossiter. 2011. "Unstable Properties: British Columbia, Aboriginal Title, and the New Relationship." *Canadian Geographer* 55 (4): 407–25.

Business Council of British Columbia. 2012. "A Decade by Decade Review of British Columbia's Economic Performance." http://www.bcbc.com/content/641/Decade%20by%20Decade%20Review%20of%20BC%20Economic%20Performance.pdf.

Butterwick, S., and C. White. 2006. *A Path Out of Poverty: Helping BC Income Assistance Recipients Upgrade their Education*. Ottawa: Canadian Centre for Policy Alternatives.

Buttle, J. 1989. "Campbell Booed by Disgruntled Merchants." *Vancouver Sun*, 16 June.
– 1990. "City's Joint Planning Process under Fire." *Vancouver Sun*, 7 August.

Calvert, J. 2007. *Liquid Gold: Energy Privatization in British Columbia*. Halifax: Fernwood.

Camfield, D. 2006. "Neoliberalism and Working-Class Resistance in British Columbia: The Hospital Employees Union Struggle, 2002–2004." *Labour/Le Travail* 57: 9–41.
– 2009. "Sympathy for the Teacher: Labour Law and Transgressive Workers' Collective Action in British Columbia, 2005." *Capital and Class* 33: 81–107.
– 2011. *Canadian Labour in Crisis: Reinventing the Workers' Movement*. Halifax: Fernwood.

Campbell v. British Columbia (Attorney General). 2000. BCJ. No. 1524. http://indigenouspeoplesdevelopment.com/wp-content/uploads/2013/09/Westlaw_Document_18_56_21.pdf.

Campbell, G. 1976. "Review of *Vancouver Ltd.*" *BC Studies* 30: 86–9.
– 2001. "Premier Gordon Campbell Speech at Cabinet Swearing-In Ceremony." http://www.gov.bc.ca/prem/popt/speech/June_5_Premier_speech.htm.
– 2002. "Post Referendum Press Conference." 3 July. http://www.gov.bc.ca/prem/down/premiersspeeches/post-referendumspeech_07_03.pdf.
– 2008. UBCM Convention Address. http://www.ubcm.ca/assets/library

//Publications/Convention~Minutes/2008/I%20-%20Premiers %20Address.pdf.

Campbell River. 2007. *Culture and Heritage Plan.* http://infilm.ca/files/ CRCICResources/FinalC&HPlan.pdf.

Canadian Conference of the Arts. 2013. *Analyses of Provincial and Territorial Budgets 2012-2013 from the Perspective of Arts, Culture and Heritage.* Ottawa: University of Ottawa, Centre on Governance.

Canadian Institute for Health Information. 2008. *Physicians in Canada: The Status of Alternative Payment Programs, 2005-06.* Ottawa: CIHI.

– 2011a. *Health Care Expenditures in Canada.* Ottawa: CIHI.

– 2011b. *Physician Workforce Report, 2007–2011.* Ottawa: CIHI.

– 2011c. *Nursing in Canada, 2007–2011.* Ottawa: CIHI.

Canadian Medical Association. 2012. *Annual Report Card on Health Care in Canada.* http://www.cma.ca.

Canadian Press. 1990. "Vancouver Mayor Won't Run Federally." *Ottawa Citizen,* 22 April.

Carlson, K. 2010. *The Power of Place the Problem of Time: Aboriginal Identity and Historical Consciousness in the Cauldron of Colonialism.* Vancouver: UBC Press.

Carroll, W.K., and R.S. Ratner. 1989. "Social Democracy, Neo-Conservatism and Hegemonic Crisis in British Columbia." *Critical Sociology* 16 (29): 29–53.

– 2005. "The NDP Regime in British Columbia, 1991–2001: A Post Mortem." *Canadian Review of Sociology and Anthropology* 42 (2): 167–96.

Casebeer, A. 2004. "Regionalizing Canadian Healthcare: The Good – the Bad – the Ugly." *Healthcare Papers* 5 (1): 88–93.

Casebeer, A., C. Scott, and K. Hannah. 2000. "Transforming a Health Care System: Managing Change for Community Gain." *Canadian Journal of Public Health* 91 (2): 89–93.

Cashore, B., G. Hoberg, M. Howlett, J. Rayner, and J. Wilson. 2001. *In Search of Sustainability: British Columbia Forest Policy in the 1990s.* Vancouver: UBC Press.

Cassidy, O. 2013. "Critics Pan Liberals' $6.2m Arts Plan; Minister's Three-Point Strategy Aimed at Bolstering Province's 'Creative Economy.'" *Province,* 1 February.

Castells, M. 1992. *The Informational City: Economic Restructuring and Urban Development.* Hoboken, NJ: Wiley-Blackwell.

Cernetig, M. 2005. "Give Natives a Seat at the Premiers' Conference, Campbell Urges." *Vancouver Sun,* 10 August.

– 2006. "Recognize Aboriginals as Nation in Canada, Campbell Says." *Vancouver Sun,* 27 November.

– 2009. "The Pragmatism of Campbellism." *Vancouver Sun*, 16 May.

Chow, W. 2001. "Creating High-Tech Mecca New BC Council's Mandate." *Vancouver Sun*, 21 August.

Church, J., and P. Barker. 1998. "Regionalization of Health Services in Canada: A Critical Perspective." *International Journal of Health Services* 28 (3): 467–83.

Church, J., and T. Noseworthy. 1999. "Fiscal Austerity through Decentralization." In *Health Reform: Public Success, Public Failure*, ed. D. Drache and T. Sullivan, 186–203. London: Routledge.

Clark, D. 2004. "Implementing the Third Way: Modernizing Governance and Public Services in Quebec and the UK." *Public Management Review* 6 (4): 493–510.

Clark, T.N., R. Lloyd, K.K. Wong, and P. Jain. 2003. "Amenities Drive Urban Growth: A New Paradigm and Policy Linkages." In *The City as an Entertainment Machine*, ed. T.N. Clark, 291–321. Bingley, UK: Emerald Group Publishing.

Coalition of BC Businesses. 2004. *BC's Labour Code Changes: Assessing the Impact*. http://www.coalitionbcbusiness.ca/pdf/lbr_code_report_05-2004.pdf.

– 2006. *Proposed Amendments to the BC Labour Relations Code*. 2016. http://www.coalitionbcbusiness.ca/pdf/LabourCodeWebFinal10_11.pdf.

Cobb, R., and C. Elder. 1971. "The Politics of Agenda Building: An Alternative Perspective for Modern Democratic Theory." *Journal of Politics* 73 (4): 892–915.

Cohen, M. 2004. *A Return to Wage Discrimination: Pay Equity Losses Through the Privatization of Health Care*. Ottawa: Canadian Centre for Policy Alternatives.

Cohen, M., J. Murphy, K. Nutland, and A. Ostry. 2005. *Continuing Care Renewal or Retreat? BC Residential Care and Home Care Restructuring, 2001–2004*. Vancouver: Canadian Centre for Policy Alternatives (BC Office). https://www.policyalternatives.ca/sites/default/files/uploads/publications/BC_Office_Pubs/bc_2005/continuing_care.pdf.

Cohen, M.G. 2002a. "Public Power and the Political Economy of Electricity Competition: The Case of BC Hydro." Vancouver: Canadian Centre for Policy Alternatives.

– 2002b. "Electricity Deregulation, Privatization and Continental Integration: GATS and the Restructuring of Canadian Electrical Utilities." Ottawa: Canadian Centre for Policy Alternatives.

– 2003. *High Tension: BC Hydro's Deep Integration with the US through RTO West*. Vancouver: Canadian Centre for Policy Alternatives.

– 2006. "Electricity Restructuring's Dirty Secret: The Environment." In *Nature's Revenge: Reclaiming Sustainability in the Age of Corporate Globalism*, ed. J. Johnston, M. Gismondi, and J. Goodman, 73–95. Peterborough, ON: Broadview Press.

Cohen, M.G., and J. Calvert. 2012. "Assessing BC Electricity Policy since 2002 and the Government's 2011 Review of BC Hydro." *BC Studies* 174: 14.

Cohn, Daniel. 2008. "British Columbia's Capital Asset Management Framework: Moving from Transactional to Transformative Leadership on Public-Private Partnerships, or a 'Railroad Job?'" *Canadian Public Administration* 51 (1): 71–97.

Collin, C., and H. Jensen. 2009. *A Statistical Profile of Poverty in Canada*. Ottawa: Library of Parliament.

Comunian, R. 2009. "Questioning Creative Work as Driver of Economic Development: The Case of Newcastle-Gateshead." *Creative Industries Journal* 2 (1): 57–71

Cornwall, C. 2004. "Olympian Fight over Sea-to-Sky Fix." *Tyee*, 15 July. https://thetyee.ca/News/2004/07/15/Olympian_Fight_over_Sea-to-Sky_Fix/.

Costar, B., and N. Economou, eds. 1999. *The Kennett Revolution: Victorian Politics in the 1990s*. Sydney: University of New South Wales Press.

Cox, S. 1987. "Campbell Called a One-Man Show – Some Aldermen Find Fault with Mayor's Style." *Vancouver Sun*, 2 December.

– 1988. "Two Factions Intent on Making Civic Election Expenses Public." *Vancouver Sun*, 8 April.

Cox, S., and R. Palmer. 1987. "Cutbacks Justified, Says Mayor." *Vancouver Sun*, 12 May.

Craig, G.M., ed. 1982. *Lord Durham's Report*. Ottawa: Carleton University Press.

Creigh-Tyte, S. 2001. "Why Does Government Fund the Cultural Sector?" In *The UK Cultural Sector Profile and Policy Issues*, edited by S. Selwood, 173. London: Policy Studies Institute.

Cross, P. 2013. "Should the Rich Pay More? Not Necessarily." *Globe and Mail*, 30 May. http://www.theglobeandmail.com/commentary/should-the-rich-pay-more-not-necessarily/article12245332/.

Cruickshank, J. 1986. "No Middle Ground in Vancouver Race." *The Globe and Mail*, 11 November.

Cwi, D. 1980. "Public Support of the Arts: Three Arguments Examined." *Journal of Cultural Economics* 4(2), 39–62.

Dabbs, Frank. 1995. *Ralph Klein: A Maverick Life*. Vancouver: Greystone Books.

Dacks, G. 2002. "British Columbia after the *Delgamuukw* Decision: Land Claims and Other Processes." *Canadian Public Policy* 28 (2): 239–55.

- 2004. "First Nations-Crown Relations in British Columbia in the Post-*Delgamuukw* Era." In *Advancing Aboriginal Claims: Visions/Strategies/Direction*, ed. Kerry Wilkins, 271–87. Saskatoon: Purich.

Dahl, R.A. 1989. *Democracy and Its Critics*. New Haven: Yale University Press.

- 2006. *On Political Equality*. New Haven: Yale University Press.

Danard, Susan. 2001. "Cabinet Opens Door, Keeps Pocketbook Closed." *Times Colonist*, 28 June.

Danzo, J. 2010. "Jane Danzo, Chair of BC Arts Council, Resigns with Damning Letter." http://stopbcartscuts.wordpress.com/2010/08/17/jane-danzo-chair-of-bc-arts-council-resignation-letter/.

Davidson, A. 2004. "Dynamics without Change: Continuity of Canadian Health Policy." *Canadian Public Administration* 47: 251–79.

- 2008. "Sweet Nothings? The BC Conversation on Health." *Healthcare Policy* 3 (4): 33–40.

- 2010. "The Politics and Policies of Health-Care Privatization in BC." In *British Columbia Politics and Government*, ed. M. Howlett, D. Pilon, and T. Summerville, 289–307. Toronto: Emond-Montgomery.

Dehaas, J. 2008. "BC Premier Grilled on Gutted Grant System." *Maclean's*, 4 November. http://oncampus.macleans.ca/education/2008/11/04/bc-premier-grilled-on-gutted-grant-system/

Delacourt, S. 2013. *Shopping for Votes: How Politicians Choose Us and We Choose Them*. Madeira Park, BC: Douglas and Mcintyre.

De Leeuw, S. 2004. "Across a Boundary of Lava: Evaluating Race-Based Antagonism towards the Nisga'a Land Claims Treaty." In *Racism, Eh? A Critical Inter-Disciplinary Anthology of Race and Racism in Canada*, ed. C. Nelson and C.A. Nelson, 122–34. Don Mills, ON: Captus Press.

Deloitte. 2015. "Trending P3: The Evolving Role of Value-for-Money Analysis in Supporting Project Delivery Selection." 13 March. www.infrastructure ontario.ca/WorkArea/DownloadAsset.aspx?id=2147492666.

Deveau, S. 2004. "Film Fund Cut Clobbers BC Projects." *Tyee*, 19 April. http://thetyee.ca/News/2004/04/19/Film_Fund_Cut_Clobbers_BC_Projects/.

Dickie, P. 2005. *The Crisis on Union Organizing under the BC Liberals*. Hastings Labour Law Office. https://www.freelists.org/archives/turc/07-2015/pdfTPN_fqgO65.pdf.

Dieticians of Canada. 2012. *Cost of Eating in British Columbia 2011*. Vancouver: Dieticians of Canada BC Region.

Dreier, P., J. Mollenkopf, and T. Swanstrom. 2001. *Place Matters: Metropolitics for the Twenty-First Century*. Lawrence: University Press of Kansas.

Dunning, D. 2011. "The Dunning-Kruger Effect: On Being Ignorant of One's

Own Ignorance." In *Advances in Experimental Social Psychology*, vol. 44. ed. J. Olson and M.P. Zanna, 247–96. New York: Elsevier.

Dunning, D., K. Johnson, J. Ehrlinger, and J. Kruger. 2003. "Why People Fail to Recognize Their Own Incompetence." *Current Directions in Psychological Science* 12 (3): 83–7.

Dye, T.R. 2014. *Who's Running America: The Obama Reign.* New York: Routledge.

Edmonton Journal. 2002. "A Phony BC Referendum." 4 July.

Edwardson, R. 2012. *Canadian Content: Culture and the Quest for Nationhood.* Toronto: University of Toronto.

El Akkad, O. 2005. "New Approach to Native Relations Urged." *Globe and Mail*, 15 October.

Elgie, S., and J. McClay. 2013a. "Policy Commentary: BC's Carbon Tax Shift Is Working Well after Four Years (Attention Ottawa)." *Canadian Public Policy* 39 (2): 1–10.

– 2013b. *The BC Carbon Tax after Five Years: Results – An Environmental Success Story.* Ottawa, Ontario: Sustainable Prosperity. http://www.cmc-nce.ca/wp-content/uploads/2013/07/BCs-Carbon-Tax-Shift-after-5-Years-Results.pdf.

Fairey, D. 2005. *Eroding Worker Protections: British Columbia's New Flexible Employment Standards.* An Economic Security Project Report. Vancouver: Canadian Centre for Policy Alternatives.

– 2006. "The Erosion of Employment Standards." *BC Commentary: A Review of Provincial Social and Economic Trends* 9 (1): 1.

Fairey, D., C. Hanson, G. MacInnes, A. McLaren, G. Otero, and M. Thompson. 2008. *Cultivating Farmworker Rights.* An Economic Security Project Report, 1–76. Vancouver: Canadian Centre for Policy Alternatives.

Fairey, D., and S. McCallum. 2007. *Negotiating without a Floor: Unionized Worker Exclusion from BC Employment Standards.* Ottawa: Canadian Centre for Policy Alternatives.

Fairey, D., T. Sandborn, and J. Peters. 2012. "The Biggest Roll-Back of Worker Rights in Canadian History." In *Boom, Bust and Crisis: Labour, Corporate Power and Politics in Canada*, ed. J. Peters, 104–24. Halifax: Fernwood.

Farquharson, D. 1986a. "Candidates Are Poles Apart in Vancouver Mayoral Vote." *Montreal Gazette*, 15 November.

– 1986b. "Vancouver Veers Right." *Windsor Star.* 17 November.

– 2001. "BC Liberals' TV Cabinet Meeting a Yawn: Serious Debate Still Likely to Take Place Out of the Public Eye; The Rest Simply Stagecraft." *Edmonton Journal*, 2 July.

Fawkes, T. 1983. *Assault from the Right.* Vancouver: BC Federation of Labour, BC and Yukon Building Trades Council.

Fayerman, P. 1988. "Voters Have Clear Choice for Mayor of Vancouver." *Vancouver Sun*, 5 November.

– 1990. "Pondering Greener Pastures: Failed Mayoral Bid Leaves Green 'Open to New Things.'" *Vancouver Sun*, 19 November.

Ference Weicker and Company (Management Consultants). 2003. "Vancouver Agreement – Community Assessment of the 2010 Olympic Winter Games and Paralympic Games on Vancouver's Inner-City Neighborhoods." http://www.fin.gov.bc.ca/reports/Community_Assessment.pdf.

Finlayson, J., and K. Peacock. 2010. "HST Misconceptions." Business Council of British Columbia. https://www.scribd.com/document/39679284/HST-Misconceptions-FINAL.

First Nations of British Columbia, the Government of British Columbia, and the Government of Canada. 1991. *The Report of the British Columbia Claims Task Force*, 28 June. http://www.fns.bc.ca/pdf/BC_Claims_Task_Force_Report_1991.pdf

First Nations Health Council, Government of Canada, and BC Ministry of Health Services. 2012. *Health Partnership Accord*. Victoria: The Tripartite Parties.

First Nations Health Council, Government of Canada, and Government of BC. 2007. *Tripartite First Nations Health Plan*. Victoria: The Partners.

First Nations Leadership Council and Government of BC. 2006. *Transformative Change Accord: First Nations Health Plan*. Victoria: The Partners.

Flew, T. 2012. *The Creative Industries*. London: Sage.

Florida, R.L. 2002. *Rise of the Creative Class: And How It's Transforming Work, Leisure, Community and Everyday Life*. New York: Basic Books.

Florida, R., and G. Gates. 2003. "Technology and Tolerance: The Importance of Diversity to High-Technology Growth." In *The City as an Entertainment Machine*, ed. Terry Nichols Clark, 199–219. Bingley, UK: Emerald Group Publishing.

Fong, Petti. 2001. "Treaty Referendum in Early 2002: Natives Urge Boycott of Poll Promised by Liberals." *Vancouver Sun*, 18 August.

Food Banks of Canada. 2011. "Hunger Count 2011: A Comprehensive Report on Hunger and Food Bank Use in Canada, and Recommendations for Change." Toronto: Food Banks of Canada.

Forest Practices Board. 2011. *Forest Resources and the Montrese Creek Hydro Electric Project*. https://www.bcfpb.ca/sites/default/files/reports/IRC175%20-%20Forest%20Resources%20and%20the%20Toba%20Montrose%20Creek%20Hydroelectric%20Project.pdf.

Forsyth, J., G. Hoberg, and L. Bird. 2013. "In Search of Certainty: A Decade of Shifting Strategies for Accommodating First Nations in F orest Policy, 2001–2011." In *Aboriginal Peoples and Forest Lands in Canada*, ed. D.B. Tindall, R.L. Trosper, and P. Perreault, 299–312. Vancouver: UBC Press.

Fortin, N., D. Green, T. Lemieux, K. Milligan, and W.C. Riddell. 2012. "Canadian Inequality: Recent Developments and Policy Options." *Canadian Public Policy* 38 (2): 121–45.

Fotheringham, A. 1994. "This Pundit Still Putting Money on NDP Premiers." *Financial Post*, 22 February.

Francis, R. 2005. "A Government More Closed, Less Accountable." In *Liberalized*, ed. D. Beers, 71–91. Vancouver: New Star.

Frankish, J., B. Kwan, and R. VanWynsberghe. 2010. "'Two Solitudes': The 2010 Vancouver Olympics and Inner City Inclusivity Commitments." Centre for Population Health Promotion, University of British Columbia. http://blogs.ubc.ca/frankish/files/2012/10/ICS-FINAL-report.pdf.

French, S.P., and M.E. Disher. 1997. "Atlanta and the Olympics: A One-Year Retrospective." *Journal of the American Planning Association* 63 (3): 379–92.

Frug, G. 2005. "Governing Global Cities: Who Decides?" YouTube, uploaded 9 September 2011. http://www.youtube.com/watch?v=Ds9iIi4_YZQ.

Fuller, S. 2003. *Fair Pharmacare? A Backgrounder on the Government's Changes to BC's Pharmacare Program*. Vancouver: Canadian Centre for Policy Alternatives.

– 2005. "Public-Sector Employment and Gender Wage Inequalities in British Columbia: Assessing the Effects of a Shrinking Public Sector." *Canadian Journal of Sociology* 30 (4): 405–39.

Fuller, S., and L. Stephens. 2004. *Women's Employment in BC: Effects of Government Downsizing and Employment Policy Changes, 2001–2004*. Ottawa: Canadian Centre for Policy Alternatives.

Fullerton, D. 1991. "On Justification of Public Support of the Arts." *Journal of Cultural Economics* 15(2): 67–82.

GamesBids.com. 2002a. "Vancouver's Mayor-Elect Steps Back Slightly on Bid Referendum." 17 November. http://gamesbids.com/eng/other-news/vancouvers-mayor-elect-steps-back-slightly-on-bid-referendum/.

– 2002b. "Reaction to Vancouver 2010 Referendum." 9 November. http://gamesbids.com/eng/other-news/reaction-to-vancouver-2010-referendum/.

Gawthrop, Daniel. 1996. *Highwire Act: Power, Pragmatism, and the Harcourt Legacy*. Vancouver: New Star.

Gibson, G. 2001. "Clear the Air on Native Treaties." *National Post*, 19 March.

Giddens, A. 1998. *The Third Way: The Renewal of Social Democracy*. Cambridge, UK: Polity Press.

– 2014. *Turbulent and Mighty Continent: What Future for Europe?* Cambridge, UK: Polity Press.

Glyn, A. 2008. *Capitalism Unleashed: Finance, Globalization, and Welfare*. Oxford: Oxford University Press.

Golombek, J. 2013. "Here's What the Wealthiest of the Wealthy in Canada Earn – and Pay in Taxes." *Financial Post*, 16 March. http://business.financial post.com/2013/03/16/heres-what-the-wealthiest-of-the-wealthy-in-canada-earn-and-pay-in-taxes/.

Government of British Columbia. 2002. *Energy for Our Future: A Plan for BC*. http://www.bcenergyblog.com/uploads/file/2002%20BC%20Energy%20Plan.pdf.

– 2003a. Significant Projects Streamlining Act, S.BC (Bill 75). http://www .bclaws.ca/civix/document/id/consol18/consol18/00_03100_01.

– 2003b. "Community Charter: A New Legislative Framework for Local Government." http://www.bclaws.ca/civix/document/id/complete/ statreg/03026_00.

– 2004. Forest and Range Practices Act Forest Planning and Practices Regulation. BC Reg. 14/2004 http://www.bclaws.ca/civix/document/id/loo83/ loo83/12_14_2004.

– 2007a. Speech from the Throne. Third Session, Thirty-Eighth Parliament. 13 February. https://www.leg.bc.ca/content/legacy/web/38th3rd/ Throne_Speech_2007.pdf.

– 2007b. *BC Energy Plan: A Vision for Clean Energy Leadership*. http://www2.gov.bc.ca/assets/gov/farming-natural-resources-and-industry/electricity-alternative-energy/bc_energy_plan_2007.pdf.

– 2008. *British Columbia: Climate Action for the 21st Century*. Victoria: Government of British Columbia. http://www.gov.bc.ca/premier/attachments/climate_action_plan.pdf.

– 2010. "Bill 17 – 2010 *Clean Energy Act*." http://www.leg.bc.ca/39th2nd/ 1st_read/gov17-1.htm.

– 2011. *Review of BC Hydro*. http://www.newsroom.gov.bc.ca/downloads /bchydroreview.pdf.

– 2016. Great Bear Rainforest Order. January. https://www.for.gov.bc.ca/tasb/slrp/lrmp/nanaimo/CLUDI/GBR/Orders/ GBR_LUO_Signed_29jan2016.pdf.

Government of Canada. 1986. Department of External Affairs. "General Report on the 1986 World Exposition." 2 May–13 October. n.p.

Graham, S., J. Atkey, C. Reese, and M. Goldberg. 2009. *The Best Place on Earth?: Contemporary and Historical Perspectives on Poverty Reduction Policies and Programs in British Columbia*. Ottawa: Canadian Council on Social Development.

Gram, Karen. 1991. "Campbell Elected to Chair GVRD's Board of Directors." *Vancouver Sun*, 7 January.

Grant, Tavia. 2011. "Income Inequality Rising Quickly in Canada." *Globe and Mail*, 13 September.

Gray, J. 2009. *False Dawn: The Delusions of Global Capitalism*. London: Granta Books.

Greenstone, M., D. Koustas, K. Li, A. Looney, and L.B. Samuels. 2012. "A Dozen Economic Facts about Tax Reform." The Hamilton Project Policy Memo. http://www.hamiltonproject.org/assets/legacy/files/downloads_ and_links/05_economic_facts_tax_reform.pdf.

Guenther, S., J. Patterson, and S. O'Leary. 2008. *Insult to Injury: Changes to the BC Workers' Compensation System (2002–2008): The Impact on Injured Workers*. A Report to the BC Federation of Labour, November (1–16). http://bcfed.ca/sites/default/files/attachments/1520-09br-Insult%20to %20Injury.pdf

Gurstein, P., and S. Murray. 2007. "From Public Servants to Corporate Employees: The BC Government's Alternative Service Delivery Plan in Practice." Vancouver: Canadian Centre for Policy Alternatives.

Gutstein, Donald. 1986. "The Impact of Expo on Vancouver." In *The Expo Story*, edited by Robert Anderson and Eleanor Wachtel, 65–100. Madeira Park, BC: Harbour Publishing.

– 2014. *Harperism: How Stephen Harper and His Think Tank Colleagues Have Transformed Canada*. Toronto: Lorimer.

Haida Nation v. British Columbia (Minister of Forests) [2004] S.C.C. 73 [2004] 3 S.C.R. 511.

Hale, G. and Y. Belanger. 2015. *From "Social License" to "Social Partnership?": Promoting Win-Win Cultures for Resource and Infrastructure Development*. Ottawa: C.D. Howe Institute.

Hall, N. 2004. "Hugs, Tears as Assembly Says Farewell." *Vancouver Sun*, 29 November.

Hanlon, N. 2001. "Hospital Restructuring in Smaller Urban Ontario Settings: Unwritten Rules and Uncertain Relations." *Canadian Geographer* 45 (2): 252–67.

Hanlon, N., and G. Halseth. 2005. "The Greying of Resource Communities in Northern British Columbia: Implications for Health Care Delivery in Already Under-Serviced Communities." *Canadian Geographer* 49 (1): 1–24.

Hanlon, N., and M. Rosenberg. 1998. "Not So New Public Management and the Denial of Geography: Ontario Health Care Reform in the 1990s." *Environment and Planning C: Government and Policy* 16 (5): 559–72.

Hansen, C. 2009. "Swift Action to Protect Jobs and Families during Turmoil." *Vancouver Sun*, 18 February, A11.

Harnett, C. 2002. "Native Leaders Look for Progress on Treaty Talks." *National Post*, 10 July.

Harper, T. 1986. "Vancouver: Left, Right Left, Right." *Toronto Star*, 15 November.

Harris, C. 2002. *Making Native Space: Colonialism, Resistance, and Reserves in British Columbia*. Vancouver: UBC Press.

Harrison, K. 2012. "A Tale of Two Taxes: The Fate of Environmental Tax Reform in Canada." *Review of Policy Research* 29: 383–407.

Harvey, David. 1987. "Flexible Accumulation: Through Urbanization Reflections on "Post-Modernism" in the American City." Paper presented at the Developing the American City, Society and Architecture in the Regional City Symposium, Yale School of Architecture, February.

– 1989. "From Managerialism to Entrepreneurialism: The Transformation in Urban Governance in Late Capitalism." *Geografiska Annaler Series B Human Geography* 71 (1): 3–17.

– 2005. *A Brief History of Neoliberalism*. Oxford: Oxford University Press.

Hauka, D. 1992. "Municipal Leaders Fear Deal Frees Natives of Civic Laws." *Province*, 8 October.

– 1993. "Campbell Clams Up on Donations." *Province*, 12 August.

Hayter, R. 2003. "'The War in the Woods': Post-Fordist Restructuring, Globalization, and the Contested Remapping of British Columbia's Forest Economy." *Annals of the Association of American Geographers* 93 (3):706–29.

Health Canada. 2012. "Description of the Household Insecurity by Province and Territory, 2009–2010." http://www.hc-sc.gc.ca/fn-an/surveill/nutrition/commun/insecurit/prov_ter_longdesc-eng.php.

Hesmondhalgh, D. 2012. *The Creative Industries*, 3rd ed. London: Sage.

Hoberg, George. 2009. "Lament for the Great Bear Rainforest." *GreenPolicyProf*. 2 April. http://greenpolicyprof.org/wordpress/?p=109.

– 2010. "Bringing the Market Back In: BC Natural Resource Policies During the Campbell Years." In *British Columbia Politics and Government*, ed. M. Howlett, D. Pilon, and T. Summerville, 331–52. Toronto: Emond Montgomery.

Hoberg, George, and Leah Malkinson. 2013. "Challenges in the Design of Performance-Based Forestry Regulations: Lessons from British Columbia." *Forest Policy and Economics* 26: 54–62.

Hoberg, George, Leah Malkinson, and Laura Kozak. 2016. "Barriers to Innovation in Response to Regulatory Reform: Performance-based Forest Practices Regulation in British Columbia." *Forest Policy and Economics* 62: 2–10.

Hoberg, George, and S. Taylor. 2010. "One Land Manager, or Seven? The 2010 Reorganization of Natural Resource Management in BC." *GreenPolicy Prof*. 27 October. http://greenpolicyprof.org/wordpress/?p=458.

Hoekstra, G., P. O'Neil, D. Penner, and R. Shaw. 2014. "Enbridge Jumps a Hurdle, Many More to Come." *Vancouver Sun*, 18 June.

Hon, D. 2005. "The Orphaning of STV: A Tale of Two Referendums Promised by the BC Liberals." *TheTyee.ca*, 18 May.

Horn, W. 1992. "People Power: Renaissance of Neighborhood Activism Shakes Up the Way Things Are Done at, by City Hall." *Vancouver Sun*, 14 April.

Howe, B., and F. Klassen. 1996. *The Case of BC Hydro: A Blueprint for Privatization.* Vancouver: Fraser Institute. http://oldfraser.lexi.net/publications/critical_issues/1996/bc-hydro/.

Howlett, M., J. Rayner, and C. Tollefson. 2009. "From Government to Governance in Forest Planning? Lessons from the Case of the British Columbia Great Bear Rainforest Initiative." *Forest Policy and Economics* 11: 383–91.

Hume, M. 2008a. "From Hope to Hard Feelings." *Globe and Mail*, 1 March.

– 2008b. "Native Leaders Feel the Sting of Broken Promises." *Globe and Mail*, 25 February.

Hume, S. 2002a. Campbell's Referendum Folly Hasn't a Legal Leg to Stand On." *Vancouver Sun*, 14 March.

– 2002b. "The Referendum Five." *Vancouver Sun*, 4 May.

Hungerford, T.L. 2012. "Taxes and the Economy: An Economic Analysis of the Top Tax Rate Since 1945." Congressional Research Service (7-5700). https://fas.org/sgp/crs/misc/R42729.pdf.

Hunter, J. 1994. "Law Would Give Voters Power to Fire Politicians." *Vancouver Sun*, 17 June.

– 1996. "Warnke's Move from Liberals Stuns Campbell, Cheers NDP: Departure Tied to Issue of Campbell's Leadership." *Vancouver Sun*, 29 April.

– 2009. "Two Years of Deficit, Public Sector Battle Brews." *Globe and Mail*, 18 February.

– 2011. "Gordon Campbell's Greatest Regret." *Globe and Mail*, 18 February.

Ibbitson, John. 1997. *Promised Land: Inside the Mike Harris Revolution.* Scarborough, ON: Prentice Hall Canada.

Independent Publishers Association Meeting. 1971. *SFU Archives and Records Management Dept Online Finding Aids/F-57 Assoc of Canadian Publishing fonds.*, 2013, from http://www.sfu.ca/archives2/F-57/F-57.html.

Integrated Land Management Bureau. 2006. *A New Direction for Strategic Land Use Planning in BC.* Victoria: Government of British Columbia. https://www.for.gov.bc.ca/tasb/slrp/policies-guides/new%20direction%20synopsis.pdf.

International Labour Organization (ILO). 2013. "ILO Calls for Urgent Global

Action to Fight Occupational Diseases." 26 April. http://www.ilo.org/
global/about-the-ilo/media-centre/press-releases/WCMS_211627/lang—
en/index.htm.

Ipsos Reid. 2007. "British Columbians Back BC Liberals." 17 April.
http://www.ipsos-na.com/news-polls/pressrelease.aspx?id=3445.

Isitt, B., and M. Moroz. 2007. "The Hospital Employees' Union Strike and the
Privatization of Medicare in British Columbia, Canada." *International
Labor and Working-Class History* 71: 91–111.

Ivanova, Iglika, and Seth Klein. 2013a. *Progress Tax Options for BC: Reform
Ideas for Raising New Revenues and Enhancing Fairness.* Canadian Centre for
Policy Alternatives. http://www.policyalternatives.ca/sites/default/files/
uploads/publications/BC%20Office/2013/01/CCPA-BC-Tax-Options_0.pdf.

– 2013b. "Working for a Living Wage: Making Paid Work Meet Basic Family
Needs In Metro Vancouver, 2013 Update." Toronto: Canadian Centre for
Policy Alternatives.

Jaccard, M. 1998. "Reforming British Columbia's Electricity Market: A Way
Forward." In *British Columbia Task Force on Electricity Market Reform: Final
Report.* http://www.emrg.sfu.ca/media/publications/1998/TaskForceon
ElectricityMarketReform.pdf.

Jackson, A. 2000. "Tax Cuts: The Implications for Growth and Productivity."
Canadian Tax Journal 48 (2): 276–302.

James, A. 1999. "Closing Rural Hospitals in Saskatchewan: On the Road to
Wellness?" *Social Science and Medicine* 49 (8): 1021–34.

Jang, B. 2003a. "BC Recall Laws Being Abused, Liberal Says." *Globe and Mail*,
29 January.

– 2003b. "BC Voters Launch Drive to Oust Campbell." *Globe and Mail*, 7 March.

Jeffery, B. 2015. *Dismantling Canada: Stephen Harper's New Conservative
Agenda.* Montreal and Kingston: McGill-Queen's University Press

John, G.C.E. 2000. "Liberals Should Abide by Ruling on Nisga'a Treaty."
Vancouver Sun, 28 July.

Judd, D.R., and Susan Fainstein. 1999. *The Tourist City.* New Haven, CT: Yale
University Press.

Kamloops Daily News. 2001. "Chretien, Premiers Go After More Hollywood
Productions." 30 November. http://proxy.lib.sfu.ca/login?
url=http://search.proquest.com.proxy.lib.sfu.ca/docview/358293538
?accountid=13800

Kavanagh, J. 1990. "Campbell to Examine Environment: Groups Commend
Mayor's Initiative." *Vancouver Sun*, 15 January.

Kazin, Michael. 1998. *The Populist Persuasion: An American History.* New York:
Cornell University Press.

Kershaw, P. 2007. "Measuring Up: Family Benefits in British Columbia and Alberta in International Perspective." *IRPP Choices* 13 (2): 33.

Kesselman, J.R. 2002. "Fixing BC's Structural Deficit: What, Why, When, How? and for Whom? *Canadian Tax Journal* 50 (3): 884–932.

– 2010. "The Harmonized Sales Tax: Through an Economic Prism." *Policy Perspectives* 17 (2): 1–8.

– 2011. "Consumer Impacts of BC's Harmonized Sales Tax: Tax Grab or Pass-Through?" *Canadian Public Policy* 37 (2): 139–62.

Kieran, B. 1994. "Campbell, Grits Lacking in Vision." *Province*, 2 October.

Kines, L., and J. Rudd. 2004. "Campbell Rules by Intimidation, Says MLA." *Vancouver Sun*, 24 March.

Klein, S., and A. Smith. 2006. "Budget Savings on the Backs of the Poor: Who Paid the Price for Welfare Benefit Cuts in BC?" *Behind the Numbers*. Canadian Centre for Policy Alternatives. https://www.policyalternatives.ca/sites/default/files/uploads/publications/BC_Office_Pubs/bc_2006/BTN_welfare_cuts.pdf.

Klein, Seth, M.G. Cohen, T. Garner, I. Ivanova, M. Lee, B. Wallace, and M. Young. 2008. *A Poverty Reduction Plan for BC*. Vancouver: Canadian Centre for Policy Alternatives. https://www.policyalternatives.ca/sites/default/files/uploads/publications/BC_Office_Pubs/bc_2008/ccpa_bc_poverty_reduction_full.pdf.

Kukucha, Christopher J. 2004. "The Role of the Provinces in Canadian Foreign Trade Policy: Multi-Level Governance and Sub-National Interests in the Twenty-First Century." *Policy and Society* 23 (3): 113–34.

Lacharite, J. 2008. "Implications of Electronic Commerce for Tax Collection in British Columbia. *BC Studies Quarterly* 158 (2): 93–113.

Lahey, K. 2009. *Gender Analysis of Budget 2009*. The Progressive Economics Forum. http://www.progressive-economics.ca/2009/01/31/gender-analysis-of-budget-2009/

Lamb, J. 1989. "Whither Gordon Campbell? Put Nicely: Go Fly a Kite." *Vancouver Sun*, 21 January.

Lamb, Jamie. 1990. No headline. *Vancouver Sun*, 4 December, B1.

Lambertus, S. 2004. *Wartime Images, Peacetime Wounds: The Media and the Gustafsen Lake Standoff*. Toronto: University of Toronto Press.

Lammam, C., and H. MacItyre. 2013. "Return of the PST Darkens the BC Economy." *Fraser Forum*. https://issuu.com/fraserinstitute/docs/fraserforum_mayjune2013.

Lavoie, J., and M. Sekeres. 2002. "Campbell Vows to Ignore Ballot-Burning Protesters." *Times Colonist*, 6 April.

Laycock, D. 1994. "Reforming Canadian Democracy? Institutions and Ideology in the Reform Party Project." *Canadian Journal of Political Science* 27 (2): 213–47.

Lederman, M. 2013. "Note to VAG, Consider Staying Put." *Globe and Mail*, 4 May.

Lee, Jeff. 1988a. "Campbell Launches Bid for Re-Election by Knocking Politics of Confrontation." *Vancouver Sun*, 16 September.

– 1988b. "Appointments Anger Cope Aldermen." *Vancouver Sun*, 6 December.

– 1988c. "Planner Quits, Citing Friction with Council." *Vancouver Sun*, 9 December.

– 1988d. "NPA Funds Non-Issue, Mayor Says." *Vancouver Sun*, 15 November.

– 1988e. "Tough Choices Await NPA." *Vancouver Sun*, 21 November.

– 1988f. "Campbell Shakes Up Committee System." *Vancouver Sun*, 6 December.

– 1990a. "Green Mayoralty Bid Hangs on Davies." *Vancouver Sun*, 28 September.

– 1990b. "Housing Issue Key to Vancouver Election Campaign." *Vancouver Sun*, 20 October.

– 1990c. "A Tale of Two Candidates: 'Teflon Man' Cites Action, Not Words." *Vancouver Sun*, 20 October.

– 1990d. "Mayor Hails NPA's 'Affordable Government." *Vancouver Sun*, 2 November.

– 1992a. "Campbell Tells Ottawa, Victoria: Don't Dump Money Woes on Us: State of the City Report Pledges Vancouver-Wide Hot-Topic Talks." *Vancouver Sun*, 16 January.

– 1992b. "Municipalities Want to Be Part of Talks." *Vancouver Sun*, 23 September.

– 1993a. "Harcourt Told to Keep Hands Off Property." *Vancouver Sun*, 22 January.

– 1993b. "An Impatient Campbell Says He'll Tell Us 'When.'" *Vancouver Sun*, 6 March.

– 1993c. "Campbell Called Front Man for Pro-Coalition Clique." *Vancouver Sun*, 5 May.

– 1993d. "Campbell Launches Liberal Bid with Road Trip." *Vancouver Sun*, 6 May.

– 2005. "Developer Drops Out of Olympics Work." *Vancouver Sun*, 6 October.

Lee, M., and M. Cohen. 2005. *The Hidden Costs of Health Care Wage Cuts in BC*. Ottawa: Canadian Centre for Policy Alternatives.

Lee, M., I. Ivanova, and S. Klein. 2011. "BC's Regressive Tax Shift: A Decade of

Diminishing Tax Fairness, 2000 to 2010." *Behind The Numbers*. Canadian Centre for Policy Alternatives (BC Office). http://www.policyalternatives .ca/sites/default/files/uploads/publications/BC%20Office/2011/06/CCPA _BC_regressive_tax_shift.pdf.

Lee, M., S. Murray, and B. Parfitt. 2005. *BC's Regional Divide: How Tax Spending Policies Affect BC Communities*. Ottawa: Canadian Centre for Policy Alternatives.

Legislative Assembly of British Columbia. 2003. *Speech from the Throne*, 11 February. https://www.leg.bc.ca/content/Hansard/37th4th/h30211p.htm.

Lenskyj, H.J. 1996. "When Winners Are Losers: Toronto and Sydney Bids for the Summer Olympics." *Journal of Sport and Social Issues* 20, (4): 392–410.

Leonhardt, D. 2012. "Do Tax Cuts Lead to Economic Growth?" *New York Times*, 15 September. http://www.nytimes.com/2012/09/16/opinion/sunday/do-tax-cuts-lead-to-economic-growth.html.

Leslie, D., and N.M. Rantisi. 2012. "The Rise of a New Knowledge/Creative Economy: Prospects and Challenges for Economic Development, Class Inequality, and Work." In *The Wiley-Blackwell Companion to Economic Geography*, edited by T.J. Barnes, J. Peck, and E. Shepperd, 458–72. Hoboken, NJ: Wiley-Blackwell.

Leslie, J., and R. Maguire. 1978. *The Historical Development of the Indian Act*. Ottawa: Treaties and Historical Research Centre.

Lewis, S., and D. Kouri. 2004. "Regionalization: Making Sense of the Canadian Experience." *Healthcare Papers* 5 (1): 12–31.

Liedtke, M. 2001. "Action on Energy Trading Floors Reverberate in Power-Hungry California." The Associated Press, 17 April. http://jacksonville .com/tu-online/stories/041901/bus_5950798.html#.WPe71_nyuUl.

Lomas, J. 1997. "Devolving Authority for Health Care in Canada's Provinces: Emerging Issues and Prospects." *Canadian Medical Association Journal* 156: 817–23.

Low, D. 2010. "The 2010 Cultural Olympiad Impact Study." Master of urban studies dissertation, Simon Fraser University, Vancouver.

– 2012. "Content Analysis and Press Coverage: Vancouver's Cultural Olympiad." *Canadian Journal of Communication* 37 (3): 505–12.

Luke, H., and G. Moore. 2004. *Who's Looking Out for Our Kids? Deregulating Child Labour Law in British Columbia*. A Canadian Centre for Policy Alternatives-BC Policy Brief, March. https://www.policyalternatives.ca/publications/reports/whos-looking-out-our-kids.

Lund, Brian. 2008. "Major, Blair and the Third Way in Social Policy." *Social Policy and Administration* 42 (1): 43–58.

Lunman, K. 2001a. "Campbell Asks BC to Put Faith in Liberals." *Globe and Mail*, 6 June.

– 2001b. "Meet Gordon Campbell, Efficiency Expert." *Globe and Mail*, 3 September.

– 2001c. "Ottawa Opposed Treaty Referendum in BC, Nault says." *Globe and Mail*, 26 July.

MacDonald, D. 2002. *More Labour Code Amendments Invite Increased Confrontation: A Backgrounder on BC's Proposed Changes to the Labour Relations Code*. Vancouver: Canadian Centre for Policy Alternatives.

MacDonald, F. 2011. "Indigenous Peoples and Neoliberal 'Privatization' in Canada: Opportunities, Cautions and Constraints." *Canadian Journal of Political Science* 44 (2): 257–73.

Macdonald, N. 2011. "Q & A: Gordon Campbell." *Maclean's Magazine*, 16 February. Accessed 21 November 2016. http://www.macleans.ca/general/on-right-and-wrong-politics-arnold-schwarzenegger-and-his-worst-day-in-office/.

Macklem, P. 2001. *Indigenous Difference and the Constitution of Canada*. Toronto: University of Toronto Press.

MacLeod, A. 2008. "Voting Reform to Die?" *TheTyee.ca*, 7 February.

Macqueen, K. 2002. "Referendum Madness." *Maclean's* 115 (19): 42.

MacPhail, F., and P. Bowles. 2007. "From Casual Work to Economic Security: The Case of British Columbia." *Social Indicators Research* 88 (1): 97–114.

Macpherson, C.B. 1977. *The Life and Times of Liberal Democracy*. Oxford: Oxford University Press.

Magnusson, W., W.K. Carroll, C. Doyle, M. Langer, and R.B.J. Walker, eds. 1984. *The New Reality: The Politics of Restraint in BC*. Vancouver: New Star.

Markey, S., G. Halseth, and D. Manson 2006. "The Struggle to Compete: From Comparative to Competitive Advantage in Northern British Columbia." *International Planning Studies* 11 (1): 19–39.

– 2008. "Challenging the Inevitability of Rural Decline: Advancing Policy of Place in Northern British Columbia." *Journal of Rural Studies* 24: 409–21.

Markle, T. 2011. "City Seizes Millennium Assets, Anticipates over $100m in Profits from Social Housing Sell Out." *The Mainlander.com*, 9 April. http://themainlander.com/2011/04/09/city-seizes-millenium-assets-anticipates-140m-profits-from-social-housing-sell-out/.

Marland, A., T. Giasson, and J. Lees-Marshment, eds. 2012. *Political Marketing in Canada*. Vancouver: UBC Press.

Martin, Don. 2002. *King Ralph: The Political Life and Success of Ralph Klein*. Toronto: Key Porter.

Martin, D., and C. Adams. 2002. "Canadian Public Opinion Regarding Aboriginal Self-Government: Diverging Viewpoints as Found in National Survey Results." *American Review of Canadian Studies* 30 (1): 79–88.

Martineau, P. 2005. "Federal Personal Income Tax: Slicing the Pie." *Statistics Canada Analytical Paper*. http://www.michelbeauregard.com/11-621-MIE2005024.pdf.

Matas, R. 2001. "Treaty Vote Waste of Money, Polls Says." *Globe and Mail*, 20 December.

May, J., P. Cloke, and S. Johnsen. 2005. "Re-Phasing Neo-Liberalism, from Governance to 'Governmentality': New Labour and Britain's Crisis of Street Homelessness." *Antipode* 37 (4): 703–30.

McBride, S., and K. McNutt. 2007. "Devolution and Neoliberalism in the Canadian Welfare State: Ideology, National and International Conditioning Frameworks and Policy Change in British Columbia." *Global Social Policy* 7 (2): 177–201.

McChesney, R. 1999. "Introduction." In Noam Chomsky, *Profit over People: Neoliberalism and the Global Order*. New York: Seven Stories Press.

McCune, S. 1990. "Subtle Changes in the Body Politic." *Province*, 19 November.

McGrady, Leo, and Sonya Sabet-Rasekh. 2016. "A Guide to the Law of Organizing in British Columbia." Vancouver. http://mcgradylaw.ca/pdfs/Law%20Of%20Organizing%20Revised%202nd%20ed%20October%2015%202016.pdf.

McGuigan, J. 2005. "Neo-liberalism, Culture and Policy." *International Journal of Cultural Policy* 11 (3): 229–41.

McInnes, C. 1995. "Campbell Has the 'Scent of Power' about Him." *Globe and Mail*, 17 July.

– 2001. "Campbell Hikes Cabinet Accountability." *Calgary Herald*, 5 June.

– 2003. "Tossing Out Politicians by Recall Is a Long-Odds Tactic." *Vancouver Sun*, 16 April.

– 2004. "Political Honesty Takes a Beating in Canada, Too." *Vancouver Sun*, 4 November.

– 2005. "After a Bit of a Workout, Recall Legislation Has Lost Its Luster." *Vancouver Sun*, 17 March.

McKee, C. 2009. *Treaty Talks in British Columbia: Building a New Relationship*. Vancouver: UBC Press.

McLintock, B. 2003. "Citizens to Drive Electoral Change." *Province*, 29 April.

McLintock, B., and T. Hawthorn. 1993. "Campbell Rides New Grit Wave: First-Ballot Victory for Mayor." *Province*, 12 September.

McMartin, P. 1987a. "Playing the Numbers Game at City Hall." *Vancouver Sun*, 4 February.

– 1987b. "Prepare for the Invasion of the Megamarket." *Vancouver Sun*, 16 March. http://www.vancouversun.com.

– 1987c. "Fireboat Affair Typifies Style of City's Mayor." *Vancouver Sun*, 4 May.

– 1987d. "Mayor Counted One Nose Too Few." *Vancouver Sun*, 30 July.

– 1995. "The Very Private Gordon Campbell." *Vancouver Sun*, 29 November.

Menzies, G. 2012. "Vancouver Was Home to the First Social Media Olympics, Not London." *Vancouver Sun*, 24 July. http://www.vancouversun.com/ sports/2012-summer-games/Vancouver+home+first+social+media +Olympics+London/6978173/story.html.

Messere, Ken, Flip de Kam, and Christopher Heady. 2003. *Tax Policy: Theory and Practice in OECD Countries*. Oxford: Oxford University Press.

Mickleburgh, R. 2000a. "Ex-Premier Clark Charged in BC Casino Controversy," *Globe and Mail*, 21 October. http://www.theglobeandmail.com/news/ national/ex-premier-clark-charged-in-bc-casino-controversy/article1043140/.

– 2000b. "BC Liberals Challenge Aboriginal Self-Government." *Globe and Mail*, 16 May.

– 2003. "Ignominious End to BC Ferry Saga." *Globe and Mail*, 22 March. http://www.theglobeandmail.com/news/national/ignominious-end-to-bc-ferry-saga/article4127808/.

– 2009. "Chief's Public Support for NDP Irks Native Community." *Globe and Mail*, 11 May.

– 2011. "Predictions of Post Olympic Jump in Visitors Are Fading." *Globe and Mail*, 26 October, P: A15.

Milke, M. 2002. *Tax Me I'm Canadian: Your Money and How Politicians Spend It*. Toronto: Thomas and Black.

Ministry of Community, Aboriginal and Women's Services. 2002. *The Community Charter: A New Legislative Framework for Local Government*. Victoria: Queen's Printer.

Ministry of Competition, Science and Enterprise (Capital Projects Branch, Province of British Columbia). 2002. *The Economic Impact of the 2010 Winter Olympic and Paralympic Games – Initial Estimates*. http://www.fin.gov .bc.ca/reports/ecimpact2002.pdf.

Ministry of Energy, Mines and Petroleum Resources, BC Hydro. 2010. "New Act Powers Forward with Clean Energy and Jobs." http://www2 .news.gov.bc.ca/news_releases_2009-2013/2010PREM0090-000483.htm.

Ministry of Forests, Lands, and Natural Resource Operations. 2010. *The State of British Columbia's Forests – 2010 Report*. Victoria: Government of British Columbia. http://www.for.gov.bc.ca/hfp/sof/#2010_report.

– 2011. *Revised 2011/12–2013/14 Service Plan*. Victoria: Government of British Columbia. http://www.for.gov.bc.ca/hfd/pubs/docs/mr/plans/ 2011_12/flnr.pdf.

Mintz, J. 2010. "British Columbia's Harmonized Sales Tax: A Giant Leap in the Province's Competitiveness." *University of Calgary School of Public*

Policy Briefing Papers 3 (4): 1–15. http://www.fin.gov.bc.ca/Mintz
_report.pdf.

Miraftab, F. 2004. "Public-Private Partnerships: The Trojan Horse of Neoliberal Development?" *Journal of Planning Education and Research* 24: 89–101.

Mitchell, D.A., and P. Tennant. 1996. "Government to Government: Aboriginal Peoples and British Columbia." In *For Seven Generations: An Information Legacy of the Royal Commission on Aboriginal Peoples*. Ottawa: Canada Communications Group.

Mitchell, David. 1983. *W.A.C. Bennett and the Rise of British Columbia*. Scarborough, ON: HarperCollins Canada.

Molloy, T. 2006. *The World Is Our Witness: The Historic Journey of the Nisga'a into Canada*. Calgary: Fifth House.

Montani, A., and A. Perry. 2013. *Child Labour Is No Accident: The Experience of BC's Working Children*. First Call – BC Child and Youth Advocacy Coalition, Vancouver, BC, 9 May. http://firstcallbc.org/wordpress/wp-content/uploads/2015/08/Child-Labour-Is-No-Accident-FirstCall-2013-05.pdf.

Moran, M. 1999. *Governing the Health Care State: A Comparative Study of the United Kingdom, the United States and Germany*. Manchester: Manchester University Press.

Moretti, E. 2012. *The New Geography of Jobs*. New York: Houghton Mifflin Harcourt.

Morgan, S., M. Barer, and J. Agnew. 2003. "Whither Seniors' Pharmacare: Lessons from (and for) Canada." *Health Affairs* 22 (3): 49–59.

Morgan, S., and M. Coombes. 2006. "Income-Based Drug Coverage in British Columbia: Towards an Understanding of the Policy." *Healthcare Policy* 2 (2): 92–108.

Morgan, S., R. Evans, G. Hanley, P. Caetano, and C. Black. 2006. "Income-Based Drug Coverage in British Columbia: Lessons for BC and the Rest of Canada." *Healthcare Policy* 2 (2): 115–27.

Moya, M. 1984. "New Alderman Wants to Lure Development Investment." *Vancouver Sun*, 19 November.

Mulgrew, I. 2001. "Liberal Candidates Kept on Short Leashes." *Vancouver Sun*, 9 May.

– 2011. "Natives Promise 'Chaos' for BC if Campbell Allows Treaty Referendum." *Vancouver Sun*, 12 March.

Multi-Party Agreement 2002. Multi Party Agreement for the 2010 Olympic and Paralympic Games. http://www.fin.gov.bc.ca/reports/Multiparty agreementEnglish.pdf.

Murray, K.B. 2008. "The Realignment of Government in the Provinces." In *Canadian Provincial Politics*, 2nd ed., ed. C. Dunn, 415–34. Toronto: University of Toronto Press.

Murray, S. 2005. "Shifting Costs: An Update on How Tax and Spending Cuts Impact British Columbians." *Behind the Numbers*. Canadian Centre for Policy Alternatives. http://www.policyalternatives.ca/sites/default/files/uploads/publications/BC_Office_Pubs/bc_2005/shifting_costs.pdf.

– 2007a. "Who Gets What from the 2007 BC Tax Cut?" *Behind the Numbers*. Canadian Centre for Policy Alternatives. https://www.policyalternatives .ca/sites/default/files/uploads/publications/BC_Office_Pubs/bc_2007/bc _tax_btn.pdf.

– 2007b. "Time to Raise BC's Minimum Wage." *BC Commentary: A Review of Provincial Social and Economic Trends* 10 (2): 1.

Nanaimo. 2008. *Cultural Strategy.* https://www.nanaimo.ca/assets /Departments/Parks~Rec~Culture/Publications~and~Forms/Cultural Strategy.pdf.

Napoleon, V. 2004. "Who Gets to Say What Happened? Reconciliation Issues for the Gitxsan." In *Intercultural Dispute Resolution in Aboriginal Contexts,* ed. C. Bell and D. Kahane, 176–95. Vancouver: UBC Press.

Needham, Phil. 1993. "Campbell Promises to Be Accountable." *Vancouver Sun,* 19 October.

Nelles, J., and C. Alcantara. 2011. "Strengthening the Ties That Bind? An Analysis of Aboriginal-Municipal Inter-Governmental Agreements in British Columbia." *Canadian Public Administration* 54 (3): 315–34.

OECD. 2001. *Tax and the Economy: A Comparative Assessment of OECD Countries.* Paris: OECD Publishing.

– 2003. "Enhancing the Cost Effectiveness of Public Spending." *OECD Economic Outlook* 74: 161–75.

– 2012a. *Revenue Statistics – 1965–2011.* Paris: OECD Publishing.

– 2012b. *Consumption Tax Trends: VAT/GST and Excise Rates, Trends, and Administration Issues.* Paris: OECD Publishing.

Office of the Premier. 2006. "Province and City Plan New Vancouver Cultural Precinct." http://www2.news.gov.bc.ca/news_releases_2005-2009/2006 TSA0013-000382.htm.

Olynyk, J.N. 2005. *The Haida Nation and Taku River Tlingit Decisions: Clarifying Roles and Responsibilities for Aboriginal Consultation and Accommodation.* http://www.lawsonlundell.com/media/news/236_Negotiatorarticle.pdf.

O'Neill, T. 2013. "BC Budget 2013 Economic and Revenue Forecasts: Review and Assessment, Independent Report to the BC Minister of Finance." February. http://www.bcbudget.gov.bc.ca/2013/reports/2013_oneill _report.pdf.

Otero, G., and K. Preibisch. 2009. *Farmworker Health and Safety: Challenges for British Columbia.* A draft report. October (1–98). http://www.sfu.ca/~otero/ docs/Otero-and-Preibisch-Final-Nov-2010.pdf

Palmer, B. 1987. *Solidarity, the Rise and Fall of an Opposition in British Colum-bia*. Vancouver: New Star Books.

Palmer, Vaughn. 1993a. "One-Vote Margin Puts Campbell One Up on Rivals." *Vancouver Sun*, 3 August.

– 1993b. "Is Campbell Really the Best We Can Do?" *Vancouver Sun*, 9 Sep-tember.

– 1993c. "A Victory for Quiet, Ruthless Efficiency." *Vancouver Sun*, 13 Septem-ber.

– 1994a. "Mr. Campbell a Team Player – His Team." *Vancouver Sun*, 3 Febru-ary.

– 1994b. "Tough Talk Came Too Late to Snare Fox." *Vancouver Sun*, 16 March.

– 1995. "Old-Time Liberal Feels Alienated by Party's New Leader." *Vancouver Sun*, 3 May.

– 1996. "BC Liberals Show No Sign of Doing Politics Differently." *Vancouver Sun*, 23 March.

– 1999. "Campbell's Proposals Would Have a Major Impact." *Vancouver Sun*, 19 April.

– 2000a. "Campbell's Ready and Waiting. And Waiting." *Vancouver Sun*, 19 October.

– 2000b. "Campbell Plan Upsets Native Indian Readers." *Vancouver Sun*, 20 October.

– 2000c. "The Liberal Case for Open Government." *Vancouver Sun*, 21 No-vember.

– 2001a. "Campbell Tap Dances over Shifting Ground." *Vancouver Sun*, 25 July: A14.

– 2001b. "BC Liberal Gimmicks or Small 'r' Reforms?" *National Post*, 3 March.

– 2001c. Campbell's Quiet Shift on the Referendum Issue." *Vancouver Sun*, 7 April.

– 2002a. "Recall Law No Longer on Liberals' Agenda." *Vancouver Sun*, 26 Feb-ruary.

– 2002b. "'Gord's Baby' a Staggering Work in Progress." *Vancouver Sun*, 7 June.

– 2002c. "BC's People Speak Decisively." *National Post*, 4 July.

– 2003a. "Community Charter = Hang On to Your Wallet." *Vancouver Sun*, 12 March.

– 2003b. "Campbell's 'Open' Cabinet Pure Infomercial." *Vancouver Sun*, 15 March.

– 2003c. "Hypocritical Liberals Assail Recall 'Onslaught.'" *Vancouver Sun*, 6 May.

– 2005a. "BC Plans to Restrict Ads." *Regina Leader Post*, 12 January.

– 2005b. "'Plain and Simple' Truth Rare in Liberal Lexicon." *Vancouver Sun*, 18 February.

– 2006. "Campbell 'Blisters' Federal Conservatives to Applause All Round." *Vancouver Sun*, 5 May.

– 2008a. "Campbell Locks Horns with Business over One of His 'Four As.'" *Vancouver Sun*, 12 February.

– 2008b. "Campbell Rebuffs Native Leaders on Timetable for Recognition Act." *Vancouver Sun*, 26 February.

– 2009a. "Liberals and Native Leaders Press 'Recognition' Agenda." *Vancouver Sun*, 26 February.

– 2009b. "Campbell Gets Time to Get It Right." *Vancouver Sun*, 18 March.

Panitch, L., and D. Swartz. 2003. *From Consent to Coercion: The Assault on Trade Union Freedoms*. Aurora: Garamond Press.

Patten, S. 1996. "Preston Manning's Populism: Constructing the Common Sense of the Common People." *Studies in Political Economy* 50: 95–132.

Patterson, L.L. 2006. *Aboriginal Roundtable to Kelowna Accord: Aboriginal Policy Negotiations, 2004–2005*. Ottawa: Political and Social Affairs Division.

Peacock, A. 1969. "Welfare Economics and Public Subsidies to the Arts." *Journal of Cultural Economics* 18 (2): 323–35.

Peck, Jamie, and Adam Tickell. 2002. "Neoliberalizing Space." *Antipode* 34 (3): 380–404.

Peckham, S., M. Exworthy, I. Greener, and M. Powell. 2005. "Decentralizing Health Services: More Local Accountability or Just More Central Control?" *Public Money and Management* 25 (4): 221–8.

Penikett, T. 2006. *Reconciliation: First Nations Treaty Making in British Columbia*. Vancouver: Douglas and McIntyre.

Penner, Derrick. 2003. "Tomato King Cheers Right to Burn Wood: Court Overturns Bylaw That Restricted Growers Fuel – Delta Bylaw 'Set Undue Restrictions.'" *Vancouver Sun*, 19 April, C1–2.

Phillips, Stephen. 2010. "Party Politics in British Columbia: The Persistence of Polarization." In *British Columbia Politics and Government*, ed. M. Howlett, D. Pilon, and T. Summerville, 109–29. Toronto: Emond Montgomery.

Pilon, D. 2006. "Explaining Voting System Reform in Canada: 1874 to 1960." *Journal of Canadian Studies* 40 (3): 135–61.

– 2007. "Presentation to the Ontario Legislative Committee Hearings on Bill 155." http://www.ontla.on.ca/committee-proceedings/transcripts/files _html/05-

– 2009. "Democracy, BC-style." In *Politics and Government in British Columbia*, ed. M. Howlett, D. Pilon, and T. Summerville, 87–108. Toronto: Emond Montgomery.

– 2010. "The 2005 and 2009 Referenda on Voting System Change in British Columbia." *Canadian Political Science Review* 4 (2–3): 73–89.

– 2013. *Wrestling with Democracy: Voting Systems as Politics in the Twentieth-Century West.* Toronto: University of Toronto Press.

Plecas, B. 2006. *Bill Bennett: A Mandarin's View.* Madeira Park, BC: Douglas and McIntyre.

Ponting, J.R. 2006. *The Nisga'a Treaty: Polling Dynamics and Political Communication in Comparative Context.* Peterborough: Broadview Press.

Potts, J. 2011. *Creative Industries and Economic Evolution.* Cheltenham, UK: Edward Elgar.

Poverty Olympics. 2010. http://povertyolympics.ca.

Powell River. 2012. *Powell River Arts and Culture Initiative.* https://powellriver .civicweb.net/document/2578.

Pralle, S. 2003. "Venue Shopping, Political Strategy, and Policy Change: The Internationalization of Canadian Forest Advocacy." *Journal of Public Policy* 23 (3): 233–60.

Price, K., A. Roburn, and A. MacKinnon. 2009. "Ecosystem-Based Management in the Great Bear Rainforest." *Forest Ecology and Management* 258: 495–503.

PriceWaterhouseCoopers. 2009. BC *Treaty Commission: Financial and Economic Impacts of Treaty Settlements in* BC(*November*). http://www.bctreaty.net/ sites/default/files/BC-Treaty-Commission-PricewaterhouseCoopers-Report .pdf.

Proctor, J. 1997. "Pick Unity Panel at Random: Campbell." *Province*, 12 October.

Province. 1994. "Silent Partner." 10 February.

– 2001. "Campbell's 'Open,' Says Me, Not All It's Cracked Up to Be." 23 July.

– 2002. "Liberals Slow to Pick up Recall Bill." 12 November.

Pulkingham, J. 2006. "Bucking the National Trend: The Campbell Cuts and Poverty among Lone Mothers in BC." *SPARC BC News*, 6.

Punter, John. 2003. *The Vancouver Achievement: Urban Planning and Design.* Vancouver: UBC Press.

Pupo, N., and M. Thomas, eds. 2010. *Interrogating the New Economy: Structuring Work in the 21st Century.* Toronto: University of Toronto Press.

Rabe, B.G., and C.P. Borick. 2012. "Carbon Taxation and Policy Labelling: Experience from American States and Canadian Provinces." *Review of Policy Research* 29 (3): 358–82.

Rasmussen, M. 2008. "Legislatures in Saskatchewan: A Battle for Sovereignty." In *Saskatchewan Politics: Crowding the Centre*, ed. H. Lesson, 37–60. Regina: Canadian Plains Research Centre.

Rebick, Judy. 2012. *Occupy This!* Penguin Books. Ebook.

Record New Westminster, The. 2004. "$12 Million Avaible to the Arts to Help Prepare for 2010." 18 December.

Redekop, J.H. 2005. "Commentary: An Assessment of the BC Citizens' Assembly." *BC Studies* 147: 89–102.

Rees, A. 2005. "Tracking, and Stalling, Muckrakers." In *Liberalized*, edited by D. Beers, 76–9. Vancouver: New Star.

Regional Steering Committee on Homelessness. 2012. *One Step Forward ... Results of the 2011 Metro Vancouver Homeless Count*. http://homelesshub.ca/resource/one-step-forward...-%EF%BB%BFresults-2011-metro-vancouver-homeless-count.

Reid, A. 2002. "Treaty Referendum Is No Laughing Matter." *Vancouver Sun*, 5 April.

Resnick, P. 1987. "Neo-Conservatism on the Periphery: The Lessons from BC." *BC Studies* 75: 3–23.

Robertson, G. 2010. "Olympic Village Greenest Neighborhood in the World." Vancouver Mayor's Office, 16 February. http://www.mayorofvancouver.ca/olympic-village-greenest-neighbourhood-in-the-world.

Ross, M.L. 2005. *First Nations Sacred Sites in Canada's Courts*. Vancouver: UBC Press.

Rossiter, D., and P.K. Wood. 2005. "Neo-liberal Responses to Aboriginal Land Claims in British Columbia." *Canadian Geographer* 49 (4): 352–66.

Roy, F. 2006. "From She to She: Changing Patterns of Women in the Canadian Labour Force." *Canadian Economic Observer*. Statistics Canada, catalogue number 11-010-X, 3-1 to 3-10.

Royal Bank. N.d. *Striving for Excellence: Your Guide to Business Opportunities for the 2010 Winter Games*. http://www.rbcroyalbank.com/commercial/campaign/olympicbusiness/pdf/2010_olympic_bus_guide.pdf.

Royal Commission on Financial Management and Accountability (Lambert Commission). 1979. *Report*. Ottawa: Queen's Printer.

Royal Commission on Workers' Compensation in British Columbia. 1998. "PRAXIS Background Paper: Benefits." http://www.qp.gov.bc.ca/rcwc/research/praxis03benefits.PDF.

Ruff, Norman. 2004. "Electoral Reform and Deliberative Democracy: The British Columbia Citizens' Assembly." In *Steps Toward Making Every Vote Count: Electoral Reform in Canada and its Provinces*, edited by H. Milner, 235–48. Peterborough: Broadview Press.

– 2010a. "New Era, Old Reality: The BC Legislature and Accountable Government." In *British Columbia Politics and Government*, edited by M. Howlett, D. Pilon, and T. Summerville, 191–203. Toronto: Emond Montgomery.

– 2010b. "Executive Dominance: Cabinet and the Office of the Premier in British Columbia." In *British Columbia Politics and Government*, ed. M. Howlett, D. Pilon, and T. Summerville, 205–16. Toronto: Emond Montgomery.

Sallot, J. 2004. "Aboriginals to Receive $700 Million." *Globe and Mail*, 14 September.

Samuelson, P.A. 1954. "The Pure Theory of Public Expenditure." *The Review of Economic and Statistics* 36 (4): 387–9.

Sandborn, T. 2007. "Campbell Government Violated Charter Rights: Supreme Court." *Vancouver Sun*, 8 June.

– 2010. "The Biggest Rollback of Workers' Rights in Canadian History." *Tyee*, 7 September.

Sandler, J. 2001. "Natives Call for Boycott over Treaty Referendum." *Vancouver Sun*, 23 June.

Sarti, R. 1990. "NPA to Spend $400,000 on Campaign, Party Says." *Vancouver Sun*, 5 November.

Saskia, S. 2000. *Cities in the World Economy*, 2nd edition. Thousand Oaks, CA: Sage/Pine Forge Press.

Saul, J.R. 1997. *Reflections of a Siamese Twin: Canada at the End of the Twentieth Century*. Toronto: Penguin.

– 2008. *A Fair Country: Telling Truths about Canada*. Toronto: Viking Canada.

Savitch, H., and P. Kantor. 2002. *Cities in the International Market Place*. Princeton: Princeton University Press.

Savoie, D.J. 1999. *Governing from the Centre: The Concentration of Power in Canadian Politics*. Toronto: University of Toronto Press.

Sayers, C.J. 2001. "Don't Forget Treaty Issues." *Vancouver Sun*, 12 May.

Sayre, W.S., and H. Kaufman. 1960. *Governing New York City*. New York: Sage.

Schlosser, T., D. Dunning, K. Johnson, and J. Kruger. 2013. "How Unaware Are the Unskilled? Empirical Tests of the 'Signal Extraction' Counter-Explanation for the Dunning-Kruger Effect in Self-Evaluation of Performance." *Journal of Economic Psychology* 39: 85–100.

Shaw, C.A. 2008. *Five Ring Circus: Myths and Realities of the Olympic Games*. Gabriola Island, BC: New Society Publishers.

Shaw, K. 2004. "The Global/Local Politics of the Great Bear Rainforest." *Environmental Politics* 13 (2): 373–82.

Sheaffer, M. 2007. *Lost in Transmission: A Comprehensive Critique of the BC Energy Plan*. Vancouver: Canadian Office and Professional Employees Union Local 378.

Siemiatycki, M. 2005. "City: Analysis of Urban Trends, Culture, Theory, Policy, Action." *City* 9 (1): 9–22.

Simoski, K. 2009. "First Nations, Government Agree to Delay Historic Bill." *Vancouver Sun*, 16 March.

Simpson, J. 2012. *Chronic Condition: Why Canada's Health Care System Needs to Be Dragged into the 21st Century*. Toronto: Allen Lane Canada/Penguin.

Singer, D. 2000. "The Third Way and a New Left." *Journal of World Systems Research* 1 (3): 692–704.

Slattery, B. 2005. "Aboriginal Rights and the Honour of the Crown." *Supreme Court Law Review* 29: 433–45.

Smith, C. 2004. "Union Leaders' Firm Backed BC Liberals." *Georgia Straight*, 13 May. http://www.straight.com/article/union-leaders-firm-backed-b-c-liberals.

Smith, M. 1995. *Our Home or Native Land? What Governments' Aboriginal Policy Is Doing to Canada*. Toronto: Stoddart.

Smith, P. 2017. "Vancouver." In *The Rise of Cities*, edited by Dimitri Roussopoulos, 151–98. Montreal: Black Rose Books.

Smith, P., K. Ginnell, and M. Black. 2010. "Local Governing and Local Democracy in British Columbia." In *British Columbia Politics and Government*, ed. M. Howlett, D. Pilon, and T. Summerville, 245–66. Toronto: Emond Montgomery.

Smith, P., and K. Stewart. 2007. "Unaided Politicians in Unaided City Councils: Explaining Policy Advice in Canadian Cities." In *Policy Analysis in Canada: The State of the Art*, edited by M. Howlett and L. Dobuzinskis, 265–87. Toronto: University of Toronto Press.

– 2009. "British Columbia." In *Foundations of Governance: Muncipal Governance in Canada's Provinces*, ed. Andrew Sancton and Robert Young, 282–313. Toronto: University of Toronto Press.

– 2010. *Making Local Election Financing Work in BC*. Brief for the BC Local Government Election Task Force. Richmond: UBCM.

Smith, P.J. 1998. "Local Government: An Introduction." In *The Puzzles of Power: An Introduction to Political Science*, 2nd ed., ed. M. Howlett and D. Laycock, 393–403. Toronto: Oxford University Press.

– 2008. "British Columbia Changes Metro Vancouver's Transportation Governance: A Re-Examination of Peter Self's Dilemma Thesis – Efficiency vs. Accountability?" *Local Matters* 2: 2–5.

– 2009. "Even Greater Vancouver: Metropolitan Morphing in Canada's Third Largest City Region." In *Who Will Govern Metropolitan Regions in the 21st Century?*, ed. D. Phares. Armonk, NY: M.E. Sharpe.

Smith, P.J., and H.P. Oberlander. 1993. "Governing Metropolitan Vancouver: Regional Intergovernmental Relations in British Columbia." In *Metropolitan Governance: American/Canadian Intergovernmental Perspectives*, ed. D.

Rothblatt and A. Sancton, 329–73. Berkeley, University of California: Institute of Governmental Studies.

– 1998. "Restructuring Metropolitan Governance: Greater Vancouver— British Columbia Reforms." In *Metropolitan Governance Revisited: American/Canadian Intergovernmental Perspectives*, ed. D. Rothblatt and A. Sancton, 371–406. Berkeley, University of California: Institute of Governmental Studies.

Smyth, M. 2001. "Liberal MLAs Gagged before Election." *Province*, 6 April.

– 2003a. "Muffling Watchdogs Yet Another Low Olow from the Liberals." *Province*, 23 January.

– 2003b. "Would We Be in This Process If Campbell Had Won in 1996?" *Province*, 29 April.

– 2003c. "Campbell's 'Open Government' Pledge Is a Joke." *Province*, 18 July.

– 2003d. "BC's Top Bureaucrat Needs a Reminder Who He Works For." *Province*, 3 October.

– 2003e. "If It Was Wrong When the NDP Spent Your Money on Ads ..." *Province*, 4 December.

– 2005a. "Campbell Changes Tune on Native Affairs." *Province*, 21 June.

– 2005b. "Lift Question Period Limits, Mr. Premier." *Province*, 29 May.

Snowball, J.D. 2005. "Arts for the Masses? Justification for the Public Support of the Arts in Developing Countries – Two Arts Festivals in South Africa." *Journal of Cultural Economics* 29: 107–25.

– 2008. *Measuring the Value of Culture.* Springer.

Snowball, J., and Antrobus, G.G. 2002. "Valuing the Arts." *South African Journal of Economics* 70 (8): 1297.

Spector, N. 2001. "Campbell Should Admit His Error on NDP Status." *Times Colonist*, 31 May.

Spencer, Kent. 2012. "Human Rights Activist, Politician Jim Green Dead at 68." *Province*, 28 February.

Spoehr, J., ed. 2003. *Power Politics: The Electricity Crisis and You.* Australia: Wakefield Press.

Stanford, J. 2008. *Economics for Everyone: A Short Guide to the Economics of Capitalism.* Halifax: Fernwood.

Statistics Canada. 2009. "Provincial and Territorial General Government Revenue and Expenditures, By Province and Territory. (Alberta, British Columbia, Yukon, Northwest Territories)." Accessed 19 April 2017. http://www.statcan.gc.ca/tables-tableaux/sum-som/lo1/csto1/govto8c-eng.htm.

– 2011. *Women in Canada: A Gender-Based Statistical Report.* Ottawa: Ministry of Industry.

Stewart, K. 2003. *Think Democracy: Options for Local Democratic Reform in Vancouver*. Vancouver: IGS Press.

Strong-Boag, Veronica. 2011. *Fostering Nation? Canada Confronts Its History of Childhood Disadvantage*. Waterloo: Wilfrid Laurier University Press.

Sullivan, P. 2000. "The Passing of a Passionate BC Warrior of Words." *Globe and Mail*, 7 September.

Sullivan, S. 2005. "Inaugural Address to the City's Councillors." 5 December. http://vancouver.ca/files/cov/Mayor-Sam-Sullivan-2005-inaugural-speech.pdf.

Summerville, Tracy, and Gary Wilson. 2015. "Globalization and Multilevel Governance in Northern British Columbia: Opportunities and Challenges." In *Globalizing Northern British Columbia: Development, Agency and Contestation in a Resource-Based Economy*, edited by Paul Bowles and Gary Wilson, 109–35. Vancouver: UBC Press.

Summerville, Tracy, Gary N. Wilson, and John F. Young. 2013. "Federal Property in British Columbia: Dynamic Changes and Perennial Issues." In *Federal Property Policy in Canadian Municipalities*, edited by Michael C. Ircha and Robert Young, 37–61. Montreal: McGill-Queen's University Press.

Sustainable Prosperity. 2012. "British Columbia's Carbon Tax Shift: The First Four Years." Research Report. https://www.skepticalscience.com/print.php?n=2076.

Taft, Kevin. 1997. *Shredding the Public Interest: Ralph Klein and 25 Years of One-Party Government*. Edmonton: University of Alberta Press.

Taku River Tlingit First Nation v. British Columbia (Project Assessment Director). 2004. S.C.C. 74 [2004]; 3 S.C.R. 550.

Teghtsoonian, K. 2010. "Social Policy in Neoliberal Times." In *British Columbia Politics and Government*, edited by M. Howlett, D. Pilon, and T. Summerville, 309–30. Toronto: Emond Montgomery.

Telford, Hamish. 2010. "BC as an Intergovernmental Relations Player: Still Punching Below Its Weight?" In *British Columbia Politics and Government*, edited by M. Howlett, D. Pilon, and T. Summerville, 33–52. Toronto: Emond Montgomery.

Tennant, P. 1980. "Vancouver Civic Politics, 1929–1980." *BC Studies* 46: 3–27.

Tennant, P., and D. Zirnhelt. 1973. "Metropolitan Government in Vancouver: The Politics of 'Gentle Imposition.'" *Canadian Public Administration* 16: 124–38.

Throsby, D. 1994. "The Production and Consumption of the Arts: A View of Cultural Economics." *Journal of Economic Literature* 9(2): 1–28.

– 2010. "Tourism: The Economics of Cultural Policy." In *The Economics of Cultural Policy*, 146–57. Cambridge: Cambridge University Press.

Times-Colonist. 1994. "Campbell Urges Free Votes: Lauds NDP." 8 April.

– 2001. "NDP Deserves Official Status." 14 July.

– 2002. "Recall Bids Are a Tough Challenge: Legislation Is Designed to Be Used in Extreme Cases, Not Simply to Change Election Results." 19 November.

Tiongson, E. 1997. "Baumols Cost Disease Reconsidered." *Challenge* 40(6): 117–23.

Toronto Star. 1987. "Developer New Mayor of Vancouver." 17 November.

Touati, N., D. Roberge, J.-L. Denis, R. Pineault, and L. Cazale. 2007. "Governance, Health Policy Implementation and the Added Value of Regionalization." *Healthcare Papers* 2 (3): 97–114.

Treff, K., and D. Ort. 2013. *Finances of the Nation 2012.* Toronto: Canadian Tax Foundation.

Trottier, L.-H., F. Champagne, A.-P. Contandriopolous, and J.-L. Denis. 1999. "Contrasting Visions of Decentralization." In *Health Reform: Public Success, Private Failure*, edited by D. Drache, D. Sullivan, and T. Sullivan, 147–65. London: Routledge.

Tuoy, C.J. 1999. *Accidental Logics: The Dynamics of Change in the Health Care Arena in the United States, Britain and Canada.* New York: Oxford University Press.

Tyson, Laura D'Andrea and Owen Zidar. 2012. "Tax Cuts for Job Creators." *New York Times*, 19 October.

UBCIC. 2005. "Resolution of the Special Joint Assembly of First Nations Chiefs in British Columbia." http://www.ubcic.bc.ca/files/PDF/joint _res_NewRelationship_May2005.pdf.

– 2009. "Discussion Paper on Instructions for Implementing the New Relationship." Accessed 21 November 2016. http://www.ubcic.bc.ca/files/PDF/ Discussion_ImplementingNR_190209.pdf

Union of British Columbia Municipalities. 2003. Press Release. 7 November.

United Nations. 2011. *The United National Human Development Index, 2011.* New York: United Nations. http://www.undp.org/content/undp/en/ home/librarypage/hdr/human_developmentreport2011.html.

Vancouver Board of Trade. 2005. Summary of Gordon Campbell's talk, http://www.boardoftrade.com/events/event-highlights/spirit-of-vancouver/3441890234.aspx.

Vancouver Foundation. 2007. Metro Vancouver's Vital Signs 2007. http://2007.vancouverfoundationvitalsigns.ca/?q=node/16.

– 2010. *Vancouver Foundation's Vital Signs for Metro Vancouver 2010: On the Road to Vitality.* https://www.vancouverfoundation.ca/sites/default/ files/publications/Vancouver%20Foundation%20Metro%20Vancouver %20Vital%20Signs%202010_cc%204.0.pdf

Vancouver Sun. 1987a. "Gay Games Welcomed." 24 October.
- 1987b. "Longer Civic Terms Welcome." 24 March.
- 1993. "Campbell Keeps Us Guessing." 19 April.
- 1994a. "Politicians' Donors Should Be Named." 22 February.
- 1994b. "Campbell Releases List of Contributors to His By-election Campaign." 24 March.
- 1995. "Liberals Introduce Bill to Make Launching a Referendum Easier." 11 July.
- 2001. "Liberal Victory Gives BC Chance For Renewal: NDP Deserves Opposition Status However Small the Numbers." 17 May.
- 2002. "Province in 'Financial Mess': In This Text of His TV Address, Premier Gordon Campbell Warns of Cuts to Come." 14 February.
- 2003. "Recall Legislation Must Be Repealed: It's Being Used Too Often for the Wrong Reasons." 3 February.
- 2004. "An Election Promise Campbell Should Keep." 12 January.
- 2005. "Olympic Construction Costs Soar." 26 November.

Van Wynsberghe, R. 2013. "Olympic Games Impact (OGI) Study for the 2010 Olympic and Paralympic Winter Games: Post-Games Report." http://css.ubc.ca/projects/olympic-games-impact-study/ogi-reports/.

Veldhuis, N., C. Lammam, and M. Palacios. 2011. "Mitigating the Crushing Blow to BC's Competitiveness." *Fraser Forum.* https://www.fraserinstitute.org/research/fraser-forum-novemberdecember-2011-how-canadas-premiers-stack.

Vogel, D. 2003. *Challenging Politics: COPE, Electoral Politics and Social Movements.* Halifax: Fernwood.

Volkart, C. 1987a. "Campbell Urges Plebiscite in Welcoming Ward Legislation." *Vancouver Sun,* 15 May.
- 1987b. "Fall Ballot on Wards Too Fast to Suit Davies." *Vancouver Sun,* 23 July.
- 1988. "Caucus Talks with MPs, MLAs Called Useless; Mayor's Caucus Talks Useless, Eriksen Says." *Vancouver Sun,* 25 January.

Volkart, C., and S. Cox. 1987. "Headlines, Howls Mark NPA Council's First Six Months." *Vancouver Sun,* 20 June.

Walden, D. 2012. *Paradigm Shift in the Arts and Cultural Heritage: From Supply to Demand and the Demand to Supply.* http://canadacouncil.ca/council/news-room/news/2012/david-a-walden-(2012).

Wallace, B., S. Klein, and M. Reitsma-Street. 2006. *Denied Assistance: Closing the Front Door on Welfare in BC.* Ottawa: Canadian Centre for Policy Alternatives.

Ward, D. 1990. "Going Gala: An Innocent Finds Class Solidarity in the Charity Circuit Status-Sphere." *Vancouver Sun,* 20 October.

- 1994. "Disclose Backers Now, Campbell Foes Say: Funded by Special Interest Groups, Social Credit, NDP Candidates Claim." *Vancouver Sun*, 15 February.
- 2010. "Gordon Campbell Canada's Most Unpopular Premier." *Vancouver Sun*, 13 September.

Warren, M.E., and H. Pearse, eds. 2008. *Designing Deliberative Democracy: The British Columbia Citizens' Assembly*. Cambridge: Cambridge University Press.

Weaver, S. 1984. "Indian Government: A Concept in Need of a Definition." In *Pathways to Self-Determination: Canadian Indians and the Canadian State*, edited by L. Little Bear, M. Boldt, and J.A. Long, 65–8. Toronto: University of Toronto Press.

Wells, M., and J.W. Berry. 1992. "Attitudes toward Aboriginal Self-Government: The Influences of Knowledge, and Cultural and Economic Security." *Canadian Journal of Native Studies* 12 (1): 75–93.

White, F., and D. Nanan. 2009. "A Conversation on Health in Canada: Revisiting Universality and the Centrality of Primary Healthcare." *Journal of Ambulatory Care Management* 32 (2): 141–9.

White, Scott. 1993. "BC Liberals Dump Wilson for Mayor of Vancouver." *Montreal Gazette*, 12 September.

Whitson, David. 2004. "Bringing the World to Canada: 'The Periphery of the Centre.'" *Third World Quarterly* 25 (7): 1215–32. doi:10.1080/01436590420028I230.

Wilderness Committee. 2012. *BC Species at Risk – There Ought to Be a Law*. http://wildernesscommittee.org/sites/all/files/publications/2012_bc-species-paper-web.pdf.

Willcocks, Paul. 2001. "BC Cabinet Given Marching Orders." *Regina Leader Post*, 14 July.
- 2003. "Critics of Recall Have Short Memories." *Vancouver Sun*, 10 March.
- 2006. "On the Ledge: Jessica McDonald." *BC Business*, 1 February. http://www.bcbusiness.ca/on-the-ledge-jessica-mcdonald.

Williams, E.F., J. Kruger, and D. Dunning. 2013. "The Hobgoblin of Consistency: Algorithmic Judgment Strategies Underlie Inflated Self-Assessments of Performance." *Journal of Personality and Social Psychology* 104 (6): 976–94.

Wolin, S.S. 2010. *Democracy Incorporated: Managed Democracy and the Specter of Inverted Totalitarianism*. Princeton: Princeton University Press.

Woolford, A. 2005. *Between Justice and Certainty: Treaty Making in British Columbia*. Vancouver: UBC Press.

World Economic Forum. 2011. *The Global Gender Gap Report 2011*. http://www3.weforum.org/docs/WEF_GenderGap_Report_2011.pdf.

Yaffe, B. 1994. "Gordon Campbell: His Game, His Rules." *Vancouver Sun*, 14 June.

– 1996. "The Question of Citizens vs. the Constitutional Question." *Vancouver Sun*, 6 February.
– 2001a. "And Now We Present – Unreality Television." *Vancouver Sun*, 27 June.
– 2001b. "Campbell Needs to Retreat on Referendum." *Vancouver Sun*, 14 March.
Yeager, S. 1995. "Liberal Leader Faces Growing Unrest." *Vancouver Sun*, 19 May.

Contributors

DR YALE BELANGER is a professor of political science at the University of Lethbridge. His PhD (Trent) explored the evolution of Aboriginal political organizations between 1870 and 1951. He has written or edited numerous books and articles about Aboriginal self-government, Aboriginal housing and homelessness, Indigenous activism, and First Nations casino development and the gaming industry.

EMMANUEL BRUNET-JAILLY is a professor of public policy at the University of Victoria, BC, where he is Jean Monnet Chair in Innovative Governance (2016–19) and director of the university's European Union Jean Monnet Centre of Excellence. He studied law and political science at Paris IV – Sorbonne and completed his PhD in political science at the University of Western Ontario. He is the author of about ninety articles and chapters, and eight books and special issues of scholarly journals in urban and border studies. His most recent publications include *Border Disputes: A Global Encyclopedia* (2015). Currently, he is the principal investigator for Borders In Globalization, a research program funded by the Social Science and Humanities Research Council of Canada (2013–19) and the European Union (2016–19). As well, he is the chief editor of the *Journal of Borderland Studies* and of the Canadian American Public Policy series.

MARJORIE GRIFFIN COHEN is professor emeritus at Simon Fraser University and writes on issues related to political economy and public policy with special emphasis on the Canadian economy, women, labour, electricity deregulation, and climate change. Her most recent book is *Climate Change and Gender in Rich Countries*. Professor Cohen has been on the board of directors of NewGrade Energy (Saskatchewan), BC Hydro, and BC Power Exchange. She was also instrumental in establishing the Canadian Centre for Policy Alternatives in BC and was its first chair.

GILLIAN CREESE is a professor in the Department of Sociology and the Institute for Gender, Race, Sexuality, and Social Justice at the University of British Columbia. Her most recent books include *The New African Diaspora in Vancouver: Migration, Exclusion, and Belonging* (2011), and (with Wendy Frisby) *Feminist Community Research: Case Studies and Methodologies* (2011). Her current research explores the gendered and racialized experiences of growing up African-Canadian in Metro Vancouver.

KEVIN GINNELL completed his PhD in political science at Simon Fraser University. He has authored numerous articles and chapters in books and conducted research on such issues as multi-level governance, Canadian urban/metropolitan government, global cities, public policy, global political economy, and Aboriginal politics. He is currently a member of the Department of Political Science at Douglas College in Vancouver, BC, and is also an adjunct professor at Simon Fraser University.

NEIL HANLON is a professor of geography at the University of Northern British Columbia. His research looks at rural and remote health service provision, regional health governance, and community-level responses to socio-demographic change.

GEORGE HOBERG is a political scientist and professor in the School of Public Policy and Global Affairs at the University of British Columbia. He is a specialist on energy, environment, and natural resource policy and governance. He has written books on BC and Canadian forest policy, environmental policy in the US, and toxic substances regulation and has edited two books on comparative Canada-US policies and the US influence on Canada. His current research focuses on the clean energy transformation.

J.R. LACHARITE is an assistant professor in the Department of Political Science and Global Studies at the University of Northern British Columbia, Prince George, BC. His teaching and research interests and focus include Canadian politics and policy, e-democracy, comparative tax policy, Canadian security and national defence issues, and Chinese politics and society.

DR DUNCAN LOW worked for many years in the professional arts in the UK and Canada. In 2008 he entered SFU's Urban Studies program where he examined Vancouver's 2010 Cultural Olympiad. He has authored several articles on the impact of the 2010 Olympics on the arts community; he has also given numerous presentations on the subject including at the London 2012 cultural planners meeting. He completed his PhD at SFU's School of Communication in 2016. His dissertation is entitled "Federal Arts Policy 1957–2014: The Rhetoric and the Reality." He was recently awarded a 2017/2018 Mitacs Canadian Science Policy Fellowship attached to the Research and Analysis Unit at the BC Ministry of Advanced Education.

DENNIS PILON is an associate professor in the Department of Politics at York University in Toronto, Ontario. He is the author of *Wrestling with Democracy: Voting Systems as Politics in the Twentieth Century West* and *The Politics of Voting: Reforming Canada's Electoral System*, as well as co-editor of *British Columbia Politics and Government*, with Michael Howlett and Tracy Summerville. His research focuses on voting systems and their reform and democratization processes more broadly, in both Canadian and comparative contexts, as well as comparative social democracy and class analysis.

PATRICK J. (PADDY) SMITH is the director of the Institute of Governance Studies and professor of political science and of urban studies at Simon Fraser University in Vancouver, BC. He has authored/edited several books and numerous articles on such issues as political parties and elections, the Canadian constitution, security intelligence, anti-terrorism and human rights, urban and metropolitan governance, public policy, open government, public sector ethics, Aboriginal justice, global cities and cross-border issues, multi-level governance, gender and politics, and democratic reform.

VERONICA STRONG-BOAG is an FRSC Professor Emerita in women's studies at UBC and director of the website http://womensuffrage.org. She received the Tyrrell Medal in Canadian History from the RSC in 2012 and is a former president of the Canadian Historical Association (1993–94). She is currently writing the biography of Laura Marshall Jamieson (1882–1964 – a former BC suffragist and CCF MLA), and acts as the general editor of the UBC Press series Women's Suffrage and the Struggle for Democracy in Canada.

TRACY SUMMERVILLE is an associate professor of political science at the University of Northern British Columbia. Her research work includes the impacts of globalization on resource communities.

GARY TEEPLE is a professor of sociology and teaches in the Department of Sociology and Anthropology at Simon Fraser University. He is also the former director of the Labour Studies Program at SFU. He received a DPhil from the Department of Comparative Politics at the University of Sussex in the UK and an MA from the Department of Sociology at the University of Toronto. His publications include *Relations of Global Power: Neo-liberal Order and Disorder* (2011, co-edited with S. McBride); *The Riddle of Human Rights* (2004); *Globalization and the Decline of Social Reform* (1995/2000); *Marx's Critique of Politics, 1842–47* (1984); and (editor) *Capitalism and the National Question in Canada* (1972). His research interests lie in the global division of labour, human rights, critical theory, Hegelian and Marxist philosophy, and the sociology of art. Currently, he is working on a book-length introduction to labour studies and a critical analysis of modern liberal democracy.

Index

Abbotsford Regional Hospital, 99
Aboriginal, First Nations, 3, 11–12, 61–87, 89, 100–3, 107–8, 156, 168, 188, 193, 195, 222, 226; BC Assembly of First Nations, 82; BC Claims Task Force, 80; BC Ministry of Aboriginal Affairs, 65, 68, 73; BC Ministry of Aboriginal Affairs and Reconciliation, 78; BC Ministry of Community, Aboriginal and Women's Services, 211–12, 214–15; BC Treaty Commission, 63–5, 69–74, 77, 80–1; Citizen's Voice on Native Claims Federation, 64; First Nations Health Accord, 151, 156–7, 164; First Nations Health Council, 156; First Nations Leadership Council, 82–3, 156; Indigenous Recognition and Reconciliation Act, 62, 81–4; Missing Women Commission of Inquiry, 171; Olympics art gallery, 245, 269–70; poverty, 172–4; Royal Proclamation (1763) on Aboriginal rights, 71; self-government, 62–4, 66, 68, 80–1, 84, 86n6, 102–3, 107; Transformation Change Accord, 156;

treaties, 9, 44–5, 47–8, 50, 61–87, 101, 103, 188, 222. *See also* Carrier Sekani; Clayoquot Sound; Delgamuukw decision; Great Bear Rainforest; Gustafsen Lake; Haida Gwaii; Haida Nation; Inuit; Kamloops Indian Band; Kwakwaka'wakw; Lil'wat Nation; Métis; Nisga'a; Squamish; Sto:lo; Taku River Tlingit; Tsawwassen; Tsleil-Waututh; Ucluelet; Union of BC Indian Chiefs; Westbank
abortion. *See under* women
Accenture, 200
Action Democratique Party, Quebec, 41
acts, laws, BC: Clean Energy Act, 203–4; Community Charter Act, 214–15, 217; Employment Standards Act (ESA), 129, 136–8, 141, 143, 169; Forest and Range Practices Act, 183, 185, 187; Greenhouse Gas Reductions Target Act, 179; Growth Strategies Act, 227; Health and Social Services Delivery Improvement Act, 169; Health Care Services Continua-